Effective Help Desk Specialist Skills

Darril R. Gibson

PEARSON IT CERTIFICATION

800 East 96th Street
Indianapolis, Indiana 46240 USA

Effective Help Desk Specialist Skills

Copyright © 2015 by Pearson Education, Inc.

ISBN-13: 978-0-7897-5240-6

ISBN-10: 0-7897-5240-9

Library of Congress Control Number: 2014949750

Printed in the United States of America

Second Printing: July 2016

Trademarks

Warning and Disclaimer

Special Sales

For information about buying this title in bulk quantities, or for special sales opportunities (which may include electronic versions; custom cover designs; and content particular to your business, training goals, marketing focus, or branding interests), please contact our corporate sales department at corpsales@pearsoned.com or (800) 382-3419.

For government sales inquiries, please contact governmentsales@pearsoned.com.

For questions about sales outside the U.S., please contact international@pearsoned.com.

Associate Publisher
Dave Dusthimer

Acquisitions Editor
Betsy Brown

Development Editor
Box Twelve Communications

Managing Editor
Sandra Schroeder

Project Editor
Mandie Frank

Copy Editor
Katie Matejka

Indexer
Heather McNeill

Proofreader
Sarah Kearns

Technical Editor
James Anthos

Publishing Coordinator
Vanessa Evans

Interior Designer
Mark Shirar

Cover Designer
Alan Clements

Compositor
Studio Galou

Contents at a Glance

Table of Contents

About the Author

Darril Gibson is the CEO of YCDA, LLC (short for You Can Do Anything). He regularly writes and consults on a wide variety of technical and security topics and holds several certifications including MCSE, MCDBA, MCSD, MCITP, ITIL v3, Security+, and CISSP. He has authored or coauthored more than 30 books including the best-selling *Security+: Get Certified, Get Ahead* series. Darril regularly blogs at http://blogs.getcertifiedgetahead.com/.

Dedication

To my wife, Nimfa, who has enriched my life in so many ways over the past 22 years.

Acknowledgments

A book of this size takes a lot of effort from many people working behind the scenes and I'm grateful for all the work they did. James Anthos provided excellent feedback as a technical editor, and Jeff Riley was great as a development editor. While I know many more people contributed to the book, they often did so without any interaction from me (which I love), and I don't know their names. I appreciate their efforts just the same. I would also like to thank Betsy Brown at Pearson for the opportunity to write this book.

About the Technical Reviewer

James Anthos is the Program Director for the South University Information Technology department in Columbia, S.C. James joined South University in 2000 after a 30-year career as an information technology professional at several companies. He earned his MBA at West Virginia Wesleyan College in Buckhannon West Virginia in 1993, completed an MS in Computer Information Systems at The University of Phoenix in 2005, and is currently pursuing a doctorate in business administration at Argosy University. He graduated from Strayer University, Washington D.C. in 1980 with a BS in Data Processing Management.

James began his information technology career as a computer operator for Electronic Industries Association in Washington, D.C. in 1968. Next, he worked for more than nine years at Airline Pilots Association as a Sr. Systems Analyst, and then spent three years as the director of the computer data center at Salem College in Salem, W.V. While working at Salem College, Anthos began teaching part-time, an endeavor he has continued since 1981. In 1983, Anthos redesigned the Salem College Computer Technology degree to include three new tracks of specialization. The first specialty was in Office Automation, the second was Robotics, and the third was Computer Programming.

In 1984, Anthos joined Consolidated Natural Gas in Clarksburg, W.V., as a Systems Analyst. He was promoted to Sr. Systems Analyst in 1987 and held that position until 1998 when he accepted a position with Blue Cross Blue Shield of South Carolina as a Project Manager. He worked for BCBS of South Carolina until 2003, when he accepted a full-time teaching position at South University.

His major contribution to the teaching profession is his dedication to the students, and his desire to produce graduates with adequate skills to succeed in their chosen profession.

We Want to Hear from You!

As the reader of this book, *you* are our most important critic and commentator. We value your opinion and want to know what we're doing right, what we could do better, what areas you'd like to see us publish in, and any other words of wisdom you're willing to pass our way.

We welcome your comments. You can email or write to let us know what you did or didn't like about this book—as well as what we can do to make our books better.

Please note that we cannot help you with technical problems related to the topic of this book.

When you write, please be sure to include this book's title and author as well as your name and email address. We will carefully review your comments and share them with the author and editors who worked on the book.

Email: feedback@pearsonitcertification.com

Mail: Pearson IT Certification
      ATTN: Reader Feedback
      800 East 96th Street
      Indianapolis, IN 46240 USA

Reader Services

Visit our website and register this book at www.pearsonitcertification.com/register for convenient access to any updates, downloads, or errata that might be available for this book.

Introduction

The term "help desk" means different things depending on the context. At the core, help desk professionals provide services to customers. These customers might be internal employees or external customers of products or services, but they are all customers. In a small organization, the help desk might be a single person doing everything. In an organization with a large IT department, the help desk might be a large division of personnel dedicated to helping personnel within the organization. Some organizations, such as Internet service providers (ISPs), provide services to their customers via a help desk.

However, in any of these situations, help desk professionals require a core set of skills to succeed. Many people think that technical and troubleshooting skills are enough, but they aren't. Instead, help desk professionals require a broad set of both hard and soft skills:

- Hard skills are specific, measurable skills such as configuring and troubleshooting systems. Some specific hard skills help desk professionals need are technical skills related to the systems they support, troubleshooting skills to correct problems, security skills to recognize and correct security issues, and business skills to use the tools within the business.

- Soft skills refer to the ability to communicate effectively with others. Communication skills are of primary importance, especially when communicating with customers and personnel within an organization, but additional soft skills are also required. Personal skills help individuals manage their time, stress, and career. Writing and training skills help individuals pass their knowledge onto others.

While this knowledge is important for anyone pursuing a career in an IT help desk position, it is also important for anyone pursuing a career that will oversee help desk professionals. This includes IT managers and C-level executives such as chief executive officers (CEOs) and chief technology officers (CTOs). Many times, help desk professionals provide the first impression of an organization. If they are technical people without any personal skills, it can negatively affect the organization's success and bottom line.

Organization of the Text

The book begins with the assumption that students are not familiar with the help desk role and how it operates in many organizations. It covers a combination of both hard skills and soft skills that help desk personnel need to succeed:

- Chapter 1 provides an overview of the help desk support role, required skill-sets, user categories and characteristics, and the flow of a typical incident.

- Chapters 2, 3, 7, and 8 provide information on soft skills. These topics include communication skills, personal skills, writing skills, and training skills.

- Chapters 4, 5, 6, and 9 provide information on hard skills. These topics include technical skills, security skills, troubleshooting skills, and business skills.

- Chapter 10 provides information on how to calculate the value of the help desk using metrics, and on comparing costs in a cost benefit analysis.

Each chapter has the same organization, starting with an introduction, a list of learning objectives, and a list of key terms that are important within the chapter. Chapter review activities are included at the end of the chapter. These include questions, a list of key terms and acronyms, and exercises such as mind map suggestions or case studies. Your instructor might want you to read all the sections of a chapter and use all of the review tools. It's also possible your instructor only wants you to read specific sections and use specific review tools. It's best to check the syllabus to identify which parts of the book to use.

Key Pedagogical Features

To begin the chapter:

Each chapter begins with a few features that help direct you as to what the chapter discusses, before getting into the core topics of the chapter:

- Chapter Introduction describes the big ideas in the chapter, with perspective on how it fits with the other chapters.

- Chapter Outline lists the titles of the (usually three or four) major sections in each chapter, with a short description.

- Chapter Objectives list the most important student results from using this chapter as part of a course.

- Key Terms list the terms for the most important concepts in the chapter. These terms and their related concepts should be the reader's top priority for what to understand and recall from this chapter. As a suggestion, while reading the chapter, make notes about each of these terms.

In the core of the chapter:

The majority of each chapter, following the chapter introduction, uses text, tables, lists, and figures to explain various topics. Along with those descriptions, the core topics also use the following features:

- **Key Terms:** Inside the chapter, the key terms are noted in a large, bold font so that they can be easily found.

- **Author's Note:** These notes list topics that the author wants to draw particular attention to, but which you can skip when reading if you want to maintain the flow. Author notes typically list some deeper fact about the current topic or some fact that may be a little off-topic. Read these notes either during your first read of the chapter or when reviewing and studying.

- **On the Side:** These notes list topics that add interest to the topic, but which your instructor probably will not require you to know for tests. (Check with your instructor.)

In the chapter-ending Chapter Review section:

The end of each chapter closes with a Chapter Review section, which has tools and activities that you can use to review the reading from inside the chapter:

- **Answer These Questions:** These multiple-choice questions help you review topics in the chapter.

- **Define the Key Terms:** This heading lists the same key terms listed in the beginning of the chapter. The section reminds you of the terms and suggests an activity where you write the definition for these terms in your own words. You can then compare your definition with the definitions in the glossary.

- **List the Words Inside Acronyms:** As a simple review, take this list of acronyms from the chapter and write out the words represented by the acronym. Then, check the acronyms in the glossary.

- **Create Mind Maps:** This heading suggests a few mind-mapping activities to help you mentally review the chapter.

- **Define Other Terms:** As a simple review, take this list of other terms from the chapter, beyond the list of key terms, and write out a definition for each. You can then compare your definition with the definitions in the glossary.

Other features outside each chapter:

Beyond the features in each chapter, this book comes with other helpful features as well:

- **Glossary and Index:** The glossary lists the various terms used in the book, with definitions, while the index lists page references for the most common of those terms.

A Brief Word on Mind Mapping

Mind maps are a type of graphic organizing tool that give learners a visual way to learn, take notes, organize thoughts, and think. Each chapter includes some suggested mind-mapping exercises as a way to help you think about the topics in that chapter.

With the mind-mapping exercises in these chapters, the goal is not for you to create the exact same mind map that the author had in mind when creating the activity. Instead, the point of the activity is what happens to your own mind and memory by simply doing the activity. These activities help you to:

- Organize the topics in your own mind and your own words.

- Improve your memory of the concepts and terms.

- Build a stronger understanding of how the ideas relate to each other.

- Build a stronger understanding of what topics go together, and which topics differ.

You can create mind maps with software, or just with pencil and paper. When using pencil and paper, start by creating a circle or box and write the main topic within it. Next, think of a related topic, create another circle, and write this topic within it. Then, connect the topics with a line. Continue the process until you've exhausted your knowledge.

The main point is that you list the topics and show their relationships with connecting lines. As an example, imagine you're asked to list the skills required of support personnel, and organize these skills into two categories. Figure I-1 shows one possible result.

FIGURE I-1

Sample mind map.

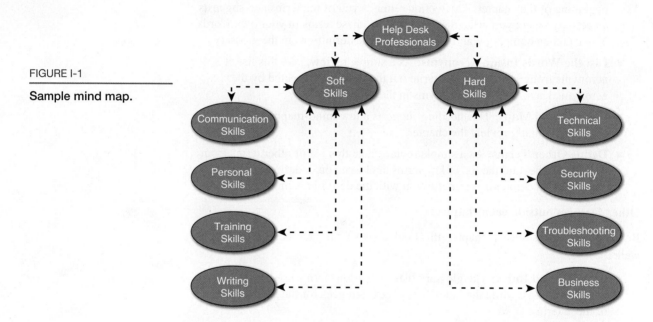

If you just glance at the figure, and see the somewhat basic ideas and terms and stop there, you miss the whole point of the mind-map exercise. First, think about the core idea, listed in the center as "Help Desk Professionals." Would you use this term for support personnel or some other term? The mind map starts with a blank sheet of paper, so you have to choose. What other categories might you use instead of "Soft Skills" and "Hard Skills?" If you thought of several, you could add a list of synonyms or alternatives to the mind map, but it gives you the chance to think about what terms to use.

Think about the next level of organization, listing individual soft skills and individual hard skills. Can you think of others to add to the list? Also, you might consider some skills to be in both categories. For example, you might think of some individual business skills that are hard skills while others are soft skills. You could add an extra line from "Business Skills" to the "Soft Skills" heading. However, making the decision to add the extra line requires you to think about how a business skill could be a soft skill in addition to a hard skill.

Finally, consider the core topic of "Help Desk Professionals." You could include subcategories, depending on how they communicate to customers such as in-person, over the phone, via email, or online instant messaging chat windows. For some of these, you might consider some skills to be more important than others and put them in a different order.

The point of these exercises for this book is not the finished mind map as much as the process. While creating the mind map, you might add or change items, move items, or add and erase lines. (Using a pencil rather than a pen, or software, really is preferred so that you can make changes.) Each time you write something and see the correct relationship, it reinforces your memory. Each time you write something and start to question it, it helps you uncover where you have questions. As you pursue answers, your level of knowledge will become much deeper.

Conclusion

Help desk support is an important element of any organization. Organizations historically filled this role with technical personnel that knew a little about computers. However, organizations now look for personnel with a broad set of skills including both hard skills and soft skills. I hope you enjoy learning about core skills sets required by help desk professionals (and many other IT professionals) as you work through this text.

Chapter 1

Introduction to Help Desk Support Roles

Help desk specialists require a wide range of skills to be successful. Their primary job is to help users, and the obvious skills they need are technical so that they can troubleshoot and resolve problems. However, they also need to have other skills and knowledge to be effective on the job.

This chapter introduces the support center, help desk professionals, users, and incidents (or problems) in four major sections:

- The first section, "Understanding the Support Center," provides some history related to computers and information technology (IT) and how the support center has evolved over the years. It also identifies services provided to the users.

- Next, "The Role of the Help Desk Professional" section identifies the role of IT workers working as help desk professionals. These professionals are the first line of support for users, and they routinely assess problems and identify solutions. While the job is technical in nature, technicians on the help desk also require skills beyond technical and troubleshooting skills. This section introduces many of the skillsets needed by the help desk professional.

- The "Understanding Users" section describes many common user categories and some of their common characteristics. By understanding the user, help desk professionals are better able to recognize their needs.

- Last, the "Typical Incident Process" section lists the steps for a typical incident. It also explains the importance of tracking incidents and some of the metrics that can be used to determine the effectiveness of a help desk center.

This chapter lays the foundation for the rest of this book by introducing many of the core skills and common tasks of help desk specialists. Other chapters in the book delve into many of these topics at a deeper level.

Chapter Outline

Objectives

- Define the key terms related to help desk support roles
- Describe the primary role of the support center
- Summarize the services provided to users
- List and compare the different tiers of support
- Describe the skillsets required of successful help desk professionals
- Compare different user categories
- List and describe the steps in a typical incident process
- Explain the benefits of tracking incidents

Key Terms

business skills	Internet service provider (ISP)	service level agreement (SLA)
cost center	malware	technical skills
escalate	metric	technical support
help desk	profit center	ticket
incident	security skills	troubleshooting skills
incident management		

Understanding the Support Center

AUTHOR'S NOTE:
The primary purpose of the help desk is to assist users, and in this context, the users are customers. This is obvious when users are purchasing a product or service from the organization, and aren't employed by the organization. However, users within an organization are also customers. The help desk is providing a service to these users and needs to ensure they are satisfied just as if they were paying customers.

The purpose of an IT support center is to provide **technical support** to users. This includes starting (or booting) a computer, logging on, configuring a computer, configuring and running applications, and accessing network resources. The support center might support users within the same organization or, in other cases, the support center might support external customers of the organization.

For example, large organizations have in-house IT departments to assist users within the organization. Help desk employees working in a support center division of the IT department assist other employees in the same organization. In contrast, **Internet service providers (ISPs)** provide Internet access to their subscribers and employ help desk personnel to assist ISP subscribers. Customers that are having problems accessing the Internet or using any of the ISP services contact the support center for assistance.

A Little History

Prior to the 1970s, computers used within an organization were restricted to mainframes that typically took up a full room. Many were the size of a large refrigerator and had only a fraction of the computing ability of today's computers. Organizations lucky enough to have these computers employed a few highly qualified personnel to maintain and operate them.

In 1976, Steve Jobs and Steve Wozniak started Apple and began selling the first computer for home use, the Apple I. In 1981, IBM created the IBM Personal Computer (or IBM PC), which became a standard used in many organizations by regular employees. IBM contracted with a small start-up company called Microsoft, founded by Bill Gates and Paul Allen, to provide the disk operating system (DOS) for the IBM PC. Back then, Bill Gates had a vision of "a computer on every desk and in every home" and used this DOS as a starting point.

The DOS used on IBM PCs included a disk operating system called PC-DOS. However, Microsoft retained the rights to the software and began selling it as MS-DOS (Microsoft Disk Operating System). Several other manufacturers began creating their own PCs running MS-DOS, and these PCs provided much of the same functionality as IBM PCs. These IBM PC-compatible computers came to be known as clones, and in time, the clones overtook IBM's market share. IBM no longer manufactures PCs, but the combination of these events helped the PC market expand exponentially.

Today's world is much closer to Bill Gates's vision of a computer on every desk and in every home. Moreover, it is very common for almost every employee within many organizations to have a PC. Over time, Microsoft developed increasingly more sophisticated Windows operating systems and applications. Additionally, many other companies developed highly useful applications that streamlined work processes, steadily increasing overall employee productivity.

In 1969, the Advanced Research Projects Agency Network (ARPANET) started developing a network used by universities and research laboratories in the United States to share information between each other over long distances. This morphed into the Internet in the 1980s, and eventually became a network accessible by users around the world. Currently, it's estimated that more than 2 billion users have access to the Internet.

Along with the explosion of the Internet, organizations began connecting computers and other resources together in local area networks (LANs). Large organizations with multiple buildings spread across a campus connected the building LANs together in metropolitan area networks (MANs). Organizations with buildings or campuses in multiple locations connected their LANs together in wide area networks (WANs).

Note that in the span of just a couple of decades (from the '70s to the '90s), computer usage within organizations sharply increased. Previously, organizations used very few computers and needed very few IT support personnel. However, as the IT usage grew, there became an obvious need for more IT support personnel.

The Evolution of the Support Center

While the growth of computer use, networks, and the Internet has provided significant benefits for organizations, these computers, applications, and networks have become increasingly complex. Ideally, they work as expected all the time. In reality, computers and networks display a wide range of problems from minor operability problems to complete failure. Users cannot be expected to know all the technical details required to maintain and troubleshoot computers and networks any more than they can be expected to know everything about phones and all the details about the plain old telephone system (POTS) or the more sophisticated Integrated Services Digital Network (ISDN). Instead, organizations realized that they needed specialists within an IT support center to maintain the computers and networks, and help the users when necessary.

The support center role has evolved over time. When an organization had only a few desktop computers, the support center was typically one or two computer experts. These experts did everything related to the computers. As computer use grew, it was apparent this model was no longer effective. Instead, organizations began to separate the roles of the IT personnel based on different needs.

It's important to understand that the help desk is a cost center instead of a profit center. A **profit center** generates revenue for a company and includes departments such as sales and marketing. These departments generate sales and help earn profits for the company. A **cost center** generates additional costs for a company without bringing in any direct revenue. For example, the IT department does not generate any sales, so it does not bring in any additional revenue. Instead, it only generates costs for IT hardware, software, and services.

ON THE SIDE: Understanding the difference between profit centers and cost centers is important for IT professionals if they want to speak the language of senior management. Senior management will often respond to saving funds by investing in IT support. In contrast, IT personnel that simply ask for more money without showing the benefits to the organization often walk away empty-handed.

Companies that care about the bottom line focus on increasing revenue and decreasing costs, so the idea of creating or expanding a help desk isn't always embraced. However, over time, many organizations realize that providing IT support to users significantly improves their overall productivity—but the value of the help desk still needs to be justified. One way costs are justified is through metrics discussed in the Typical Incident Process section later in this chapter.

Understanding an Incident and Incident Management

When talking about a help desk and its functions, it's important to understand two key terms: **incident** and **incident management**. In simple terms, you can think of an incident as a problem. Customers typically report the problem to the help desk and the help desk technicians take steps to resolve it. An organization implements incident management processes to ensure that all incidents are resolved to the best ability of the organization.

However, there are definitions that are more specific. Chapter 9, "Business Skills," includes information on the Information Technology Infrastructure Library (ITIL). ITIL is a group of books written and published by the United Kingdom's Office of Government and Commerce (OGC). It has been around since the 1980s and has improved and matured since then. ITIL provides organizations with a collection of good practice concepts that can improve IT processes within any IT organization. Its goal is to help organizations identify functions, roles, and processes that can benefit from these concepts to ensure IT services remain available on a consistent basis.

ITIL provides the following paraphrased definitions for an incident and incident management:

- **Incident.** An incident is an unplanned interruption or a reduction in the quality of an IT service. It can also be the failure of a fault tolerant or redundant solution designed to increase the availability of a service. For example, the failure of one disk in a mirror set is an incident.
- **Incident Management.** This includes all processes and procedures used to deal with incidents. Incidents might be reported by users, by technical staff, or from automated tools that perform event monitoring and reporting.

The Role of the Support Center

Organizations often divide an IT department into several different divisions. Personnel working within these divisions are able to focus on specific IT requirements and become experts within that area. While the following list is not inclusive, it does identify many of the common divisions:

- Help Desk
- Infrastructure

- Servers
- Security
- Software

Help Desk

The **help desk** provides direct support to the end users. Support provided by the help desk varies between organizations; later in this chapter, the section "Services Provided to Users" explains many of the common services organizations choose to provide. Overall, this book focuses on the help desk division, or the help desk function, within an IT department.

Infrastructure

Large networks have dedicated technicians and administrators to maintain the network infrastructure. This includes network connections and hardware such as routers and switches, and access to other networks such as the Internet. If an organization doesn't have a dedicated security team, technicians maintaining the network would also maintain firewalls and proxy servers that are connected to the Internet. In some smaller organizations, infrastructure technicians are part of another division, such as the servers division.

Servers

Organizations typically have one or more servers that require some advanced knowledge to configure and maintain. Some examples are file servers where users store and access files, mail servers used for email, and web servers used to host web sites. Administrators that maintain these servers might also work on the network infrastructure.

Security

Security has become increasingly important to organizations due to the frequency of attacks and the high level of threats. Criminals often attack networks trying to steal data such as customer information or company secrets. In other cases, criminals launch sophisticated denial of service (DoS) attacks with the goal of taking down a server, network, or any type of service provided by the company.

Malicious software (**malware**) includes viruses, worms, Trojans, logic bombs, and more. Antivirus software helps protect against malware but it is only useful when all appropriate systems have antivirus software installed, and it is kept up-to-date. Years ago, organizations depended on employees to maintain and update antivirus software, but this rarely worked. Today, security experts deploy, update, and maintain this software remotely.

Network security experts maintain firewalls and Internet-facing servers to provide a level of protection for the internal network. In many cases, these network security experts also manage the antivirus software for the company. Proactive organizations task these security experts with performing vulnerability assessments and risk analysis. Even if an organization doesn't have a dedicated team of security professionals, technicians in other areas of the company will still be responsible for maintaining IT security.

Software

Some organizations develop their own software. They have dedicated programmers to create, maintain, and troubleshoot these applications. Programmers rarely work on regular servers or the network infrastructure, though they might be responsible for the configuration and maintenance of web servers and database servers.

An effective IT department has a team mentality and recognizes the need for the different divisions to work together. Even though the separate divisions have different responsibilities, they frequently interact with other.

IT Tiers within an Organization

Organizations typically organize support to their customers in separate levels, or tiers. Most organizations that use tiers have three internal tiers, and some identify a fourth external tier. Technicians at lower-level tiers try to resolve the problem to the best of their ability. If they are unable to resolve the problem, they **escalate** the problem. In other words, they pass the problem on to a technician at a higher tier to resolve the problem.

Support personnel at each tier might work on the same **incident** or trouble call. For example, when the customer makes initial contact with a tier 1 technician, this technician logs it as an incident and begins working on it. If the tier 1 technician cannot resolve the incident, this technician escalates the incident to a higher tier. As the incident escalates through the tiers, technicians at each level review past activity and log their actions. This ensures that all technicians are able to see the full scope of the problem and the previous actions taken to resolve it.

Figure 1-1 shows an overview of the tiers, and the following bullets describe them in more depth.

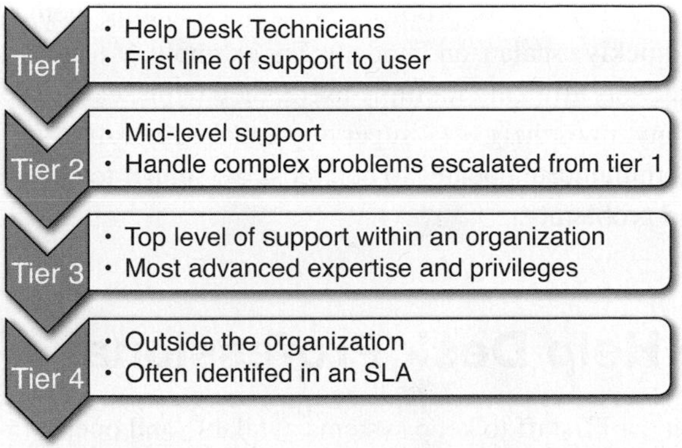

FIGURE 1-1

Four tiers of support within an organization.

Tier 1	• Help Desk Technicians • First line of support to user
Tier 2	• Mid-level support • Handle complex problems escalated from tier 1
Tier 3	• Top level of support within an organization • Most advanced expertise and privileges
Tier 4	• Outside the organization • Often identifed in an SLA

- **Tier 1.** Help desk personnel are tier 1 and provide basic support to users. Technicians have basic skills, knowledge, and privileges to resolve simple and common problems.

- **Tier 2.** Technicians with a higher level of knowledge, experience, and permissions work at tier 2 and can assist tier 1 technicians resolve more complex problems. These technicians often have experience at the tier 1 level, or at least have experience providing direct assistance to users. In most cases, these technicians have dedicated jobs in other areas of the IT department, such as maintaining servers or the network infrastructure.

- **Tier 3.** The highest tier in most organizations is tier 3. Administrators and technicians at this tier troubleshoot and resolve the most difficult or complex problems. Just as tier 2 technicians have other job responsibilities, tier 3 technicians also have other responsibilities. For example, they might be working on IT projects related to expanding IT services or migrating older systems and data to newer systems.

- **Tier 4.** Many organizations have **service level agreements (SLAs)** with outside organizations. An SLA stipulates the performance expectations and identifies support services provided by the vendor. When certain problems appear, they contact the outside entity to resolve them. For example, an organization could have an SLA with Microsoft and work with Microsoft personnel to resolve problems related to Microsoft operating systems and software. Similarly, they might have an SLA with Dell to replace failed hardware.

ON THE SIDE: Not all service level agreements are external to an organization. For example, two departments or subsidiaries of the same organization can use a memorandum of understanding (MOU) or memorandum of agreement (MOA) as an agreement to provide a certain level of service. One entity provides assurances to the other entity that they will meet performance expectations. The major difference is that an SLA typically includes monetary penalties if the vendor does not meet the performance expectations. In contrast, an MOU or MOA does not include penalties but instead indicates that each party will employ their best efforts to uphold the agreement.

While tier 1 technicians will try to handle most problems without escalating them, there are situations when they quickly escalate an incident. For example, if technicians realize that the same incident is affecting multiple users, they will escalate the incident to a higher tier. Many times, help desk supervisors make the call to escalate an incident and then communicate updates to help desk personnel to ensure they don't work on an escalated problem.

The Role of the Help Desk Professional

Customers and users depend on the IT staff to keep systems available and operational. In this context, the IT staff includes all of the personnel that work directly with users and customers, and all of the personnel that are working behind the scenes to keep the servers and network infrastructure operational. This requires a significant amount of technical expertise by the technical staff combined with a dedication to the job. The help desk professional is often the "face" of the IT staff that customers see and, right or wrong, customers often make judgments about the entire organization based on their interactions with a help desk professional.

With this in mind, it's important for help desk professionals to understand their role within the organization and especially their role to customers. In additional to having a strong set of technical skills, help desk technicians also need to have a strong set of soft skills.

First Line of Support for Users

While most organizations have several tiers or levels of support personnel, the help desk is the first line of support for users. When users experience a problem, they contact the help desk first for assistance. Ideally, the help desk can resolve the problem and the customer will be satisfied. Even if help desk personnel cannot fully resolve the problem, they need to provide assistance in such a way that leaves the customer with a favorable impression of the organization. In order to do so, help desk personnel need to have strong communication skills and understand the organization's goals related to customer service.

Assessing Problems and Identifying Solutions

The primary reason customers contact the help desk is because they have problems they want to resolve. Help desk specialists focus on assessing problems and identifying solutions during the majority of their workdays. This indicates that their primary skills are technical, but this isn't always the case.

Certainly, help desk personnel need to have technical knowledge and the ability to troubleshoot problems. However, assessing problems and identifying solutions for help desk customers goes well beyond the technical skills. For example, they also need to communicate effectively with the customer to understand the problem and communicate the solution. Also, some people are energized by problems and the challenge to solve them. In addition to helping the customer, they really enjoy the satisfaction of identifying solutions and solving problems. In contrast, some people are troubled by problems and view them as obstacles and irritations. Their goal is often to just get rid of the problem as soon as possible rather than ensuring the problem is resolved.

Recognizing Required Skillsets

Many people think that help desk technicians only need the technical skills required to solve problems. However, successful help desk technicians require a wide range of skillsets. These skillsets are often categorized as hard skills and soft skills.

Hard skills are specific, measurable skills such as configuring and troubleshooting systems. **Soft skills** refer to the ability to communicate effectively with others. In short, hard skills can often get you an interview while soft skills can get you the job. After landing any technical job, a good mix of both hard and soft skills help individuals move up into higher-level positions. In contrast, a lack of a mix of skills in both skillsets either prevents people from getting jobs or keeps them stuck in the same position much longer than personnel with a good mix of hard and soft skills.

> **ON THE SIDE:** Hiring managers often talk about the lack of qualified candidates to perform jobs, but they aren't always talking about hard skills qualifications. For example, a survey in 2013 by the Society for Human Resource Management indicated, "Nearly one-half (49%) believe 2013 college graduates are lacking the knowledge/basic skill of writing in English." Hiring managers viewed these candidates as unqualified due to their lack of soft skills. You can access the survey here: http://www.shrm.org/Research/SurveyFindings/Articles/Pages/Hiring2013CollegeGraduates.aspx.

Hard Skills

Hard skills are specific abilities that can be taught and measured. For example, someone might take a class to learn about security topics and then pass the CompTIA Security+ exam, earning the CompTIA Security+ certification. The certification indicates that the individual has specific competencies related to IT security. Some of the common hard skills needed by help desk technicians are technical skills, security skills, troubleshooting skills, and business skills (later chapters will discuss these topics more in-depth).

- **Technical skills** refer to the technician's ability to configure, maintain, and troubleshoot IT systems. These skills vary between organizations and even between specific jobs within an organization. For example, a help desk technician working at tier 1 needs to have in-depth knowledge about the systems and products that end users operate. This knowledge ensures these technicians can help the end users. A tier 2 technician needs to have in-depth knowledge about much more, such as the network infrastructure and servers operating within the organization. (See Chapter 4, "Technical Skills.")

- **Security skills** have become more and more important in recent years. Attackers and criminals are constantly waging attacks on individuals and organizations of all sizes. For example, malware is a common threat and technicians need to be able to recognize malware symptoms and resolve them. Employees that understand the relationship between vulnerabilities, threats, and risks are much more likely to recognize attacks when they occur. Additionally, these employees are much more likely to understand and readily comply with an organizations security policies. (See Chapter 5, "Security Skills.")

- **Troubleshooting skills** refer to the ability of a technician to identify and resolve a problem. The highest tier in most organizations is tier 3 and administrators and technicians at this level troubleshoot and resolve the most complex problems. However, tier 1 technicians should be able to perform some basic troubleshooting steps to narrow the problem. (See Chapter 6, "Troubleshooting Skills.")

- **Business skills** refer to the technician's understanding of the organization's vision, mission, and values, in addition to the ability to use tools available within the organization. Successful technicians understand the elements of a business and their role within the business. Businesses often deploy tools such as help desk applications, and technicians need to be able to use them. For example, technicians should be able to enter all appropriate information into a help desk application and use it to search for previously known problems so that they can quickly resolve some problems for users. (See Chapter 9, "Business Skills.")

Soft Skills

Soft skills are much more subjective than hard skills. They are typically associated with personal attributes and indicate how successfully individuals are able to work with other people in teams and how effectively they are able to interact with users. Each soft skill will be discussed in more depth in later chapters.

- **Communication skills**. Effective communication is extremely important in IT support job roles. Technicians need to be able to question the user to get adequate information on a problem without taking on a tone of interrogation. Two important communication skills are using open-ended questions and active listening. (See Chapter 2, "Communication Skills.")

- **Personal skills**. Personal skills refer to someone's ability to manage different situations and manage themselves. A core personal skill is attitude, which includes maintaining a positive attitude in general and evoking an attitude of service toward the customer. Other elements of personal skills include the ability to manage personal time, stress, and an individual's career. (See Chapter 3, "Personal Skills.")

- **Writing skills**. Superior written communication is one of the most important soft skills for help desk technicians, especially in organizations that use a searchable knowledge base. Technicians and administrators use these systems to search for common problems and how to resolve them. In order for this database to be useful, support technicians must document their actions after they resolve a problem, and so strong writing skills are important. (See Chapter 7, "Writing Skills.")

- **Training skills**. In many cases, technicians provide training to users so that the users can resolve problems on their own the next time they occur. This can be informal one-on-one training or in some cases formal classroom training. When an organization deploys new operating systems or applications, they often provide formal classroom training to the users before the deployment. The goal is to help the users understand the product and reduce the load on the help desk after the deployment. Senior technicians are also expected to provide training to newer technicians. (See Chapter 8, "Training Skills.")

AUTHOR'S NOTE: I sometimes hear from readers complaining that they can't get a job or aren't getting any callbacks for interviews and imploring me to help. To me, the reason is obvious—a lack of adequate soft skills. As an example, here is a snippet of a recent email I received from someone named "Bob" (not his real name).

"The subject of my email is that I need help, the help I need from you is job. I know you know and have made a lot of contact over the years through out your career and it looked like these days you have to know somebody to be able to get a job."

I never met Bob, but I would guess that a lack of communication and writing skills is preventing him from getting interviews and job offers. I tried to explain this in my response but never heard from him again. Maybe he understood and chose to improve his soft skills. He also could have decided to ignore my advice and might still be trying to break into the IT field.

Critical Thinking

Critical thinking is another soft skill that makes a world of difference in job performance. Unlike the other hard and soft skills mentioned in this chapter, it is not covered in a specific chapter within this book, so it is expanded here. Critical thinking includes the following activities:

- **Actively thinking**. A person uses their intelligence, experience, knowledge, and skills to explore a problem and identify a solution.

- **Asking**. Critical thinkers often ask themselves questions about a problem or challenge, and then seek out the answer.

- **Changing perspectives**. Many problems are easily resolved by looking at them from a different perspective.

- **Evaluating evidence or symptoms**. The critical thinker is able to use reason to evaluate existing facts to come to a substantiated conclusion.

Many organizations use flow charts with simple yes and no questions or predefined procedures that technicians can use to identify problems, but creating these flow charts takes time and money, and they can't be created for every possible situation. As an example, Figure 1-2 shows a simple flow chart that can be used when a user complains that the "computer broke." The technician can ask simple questions such as "Do you see anything displayed on the monitor?," "Do you see the monitor power LED?," and "Do you see the computer LED?." Based on the user's responses, the technician can then either ask more questions or follow a predefined process to resolve the problem. Admittedly, the flow chart shown in Figure 1-2 is simplistic, but many times the problems are simple. A simple flow chart helps technicians resolve these problems quickly.

FIGURE 1-2

Sample flow chart.

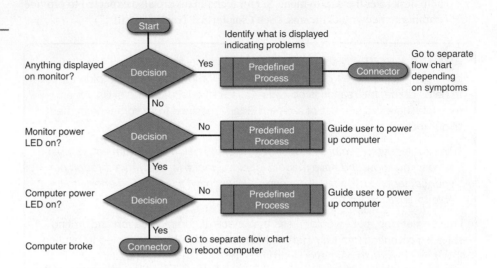

When the problems aren't simple and flow charts aren't available to assist the help desk technicians, critical thinking skills are important. Many complex problems have multiple symptoms, and help desk technicians are required to evaluate each of them and separate the relevant symptoms from the non-relevant symptoms. Critical thinking skills help them to evaluate a problem and compare it to past problems they've seen. They can then draw on their experience to troubleshoot and resolve different and more complex problems.

For example, imagine a user complains that a computer lost network connectivity. There are several possible reasons for the problem. It could be due to a physical issue, such as a cable break or a faulty network device (like a switch or router). It could be due to a faulty configuration on the computer or a network device. It could be that the user lost network connectivity to one network resource such as email, but assumed that all network connectivity was lost. The problem might be affecting a single user, a small group of users, or all of the users. Successful technicians use critical thinking skills to formulate questions, gather information, and determine what is relevant.

Many colleges and technical training providers offer critical thinking and problem solving courses to help students develop critical thinking skills. These courses can often be the most beneficial for students well beyond their college years because they help them to think on their own.

ON THE SIDE: A simple way to build critical thinking skills is to simply ask yourself questions on any topic that isn't completely clear to you. First, by writing the question in a coherent sentence, it forces you to identify what isn't clear. Then, by investigating the answer to your question, you end up learning the topic at a much deeper level. During this process, you might indeed come up with more questions, but if you write these down and answer them, you will learn and exercise your critical thinking skill abilities.

Understanding Users

A primary purpose of help desk professionals is to support users. With this in mind, it's important to understand them. Different types of users have different needs and skillsets, and will have a wide variety of different problems. When the help desk understands the users, their common characteristics, and their needs, they are better equipped to help them.

As an example, an ISP providing end user support for customers recognizes that many of these customers use their computers for simple tasks such as accessing their email and browsing the Internet. Common problems for these users are computer configuration to access the Internet, ensuring the proper hardware is in place and is configured correctly, and possibly configuring basic applications for Internet use.

In contrast, employees within an organization use their computers for work tasks. Employees typically use basic applications such as email programs but might also use highly complex applications such as computer aided design (CAD) or data mining programs. These employees contact the help desk for assistance when they are unable to perform their work tasks due to a computer or network issue.

User Categories

One way of understanding users is with user categories. User categories can vary widely, but some common categories are related to their knowledge level, the applications they use, and where they are using the computers.

When an organization understands the users, it can ensure that help desk technicians are prepared to help them. The organization is able to hire the technicians with the appropriate skill levels and provide the needed training to ensure these technicians provide the best possible support to the customers.

Internal or External

One of the simple user categories is based on the user's relationship to the organization. Internal users work in the same organization as the help desk, and help desk personnel typically prioritize incidents based on the user requesting assistance.

For example, when an executive has an IT problem, this is often a high priority for the help desk. Similarly, if product sales is considered a critical business function, users working in the sales department might be given preferential treatment when they contact the help desk.

External users are customers of the organization. Often, an organization is selling some other product or service and the help desk technicians assist customers having a problem with the product or service. An ISP is an obvious example of help desk personnel assisting external users. As another example, an organization might sell an online application and then assist customers that have purchased the application. This assistance might be via email, chat, or phone.

IT Knowledge Level

It's important to realize that just because users have computers, that doesn't mean they have intricate knowledge of how they work or how they are connected to networks. Some users grew up with computers in their home and have in-depth knowledge of computers and networks, while other users rarely use them and don't understand many of the details.

As an example, one help desk professional was working at an ISP assisting home users. Many home users installed wireless routers in their home, sharing Internet access among multiple users within their home, and they had a high level of IT knowledge. One day, a user from Virginia called and complained that he lost his Internet connection on his laptop computer. After some discussion, the technician discovered that the customer was a long-distance truck driver and was trying to connect his laptop computer from his current location in Oklahoma to his wireless network in Virginia. Experienced personnel working with computers know that wireless transmissions used within a house have a very limited range and certainly wouldn't travel from Virginia to Oklahoma. However, not everyone has that same level of knowledge, so it's important to gauge the user's knowledge level during a trouble call.

Computer Usage

Another way of classifying users is based on how they use their computers. Some users operate a single application on their computer and rarely do anything else. Other users might have five or more applications open at any given time. By understanding common usage by help desk customers, the technicians have a better chance of predicting common problems. As an example, many home users run web browsers, email applications, and games, but do little else. These users have many common problems that typically aren't seen by an in-house help desk.

In contrast, employees within a company will typically run word processing, spreadsheet, database, email, and other applications. Additionally, many organizations have dedicated applications for specific purposes. For example, sales people within an organization might use software to check inventory, track sales, and access customer information. Help desk personnel assisting these users need to have in-depth knowledge of these specialized applications so they can effectively help the users.

Location or Environment

Identifying where the customer is using the computer also helps to understand the potential issues they might have. The two primary locations or environments are home and within an organization. Home users will typically have basic issues with their computers and a help desk will often provide generic support to them. Users within an organization will have issues related to the computers and applications used in support of the organization's mission. Internal users might have generic problems just as home users do, but they will also have specific issues related to accessing resources within the organization.

An additional location is mobile or remote. For example, personnel within a company might routinely travel as part of their job but still need access to the company network. Similarly, organizations might allow users to work from home. A common way these personnel access the network from remote locations is via a **virtual private network (VPN)**.

A VPN provides access to a private network through a public network such as the Internet, as shown in Figure 1-3. Once configured, remote users connect to the Internet via an ISP and are then able to connect to the organization's private internal network. In many cases, the VPN users are able to access resources through the VPN just as if they were accessing the private network from within the organization. It gives remote users access to the internal network from almost anywhere in the world, as long as they have Internet access. The primary issue for traveling or remote users is likely to be related to connecting to the company network through the VPN, so it's important for help desk personnel to understand what a VPN is and how it is configured within an organization.

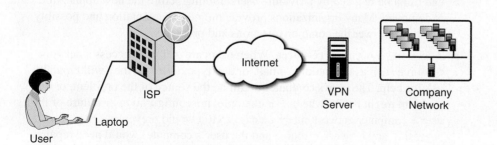

FIGURE 1-3

User accessing company network via a VPN.

Services Provided to Users

Many users view the computer as a tool or resource they use to accomplish tasks. When computer problems prevent them from accomplishing these tasks and they can't resolve these problems on their own, they ask for help. There are many reasons why users call the help desk. Some of them include:

- **Logging on**. This can include problems related to a forgotten username or password, and locked accounts. Many organizations employ automated methods to assist external users, but they assist internal users directly. One common source of login problems is the CAPS LOCK key, which has been preventing successful logins for decades.

- **Asking for information**. Users often call the help desk for information about a product or service. Help desk technicians will typically have some knowledge about products and services and have the ability to transfer the user to another area of the company if necessary. For example, if a customer calls about a product and wants to order it, the technician can transfer the call to the sales department.

- **Starting an application**. Users sometimes have problems starting an application because they can't find it or due to a software issue. For example, if the application has a problem such as a corrupt file or incorrect configuration, it might not start properly and terminate with an error.

- **Installing or upgrading software**. When users are responsible for installing or upgrading operating systems and applications, they often need assistance. For example, users might have problems installing updates to the operating system or a specific program. Many times the instructions are available, but in some situations, the users simply can't find or understand the instructions. In other situations, their system has other problems preventing the instructions from succeeding.

- **Configuring or troubleshooting hardware**. If users are responsible for configuring or troubleshooting hardware, they might have problems and call the help desk for assistance. Printers often account for many hardware trouble calls within an organization, but other hardware problems related to mice, keyboards, hard drives, displays, sound cards, and speakers are common.

- **Using or performing a task with an application**. Many times users are unable to perform specific tasks within an application. For example, when an organization deploys a new email application, users might not be able to do familiar tasks and ask for assistance. In this example, the help desk calls can often be reduced by providing users training before the new application is deployed. Many organizations provide online documentation and possibly videos to answer the common questions and problems.

- **Accessing a network resource.** When users are unable to access a network resource such as the Internet, email, or any type of server, they will typically ask for help. The user's computer might be the source of the problem, or the problem might be elsewhere. For example, misconfiguration or failure of the user's computer network interface card (NIC) would prevent the user from accessing any network resource and the user's computer would need repairs. If a network device such as a switch or router failed, a user won't be able to access the resource, but the user's computer isn't at fault. Either way, help desk technicians are able to address the problem and take steps to resolve it.

- **Removing viruses or other malware**. Malware causes a wide variety of problems, including system slowdowns, random reboots, lost files, errors, and more. Ideally, users will have up-to-date antivirus software running on their systems to prevent infections, but when a system is infected, users often need assistance removing the malware.

- **Recovering data**. If you've never lost a file due to corruption, malware infection, or simply because you cannot locate it, you probably haven't been using computers for very long. Almost everyone has lost a file at some time or another. If the file is important, users might call for help recovering it. If the file is corrupt, technicians might be able to restore it using special file recovery tools. If the file is backed up, technicians might be able to restore it from a backup. If the file is not backed up, technicians can use the problem as a teaching opportunity to stress the importance of creating backups. Some people simply never back up their data until they lose important files.

- **Rolling back changes**. Users sometimes want to undo a change to their system. This might be uninstalling software, removing a recent operating system or application update, or rolling back a hardware driver. Operating systems and applications typically have methods to perform each of these tasks, but they are sometimes beyond the technical ability of common users.

- **Understanding errors and messages**. Cryptic errors and messages can overwhelm users. Many of these are unclear and users aren't sure if they should take action in response to them, or just ignore these errors and messages.

ON THE SIDE: It's possible to avoid many of these types of help desk calls with effective documentation. If users have access to clear documentation that is easy to find, many will use it instead of contacting a technician for help. This isn't universal, though. Many users choose instead to call for help first and check documentation later. Chapter 7 covers the importance of writing skills, including technical writing for different audiences. When users successfully get the information they need from documentation one time, they are more likely to use it again.

Typical Incident Process

Most organizations have a formal process that technicians follow for any incident. An incident typically starts with a user reporting an issue and ends with a help desk technician closing it after the issue is resolved. However, there are many steps between the first and last step.

Steps in a Typical Incident Process

While not every organization uses the same process to manage incidents, there are many similarities between different processes. Organizations define the process internally and might combine or omit steps based on their needs. However, by reviewing a typical incident process, you are able to identify many of the common elements. As an introduction, Figure 1-4 shows the steps in a typical incident process and the following sections describe them in more depth.

FIGURE 1-4

Typical steps in an incident process.

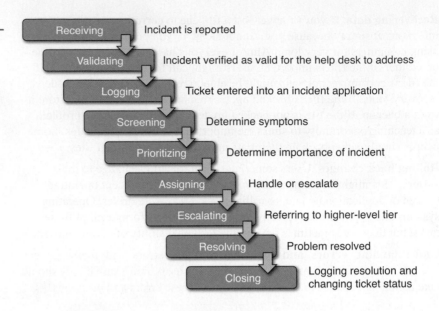

Receiving — Incident is reported

Validating — Incident verified as valid for the help desk to address

Logging — Ticket entered into an incident application

Screening — Determine symptoms

Prioritizing — Determine importance of incident

Assigning — Handle or escalate

Escalating — Referring to higher-level tier

Resolving — Problem resolved

Closing — Logging resolution and changing ticket status

Receiving Incidents

In the first step, the help desk receives the incident from a user reporting it. The method of reporting could be in person or via telephone, email, a chat page, or a web-based reporting tool.

When users report the incident via telephone, many organizations record the entire conversation. From a legal perspective, the organization normally has a requirement to notify users that the conversation is being recorded, and many automated help desk phone systems notify users prior to connecting them with technicians. Many electronic methods such as chat pages and web pages include a legal statement with a requirement for the user to check a box agreeing to the process.

One of the most important elements of success when receiving an incident is to respond appropriately and begin to establish rapport. Users often don't have the right words to report the issue, so they might need to be coaxed into providing all the relevant information. Creating a friendly, helpful atmosphere will help the technician during the process.

Consider if you called your ISP for help and a technician responded with one of the following two phrases:

- "What do you want?"
- "Hello. My name is Sally. How can I can help you?"

Many people would likely respond with anger from the first greeting while the second greeting is warm and indicates a sincere desire to help. While this is obvious when you read it, it isn't so obvious to all help desk technicians on the job. Organizations often provide help desk professionals with a script when starting a conversation, giving them the words to let the customer know they are there to help. For example, at least one ISP has their technicians answer the phone with these words: "Hello. My name is _____ and I can help you." Help desk technicians will typically memorize the greeting after repeating it a few times so they don't have to keep reading it.

Similarly, when communicating with users via email or chat pages, technicians often have pre-created scripts that they can cut and paste into the email or chat pages. These scripts typically include a greeting such as hello, an introduction including the technician's name, and an offer to help. In the technician's first response, they will typically include words expressing empathy along with confirmation that they can help. For example, they might say, "I'm sorry you're having problems but I can help you resolve this."

Validating Incidents

After the initial greeting, the customer reports the problem they are having. In this phase of the call, the technician attempts to verify it is a valid incident that the help desk should address, or if the call should be referred elsewhere.

Many organizations include an authentication procedure in this phase to ensure that the help desk is authorized to help the user. For example, an ISP help desk assists ISP customers so one of the first things that the technician does is to verify the customer's identification number. Automated phone systems often verify the customer's identification number prior to forwarding the call to a technician.

Organizations need to have clear guidelines in place on what support help desk technicians should provide. For example, if the help desk technicians are providing help to internal employees, they typically assist users with any type of problem with their computer or other IT resources.

In contrast, ISP help desk technicians only assist customers with IT problems related to the services provided by the ISP. For example, ISP technicians would assist customers having problems accessing the Internet through the ISP. However, users calling with a problem related to their printer would be told that the ISP does not provide that type of assistance.

Many organizations include a listing of items that the help desk will not support. For example, the following list could be used within an organization to ensure help desk personnel focus on supported incidents:

- The help desk does not provide support for employee's personal computing devices. This includes home computers, laptops, tablets, and smartphones.
- The help desk does not provide support for any software products that were not approved by and purchased by our company.

Telling a customer "no" can be sensitive, and pre-defined scripts are useful to give technicians phrases that respectfully communicate the company policy to the customer. While technicians might think it's funny that an ISP customer would call for help with their printer, it wouldn't be appropriate to laugh. Instead, technicians would typically express empathy and then explain why they are unable to help with

ON THE SIDE: Organizations often have very strict rules governing the purchase of software. While this does help control purchase costs, a bigger issue is support of the software. Approved software requires support and this often requires training of IT personnel to ensure they know how to install, configure, troubleshoot, and maintain it.

words such as this: "I'm sorry you're having problems with your printer but we can only provide assistance related to the services we provide. I'd suggest you contact the printer manufacturer."

Logging Incidents

Once technicians validate calls as actual incidents, they begin the process of logging them. A logged incident is also known as a **ticket**, or **service ticket**. Most organizations have applications to open, track, and close tickets through front end data entry screens, with all the data stored in a back-end database. These applications ensure proper data is entered and make it easy to track the incident through its lifetime.

Organizations using help desk software decide what information is required when logging the incident prior to deploying it. Some common customer data is name, email address, phone, and a customer ID if used. Next, a subject or category selection categorizes the incident. For example, technicians can categorize incidents as operating system problems, hardware problems, or network access problems.

A ticket also has a comment or remarks section where the technician can enter notes about the problem, and some ticket systems include an additional section to enter the original symptoms. It's possible for symptoms to change while troubleshooting and clearly logging the original symptoms helps keep technicians on track. The technician's ability to write clearly and concisely is extremely important in this step.

Some ticket systems allow the technicians to enter the data in any order. For example, Figure 1-5 shows an example web-based ticket system. Help desk technicians access this system with a web browser and are able to enter the information as the user is talking. In the figure, you can see that the technician is able to enter symptoms from the customer first, but can later enter the customer ID and other customer information. This allows the technician to listen to the customer and gather some information without forcing the user to answer a series of questions. This is especially useful if a customer has been waiting on the phone for a while and finally is able to talk to a technician. After the user explains the problem, the technician can say something like, "I understand, and we can help you with this. In case we get cut off, I want to make sure I have all your information. Can I ask you a couple of questions?" The technician then fills in the other necessary data such as the Customer ID.

AUTHOR'S NOTE:
Some organizations host web sites where users can create the ticket themselves. This is very popular among organizations that support products and services sold over the Internet. The user logs onto the website and creates the ticket. In these situations, technicians receive and validate tickets after customers log them.

FIGURE 1-5

Example of web-based ticket creating system.

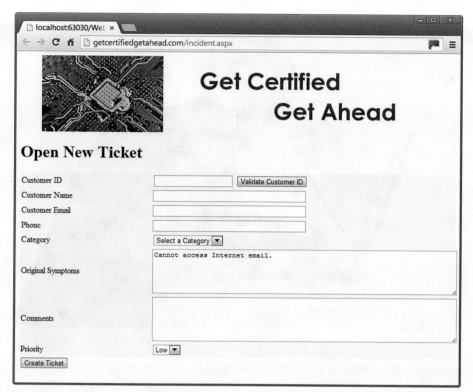

In contrast, some systems force customers to enter an account number through the automated voice mail system, but the account number is just used to authenticate the user and isn't used for further reference. After the customer waits 15 minutes or so to talk to a live person, the technician begins asking a series of questions such as account number, customer name, customer email, and so on. This often just frustrates the customer further.

When planning the process for a help desk, it's important to think about the customer's perspective. The immediate issue for the customer is the problem at hand. When the customer is forced to repeat customer data multiple times, it becomes very tedious and frustrating. For example, some help desk procedures force the customer to enter identifying data such as an account number when first calling an automated phone system. Then when a technician takes the call, the technician asks for this information again to verify the caller is a customer. Later, after the technician realizes the incident should be logged, the technician once again asks the customer for this information to enter it into a ticket. Customers can get so frustrated they want to reach through the computer and take out their frustration on the technician, as shown in Figure 1-6.

FIGURE 1-6

Ineffective logging systems can frustrate customers.

One of the most efficient methods of using a ticket system combined with an automated phone system is to ensure that they are integrated with one or more databases. The phone system prompts the caller to provide a customer number, and it validates the customer number against a customer database. The phone system only forwards calls to the help desk that are from valid customers. When the phone system forwards a call to the technician, it populates the ticket with the customer ID, along with the customer's name, email, phone number, and so on. Looking at Figure 1-5, the technician would see the ticket with most of the information filled in and can then focus on the problem.

In some cases, the user has a simple question that the technician can easily answer in less than a minute. Should the technician create a ticket for this? It depends. Most ticket applications include analysis capabilities. Management can review them periodically to extract quantifiable data and measure the performance of the help desk. However, if technicians are not creating tickets consistently, this data is not reliable. Consider these two scenarios:

First, imagine a star technician that quickly resolves user issues without taking much time at all. Without clear guidance from management, this gifted technician might not log most of these incidents, thinking that they are trivial and not worth logging. In contrast, another technician without the same level of expertise might help customers with the same types of problems, but take much longer before he can resolve them. When management later analyzes the incident logs, it might look as if the gifted technician is doing significantly less work than other technicians are, even though he is solving more customer problems.

In the second scenario, imagine that a specific user has extremely limited IT knowledge and is calling the help desk almost daily asking for help. The problems are easy to solve so technicians do not log them, but it still takes time for technicians to assist this user creating an overall help desk backlog. Help desk management might ask senior leadership for a budget increase to hire a new help desk technician. However, if these logs are analyzed, it would indicate that the help desk has enough technicians, but the technicians are not clearing many tickets.

Organizations should make it clear to technicians when to create a ticket and when tickets shouldn't be created. Junior technicians don't always understand the big picture of an organization, or even how budgets work, and without clear guidance, technicians will log tickets inconsistently. It does take time to log all problems, and technicians might think they are helping the organization by helping more customers without logging the incidents.

There aren't any rules that work for all organizations on what incidents to log. However, the key is that management needs to make a decision and communicate it to the technicians. If technicians don't have guidelines on what incidents to log, each technician will make their own decisions and these decisions might not match the goals of the organization.

Screening Incidents

Once the technician begins logging the incident, the screening phase begins. During this phase, the technician asks a series of questions about the problem. Both effective questioning techniques and active listening techniques go a long way in this step (Chapter 2 goes into these techniques in much more depth).

When screening the incident, the goal is to get the actual symptoms. Based on the symptoms, technicians determine if this is a problem they should be helping the customer with, or if they need to escalate it. Here are some examples of complaints from a customer and responses by the help desk technician:

- Customer: "The Internet is down."
- Technician: "What are you trying to do that isn't working?"

- Customer: "Why doesn't my printer work?"
- Technician: "I'm not sure. What is happening when you try to print?"

- Customer: "My computer keeps crashing."
- Technician: "That doesn't sound good. Can you explain what it does when it crashes?"

- Customer: "My account is locked and I can't log on. Can you help?"
- Technician: "I'm sorry you're having problems. I cannot unlock it, but I can connect you with technicians that have permissions to do so."

In the first three issues, the problem is very likely one that the help desk technician can help the customer resolve so the technician begin asking more questions about the problem. However, in the fourth example, the technician doesn't have adequate privileges to resolve the problem and must escalate it.

Prioritizing Incidents

Some incidents are extremely important while others are not. Most ticketing systems include the ability to assign a priority to an incident and organizations clearly define the different priorities. There isn't a universal definition that applies to all organizations, but many use simple low, medium, and high priorities.

High-priority incidents indicate problems or issues that are affecting a significant number of users and are affecting one or more mission-critical functions or services. **Mission-critical functions** or services are those that are integral to the organization performing their core business. For example, a company that primarily sells products online through a website would consider all the functions and services of the website as mission critical. This could be the website server, access to back-end database or any other services needed by the website applications, and Internet connectivity. Similarly, an ISP might consider an outage affecting hundreds of users as a high-priority issue.

Medium priority incidents prevent a single user from performing mission-critical functions or services. If a user's computer fails but the user is still able to perform tasks on another computer, it wouldn't meet this definition. Another possibility of a medium-priority issue is if an issue degrades the performance and reliability of several IT mission-critical IT services. For example, if a router failed on a network, the network might remain operational using alternate paths, but the increased traffic on these alternate paths could significantly slow down the network.

Low-priority incidents indicate issues affecting a single user or issues that are degrading the performance and reliability of non-mission-critical IT services. For example, it would be a low priority if a single user was unable to access email on one computer but can access email on another computer.

ON THE SIDE: Organizations can use any type of priority definition that meets their needs. For example, instead of High, Medium, and Low, they can use 1, 2, and 3. Similarly, instead of three levels, they can use five levels such as Critical, High, Medium, Low, and Routine. The key is that the organization has defined the priority levels and trained help desk professionals on their definitions.

Assigning Incidents

Typically, the help desk technician that receives the call will follow it through to completion. However, if the technician doesn't have the expertise or permissions to resolve the problem, it might be necessary to assign the incident to another technician. In some cases, the technicians refer the incident to another help desk technician who has specialized experience and knowledge for the problem. In other cases, the technician might need to escalate the issue to a higher-level tier.

Escalating Incidents

If technicians cannot resolve a problem, they escalate it by sending it to a higher-level tier. There are two primary reasons why help desk technicians escalate a problem:

1. The technician runs out of ideas to resolve the problem. For example, the problem might be beyond the technician's expertise level. By escalating the problem to a higher tier, a more experienced technician is able to resolve the problem for the user.

2. The technician doesn't have adequate privileges to resolve the problem. For example, the technician might realize that an account needs to be created on a server but the technician doesn't have the required privileges to create the account. Technicians at higher tier levels have progressively more privileges.

Help desk supervisors will typically monitor escalated incidents closely. If technicians are constantly escalating simple problems due to a lack of privileges, the supervisor can facilitate an increase in privileges for the technicians. This allows the problem to be resolved quicker, ensures customers are satisfied quicker, and requires less work for the upper tier levels. Additionally, if a single technician is escalating significantly more incidents than other technicians are, this technician might need additional training.

Resolving Incidents

Once the organization addresses the incident completely, it is considered resolved. In most situations, this indicates that the customer's question or problem has been answered or solved. For example, a customer reports a problem accessing the Internet, and the help desk is able to assist the customer to restore their access.

In some cases, the customer might not be satisfied but the incident is still resolved. For example, a customer might want to perform a specific task with an application and request assistance to achieve his goal. After investigating, the help desk might discover that that the application doesn't include the desired feature and communicates this to the customer. The customer might not be happy with the answer, but help desk personnel have done all they can to resolve the problem.

Closing Incidents

Technicians close the incident once the incident is resolved. This typically involves logging the resolution into the incident software and selecting the option to close it. Closed incidents are usually still accessible to help desk personnel. This way if a customer calls back after a short time, they can easily view the history and reopen it if necessary.

Help desk personnel are often provided with a script to close the ticket. For example, they might ask "Is there anything else I can help you with today?." The goal is to ensure that customers have what they need and will not be calling back in a short time.

Tracking Incidents

While most organizations recognize the need for help desks, they also want to ensure that the costs are justified. One of the primary methods of justifying costs is through metrics. A **metric** is a method of measuring something and it provides quantifiable data used to gauge the effectiveness of a process.

Some of the common metrics used to measure the effectiveness of a help desk are:

- **New incidents**. This identifies the workload imposed on the help desk team.

- **Resolved incidents**. Ideally, the help desk team should be closing about the same number of incidents as they receive. If not, it indicates there aren't enough qualified technicians to handle the workload or the technicians are not able to focus on help desk workload.

- **Backlog**. The backlog is simply the number of new incidents minus the resolved incidents. If the number of resolved incidents is consistently less than the number of new incidents, the backlog will continue to grow. Figure 1-7 shows a graph displaying new incidents, resolved incidents, and the backlog over a few weeks. Management personnel reviewing this graph can easily see that that backlog is steadily climbing and address the problem before it gets too serious.

FIGURE 1-7

Example graph of new incidents, resolved incidents, and backlog.

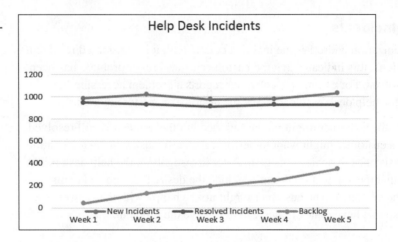

- **Reply time**. The reply time might indicate how long it takes a customer to get a response from an email or Internet-based help desk system, or how long it takes them to talk to a live help desk technician, depending on how the help desk is set up. Ideally, users will receive a quick response to let them know the incident has been received and will be worked on. If this is too long, customers will quickly become dissatisfied.

- **First resolution time**. The time between the initial incident report and its resolution is the resolution time. A challenge with this metric is that some help desk supervisors encourage technicians to resolve problems as quickly as possible so that they can help other customers. However, if the technician rushes to a resolution, the customer might not be fully satisfied and might call back.

- **Final resolution time**. Some tickets are closed prematurely, indicating a quick first resolution, but the customer soon calls back because the problem hasn't been resolved. Technicians reopen the original ticket and keep it open until it is truly resolved. Gaps between the first resolution time and the final resolution time indicate problems that management needs to investigate. For example, if one technician has a high number of tickets that other technicians are reopening when the customer calls back, it indicates the technician is not successfully helping the customers before closing the ticket the first time. This is adding additional workload onto the help desk.

- **Customer satisfaction**. The ultimate goal of the help desk is to meet the needs of the customers and you can determine this by having customers fill out short surveys and report their satisfaction with the service.

- **Technician performance**. Performance of individual technicians can be measured based on how many tickets they resolve, how many tickets they resolved but were reopened due to the customer calling back, and satisfaction ratings from the customers. Technicians with lower metrics might need additional training while technicians with superior metrics might be ready to move up to tier 2 or a help desk supervisor or management position.

Taking Ownership of Incidents

Successful help desk specialists (and employees at any job) can often enjoy great success by implementing a simple philosophy of problem ownership. The most successful technicians are diligent, tenacious, and focus on resolving all the details of an incident with a dedication to excellence. From a broader perspective, these same traits contribute to the success of people at any job.

In contrast, some technicians see incidents as problems and focus on transferring them rather than resolving. If customers are lucky, they will eventually be transferred to a technician that will take ownership of the incident and follow it through to resolution. If not, the customer will likely experience a high level of frustration and associate the bad experience with the company name.

However, this requires the organization to allow technicians to stick with a problem. Some large organizations have policies in place where technicians stick with the customer even as they transfer customers to a different area of the organization. In contrast, some large organizations have policies in place where technicians simply transfer the customer, forget about the issue, and move on to the next problem.

Here are two examples.

In one situation, I called Verizon asking for assistance with my iPad and its Internet access through the Verizon cellular network. The technician wasn't able to resolve the problem but recognized that sales personnel could resolve it. However, instead of just transferring the call, she contacted the sales personnel, explained the problem to them, and then brought them onto the line to help me. The sales personnel couldn't completely resolve the problem but instead needed to transfer me to another area. Ultimately, I was on the line for over an hour and was transferred three different times, but this technician was with me every step of the way. She expressed empathy at the difficulty we were having at resolving the problem and even though the problem wasn't completely resolved, I still ended the call with the feeling that she did everything she could.

At another time, I called a different company related to an issue I was having. I was transferred four times and each time I had to identify myself and explain the problem again. By the time I reached the fourth technician, I was extremely frustrated at the company's customer service. The technician spoke with an accent and after I told him I was having problems understanding him, he suggested I call back.

While I certainly applaud the technician in the first scenario due to her customer service capabilities, I can't completely fault the technicians in the second scenario. The company procedures were apparently reinforcing the technician actions of referring problems rather than solving them.

If a company is able to implement a simple philosophy of encouraging technicians to take ownership of problems, it can significantly increase customer satisfaction. It also places the onus of resolving the problem on the first technician that receives it. Management is better able to identify technicians that do not have the skills to resolve problems but instead transfer them whenever possible.

Chapter Review Activities

Use the features in this section to study and review the topics in this chapter.

Answer These Questions

1. Which of the following statements is MOST accurate when referring to an internal IT help desk?

   a. It is a profit center and highly valued in almost all organizations.

   b. It is a cost center and highly valued in almost all organizations.

   c. It is a profit center and its value must be justified.

   d. It is a cost center and its value must be justified.

2. Of the following choices, what is the best definition of an incident?

   a. Process of dealing with failures, questions, or queries reported by the users

   b. Process of dealing with issues automatically detected and reported by event monitoring tools

   c. An unplanned interruption to an IT service or reduction in the quality of an IT service

   d. Dealing with technical issues by technical staff

3. Of the following choices, what is the best definition of incident management?

   a. An unplanned interruption to an IT service

   b. Process of dealing with failures, questions, or queries reported by the users

   c. Failure of a configuration item that has not yet affected a service

   d. A reduction in the quality of an IT service

4. What is the primary focus of help desk personnel in a large IT department?

   a. Maintain and configure servers

   b. Maintain and configure routers

   c. Provide support to end users

   d. Install and update antivirus software

5. Which of the following is NOT a typical division in a large IT department?

   a. Help desk

   b. Training

   c. Infrastructure

   d. Security

6. Which technical support tier assists users?

  a. Tier 1

  b. Tier 2

  c. Tier 3

  d. Tier 4

7. Which of the following BEST describes an SLA?

  a. An agreement with external organization that stipulates a performance expectation

  b. An agreement with internal organization that stipulates a performance expectation

  c. A tier 1 agreement between the help desk and customers

  d. A tier 1 agreement between the help desk and vendors

8. Of the following choices, what service would help desk personnel rarely provide?

  a. Recover data

  b. Upgrade a server

  c. Remove malware

  d. Troubleshoot network problems

9. What skillsets are required for help desk technicians? (Choose the MOST correct answer.)

  a. Technical skills

  b. Soft skills

  c. A mix of hard skills and soft skills

  d. Hard skills

10. Which of the following is a typical soft skillset that successful help desk technicians possess?

  a. Technical skills

  b. Business skills

  c. Security skills

  d. Communication skills

11. Which of the following is a typical soft skill that successful help desk technicians possess?

  a. Writing

  b. Troubleshooting

  c. Implementing security

  d. Using business tools

12. An organization uses flow charts to assist technicians resolve problems. However, a technician has identified a problem but a flow chart is not available to help him resolve it. What should the technician do next?

   a. Escalate the problem.

   b. Report the lack of a flow chart to management.

   c. Use troubleshooting skills to resolve the problem.

   d. Document the resolution in the organizations incident database.

13. Of the following choices, what is the MOST likely problem that remote users of a large organization will likely have?

   a. Connecting via an organization's LAN

   b. Connecting via an organization's VPN

   c. Updating their computer

   d. Replacing their hardware

14. Of the following choices, what is the MOST likely reason a help desk professional would escalate a problem?

   a. Customer is angry

   b. Problem requires in-depth knowledge

   c. Customer lacks adequate privileges

   d. Technician lacks adequate privileges

15. At which step of an incident is a user typically authenticated as a valid help desk customer?

   a. Screening

   b. Validating

   c. Prioritizing

   d. Escalating

16. Of the following choices, what is the best method of determining the overall effectiveness of a help desk?

   a. Identifying the costs

   b. Identifying the net revenue

   c. Asking the help desk technicians

   d. Using metrics

17. How is the backlog typically measured for a help desk?

   a. Subtracting new incidents from resolved incidents

   b. Subtracting resolved incidents from new incidents

   c. Subtracting first resolution time from final resolution time

   d. Subtracting final resolution time from first resolution time

18. Of the following choices, what is the best metric to determine the overall effectiveness of a help desk?

  a. Final resolution time

  b. Backlog

  c. Customer satisfaction

  d. Resolved incidents

19. When is an incident closed?

  a. When it has been resolved to the customer's satisfaction.

  b. When it has been resolved to the best ability of the organization.

  c. When the customer chooses to do so.

  d. When the technician stops working with the customer.

20. Of the following choices, what is a simple working philosophy technicians can implement that contributes to their success and the success of the help desk?

  a. Closing as many incidents as possible

  b. Working with as many customers as possible

  c. Escalating as many incidents as possible

  d. Take ownership of incidents as much as possible

Answers and Explanations

1. d. An internal IT help desk is a cost center and its value must be justified. It does not generate any revenue so it is not a profit center. Further, because it does not generate revenue, its value is often questioned.

2. c. An incident is defined by ITIL as "an unplanned interruption to an IT service or reduction in the quality of an IT service. Failure of a configuration item that has not yet impacted service is also an incident, for example, failure of one disk from a mirror set." The other answers refer to incident management.

3. b. An incident is defined by ITIL as a "process of dealing with all incidents; this can include failures, questions, or queries reported by the users (usually via a telephone call to the Service Desk), by technical staff, or automatically detected and reported by event monitoring tools." The other answers refer to an incident.

4. c. The primary focus of help desk personnel in a large IT department is to provide support to end users. Many IT departments have administrators that maintain and configure services, as well as network infrastructure devices such as routers. These administrators might also be responsible for security tasks such as installing and updating antivirus software, or the organization might have dedicated security personnel handling this task.

5. b. A training division is not a typical division in an IT department. However, help desk personnel often provide training to users, and other help desk personnel. Help desk personnel assist users. Infrastructure technicians maintain network resources such as routers and switches. Security personnel implement and maintain measures to prevent IT security incidents and detect them when they occur.

6. **a.** Tier 1 is the first line of support for users. Tiers 2 and 3 are higher-level tiers within an organization. Some organizations identify tier 4 as an external entity.

7. **a.** A service level agreement (SLA) is an agreement with an external organization that stipulates a performance expectation. A memorandum of understanding (MOU) or memorandum of agreement (MOA) is typically used between entities within an organization instead of a SLA. When SLAs are used, they are often referred to as tier 4 support.

8. **b.** Help desk personnel would typically provide all the services mentioned except for upgrading a server. Other administrators would manage and maintain servers. Internal help desk personnel are regularly called upon to recover data and remove malware. Both internal and external help desk personnel will troubleshoot network problems preventing a user from accessing network resources.

9. **c.** It's important for help desk technicians to have a mix of both hard skills and soft skills. Without hard skills (measurable technical skills), they will be unable to troubleshoot and resolve problems. Without soft skills, they will be unable to communicate effectively to customers and within the organization.

10. **d.** Communication skills are one of the important soft skillsets required of successful help desk technicians so that they can communicate with customers. The other skills are also required but are hard skills, not soft skills.

11. **a.** Writing is a soft skill that is required of help desk technicians so that can accurately enter information such as problem symptoms and problem resolutions into an organization's incident database. The other skills listed are hard skills.

12. **c.** The technician should use troubleshooting skills to resolve the problem. It is unlikely that an organization will have flow charts for all problems, so technicians should be able to think on their own in some situations. The technician should attempt to troubleshoot the problem before escalating it. Operating procedures might require the technician to report the lack of a flow chart to management, but not before troubleshooting it. The resolution cannot be documented until it is resolved.

13. **b.** Remote users typically connect via a virtual private network (VPN) and this is the most likely problem they will have of the given choices. Remote users will not connect via the organization's local area network (LAN) to the remote location. Updating a computer and replacing hardware isn't a common occurrence and if there is a need, users can typically have it done by coming into the primary work location.

14. **d.** Help desk professionals escalate problems when they lack adequate privileges to resolve a problem. Technicians escalate the problem to the level where technicians have the appropriate privileges. Successful technicians can still help a customer, even if the customer is angry about the situation. Help desk professionals typically have in-depth knowledge about the systems they support. The privileges of the customer aren't relevant to a help desk professional resolving a problem.

15. **b.** Users are typically authenticated as valid customers in the validating step. During screening, the technician attempts to get more information on the incident, such as additional symptoms. Next, the technician prioritizes the incident based on the available information. Technicians escalate incidents if they are not able to resolve them.

16. **d.** Metrics (such as the backlog and customer satisfaction ratings) are used to measure the effectiveness of a help desk. The costs vary widely depending on customer needs and how many customers are served. A help desk is a cost center and doesn't generate revenue. Help desk technicians working at the help desk are not the best source to determine its effectiveness.

17. **b.** The backlog metric is calculated as new incidents minus resolved incidents (or subtracting resolved incidents from new incidents). Subtracting new incidents from resolved incidents would almost always give a negative number unless both are equal. Resolution times refer to the amount of time it takes to help customers and is not related to backlog.

18. **c.** Customer satisfaction is the best metric to determine the overall effectiveness of a help desk and is often measured by having customers complete short surveys. The final resolution time can be compared with the first resolution time to identify if tickets are closed prematurely but isn't the best measure of help desk effectiveness. The backlog compares new incidents and resolved incidents to determine if the workload demand is being met, but without knowing customer satisfaction it doesn't determine the overall effectiveness.

19. **b.** An incident is closed when the organization has addressed it completely to the best ability of the organization. Customers are not always satisfied because they might not be able to get the help they want simply because the organization cannot provide it. Some help desk ticket systems allow customers to close the ticket, but this isn't true for all tickets. A technician might escalate an incident or go off duty and turn it over to another technician, but this is not a reason to close an incident.

20. **d.** A philosophy of taking ownership of problems can elevate technicians above others when working on the help desk or anywhere. Just closing incidents isn't as important because they can be closed prematurely. Working with more customers isn't as important because it can result in rushed assistance with one customer, while looking forward to working with the next customer. Escalating an incident is simply handing it off to someone else and should be minimized whenever possible.

Define the Key Terms

The following key terms include the ideas most important to the big ideas in this chapter. To review, without looking at the book or your notes, write a definition for each term, focusing on the meaning, not the wording. Then review your definition compared to your notes, this chapter, and the glossary.

Key Terms for Chapter 1

business skills	Internet service provider (ISP)	service level agreement (SLA)
cost center	malware	technical skills
escalate	metric	technical support
help desk	profit center	ticket
incident	security skills	troubleshooting skills
incident management		

List the Words Inside Acronyms

The following are the most common acronyms discussed in this chapter. As a way to review those terms, simply write down the words that each letter represents in each acronym.

Acronyms for Chapter 1

ARPANET	ITIL	OGC
CAD	LAN	PC-DOS
DoS (as in DoS attack)	MAN	POTS
DOS	MOA	RAID-1
ISP	MOU	SLA
ISDN	MS-DOS	VPN
IT	NIC	WAN

Create Mind Maps

For this chapter, create mind maps as follows:

1. Create a mind map to outline the possible divisions of a large IT department. Start with a circle labeled "IT Department," draw lines outward from the circle, and label these lines with common IT divisions. Next, add notes identifying the responsibilities of these divisions.

2. Create a mind map to list the common tiers or levels of support provided by IT departments. List the knowledge and/or experience level required by technicians at each level.

3. Create two separate mind maps to list the skills required by successful help desk technicians. Use one to list the common technical or hard skills and use the second mind map to list the soft skills.

4. List as many of the steps in a typical incident process as you can remember. After you've listed them, place them in order from the beginning of an incident until the end.

Define Other Terms

Define the following additional terms from this chapter, and check your answers in the glossary:

denial of service (DoS) attack	memorandum of understanding (MOU)	mission-critical functions or services
local area network (LAN)	metropolitan area network (MAN)	virtual private network (VPN)
memorandum of agreement (MOA)		wide area network (WAN)

Case Studies

Case Study 1

Use the Internet to search "incident" and "incident management." Define each of these terms using information you find from reliable sources on the Internet.

Case Study 2

Perform a search on the Internet using the term "help desk priorities." List and compare the priority levels used by at least two organizations and their definitions. Notice that there isn't a single definition used universally. Some organizations use numbers, some use words, and they often have anywhere between three and five priority levels.

Chapter 2

Communication Skills

Many organizations consider communication to be one of the most important skills of any help desk technician. If a help desk technician is unable to communicate effectively with a customer, it can easily frustrate and anger the customer, and this single technician can give the customer an overall bad impression of the organization. Additionally, many organizations have discovered that it is often more difficult to teach communication skills to an employee than it is to teach the technical skills. Due to this, organizations typically screen prospective help desk employees, evaluating their communication skills, and will eliminate applicants that do not meet minimum requirements in this area regardless of their technical acumen.

This chapter covers communication skills in four major sections:

- The first section, "Elements of Communication," digs into verbal and non-verbal skills, effective questioning skills, active listening skills, and communication methods to improve customer interactions.

- Next, "Recognizing Communication Barriers," discusses some of the barriers that can negatively affect communication. This includes internal and external filters, previous contacts, and cultural sensitivity.

- The "Comparing Different Communication Methods" section identifies some of the differences between different communication media. This includes in-person, telephone, email, and online communication methods such as instant messaging and chats.

- Last, the "Handling Difficult Situations" section covers many of the common difficult situations along with some ideas on how to handle conflict and defuse an incident. It also covers some common guidelines organizations provide to technicians on escalating incidents due to difficult situations.

Chapter Outline

Objectives

- Define the key terms related to communication
- Describe the differences between verbal and non-verbal skills
- Define open-ended questions and identify examples
- List methods that help desk professionals can use to improve customer interactions
- Compare different external and internal filters that affect communications
- Describe the different communication methods used by help desk professionals
- List common situations that can result in a difficult situation for help desk professionals
- Discuss methods used to defuse difficult situations

Key Terms

active listening

body language

communication

filters

inflection

kinesics

non-verbal communication

open-ended question

rapport

verbal communication

vocal tone

Elements of Communication

Communication is the process of sharing information between two or more people. Primary ways people share information is through speaking, writing, and with images, but there are other ways such as through non-verbal communications. It's worth stating the obvious here: communication involves one person or entity providing information and one or more other people receiving it. If a person is providing information but it isn't received, this isn't communication. For example, a good friend of mine had a very talkative wife and he once shared with me that they had an understanding that helped them stay together for as long as they did. He understood she had a need to talk, and she understood that he didn't have a need to listen. While there was a lot of talking, there wasn't always a lot of communication.

Help desk technicians regularly interact with users and need effective communication skills in order to help these customers. Users often don't know the technical terms associated with computer problems, so they might not verbalize the problem accurately at first. However, a successful help desk technician utilizes effective communication skills to gather information from the user and communicate issues, solutions, and progress back to the user.

> **ON THE SIDE:**　As in Chapter 1, "Introduction to Help Desk Support Roles," the terms user and customer are used interchangeably in this chapter. The primary purpose of the help desk is to assist users, and these users might be external customers or internal employees. In both situations, these users are customers of the help desk.

The importance of effective communication skills for any type of customer service personnel, including help desk personnel, cannot be overstated. Indeed, many organizations struggle with the choice between hiring entry-level technicians that have minimal technical skills but strong communication skills, or hiring technicians that have strong technical skills but minimal communication skills.

Ideally, new employees would have both sets of skills, but what if they don't have both skill sets? What can the company teach them? Organizations often find that it is much easier to teach new employees technical skills than it is to teach them communication skills. Employees without strong communication skills leave customers with a bad impression of the organization, and because of this, these employees typically do not fare well in customer service positions. In contrast, employees with strong communication skills and some technical aptitude usually find it relatively easy to master the technical requirements of a help desk job.

ON THE SIDE: Brooks Trimper is the chairman of Trimper's Rides in Ocean City, Maryland. Trimper's Rides includes games, rides, restaurants, and other attractions on the Ocean City boardwalk and has been owned and operated by the Trimper family for over 100 years. At 33, Brooks Trimper is one of the youngest members of the Trimper adults working at Trimper's Rides, yet he is in charge as the chairman. When asked why he was selected as the chairman despite his younger age, he stated simply, "I communicate very well." You can bet that he and many other members of the Trimper family have strong business skills, but communication in this family-owned business is of utmost importance. The same is true in most businesses.

Verbal versus Non-Verbal Skills

Communication is much more than just the **verbal communication**, or the spoken words. Instead, it includes several **non-verbal communication** messages that combine with the spoken words in just about any conversation. People also convey many non-verbal messages through their body language and tone of voice.

UCLA professor Albert Mehrabian performed studies on communications and determined that body language accounts for 55 percent of a first impression; 38 percent comes from tone of voice, and 7 percent comes from the spoken words. It's important to note that this is for a first impression that someone forms, and people take as long as four minutes to form a first impression. Many people use these numbers to indicate that communication is only 7 percent verbal and 93 percent nonverbal. Other studies indicate different figures for verbal and nonverbal communication, but the key is that communication is much more than just the words we use.

Body Language

Body language includes facial expressions, body movement, and placement of your arms and legs. For many people, body language is subconscious behavior. In other words, people aren't thinking about their facial expressions or body movement. When you are happy, you smile. When you are angry, you frown. That doesn't mean that everyone who is smiling is happy, but we generally give more weight to someone's body language.

As a simple example, consider the man shown in Figure 2-1. You can't see his face, but it's very likely that the body language communicates something to you. The crossed arms provide a protective barrier and might indicate boredom, lack of interest or attention, defensiveness, distrust of the message, animosity toward the speaker, or even anger. The man in the figure has his hands open, but when arms are crossed and fists are clenched, it often indicates hostility.

FIGURE 2-1

Man with crossed arms.

Imagine going into a computer store and asking a technician for help. He has a scowl on his face, his arms folded over his chest, and says, "I'd be happy to help you." When you start talking, he leans back against the wall. What message would you receive? In this example, the body language and the words aren't congruent. The words by themselves indicate the technician is ready and willing to help, but body language conveys a message like, "Oh no, not another customer."

Consider the same situation but the technician is smiling with his arms at his sides. When you approach him and start talking, he leans forward toward you as he listens and he replies with, "I'd be happy to help you." In this situation, the words and the body language are congruent.

When evaluating body language, it's important to consider the context, congruence, and clusters. Context refers to the environment or the situation. Someone standing in the cold without a coat would likely cross their arms because they are cold, while someone glaring at another person with their arms crossed indicates anger. Congruence refers to how well the body language matches the words. When the body language and the words aren't congruent, people give more weight to the body language. People generally understand it's easy for someone to utter dishonest words, and they also understand that the body tells the truth. This is true even when people aren't consciously aware of incongruent messages.

Additionally, body language is expressed in clusters of different expressions and postures. A single expression doesn't necessarily convey the full message, but clusters of facial expressions and body postures that match each other combine to send a full message.

Kinesics is the study of body movements, such as gestures and facial expressions, that are a form of non-verbal communication. One of the first people to coin the term kinesics was Ray Birdwhistell who estimated that 65 to 70 percent of all communication was non-verbal. Professionals in different fields often include kinesics in their studies to gain a better understanding of others. For example, psychologists, law enforcement personnel, and anyone performing any type of interview will often draw on kinesics to help identify when an interviewee is being deceptive.

Help desk technicians do not need to be experts in kinesics or use this information to gain additional information from customers. However, they do need to be aware that their body language is sending messages to their customers. When they are conscious of their body language, they are less likely to send incongruent messages to customers.

Some common body language and their meanings are:

- **Arms at sides or on desk or lap**. The goal is to avoid placing your hands or arms in a position that communicates anything other than listening. Crossing your arms over your chest often indicates a subconscious barrier blocking the speaker. Placing your hands on your hips indicates an air of condescension. When talking, gesturing with open hands, palms facing up, communicates an honest, inviting, and receptive attitude. In contrast, palms facing down or palms facing at the other person, indicate you are unreceptive to their messages.

- **Comfortable eye contact**. Eye contact indicates interest in what another is saying. When you are truly interested, your eyes often dilate, allowing more light in so that you can see the other person better. In contrast, when you stare at people while ignoring their words, your eyes often glaze over, resulting in a blank stare. Looking elsewhere indicates you are distracted and not listening. Some cultures perceive eye contact differently, so it's important to be aware of and follow cultural norms. For example, some cultures avoid looking directly into someone's eyes out of respect, while other cultures view a lack of eye contact with distrust.

- **Head movements**. Occasionally nodding indicates you understand the other person and are following them. In contrast, tilting your head to the side might indicate boredom or a lack of understanding.

- **Smiling**. Occasional smiling indicates friendliness and warmth while excessive smiling indicates a lack of seriousness. In her book *How to Talk to Anyone: 92 Little Tricks for Big Success in Relationships*, Leil Lowndes suggests looking at the other person for a second, then after a pause, allow a big warm smile to flood over your face and into your eyes. The delay indicates your smile is not just for anyone, but especially for them. Smiling is important when talking on the phone too. People can *hear* your smile just as much as they can *hear* your frown.

- **Posture.** Sitting or standing up straight indicates attentiveness, while slouching indicates a lack of interest. Leaning in to listen to someone as they talk indicates an interest in what they are saying, while backing up or leaning away might be perceived as though you aren't interested and are trying to move away from the conversation. It's important to be considerate of personal space when leaning in, though. You only need to lean in a little to communicate interest. If you lean in too close and violate the personal space of the person, it can threaten the listener.

This list isn't a comprehensive list of all possible body language, but it should give you an idea of some simple things that help desk personnel should be aware of when interacting with customers.

On the surface, you might think that body language doesn't apply when people are only using the phone, but it does. You attitude will often follow your body language. If you are uninterested in the conversation, allow your eyes to wander, or lean back and away in your chair, your voice will communicate this lack of interest to the person on the other end of the phone line.

> **ON THE SIDE:**   I once asked a professor of a communications course for a Human Relations Master's program at the University of Oklahoma how I could become more aware of body language and the messages others are sending. She gave me the following exercises: 1) Go to the beach, sit quietly, and listen to the waves go in and out. 2) Find a quiet place and simply pay attention to your breath while repeating the word *one* as you breathe in, and *two* as you breathe out. 3) Find a place where you can observe some trees from a distance and quietly observe their movement as the wind bends the branches and moves the leaves. These weren't the answers I was looking for, but they were on target. If you want to become better at observation, take time to be quiet and practice observing simple things.

Tone

It's not just what you say, but it's also how you say it by varying the tone in your voice. **Vocal tone** refers to how you use your voice by changing the volume, pitch, and inflection of words. For example, consider the sentence, "I'd love to." Think of how you could say those three words differently to express emotions such as anger, sarcasm, fear, joy, determination, or helpfulness.

People can often determine the attitude and mindset of a person just by noticing their tone as they talk. Someone might use a conversational tone indicating friendliness, a nervous tone indicating a lack of knowledge or preparation, or an abrupt tone indicating anger. If help desk professionals aren't aware of how important their tone is, they can easily alienate customers without knowing why.

Inflection places the emphasis in a different place within a sentence to vary the meaning. Questions end with a rising inflection and signify to the listener that they should respond. For example, "Is your account activated?" ends with a rising inflection with the word *activated*. In contrast, statements end with a falling inflection and indicate a fact. For example, "Your account is activated" ends with a falling inflection on the word *activated*.

One of the problems that occur when inflections aren't used properly is when people end statements with a rising inflection. Their statements sound as if they are questions and often indicate a lack of confidence—either in themselves or in the facts that they are trying to convey. Try it by using a rising inflection on *activated* with this sentence: "Your account is activated." When inflections are used improperly, the listener can often become confused about what they are being told.

> **ON THE SIDE:** Some people consistently use a rising inflection at the end of their sentences. The result is that their statements come across as questions rather than statements. Other people often view them as timid and unsure of themselves. Just by changing the inflection, they can change the way the others perceive them.

For most people, their tone of voice reflects their true feelings and listeners develop insight into someone's attitude toward them based on their tone. Here are a few ways that a person's tone reflects their feelings.

- Consistently speaking with the same tone and volume comes across as though you are bored. It's unpleasant to listen to, and a technician speaking in a monotone will have trouble connecting with the customer.

- Speaking too sweetly with a honeyed voice and overly cheerful words comes across as though you are overcompensating. Either listeners are left with the feeling that you are dishonest or you don't have the ability to be serious. It can also come across as condescending, as though you do not respect the other person and are talking down to them.

- A loud, rough, or gruff voice comes across as angry or irritated. It can turn just about any conversation into a confrontation.

By altering your voice tone, you can easily change the course of a conversation from good to bad. It's possible for a technician to completely answer all the questions of a user, but still leave the user dissatisfied if the technician takes on a negative tone. In contrast, it's possible for a technician to leave a customer completely satisfied even when the technician can't immediately resolve a situation.

Tone isn't only related to people. If you've ever had a dog, you probably know that they recognize tone in your voice. For example, if I call one of my dogs with the word "here" in a soft voice, he might not respond unless he thinks I have a treat for him. However, if I say it loud with a voice of authority, he responds. Over time, dogs learn to recognize the words, but they also recognize the tone. Similarly, dogs use tone in their barks. I can recognize distinctive differences between an excited bark indicating someone across the street is walking their dog, and barks of alarm when a stranger is walking to our front door.

Effective Questioning Skills

Technicians often need to get customers to describe the problem or provide additional information. As an example, a customer might complain of something vague like "the server is down" or "the Internet is down." A technician might know that it's unlikely the entire Internet is down and an organization has more than one server, so these aren't valid symptoms or problems. The technician needs to ask questions to get more information and get at the root of the problem. The following sections identify some effective techniques technicians can use when questioning the user.

Ask First

One thing you can do before you start flooding the user with questions is to ask something like, "Do you mind if I ask a few questions to get a better idea of the problem?" As with other techniques, this helps establish the help desk professional as a partner involved in solving the problem. In contrast, if the technician just starts shooting questions rapid-fire at the user, the user might feel attacked and uncomfortable. Of course, a user would rarely say "No" to such a question, but it does help prepare the user for the questions.

Use Open-Ended Questions

An **open-ended question** is any question that cannot be answered with just a one- or two-word response such as "Yes" or "No." In contrast, a closed-ended question can be answered with a short one- or two-word response. Using open-ended questions is an effective questioning technique when you are trying to get more information because it forces the respondent to provide more information. The customer is more likely to provide a comprehensive answer. The following are examples of open-ended questions:

- "What symptoms are you seeing?"
- "Can you explain the problem?"
- "What applications were running on your system when you saw the problem?"

For each of these questions, the user is prompted to give a more detailed explanation.

> **ON THE SIDE:**   Sales people frequently use open-ended questions to get a dialog going between them and customers. It's easy for a customer to say "no," but when the sales person responds with something like, "That's interesting. What is preventing you from taking advantage of this offer?," the customer is pulled into a dialogue. A sale person's goal is to learn the customer's objections and remove them, while the help desk professional's goal is to identify the problem and solve it—but open-ended questions are useful in both situations.

Admittedly, there are times when a customer is very talkative and you only need to get specific information. In these cases, a closed-ended question is more appropriate. The following are examples of closed-ended questions:

- "Have you rebooted your computer?"
- "Are you currently seeing the symptoms?"
- "Have you seen this problem before?"

Don't Ask Why

Questions using the word "why" take on a tone of interrogation and confrontation. When you ask people "why," they feel attacked, as though you are challenging them to defend their thoughts or actions. Some people respond with a defensive posture and hold back, while other people take on an offensive posture and begin to attack back. If the customer becomes either defensive or offensive, it'll be more difficult for the technician to get the information they need to resolve the problem, and almost impossible to build a collaborative customer relationship.

Consider these two example questions used by technicians to get more information from a customer after the customer says, "The Internet is down":

- One technician asks: "Why do you think the Internet is down?"
- The second technician says: "What symptoms are you seeing?"

It's highly unlikely that the Internet is actually down. The customer might have lost access to the Internet, or to a specific service available over the Internet, such as web pages or email. Technicians will probably know that the Internet is not down, but their goal is still to get more information on the problem.

The first question challenges the customer to defend the statement. The customer might explain the symptoms but feel attacked. Two more questions into the conversation, the customer might sense another attack and blow up with the technician not having any idea of what happened.

In contrast, the second question attempts to build a collaborative relationship with the customer. The question indicates the technician is there to help and invites the customer to explain the problem. The technician might later point out the exact cause of the problem without pointing out that the Internet was not down and so not demeaning the customer.

You might have noticed that both questions are open-ended questions. The customer is unable to answer either one with just a one- or two-word answer. However, it's obvious that just asking an open-ended question isn't enough. The question also needs to help build rapport with the customer and questions starting with "why" rarely do so.

As a rule, it's best to avoid starting a question with "why" in just about any conversation. This is true with other relationships, not just technician/customer interactions. A simple conversation can spiral into an argument without either person fully understanding what happened. There might be times when you need to know why, but there are other ways to ask. For example, instead of asking, "Why did you do that?" you could instead ask, "Can you help me understand what led you to that action?"

Active Listening Skills

Another communication technique successful technicians use on the job is **active listening**. At the basic level of listening, you hear the words but you don't always understand the message. If you focus on the speaker using active listening techniques, you can understand the full meaning of the message. Active listeners pay attention to what someone is saying. They make eye contact, nod occasionally to indicate understanding, and occasionally respond with statements demonstrating they understand the message. When they don't understand something, they might ask questions to get clarification.

In many day-to-day conversations, the listener is simply waiting to speak rather than trying to hear and understand the speaker. This puts up a barrier to the conversation and prevents the listener from gaining a full understanding of the topic.

Think about a time when you were talking to a friend and it was apparent he or she wasn't listening. You knew it. You weren't being fooled. How did that make you feel? Ignored? Angry? Resentful? Other people (including customers) know when you aren't listening to them and they have many of the same feelings.

Consider the people in Figure 2-2. No one is looking at the speaker. Instead, they're looking down at their own devices or paperwork. The man on the right might be referring to his notes to respond, but with the speaker leaning forward, fists balled up on the table, he might not be confident the man standing will hear what he has to say. The speaker's fists can easily be interpreted as anger, so it's possible the attendees are reluctant to make eye contact, and are trying to distract themselves. The woman on the right even has her hand between her and the speaker providing a barrier, which helps to block the message.

FIGURE 2-2

Meeting participants.

In contrast, think about a time when you were talking to someone who was actively listening to you. They probably did some simple actions, such as looking at you while you talked, occasionally nodding, and responding with words and phrases indicating they understood you. If you're like most people, knowing that someone is listening to you is much more gratifying than being ignored.

When you are actively listening, you can ensure your body language matches your intent. Make comfortable eye contact, occasionally nod, and respond when appropriate to show your understanding. Some people purposely fake this by simply nodding and smiling and might even get away with it for a while. However, they usually do not hear the message, and in a technician/customer interaction, hearing the message is of paramount importance.

Figure 2-3 provides a contrast to Figure 2-2. These are the same people in the meeting, but the body language tells a much different story. The speaker is using open hand gestures and there isn't any hint of anger. The participants are looking at him and appear to be listening. The two people on the left are both leaning forward, further indicating that they are listening. Note the woman on the right. She is leaning back in her chair, which might be interpreted as a lack of interest, but her head is tilted forward, giving a subtle indication she is listening. In this case, the combination of leaning back in her chair while facing the speaker indicates she is comfortable as she is listening.

FIGURE 2-3

Meeting participants using active listening skills.

Responding to Show Understanding

Responding to the speaker helps you demonstrate that you are actively listening and you understand the message. There are three levels of responding, with each showing a different depth of understanding. As an example, consider a customer who is extremely frustrated and shows up with this complaint: "I have business reports I absolutely have to send out today, but every time I open my email program, it locks up, forcing me to reboot my computer!" An active listener might respond by repeating, paraphrasing, or reflecting:

- **Repeating**. This is where you repeat the same words back to the person. For example, you might say, "Your email program locks up."

- **Paraphrasing**. Instead of using the exact same words, you would respond with similar words and phrases to demonstrate your understanding. For example, you might say, "You can't send reports because of a problem with your email program."

- **Reflecting**. When reflecting a message, you include feelings and/or demonstrate your empathy to the person. For example, you might say, "Wow, I'm sorry you're having problems with the email program and can't get your reports sent. That must be frustrating."

One thing to be aware of when you accurately reflect feelings is that the other person will often respond with "Yes" and repeat the feeling, sometimes with more emotion. That's natural. For example, if you say, "that must be frustrating," don't be surprised if the person reiterates, "yes, it's frustrating!" The truth is people are often so grateful that someone understands them that they just emphasize it again. You can follow up with something as simple as, "I can help."

Using the LISTEN Strategy

You can use the letters in the word LISTEN to remember the different elements of active listening:

- **L. Look interested**. Ensure your body language communicates to the other person that you are actively listening.

- **I. Involve yourself in the conversation**. This includes responding, nodding, making statements, and asking questions.

- **S. Summarize**. When it's your turn to talk, summarize your understanding. You can do this by repeating, paraphrasing, and reflecting.

- **T. Test your understanding**. Periodically ask clarifying questions or restate what the person has said in your own words to ensure you do understand them.

- **E. Eye contact**. Make comfortable eye contact with the other person.

- **N. Nod**. Occasionally nod to indicate you understand.

Methods to Improve Customer Interactions

One of the best techniques help desk technicians can do to improve customer interactions is to approach the interaction as a team effort. Customers have problems that they want solved and the technicians want to help customers solve them. By starting out with a collaborative mindset, the technician guides the interaction as a team effort to solve the problem.

In contrast, unsuccessful technicians approach many customer complaints as more problems and treat customers as adversaries. They expect the customer to give them trouble instead of assistance while troubleshooting a problem, and very often, they get exactly what they expect.

The following sections identify some simple methods help desk professionals can use to create a collaborative relationship with the customer and improve overall customer interactions.

Maintain a Positive Attitude

It's important for technicians to maintain a positive attitude when talking with customers. This doesn't mean that technicians always need to be overly cheerful, but it does mean that technicians don't allow problems to irritate them.

Imagine going into your doctor and after he listens to your chest, he says, "Oh no!" That's not what you want to hear—it sounds like the problem is so bad that even the doctor is alarmed. On the hand, if the doctor maintains a positive professional demeanor, even when giving you bad news, you'll have more confidence in the doctor's ability to help you. Similarly, if a technician maintains a positive professional demeanor, customers have more confidence in the technician's ability to help them.

Customers who are experiencing problems might come across as angry or frustrated. However, it's important to realize that they aren't angry or frustrated with the technician that's trying to help them. (Or, at least they don't start out that way.) Instead, they're upset with the problem. Technicians who are able to stay focused on helping the customer resolve the problem while maintaining a positive attitude are better prepared to resolve the problem. In contrast, technicians that start out with a negative attitude often fuel the fire and find that many customers quickly begin redirecting their anger at the technician.

Build Rapport

One of the first goals of the technician during a customer incident is to build **rapport**. Rapport indicates a harmonious relationship between two or more people and it indicates they are able to relate well to each other. Rapport has three behavioral components: mutual attention, positivity, and coordination. Help desk professionals can establish and build rapport through attention (using active listening skills), positivity (maintaining a positive attitude), and demonstrating they want to create a collaborative relationship to solve the problem.

Establishing rapport doesn't mean the other person will be your best friend forever. However, the harmonious relationship will help create effective communication channels so that the technician can understand and resolve the problem as quickly as possible.

Sales-people use several different techniques to establish and build rapport that help desk professionals can mimic. They try to find common ground with the person, which can often be done with small talk to help break the ice. They try to get in step with the other person by matching their language, posture, manners, and by showing empathy. Additionally, they attempt to demonstrate a sincere understanding of the other person's point of view. When people are understood, they often feel an obligation to understand the person that sincerely tried to understand them. A primary method of demonstrating understanding is with active listening skills as described earlier in this chapter.

Simple questions such as, "How is your day going?" might sound hackneyed, but they can be effective at starting to build rapport. Many people automatically respond with something like, "Fine, and how are you?" This also gives the technician an opportunity to build the rapport with, "Good, thanks for asking." The conversation can then move into the customer's problem. This interaction might only take 20 seconds, but it is much more effective than starting the conversation with, "What's your problem?"

Even if the customer doesn't respond favorably, the interaction can still build rapport. For example, if the customer responds with something like, "Horrible. I've been fighting this problem for three hours and can't seem to get any help," the technician can still use this to build rapport. For example, the technician can respond with, "I'm sorry you're having a problem. I'm sure we can work together to resolve it."

Some other phrases technicians can use at the beginning of a conversation are:

- "I can help you."
- "How may I help you?"
- "What can I do for you today?"
- "Good morning" (or "Good afternoon" or "Good evening")

Include Words of Courtesy

Basic courtesy goes a long way toward creating a positive customer interaction. When they aren't used, they often make the speaker appear rude, uncaring, and disrespectful. In contrast, when they are used, they let others know that they are respected and appreciated. Some common words and phrases of courtesy are:

- "Thank you" (instead of "thanks")
- "Please" (instead of nothing, indicating the speaker is issuing a command instead of a request)
- "You're welcome" (instead of not acknowledging courtesy from others at all)
- "My pleasure" (instead of "you're welcome")
- "Yes" (instead of "uh huh")
- "Yes sir," "Yes miss," or "Yes ma'am" (instead of "yeah")
- "I'm sorry, I didn't hear what you said" or "pardon me" (instead of "huh")

None of these words or phrases are difficult, but they can significantly add to any interaction, not just interactions with customers. As an example, family, friends, and acquaintances appreciate a heartfelt "Thank You" just as much as a customer would appreciate it, maybe even more.

In contrast, technicians should avoid some words and phrases because they can include a lack of courtesy or lack of respect to the customer, or convey the wrong meaning. Here are a few:

- "To be honest…" This indicates that the speaker isn't always honest, but only honest when they use this phrase.

- "No worries" (or "no problem"). This comes across as minimizing the customer's problem or issue. There are times when these phrases might be appropriate, such as after someone says thank you; however, "you're welcome" or "my pleasure" is much clearer and avoids misunderstanding.

- "I only work here" (or "that's just our policy"). These phrases indicate the technician really doesn't care about the customer's problem and isn't interested in solving it. Instead, the technician comes across as making excuses. There might be times when the answer is due to a company policy, but instead of just saying "that's just our policy," the technician can explain the issue further.

- "You should" (or "you'll have to"). These phrases are directive in nature and make the technician sound like a supervisor and the customer a subordinate. Even if the customer needs to take some type of action, the technician should soften the words by saying "can you" instead of "you should." In some cases, the technician can offer the customer a choice between two or more actions that can resolve the problem. Giving the customer a choice allows the customer to maintain a sense of control in the situation.

Avoid Technical Jargon and Acronyms

Technicians commonly use technical jargon and acronyms when talking to other technicians, but when talking to customers, they should avoid it. For example, a technician might realize that a new piece of hardware is causing stop errors because the user's computer needs a firmware upgrade. Here are two ways the technician could communicate this to the customer:

- "Your BIOS needs to be flashed so that the OS can stop giving BSODs."

- "It looks like your system is having problems recognizing this new hardware, but we can resolve it by upgrading the firmware your computer uses to start."

The first example indicates that the Basic Input/Output System (BIOS) firmware needs to be upgraded in a process commonly called "flashing the BIOS" by technicians. After upgrading the firmware, the operating system (OS) will operate properly without causing a stop error commonly called a blue screen of death (BSOD). The second example provides the same answer, but in language that just about anyone can understand.

Don't Interrupt

Give customers time to explain their problem without interruption. When they're done, you can ask follow-up questions if necessary, but by letting them explain the situation you are building rapport. In contrast, if you interrupt customers in mid-stream, the phone call might easily change from a typical help desk call to one where you're dealing with a difficult situation.

Use Effective Questioning Techniques to Get More Information

It's almost a given that customers will not immediately provide all the information necessary to solve a problem. Technicians must learn how to ask questions in a way that prompts the customer to give more information. The "Effective Questioning Skills" section earlier in this chapter provides details on how to use effective questioning techniques.

Be Willing to Say "I Don't Know"

There may be times when a customer asks a question that the technician just can't answer. It is much better to simply say, "I don't know" than to try to talk through it or make up an answer. Responding with phrases such as "I think" or "I believe" indicate a lack of knowledge or self-confidence. They make technicians appear as though they are making up answers. In addition to saying "I don't know," you can respond with additional phrases such as:

- "I don't know, but I'll find out."
- "I don't know, but I can research that for you."
- "I don't know, but this is what I'm going to do."

It's important to remember that if you tell the customer that you will research it or you will find out, make sure you do. If you never get back to the customer with the answer, it indicates you aren't true to your word.

Many times customers ask questions out of curiosity and don't really need an answer. If you suspect this is the case, you can say something like, "I don't know. I can research it for you if it's important to you." If it isn't important, the customer will typically say something like, "No, I was just curious," but they will appreciate your offer just the same.

ON THE SIDE: Check out *Powerful Phrases for Effective Customer Service: Over 700 Ready-to-Use Phrases and Scripts That Really Get Results* by Renée Evenson for some excellent examples of phrases and scripts used by help desk professionals. She's also published *Powerful Phrases for Dealing with Difficult People: Over 325 Ready-to-Use Words and Phrases for Working with Challenging Personalities*, another book that is useful for help desk professionals or managers of help desks. In addition to the phrases and scripts, she also provides some insight into why these phrases work.

Recognizing Communication Barriers

Ideally, when two people communicate, the message sent is always the same message that is received. In reality, this is rarely the case. Instead, we have a variety of communication barriers that affect the communication and despite our best efforts, people often hear a completely different message than what we send. Figure 2-4 shows a simple example where one person is asking the other person to keep a secret, and the other person is hearing "new gossip."

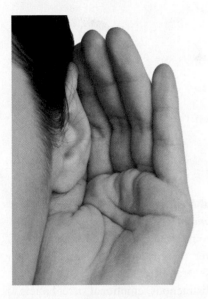

FIGURE 2-4

The received message isn't always the same as the sent message.

When you were a child, you might have played the game of telephone (also called Chinese whispers). You start with a group of people in a line or a circle. One person whispers a phrase into the ear of the person next to them, that person whispers the phrase to the next person, and so on. Errors are common in what people hear and repeat and the end message is often completely different from the original message. Some of the common reasons why the end message is different are:

- The word or phrases are unfamiliar, so the listeners change them to more familiar words and phrases.

- Sometimes listeners just don't hear the original message because the speaker didn't speak loud enough for them to hear the message. In the game, listeners are typically not allowed to ask the speaker to repeat. In real life, listeners often don't ask the speaker to repeat the message and instead simply nod and smile.

- The listener's background or culture places a different meaning on the words, and the listener adds in this meaning when they repeat the message.

- The tone or voice volume of the speaker indicated a different message to the listener and the listener changed the words to match the non-verbal message.

Filters

In a perfect world, everything that we communicate is received exactly the same way that we intend it to be received. Unfortunately, we don't live in a perfect world. Instead, there are a variety of **filters** that modify the way messages are received. Figure 2-5 gives a simple example where a man is talking to a woman and sending what he thinks is a clear message, but the woman on the right receives a completely different message.

FIGURE 2-5

Filters modify messages, changing their meaning.

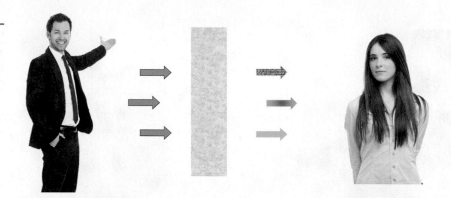

Author John Gray wrote a bestselling book titled *Men Are from Mars, Women Are from Venus: The Classic Guide to Understanding the Opposite Sex*, which describes many of the differences in men and woman and how these differences affect communication and relationships. However, these filters aren't limited to messages between men and women. There are several different communication filters that affection communication including distractions, emotional state, beliefs, and their personality traits.

Distractions

Distractions include anything that prevents the listener from focusing on or hearing the message; they can be internal or external. Examples of internal distractions include the listener being preoccupied with a different problem or issue, or that the listener is simply tired. External distractions could be background noise such as a jet flying overhead, a construction worker hammering into the cement with a jackhammer, or simply loud conversations nearby.

When speaking to another person, it's best to eliminate as many of the distractions as possible. This isn't always possible, but at the very least, the speaker can be aware of them and work around them. For example, if a loud jet is flying overhead it's best to wait until it passes. If an individual appears to have internal distractions, it's often best to address them directly with a simple question such as, "Is this a good time to talk?" It shows empathy and allows the other person to gracefully back out of the conversation. It also includes the subtle question of, "Can I have your attention?" without bluntly saying, "Listen to me!"

Emotional State

The emotional state of both the speaker and the listener can filter the message. People can be anxious, distraught, angry, happy, cheerful, and much more. If the listener is upset or angry, just about any message can be filtered and come across with a negative tone. Similarly, if the person speaking is sad or angry, these emotions often come out in the message.

Help desk technicians should be aware that upset customers can easily filter messages making them sound negative, so it is important to speak clearly and directly. If the technician is able to stay focused on the problem and build rapport with the user, the user's anger or frustration will typically fade. In contrast, technicians that don't understand how messages can be filtered might use words or phrases the amplify the user's emotions. For example, if a technician starts asking "why" questions, an irritated user might become an angry user.

Ideally, help desk personnel will compartmentalize their emotions while on a trouble call. Compartmentalizing emotions simply means that you are able to set them aside for the time being and come back to them later. Most people have this ability. Imagine you have a backpack with a dozen different pockets or compartments. While working, you learn that your pet is sick and you become worried about him. However, instead of letting this worry affect your work, you package up this emotion and store it one of the backpack's compartments. After work, you open up the backpack compartment, bring out your concern, and work through it.

> **ON THE SIDE:**   People compartmentalize emotions all the time. The only danger is if you never go back into your metaphorical backpack, pull out the stuff you stored there, and work through it. Some people try to stuff everything into their backpack and avoid dealing with it at all costs. The long-term result is an overloaded backpack that eventually weighs them down so heavily that they have trouble completing the simplest of tasks. With their backpack full, they don't have room to stuff anything else into it, so even relatively small things cause them problems.

On the other extreme, some people are unable to compartmentalize any of their emotions. They "wear their heart on their sleeve" and react immediately to every issue that appears. These people might have some phenomenal talents in other arenas, but will likely have some difficulty working as a help desk technician.

Beliefs

Beliefs represent an acceptance that something is true or it exists. The beliefs might be based on facts, as people perceive the facts, or based on their experiences. A combination of mutually supportive beliefs makes up a belief system and affects a person's perspective on the world around them. An extreme example is in the Middle East. People in different countries have grown up learning completely different belief systems based on their family, friends, schools, and their experiences. When two people from opposing countries in this region try to talk, communication is difficult, if not impossible. Instead, mediators try to interpret and translate messages between the two.

You won't need a mediator when dealing with most customers, but you should be aware that a customer's belief system could be different than yours and it can filter messages. For example, imagine a customer has the belief that a help desk professional should be able to solve any technical problem. This customer might make unreasonable demands based on this belief. In this example, the help desk technician needs to take a step backward and clarify which services the help desk provides. This can sometimes require the technician to repeat the policies two or three times before it breaks down the barrier of the customer's faulty belief. Other times, the technician might need to escalate the problem to a supervisor so that the customer can hear the same message from someone else.

Personality Traits

Some people are extreme introverts, some are extreme extroverts, and there is a wide range of people in between. Introverts tend to think more than extroverts do before they speak. Extroverts tend to express themselves verbally easier than introverts do. They are often able to draw others into a conversation by paraphrasing and asking open-ended questions. No one is completely an introvert or completely an extrovert, but instead people are a mix of both with a tendency to be more of one or the other.

There's nothing wrong with being an introvert or being an extrovert, but it is important to understand that a person's personality traits can affect their communication. Effective communicators are able to recognize differences and adapt to the communication methods used by the other person.

> **AUTHOR'S NOTE:**   Dr. Jennifer Kahnweiler, in her book *Quiet Influence: The Introvert's Guide to Making a Difference*, provides some great insight into how introverts and extroverts communicate. The book also dispels some of the misconceptions about introverts and extroverts. For example, many successful public speakers and actors are introverts.

Previous Contact

Previous contact can also be a challenge, especially if the previous contact was not a positive experience. For example, if customers have not been treated well by other help desk professionals, they will often expect to be treated poorly again. Because of this, they could easily be more confrontational and hostile than a customer that consistently had favorable experiences with the organization.

While help desk professionals cannot change experiences from previous contact, they can create a new experience from the current contact. If customers repeatedly say how poorly they were previously treated, the best course of action is to show empathy but then focus back on the current situation and demonstrate a willingness to help the customer now. Sometimes customers simply want to let someone know what happened, and after they voice their complaint, they will let it go.

Admittedly, some people just can't let an old experience go. If a customer continues to focus on the previous experience, the technician can be assertive and direct. For example, the technician could say, "I'm sorry about the problems you had. I can help you resolve your current problem but I need your help to focus on it. Or, if you'd like, I can connect you to the customer service department to file a complaint related to your previous experience." This gives the customer a choice, while also communicating that the technician wants to help but needs the customer to cooperate.

Cultural Sensitivity

Cultural differences can strongly affect communication if the speaker and listener share different cultural norms. We are strongly affected by our personal history, our country of origin, and our upbringing. Many people understand these differences and accept them, but there are times when people do not understand the differences and they cause communication problems.

As a simple example, people in Japan often avoid eye contact out of respect. Someone that makes direct eye contact might be considered rude. In contrast, people in the United States (US) make eye contact when they are actively listening. Someone that doesn't make eye contact while listening might be viewed as non-attentive. If one person from each country starts talking and they aren't aware of the cultural differences, it could significantly impact their communications.

Similarly, there are many differences in body language between cultures. In the US, a thumbs-up signal indicates "Yes" or "Good," while in Iran, it is vulgar. Forming a circle with your thumb and forefinger indicates "A-OK" in the US but is considered obscene in Germany and Brazil and represents "zero" or "worthless" in France and Belgium. In the Middle East, nodding the head down indicates agreement while nodding it up indicates disagreement. In many cultures, nodding your head up and down doesn't imply agreement at all, only that you are listening and understanding.

> **ON THE SIDE:** The book *Global Business Etiquette: A Guide to International Communication and Customs* by Jeanette S. Martin and Lillian H. Chaney provides a wealth of information on different cultural norms. This information is almost essential for international travelers.

One benefit when considering cultural differences is that when people visit another culture, they typically learn to adapt to the differences. With this in mind, you don't necessarily need to know the cultural differences in every other country in the world, but you should know that there are differences and be sensitive to them when interacting with people from different cultures.

> **AUTHOR'S NOTE:** While in the US Navy, I was stationed in Misawa, Japan and lived amongst Japanese people for about three years. They live in cramped spaces and respect other people's privacy even when standing right next to each other. Eye contact is rare. Even when speaking to you, Japanese people will often look down out of respect. I then moved to the Philippines, where people are very friendly and curious. I found that Filipino people often stared at me, and when I made eye contact, they quickly responded with a welcome smile. Coming from Japan, this was a bit of a culture shock, and confused me for a while—but only a short while.

Comparing Different Communication Methods

Many people have adopted their favorite communication method when contacting others. They might prefer to talk in person, on the telephone, via email, chat, text message, or some other method. Similarly, many organizations use one or more of these methods to communicate with customers and have their preferred method. Help desk professionals might need to work with one or all of them and should be aware of some techniques that are effective or potentially problematic with each.

In-Person

In-person communication can occur in several different environments. IT departments within a company often send technician's to the user's desk to assist. In some consumer stores, customers bring their computing equipment to the store and talk directly to technicians. For example, Apple stores have a Genius Bar where technicians talk to users face-to-face and provide direct assistance.

Communicating with people in person is often the easiest because you can take in all the body language. Similarly, the other person is able to see you and take in your body language. With this in mind, it's important to remember that in-person interactions include both verbal and non-verbal communication. As mentioned earlier, if the non-verbal communication conflicts with the verbal communication, people will typically believe the non-verbal communication. In other words, if your body language says one thing and your words say something else, people will not believe your words.

Telephone

Telephone communication is very common and can be relatively inexpensive for a company. The call center can be located in a low cost area and dozens of technicians can answer calls as they come in. As an example, many Internet service providers (ISPs) use call centers to assist subscribers. When users call in, they are routed to the next available operator.

One of the biggest things for telephone technicians to remember is to be empathetic and sound sensitive to the user frustrations. Telephone interactions don't allow people to view body language, but listeners can often take in a lot from the speaker just by listening to the tone. As an example, you can tell when someone is talking with a smile. Similarly, you can tell when they are talking with a scowl. Ideally, technicians will remain calm, positive, and sound sensitive to the user frustrations.

Users often have to wait in a queue before a technician begins helping them. A queue works just like it does when waiting in a line in a store. The difference is that while waiting in a line at a store, you can see the progress. While waiting in a telephone queue, you often don't know if you're next or if there are 20 people ahead of you. Some companies understand this and give you periodic notifications letting you know where you are in the line.

Other companies swap soft elevator music with periodic loud messages saying, "YOUR CALL IS VERY IMPORTANT TO US. ALL CALLS WILL BE RECORDED FOR TRAINING PURPOSES." The result is often a highly irritated customer once the technician finally connects.

It's common for an organization to give technicians a script to use when working with customers. This includes an initial greeting such as, "Hello. My name is _____ and I can help you," and a closing such as, "Thank you for being a loyal customer since _____. Is there anything else I can help you with today?"

> **ON THE SIDE:** Chapter 1 mentioned receiving incidents via telephone. As a reminder, many companies often record these calls. These recordings can be used for training and can also be used to review a call to determine what happened between a technician and a customer.

Text-Only Communications

Email, instant message (IM), and chat communication use only text to exchange information between two or more people. You might remember from the beginning of this chapter that in a face-to-face conversation, the words make up only about 7 percent of a message when people first meet. The remainder of the message comes through non-verbal messages.

With text-only communications, only the words are present, making it extremely important to ensure the words are clear. Also, even though only the words are present, people typically read the words with their own internal filters. Messages can come across as sarcastic, hostile, and angry even when they're not. In general, it's best to avoid joking around in text-only communications, especially when you do not know the other person; people don't always know you're joking.

> **ON THE SIDE:** It is acceptable to use abbreviations that both participants in the chat session are familiar with, but this knowledge shouldn't be assumed. One common method to ensure an acronym is clear is to spell it out the first time it's used. For example, it's possible to point out a FAQ page to the user, but the first time FAQ is used, it would be spelled out as frequently asked questions (FAQ).

Many organizations that communicate with customers with text-only communications provide help desk professionals with specific scripts. Technicians can copy and paste these scripts into the email, IM, or chat windows.

Email

Email is used by some organizations instead of phones, instant messaging, or chat windows. The benefit is that most users do not expect an immediate answer, so the organization is able to manage their technician's time. In contrast, the other methods do provide almost immediate interaction.

It's common to use an autoresponder with email. When the user sends the email, the organization's mail server receives the message and replies with an automatic response indicating the organization received the email and will address it within a certain time. This autoresponse might also include links to frequently asked question (FAQ) pages or online help pages.

When responding, it's important to address the customer's stated issue. Some technicians that reply via email get into the habit of copying canned responses that might be completely accurate, yet have nothing to do with the customer's problem.

IM and Chat

In instant message (IM) and chat windows, the scripts start off with introductory phrases such as, "Hello, my name is .... How can I help you?" or, "Hello, my name is .... I can help you." After the customer explains the problem, the technician solves it and provides feedback. During this interaction, it's important that the technician doesn't leave long pauses while they are researching something. For example, if the customer asks for help on something that the technician needs to ask about, the technician should type something like, "I don't have that answer right now, but I can find out. Do you mind if I step away for a minute to get you the answer?" Without doing this, the customer might think the link was somehow disconnected and they are waiting for someone that will never return.

When the problem is resolved, technicians should try to ensure that the customer received the help they need and close the conversation amicably. Some common phrases used to do this include:

- "Thank you. We/I appreciate your business."
- "Is there anything else that I can do for you today?"

ON THE SIDE: It's easy for technicians to assume that everyone understands some common text messaging or chat abbreviations that they use, but these aren't common to everyone, and many even have dual meanings. Technicians should avoid them and take the time to spell out their messages.

Handling Difficult Situations

Ideally, all customers are courteous, cheerful, and a pleasure to work with. In reality, many customers are less than courteous and maybe even rude, and they bring many challenges to help desk personnel. Many situations result in a difficult customer requiring extra time and attention, and some basic strategies are helpful. The goal is to guide the interaction from one where it's problematic to one where the customer's problem is resolved to the best ability of the organization and the customer is satisfied.

Here are some general guidelines that help desk professionals can adopt that will help them handle difficult situations:

- Do not argue with the customer. No matter how confrontational a customer is, arguing will only make it worse. This doesn't mean that the help desk technician needs to agree with everything that the customer says, but it does mean they should not engage in conflict. As mentioned before, it is best to focus on the problem that needs to be resolved rather than the emotions surrounding the incident.

- Avoid asking questions starting with "Why." As mentioned previously, this comes off as an attack. Customers might take on a defensive posture, or if they are already angry, they might go into an attack mode.

- Avoid being defensive or judgmental. Even if technicians avoid the use of "why" they can still sound defensive or judgmental, and thus negatively affect the interaction. Some technicians make fun of users behind their back using terms such as ID-ten-T (cryptically calling the person an "idiot") or ST-One (indicating the person is as smart as a "stone"), but this should be avoided. These terms translate into judgmental attitudes toward the customer and all teach other technicians a lack of respect for customers.

- Be aware of your posture. Sitting or standing up straight indicates attentiveness, while slouching indicates a lack of interest. Even while talking on the phone, a person's posture can affect how they respond.

- Treat every problem as important. Even if you know a problem is relatively simple to solve, treat it as important while working with the customer. For customers that turn to the help desk for help with a problem, it is important. Otherwise they wouldn't have asked for help.

ON THE SIDE: Help desk professionals are prone to burnout, especially if they are hearing the exact same problems from customers. When they hear these same issues, they might remember giving the same response 100 times before but forget that this customer never heard it. They can unconsciously take on a judgmental attitude resulting in an increase in difficult situations. Help desk supervisors often keep an eye out for burnout symptoms and take action to mitigate the problem. Chapter 3, "Personal Skills," includes information on managing stress and recognizing burnout that is useful for help desk technicians.

Expect the Best

As the old saying goes, "Expect the best, but prepare for the worst." Help desk professionals prepare for the worst by ensuing they have the skills to handle difficult situations. By expecting the best, they can often influence the outcome by amplifying the positive.

Robert Rosenthal documented what has been called the self-fulfilling prophecy in his 1968 book *Pygmalion in the Classroom*. Elementary school teachers were manipulated to believe that specific students had exceptional abilities and were expected to bloom academically and intellectually during the school year. All the students were tested, but the test results were not used to identify the "gifted" students. Instead, the researchers selected these "gifted" students randomly. Researchers tested the "gifted" students for the next two years and found that they actually did bloom. Teachers knew the identities of these students and expected the best of them. They consistently described these students more positively with a greater chance of being successful, and whether intentional or not, the teachers positively influenced the students.

Similarly, scientists learned that expectations affect outcomes and as a result, they commonly do double-blind studies. In other words, both testers and participants in a study are not aware of which participants are in an actual test group and which participants are receiving some type of placebo.

With this in mind, imagine if one help desk professional is told that all the difficult problem calls will go to him. How do you think he might handle most calls? He might be looking for any hint of problems and as soon as he senses it, he would go into a much more assertive and possibly even confrontational mode. Minor problems would easily become major issues.

In most situations, you get what you expect, so it's important for technicians to start every help desk call expecting the best possible outcome. When you expect the best, that's often what you get, and there are many underlying factors that affect this concept. For example, how does your left foot feel right now? Before reading that sentence, you probably weren't aware of your foot. Now, how does your right hand feel? Your mind cannot stay aware of everything at the same time so instead it filters your awareness based on what you're focused on. If you're focused on the best attributes of a person, the best attributes are often amplified. Similarly, if you focus on the worst attributes of a person, you can amplify these as well.

Common Situations

While it's impossible to list every possible difficult situation, there are many common difficult situations. This section includes some of these.

Angry Customer

One of the most common difficult situations is an angry customer. There are many reasons why a customer might be angry, such as dissatisfaction with a product or service. The immediate result is that the user is usually not able to communicate professionally or in a productive manner.

As mentioned previously, the biggest thing to remember here is that the customer is not angry with the technician. Instead, the customer is angry with the situation. The technician should not argue or respond to the anger but instead should stay focused on the problem. At some point, either the customer will cool off, or the technician needs to be assertive and direct by telling the user that the problem can't be solved until they are able work on a solution together.

> **ON THE SIDE:** There's a difference between being angry at the situation and abusive to the technician. Most organizations have policies in place that explicitly state that technicians do not need to tolerate abusive behavior such as inappropriate language or personal attacks. Ideally, the technician is able to defuse the abusive behavior, but they often have the option of either terminating the incident when the user crosses a pre-defined line, or referring the customer to a supervisor or someone else trained to deal with such abusive personalities.

Complainers

Some users contact the help desk and monopolize the conversation by complaining. They want to have their problem solved, but also want to voice their complaints. They typically complain about the company's product or services, and can even complain about a previous help desk contact.

The best way to handle this is by letting the customer complain and vent their feelings, at least for a little while. At some point, the help desk professional needs to guide the customer back to a resolution. A good transition method is to use empathy to express understanding, and then offer to help.

Confused Customer

One of the most challenging situations occurs when customers are upset but really do not know what they want. A help desk professional can be working with a customer to understand the problem and then get to a point where it's unclear what to do. Consider this exchange:

- Help desk professional: "What can I do to help me make this right for you?"
- Customer: "I don't know."

Did the customer just call to complain? Possibly. However, it's important for the help desk professional to address this directly. One possible reply is, "I really want to help you, but if I don't know what you want, I don't see how I can help."

The underlying problem here is most likely that the customer is irritated and confused due to the problem. After the customer vents a little, it's important for the help desk professional to focus back on the problem. Typically, the customer was unable to accomplish something and this is the cause of the problem. If the help desk professional can focus on this issue, they can determine if the problem can be resolved.

Power User

Some users are very knowledgeable and might even be more technically savvy than the help desk professional. This isn't a problem unless power users try to elevate their status during the conversation and start acting like a know-it-all. For example, if a technician tries to guide the user through a series of steps but the user starts talking about how this problem is different and these steps won't work, it prevents the technician from helping the user. No matter how savvy these power users are, it's important to remember they couldn't solve the problem on their own and that's why they're asking for help. However, the technician still has a responsibility to help the user.

A common strategy for dealing with know-it-all personalities is to enlist their help in solving the problem. Phrases such as "we can solve this" indicate a respect for the person's knowledge and ability and encourage them to collaborate with the technician.

Handling Conflict

Despite the best customer skills, help desk professionals will still come face to face with some difficult situations where a customer is upset. The customer might start out angry or become angry at some point during the incident. One of the most important techniques during these times is to address the conflict directly. This sounds obvious, but the truth is many people want to avoid conflict by either ignoring it or trying to deflect it.

Many other techniques were addressed in this chapter and are summarized here:

- **Use active listening skills**. This includes both listening and responding to show understanding. When customers recognize that they are understood, they are more willing to understand the organization's perspective.

- **Maintain a positive attitude**. This doesn't mean that the technician needs to be overly cheerful, which can easily come off as condescending. Instead, the technician needs to remain positive while evoking a sense of confidence that the problem can be solved. Simple phrases such as "I can help" or "I can solve that problem" are some examples.

- **Demonstrate empathy**. While maintaining a positive attitude, the technician should also demonstrate empathy at the customer's situation. Simple phrases like "I'm sorry," or "That must be frustrating" can go a long way toward defusing a situation.

- **Let the customer throw off some steam**. Letting the customer express some anger normally doesn't hurt anyone. As long as the customer isn't abusive or personally attacking the help desk technician, this can actually be helpful. After customers vent their anger, they are often much more receptive to working with the technician to resolve the problem.

Defusing Incidents

One important action to remember when defusing incidents is not to match the tone and volume of the customer. Think of Bob and Joe talking to each other. Bob unwittingly says something that offends Joe and Joe begins to raise his voice. If Bob matches Joe's tone and volume, Joe will very likely become louder and more boisterous. This can quickly turn into a shouting match, or worse, physical violence.

Here's the same situation handled a little differently. Bob unwittingly says something that offends Joe and Joe begins to raise his voice. Bob keeps his original tone and remains calm. Joe might continue to blow off steam for a while, but as long as Bob doesn't engage in a shouting match, Joe will eventually calm down. This doesn't mean that Bob needs to be timid. He can let Joe continue for a moment and then respond with an authoritative voice saying something like, "I need you to stop shouting," or, "Can we talk about this without shouting for a minute?"

Another way to defuse an incident where someone is yelling is to lower your voice. The louder they become, the softer you become. At some point, the other person will realize that they have lost their composure while you have kept yours, and they will typically become apologetic.

Admittedly, this only works with reasonable people. Some people have found that they can get what they want through yelling and bullying. A customer might try to bully a help desk professional by yelling, and it is unlikely that the help desk professional will be able to rationalize with this person at all. Organizations typically have specific scripts of what to say if a customer won't calm down. Some of the words that can be used include:

- "I want to help you. What is it that you want?" or "I want to help you, but it will be a lot easier if you can calm down." This can get the customer to focus back on the problem rather than the emotions.

- "You need to stop swearing at me." Help desk professionals should not be subjected to an angry customer spouting off obscenities. This sentence is simple and direct and is usually enough to get most people to stop using abusive language.

- "Would you like to talk to my supervisor?" This is often a last resort because it results in the problem getting bigger rather than getting resolved. In many organizations, help desk professionals are encouraged not to send calls to supervisors except as a last resort.

When to Escalate

Many organizations have specific guidelines in place that let help desk professionals know when to escalate a problem. Problems can be escalated due to technical reasons or due to a difficult situation caused by a problematic user.

Chapter 1 covered two primary reasons when a technician would escalate an incident due to technical reasons. In both of these situations, the technician can escalate the problem to a higher tier where more senior technicians have the ability to resolve the problem. These are:

- The problem is beyond the technical expertise of the technician and the technician has run out of ideas to resolve the problem.

- The problem requires more privileges to resolve than the technician is currently granted.

Technicians can also escalate the problem to a higher tier when they are unable to defuse a difficult situation with a customer. Many companies give technicians a lot of latitude to decide when they need to escalate a difficult situation while also making it clear to the technicians that they do not need to take any abuse from customers. In other words, the organization might give technicians the authority to escalate problems if a customer yells, uses profanity, or resorts to personal attacks. However, if a technician thinks they can defuse the situation even after the customer is abusive, they have the authority to do so.

> **ON THE SIDE:** Apple representatives providing sales information or working at the Apple Genius bar typically have a lot of latitude on deciding when and if they need to escalate a problem. One person might be able to easily handle a frustrated customer while another might need to escalate the customer's issue to someone else quickly. The key is that the Apple employee can decide when they need to call in help. Sometimes the escalation is rather subtle. Instead of saying, "I'll let you talk to my supervisor," they say, "I think John might be able to help you better," and they bring "John" into the conversation.

The key to success here is that the technicians need to know that they have the support from management. When they escalate the problem due to an abusive customer, there shouldn't be any retribution because they couldn't handle the situation.

On the other hand, if a certain technician is frequently involved in difficult situations and often needs to escalate these problems, it could be that the technician needs additional skills to avoid these types of problems. For example, the technician might unknowingly start conversations with a confrontational tone and language, causing the difficult situation to spiral out of control. Help desk technicians experiencing burnout will often be much more negative than normal and have a higher incidence of difficult situations. Because of this, it's important for technicians to manage their stress and take care of their personal health. Chapter 3, "Personal Skills" covers these topics in more depth.

Chapter Review Activities

Use the features in this section to study and review the topics in this chapter.

Answer These Questions

1. Sally and Bob were just introduced and have been talking to each other. Approximately what percentage of their communication are the actual words that they are speaking?

   a. 7%

   b. 38%

   c. 55%

   d. 93%

2. Maria took her computer into a store for repairs. Joe is the technician who is assisting Maria. While Joe's words indicate that the computer can be repaired, Maria notices his body language conflicts with Joe's words. What is Maria most likely to believe?

   a. Maria is likely to believe Joe's words.

   b. Maria is likely to believe Joe is lying.

   c. Maria is likely to believe the message she understands from Joe's body language.

   d. Maria is likely to believe Joe doesn't know how to fix the computer.

3. What does it typically convey when someone ends a sentence with a rising inflection?

   a. A statement

   b. A question

   c. Anger

   d. Happiness

4. You are assisting a customer with a problem and want to get more information by asking an open-ended question. Which of the following should you use?

   a. Are you online now?

   b. Did you have this problem yesterday?

   c. Have you ever seen this problem before?

   d. Can you explain the problem?

5. A user has called asking for assistance with email. Which one of the following questions would be the best to get additional information?

   a. What are you unable to do?

   b. Why isn't your email working?

   c. Do you have Internet access?

   d. What version of email are you using?

6. Which of the following is the WORST example of a question to ask a customer?

   a. What symptoms are you seeing?

   b. When was the first time you noticed the problem?

   c. Is your computer turned on?

   d. Why did you call?

7. Which of the following are the BEST responses when using active listening skills? (Choose three.)

   a. Staying silent

   b. Paraphrasing

   c. Reflecting

   d. Repeating

8. Which one of the following is NOT one of the behavioral components related to building rapport?

   a. Coordination

   b. Mutual attention

   c. Positivity

   d. Using open-ended questions

9. Which of the following represents the most preferable words or phrases to build a positive customer interaction when talking to a customer?

   a. Smile and nod

   b. "My pleasure"

   c. "Yeah"

   d. "Huh?"

10. When is it acceptable for a help desk technician to tell a customer "I don't know" when asked a question?

   a. Anytime the technician truly doesn't know the answer.

   b. Only when the topic is unrelated to the current problem.

   c. Only when the topic is unrelated to the user's product or service.

   d. Never.

11. Which of the following is an example of an internal filter that negatively impacts communication?

   a. Noise from a jackhammer

   b. Jet flying overhead

   c. Listener is tired

   d. Listener's child begging for attention

12. Mary has been trying to explain to Joe that his computer has a problem that will take two or three days to repair. Unfortunately, Joe is distracted with his smartphone and asked Mary again when his computer will be repaired. What is preventing effective communication in this situation?

   a. Filter

   b. Lack of rapport

   c. Technical jargon

   d. Body language

13. What is the universal body language signal to indicate that everything is OK?

   a. Making a circle with your thumb and forefinger

   b. Lightly closed fist with thumb pointing up

   c. Lightly closed fist with middle finger up

   d. None

14. Which types of communication methods can benefit from predefined scripts? Choose all that apply.

   a. Instant messaging

   b. Chat windows

   c. Email

   d. Telephone

15. When is it acceptable to use text abbreviations while communicating with users in instant messaging or chat windows?

   a. Only when they have been formally defined within the session

   b. Only when you know the age and gender of the other person

   c. Only when the other person uses them first

   d. Never

16. When is it appropriate for a help desk professional to argue with customers?

   a. Only when customers raise their voice

   b. Only when customers use profanity

   c. Only when customers personally attack the help desk professional

   d. Never

17. Which of the following responses by help desk technicians are most useful when handling most difficult situations?

   a. Maintain a defensive posture

   b. Respond to arguments

   c. Focus on the problem

   d. Build rapport by talking about previous encounters

18. Which of the following techniques is useful for getting a power user to cooperate during a help desk call?

    a. Insist the power user follows instructions explicitly.

    b. Have the power user solve the problem and call back to report the solution.

    c. Direct the power user to an online frequently asked question (FAQ) page.

    d. Involve the power user in the resolution of the problem.

19. Which of the following phrases are useful for defusing conflict by demonstrating empathy?

    a. "Don't worry, I can solve this problem for you."

    b. "I'm sorry, that must be frustrating."

    c. "Please calm down so that I can help you."

    d. "Can you explain the problem?"

20. Which of the following is a common justification for a help desk technician to escalate an incident? (Choose all that apply.)

    a. Angry customer

    b. Customer yelling

    c. Customer using profanity

    d. Customer personally attacking technician

Answers and Explanations

1. a. According to UCLA professor Albert Mehrabian, approximately 7 percent of the communication in a first interaction is the spoken words. The tone of voice makes up approximately 38 percent. Body language forms approximately 55 percent of a first impression. Combined, the tone of voice and the body language is approximately 93 percent!

2. c. When there is a conflict between the verbal message (the words) and the non-verbal message (the body language in this example), people typically believe the non-verbal message. In this example, Maria will likely believe the message she reads from Joe's body language but there isn't indication that he is lying or doesn't know how to fix the computer.

3. b. Questions typically end with a rising inflection. Statements end with a falling inflection. Rising or falling inflections at the end of a question do not indicate anger or happiness.

4. d. An open-ended question cannot be answered with just one or two words, and "Can you explain the problem?" is the only choice that meets this definition. Other answers show questions that can be answered with either yes or no.

5. a. The first question is an open-ended question and is the best of the available options. You should not start questions to users with "why." The last two questions are closed-ended questions that can be answered with a single word.

6. **d.** Questions starting with "why" take on a tone of interrogation, challenging the other person to defend an action or statement, so questions starting with "why" should be avoided. Open-ended questions cannot be answered with a single word response, so they are better choices. Closed-ended questions can be answered with a single word response and are not the best choice to get more information.

7. **b, c, d.** Paraphrasing, reflecting, and repeating are effective responses used with active listening skills. Staying silent is not an effective response, but it is useful when listening.

8. **d.** Open-ended questions are not one of the behavioral components related to building rapport. Help desk professionals can establish and build rapport through attention (using active listening skills), positivity (maintaining a positive attitude), and demonstrating they want to create a collaborative relationship to solve the problem.

9. **b.** Of the given choices, "my pleasure" is the most preferable and can be used instead of "you're welcome." Just smiling and nodding without saying anything isn't a word or phrase. Slang such as "huh" or "yeah" should be avoided.

10. **a.** If a technician does not know the answer to a question on any topic, it is preferable to say so rather than make up an answer. Technicians might add "but I'll find out" or "but I can research that for you."

11. **c.** If the listener is tired, it can distract the listener (as an internal filter) and distort the message. All of the other examples are external filters that can distract the listener and filter the message.

12. **a.** The messages Joe is receiving on his smartphone are distracting him and filtering the message from Mary. There isn't any indication that there is a lack of rapport or that Mary is using technical jargon; it could be that Joe just received significantly bad news that he's trying to process. Joe's body language indicates he's distracted, but the body language itself is not preventing effective communication.

13. **d.** There isn't a universal body language signal to indicate everything is OK. Each of the other answers can be interpreted as an obscenity in other countries.

14. **a, b, c, d.** Scripts are useful for all types of communication methods. In some methods, the technician can copy and paste the script into the email or text window. When talking, the script gives the technician thought-out words they can use during the conversation.

15. **a.** Text abbreviations can easily be misunderstood so they should be avoided unless they have been formally defined within the chat session, such as using "frequently asked questions (FAQ)" instead of just "FAQ." The age and gender of the other person do not universally indicate what text abbreviations they know. Even if the other person uses a text abbreviation, it isn't acceptable to use them throughout the chat session because they can still cause miscommunication.

16. **d.** It is never appropriate to argue with a customer. Customers might raise their voice, use profanity, and personally attack the help desk professional, but responding in kind only makes the situation worse. If necessary, help desk professionals can escalate the call to a supervisor.

17. **c.** When dealing with a difficult customer or difficult situation, the best response is to focus on the problem at hand. A defensive or judgmental posture will exacerbate the situation, and technicians should not argue with customers. A previous encounter might not have been positive, so asking about one is not necessarily a good way to build rapport.

18. **d.** A common strategy for dealing with power users (sometimes referred to as know-it-alls) is to enlist their help in solving the problem. They are often resistant to following detailed instructions. They are asking for help, so having them solve the problem and call back, or look up the problem on a FAQ page, are not the best solutions.

19. **b.** The phrases "I'm sorry" and "That must be frustrating" demonstrate empathy and are useful for defusing conflict in some situations. While it is useful for a technician to say, "I can solve this problem for you," that doesn't defuse conflict, and telling a person not to worry might make the situation worse. Similarly, telling a person to calm down does not demonstrate empathy. Open-ended questions are useful for getting more information but do not necessarily demonstrate empathy.

20. **b, c, d.** Organizations commonly give help desk technicians authority to escalate an incident if the customer is yelling, using profanity, or personally attacking the technician. Customers calling the help desk are often frustrated and can be angry at the situation, but this is not justification to escalate the incident.

Define the Key Terms

The following key terms include the ideas most important to the big ideas in this chapter. To review, without looking at the book or your notes, write a definition for each term, focusing on the meaning, not the wording. Then review your definition compared to your notes, this chapter, and the glossary.

Key Terms for Chapter 2

active listening	inflection	rapport
body language	kinesics	verbal communication
communication	non-verbal communication	vocal tone
filters	open-ended question	

List the Words Inside Acronyms

The following are the most common acronyms discussed in this chapter. As a way to review those terms, simply write down the words that each letter represents in each acronym.

Acronyms for Chapter 2		
BIOS	BSOD	IM
	FAQ	OS

Create Mind Maps

For this chapter, create mind maps as follows:

1. Create a mind map to list different types of body language that can indicate a friendly demeanor. Start with a circle labeled friendly body language, draw lines out from the circle, and label them with different postures or expressions.

2. Create a mind map to list different types of body language that can indicate a hostile or angry demeanor. Start with a circle labeled friendly body language, draw lines out from the circle, and label them with different postures or expressions.

Case Studies

Case Study 1

Work with a partner and make the following statement: "Your account is activated." First, say the statement with a rising inflection at the end and ask your partner how it sounds to them. Next, say the same statement with a falling inflection at the end and ask your partner how it sounds to them. Switch roles so that both people have an opportunity to both speak and hear the statements.

Case Study 2

Play the game of telephone with a group of five or more people. Start with phrases such as this:

- My puppy tracked mud all over the living room carpet.
- I tried bleaching my hair and it turned green.
- Maria's uncle shared his secret cinnamon apple pie recipe with me.
- Send reinforcements as quickly as possible—we're going to advance.

Case Study 3

Perform an Internet search and identify at least 10 phrases customer service personnel can use to build rapport with customers and leave them with a favorable impression of their experience and the organization.

Chapter 3

Personal Skills

Personal skills refer to an individual's ability to manage different situations and themselves. People with fine-tuned personal skills are able to interact with others with a positive attitude while also doing what's necessary to maintain their health and advance in their careers. This chapter discusses personal skills in four major sections:

- The first section, "Recognizing the Value of Attitude," stresses the importance of maintaining a positive attitude as a help desk professional. Frequently, help desk professionals are the primary individuals that customers interact with and these customers often make a judgment of the overall organization based on these interactions. This section presents information on the value of a positive attitude, compares attitude and aptitude, discusses service attitude in the context of a customer service, and ends with the value of a problem-ownership mentality.

- Any job, including jobs in help desk positions, can be stressful. Successful employees are able to recognize when they are stressed, understand the effects of distress, and manage their stress levels to prevent burnout. The "Managing Stress" section covers each of these topics and includes a list of some common signs and symptoms of stress, as well as methods to manage stress.

- Effective time management is a skill that successful people in any job must master to ensure they stay successful. The section "Managing Your Time" covers some simple habits people can adopt to better manage their time and accomplish what's important while preventing trivial tasks from consuming their days.

- While a help desk job is a good job to have early in your IT career, it is not typically a job that people stay in for their entire career. Instead, they use the job to build their skills and move up into another IT job with increased responsibilities and increased pay. The last section, "Managing Your Career," covers some topics to consider to manage your career beyond a help desk position.

Chapter Outline

Objectives

- Define the benefits of a positive attitude related to an organization's customers

- Compare the differences between aptitude and attitude

- Describe the difference between a simple positive attitude and a service attitude

- Explain the value of problem ownership

- Define and compare stress, eustress, distress, and burnout

- List some of the common signs and symptoms of distress

- Summarize some of the common causes and symptoms of burnout

- Name some simple methods of managing or reducing stress

- Describe the relationship between time management and stress

- Identify at least one method to prioritize tasks lists

- Discuss possible career paths for a help desk professional

- List some common IT certifications

Key Terms

aptitude

attitude

burnout

distress

eustress

general adaptation syndrome

self-talk

service attitude

stress

stress management

Recognizing the Value of Attitude

Many people believe that the most important skill for help desk professionals is their attitude. From the organization's perspective, employees with a positive attitude treat customers better and are more likely to have a sense of loyalty to the organization. In contrast, employees with a poor or negative attitude are less likely to treat customers consistently and less likely to have any sense of loyalty to the organization.

Loyalty to the organization is important for several reasons. From the perspective of the organization, loyal employees are more likely to stay with the organization for a longer time. Less turnover results in lower recruiting, hiring, and training costs for new employees. Also, loyal employees are more likely to ensure customers are satisfied and are more willing to take the extra steps needed to ensure customers are satisfied. From the perspective of the employee, they are only loyal to an organization that treats them well and with consistent values. When employees feel loyalty toward the organization, they are generally happier and more fulfilled.

Positive Attitude

Attitude is the way a person looks at things, such as events in their lives. It is their manner or disposition. A positive attitude is contagious, and when customers interact with help desk technicians that have a positive attitude, they tend to be more positive. While a positive attitude won't necessarily turn around an irate customer, one thing is for sure: a technician with a negative attitude is sure to cause bad situations to become worse and will often cause good situations to go bad.

Chapter 2, "Communication Skills," mentioned the importance of maintaining a positive attitude when talking with customers. As a reminder, this doesn't mean that technicians need to be overly cheerful, but it does mean they are able to look at the positive aspects of an issue, rather than focusing on the negative aspects. Customers are contacting the help desk because they need help, and many are already frustrated from the problem. If they have to deal with a technician with an attitude problem, they will get much more frustrated and it leads an overall negative view of the experience, and of the organization.

Some simple things to remember related to a positive attitude are:

- A positive attitude can convert irate customers into happy customers.
- A positive attitude can convert the customer experience from a negative one to a positive one.
- A positive attitude can convert buyers into loyal customers that keep coming back.

Even if technicians are not able to solve customer problems, they often leave customers with a favorable attitude of the organization if they maintain a positive, helpful attitude. For example, if a customer asks how to accomplish a certain task with a piece of software and the technician knows this isn't possible, the technician can provide feedback to the customer in a friendly, positive manner. Even though the customer still can't accomplish that task, they might still end the call on a positive note knowing they have been helped. In contrast, if a technician simply says, "No, can't be done," the customer is left frustrated and angry.

A key point to remember about attitude is that people have full control over their attitude. It is one of the few things that you can control. You can't control what happens to you, but you can control how you respond to these events. Imagine two people that are caught in the rain. One person becomes miserable and begins cursing at the sky. The second person starts dancing in the rain. The exact same event (the rain) occurred for both people, but one person chose to be miserable while the other person chose to dance.

Author and speaker Jack Canfield wrote about the E+R=O formula in his book *The Success Principles: How to Get from Where You Are to Where You Want to Be*. The outcome (O) of any event is determined by the individual's response. Assuming you can't control certain events such as rain, but you want a different outcome, the only choice is to modify your response.

One of the ways people can change their response is by controlling their self-talk. **Self-talk** is the voice that runs through your mind; it can be overly negative, telling you why you can't do something, or be overly positive, telling you why you can do something. The more you allow it to focus on the negative, the more negative self-talk you can expect to hear. Figure 3-1 shows an example of how a person's negative self-talk forms and reinforces a person's self-image, which affects their performance and stimulates more negative self-talk. If allowed to continue, it can continue to spiral downward until that's all a person hears.

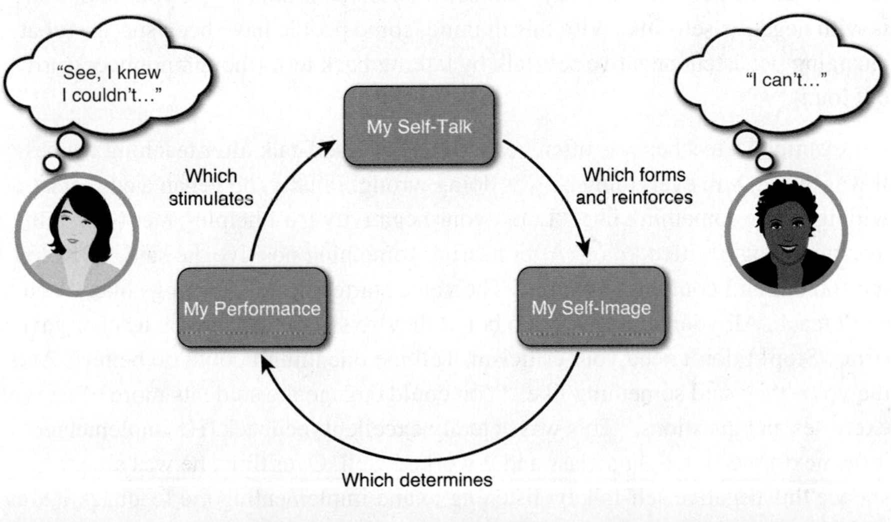

> **AUTHOR'S NOTE:**
> Jack Canfield mentions the E+R=O formula in many of his motivational speeches and courses. He attributes Dr. Robert Resnick, a psychotherapist in Los Angeles, with originally developing it and teaching it to Jack in the 70s. Many other motivational speakers and writers also use this formula.

FIGURE 3-1

Negative self-talk.

> **ON THE SIDE:**   Ask a group of your friends if they experience self-talk and almost all of them will readily admit it. The ones that don't admit it are probably hearing a steady stream of internal dialog such as this: "Self-talk? Do I have self-talk? That's crazy. I don't have voices in my head." Of course, this internal dialog is a form of self-talk itself.

However, people can take control of this self-talk and change it into positive information that will also build on itself in an upward spiral. Figure 3-2 shows an example where a person changes "I can't" into "I can," reinforcing a positive self-image, affecting their performance and stimulating more positive self-talk. This doesn't need to be difficult. It can be as simple as replacing the negative words with positive ones. For example, at the first sign of negative talk such as "I can't," replace it with positive words such as "I can."

FIGURE 3-2

Positive self-talk.

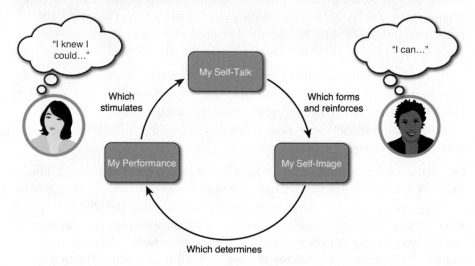

In some cases, the negative self-talk is your self-conscious or internal wisdom trying to come out and provide you feedback. Not everyone takes feedback easily, and it could be that the only way your self-conscious is able to get your attention is with negative self-talk. With this in mind, some people have been successful at changing persistent negative self-talk by talking back to it (though not necessarily out loud).

For example, a teacher was often hearing negative self-talk after teaching classes. It was telling him everything he was doing wrong. Finally, he began a conversation with it saying something like, "Look, your negativity isn't helping me. First, tell me something positive I did." After hearing something positive, he said, "OK, tell me something I could improve on." The voice started repeating things like, "You can't teach. All your students are so bored they're sleeping," and the teacher gave a firm, "Stop! I don't need your criticism. Tell me one thing I could do better." And the voice then said something like, "You could engage the students more often with exercises and questions." This was actually excellent feedback. He implemented it the next time he taught a class and it worked well. Over time, he was able to silence this negative self-talk by listening to and implementing the feedback it was providing.

Attitude versus Aptitude

Motivational speaker Zig Ziglar once said, "Your attitude, not your aptitude, will determine your altitude." This is as important for help desk professionals as it is for anyone seeking success in their lives. **Aptitude** is a person's natural ability or talent related to a particular field of study and identifies the ease with which a person can learn a topic. Someone without aptitude within a certain field can still learn it, though they will typically need to study much harder than others that have a higher level of aptitude in the field.

In contrast, people are born with an aptitude for certain topics but lack the aptitude for other topics. People can't change their natural abilities any more than they can change the natural color of their hair. However, just as people can dye their hair a different color, they can still master other skills if they spend enough time and energy to do so.

Organizations understand the value of attitude over aptitude and will typically evaluate both when screening potential employees. This is especially helpful when filling a customer service position such as a help desk position. For example, organizations often use knowledge and skills-based testing to determine a person's aptitude and knowledge of technology. These tests have technical questions with gradable answers to provide a clear indication of a person's knowledge.

Additionally, these tests can often provide some insight into a person's attitude. For example, one person might be extremely frustrated and possibly even angry when given the results of a test and choose to argue or debate certain questions and answers. Some might even attack the validity of the test and try to tell the interviewer what's wrong with the exam. Hiring managers recognize these behaviors as potential problems; they can easily result in arguing or debating with a difficult customer, resulting in a difficult situation becoming much worse.

Some organizations don't like to leave the evaluation of potential employee attitudes to chance. Instead, they test a person's ability to keep a positive attitude while under stress. One organization that provides phone-based support requires the potential employee to handle a staged phone call where the simulated customer is irate and irrational. Even when potential employees understand these are staged calls, these types of tests are often valuable in viewing how they might handle the situation and to see if they can maintain a positive attitude.

> **AUTHOR'S NOTE:** Having and keeping a positive attitude helps in many ways beyond a help desk job. Life is more enjoyable when you're able to keep a positive attitude and appreciate the positive things going on around you. In contrast, when you choose to focus on the negative, you remain miserable. Think about who you would rather spend your time with—someone able to find the positive in their life and the world around them, or someone voicing constant complaints? Most people prefer spending time with positive, joyful people and they find that by doing so, there is more joy and happiness in their life.

Service Attitude

A **service attitude** goes beyond just a positive attitude and includes a sense of caring for the customer. You can think of a service attitude as a caring attitude. Successful help desk professionals recognize they are there to provide a service for customers and their whole demeanor reflects this attitude of service. They might use the words, "What can I do to help you?" but they back it up with their behavior, their body language, and their willingness to truly understand the problem and help the customer solve it.

Flavio Martins is obsessed about customer service and writes regularly about it on his WinTheCustomer blog (http://winthecustomer.com), which is syndicated by many customer service experience networks. He sums up the importance of customer service in a simple sentence: "Satisfaction is worthless, customer loyalty is everything."

Many successful companies understand the importance of customer loyalty and remain successful because their service attitude comes through in everything they do. As an example, consider Amazon.com. Amazon is widely known for its exceptional service—everything they do is focused on what the customer wants and expects. When you order something, they send automated emails telling you when to expect delivery and typically include tracking numbers you can use to see shipping details. If the order will be delayed, they let you know. If there's a problem, they do everything they can to resolve it as quickly and painlessly as possible.

> **ON THE SIDE:**   In what has been called the Great 2013 Christmas Delivery Debacle, many packages shipped via UPS and FedEx failed to arrive in time for Christmas. Online sales for the season increased by about 15% in 2013, Thanksgiving was later than normal in November, and some major storms throughout the United States all combined to overload the shipping companies. In the week before Christmas, UPS was projected to process more than 132 million deliveries, but many simply did not arrive in time to be wrapped and placed under the tree. Was this Amazon's fault? No. However, Amazon was quick to try to make it right. For Amazon packages that UPS and FedEx didn't deliver on time, Amazon reversed the delivery charges and gave customers a $20 gift card. This is one of the many reasons why so many customers are passionately loyal to Amazon.

Alf Dunbar provides a variety of coaching, speaking, and other products centered around his "You Are The Difference" brand. He sums up what it means to have a positive service attitude using the word attitude as an acronym (see Figure 3-3). Any help desk professional can use these same principles when interacting with customers to enhance the customer's experience and leave customers with a feeling that the technician truly cared about helping them.

A Always greet your customers

T Treat your customers with respect

T Talk and chat to your customers

I Interact with customers in a relaxed way

T Turn up to work with a positive attitude

U Understand your customer's needs

D Discover the impact you have around customers

E Excite your customers about your products

FIGURE 3-3

Attitude acronym.

Problem Ownership

Chapter 1, "Introduction to Help Desk Support Roles," introduced the concept of taking ownership of incidents. If help desk specialists are encouraged to stay with a customer until a problem is resolved, they are much more likely to ensure the problem is successfully resolved.

Consider the following scenario. A help desk technician realizes that a different department must first modify the customer's account before the technician can solve the problem. For example, another department might need to modify permissions on the account and once the permissions are modified, the technician can then help the customer with final configuration steps.

When help desk technicians are able to own the problem, they can either contact the other department directly to ensure the account is correctly modified, or they can stick with the customer as the customer works with the other department. After the account is modified, the technician can then work with the customer to complete the final configuration steps. Imagine "Bob" is the customer. Bob makes one phone call, starts a conversation with "Sally" the technician, and Sally sticks with him until the problem is resolved.

In contrast, if help desk technicians are not encouraged to own problems or if they aren't able to do so, they might just transfer customers to other departments and then move on to the next customer. The same customer, Bob, calls in for help and starts a conversation with Sally, the technician. Sally transfers him to another department to get the permissions modified. Bob talks to Joe and explains he needs his permissions modified. Joe modifies the permissions and tells Bob the problem is solved. Later Bob calls the help desk back to complete the final configuration steps. Even if Bob recognizes he needs help with final configuration steps while talking to Joe, he might ask Joe for help, but since this isn't in Joe's realm of responsibility, Joe would transfer Bob back to the help desk. Bob might talk to Sally again, or he might be connected with a different help desk specialist and find that he needs to explain the problem again before he can be helped.

Which experience would you prefer if you were the customer? The one where you made one phone call and a single technician ensured the problem was resolved for you, or the one where you were shuffled between multiple people before your problem was resolved?

When people understand the full process, they understand the value of problem ownership. However, when management focuses on individual metrics such as how much time a technician spends with a single call, the value of problem ownership is sometimes lost.

Managing Stress

The Merriam-Webster dictionary defines **stress** as "a state of mental tension and worry caused by problems in your life, work, etc." and as "something that causes strong feelings of worry or anxiety." In their full definition of stress, they define it as a "constraining force or influence as a physical, chemical, or emotional factor that causes bodily or mental tension and may be a factor in disease causation."

Stress is not necessarily bad and you shouldn't try to avoid stress completely any more than you should try to avoid breathing. Stress can be very positive, and life without any stress at all can be quite boring. When a person's stress level is close to zero, they are extremely calm on the verge of peaceful sleep. In contrast, high levels of stress, especially for extended periods, can result in health problems, fatigue, and even burnout.

Psychologists Robert M. Yerkes and John Dillingham Dodson developed the Yerkes-Dodson law documenting the relationship between performance and arousal (or stress). Figure 3-4 shows a modified version of the Yerkes-Dodson Curve where you can see that when stress is low, performance is low. Performance degrades when stress is too high. The ideal is a level of stress in the middle where people are energized, focused, and enjoy optimal performance.

FIGURE 3-4

Modified Yerkes-Dodson Curve.

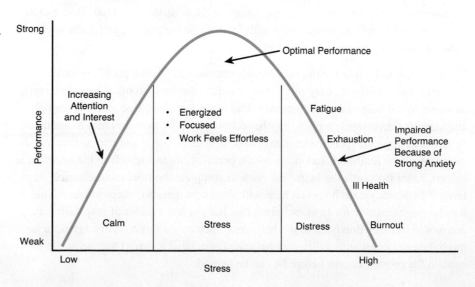

Distress vs. Eustress

Stress is often categorized as either distress or eustress, with distress generally considered negative and not helpful while eustress is considered positive, providing helpful benefits:

- **Distress** indicates anxiety or sorrow and someone experiencing distress is typically suffering from pain or even agony. This pain can be physical due to a physical ailment or emotional when the level of anxiety is consuming their thoughts. In extreme cases, distress can lead to medical problems including physical issues and psychological issues such as depression.

- **Eustress** combines the Greek prefix "eu" (meaning good or well) with stress to indicate good stress. A life event such as marriage is a very positive event, but it often results in eustress. Players on a sports team often experience eustress while practicing and competing. Similarly, many workers view tasks on the job as challenges to overcome, and the process of completing these tasks is eustress for them.

> **ON THE SIDE:**   Hans Selye, an endocrinologist, completed a significant amount of work on stressors and the response to stressors. Interestingly, he first referred to stress as "noxious agents" and later coined the term "stress." Eventually, he recognized the difference between negative stress and positive stress, and he is credited with first referring to negative stress as eustress.

Note that the same event can be distress for one person and eustress for another person. It's all in the person's perception. As an example, imagine that Bob is preparing to run in a race and perceives that his entire future is dependent on winning. If he wins, he'll get a scholarship, be able to attend the university of his choice, and live happily ever after. If he doesn't win, he imagines that he won't receive any scholarships, won't be able to attend a college or university, and will be destined to a career asking people, "Do you want fries with that?" For Bob, preparing for this race is causing distress.

In comparison, Joe is preparing for a similar race. He realizes that if he wins, he will get a scholarship and be able to attend the university of his choice. However, he isn't viewing a loss as the end of all possibilities for him. He plans to do his best and have fun in the process. If he doesn't win, he fully expects other possibilities to be available to him. The stress Joe experiences is closer to eustress.

The same situation can happen for similar tasks for people on the job. Imagine that Bob finds that he's having problems handling some trouble calls and perceives that if he is not able to successfully resolve them, he might actually lose his job on the help desk and all its benefits. Without this job, he might not be able to afford his apartment, his girlfriend might dump him, and he might end up living in the basement of his parent's home again. For Bob, these help desk calls aren't a challenge—they are a threat.

In comparison, Joe is also having problems handling some trouble calls that other help desk professionals easily handle. He recognizes that if he can't master these calls, his career with the company will likely be limited. However, he views this as a challenge and decides to do whatever he can to learn what he's missing. He asks others for help and steadily works toward mastering the needed knowledge and skills. He also recognizes that he might lose his job if he can't master this knowledge, but doesn't consider this the worst thing in the world. He knows that there are thousands of other job possibilities with many other possible career paths.

Stress and Adrenaline

The body has specific responses to distress and as an individual perceives more and more distress, the body continues to respond. As an example, Figure 3-5 shows a simplified diagram of the hypothalamic-pituitary-adrenal axis (also called the HPA).

> **AUTHOR'S NOTE:**   I certainly realize that hypothalamic-pituitary-adrenal axis is a mouthful and much more that you'll ever be expected to recite as a help desk professional. However, it is important to realize that there are specific physiological responses to stressors. When you perceive negative stress, your body responds with physical reactions.

FIGURE 3-5

HPA axis response to stressors.

When your body senses a stressor, it sends a message to the hypothalamus. The hypothalamus releases chemicals, which it sends to your pituitary gland, which then sends additional chemicals to your adrenal glands. The result is a release of adrenaline and other chemicals, which make your heart beat faster, boost your awareness, and give you more energy. In many instances, this process has given individuals super-human strength. For example, in 2012, 22-year-old Lauren Kornacki went into the garage and found her father stuck under a BMW after a jack slipped. Without giving it much thought, she lifted the car and freed her father.

The amount of chemicals released within your body varies depending on how you perceive the stressor. A little bit of stress won't give you superhuman strength. Similarly, when the crisis passes, you won't have the same level of adrenaline coursing through your body. Ask Lauren Kornacki to lift that same BMW without her father underneath the car, and she simply wouldn't be able to.

This is the same response as the fundamental "fight or flight" physiologic response. This response was useful when mankind lived in caves and was threatened by lions and tigers and bears. Nerve cells fired and the body released a cocktail of chemicals into the bloodstream to either attack the threat or run faster than the slowest cave dweller in the tribe.

However, fight or flight isn't the best response to many common day-to-day stressors. For example, if a help desk technician is experiencing a high level of stress from the job when dealing with a difficult customer, fighting or running from a customer are not good options. Still, the technician's body releases the same chemicals from the HPA axis response. If there isn't a way to release these chemicals (either by lifting a car or fighting a saber tooth tiger), they can build up and cause damage over time. The "Managing Stress" section later in this chapter provides some options to manage and reduce stress levels.

> **ON THE SIDE:** Even though you might not see obvious outward signals of stress when someone is heavily stressed, there are typically subtle indications, often with their hands and feet. For example, someone forced to listen to a difficult conversation from a customer or a supervisor might nervously bounce their feet or legs, or silently tap their fingers on a leg. Their concentration might be on maintaining a suitable facial expression, but their body still attempts to release some of the excess adrenaline and other chemicals in unconscious body movements.

General Adaptation Syndrome

Physiologists have defined the **general adaptation syndrome** (GAS) model to show how our bodies react and adapt to stressors. GAS has three phases, as shown in Figure 3-6. Notice that the line in the center shows a person's normal level of resistance to stress and represents a baseline.

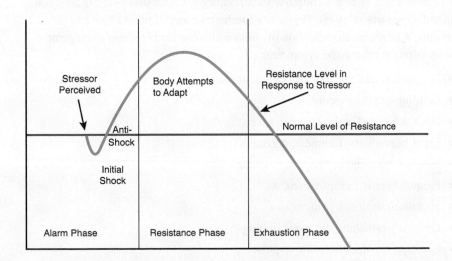

FIGURE 3-6

GAS model showing response to stress.

If the stressor isn't removed, people move through the three phases in the GAS model. The goal is to avoid the exhaustion phase by removing the stressor or reducing the effects of the stress:

- The alarm stage occurs when you first perceive the stressor. Your body experiences a momentary shock when it perceives the stressor, and your resistance is lower before your body begins to resist the stress.

- In the resistance phase, your body attempts to adapt to the stressor with a higher level of resistance.

- In the exhaustion phase, your body is no longer able to sustain the level of resistance necessary to block the stressor.

When people remain in the exhaustion phase for too long, the negative effects of stress and possibly even burnout begin to set in. You can compare this to the GAS Model in Figure 3-4, where high levels of stress result in impaired performance and physical symptoms.

Effects of Distress

Too much stress in your life can cause a wide variety of physical and psychological problems. Some common disorders linked to stress include heart problems such as hypertension and heart attacks, immune system issues causing increased infec- tions and colds, and autoimmune diseases such as rheumatoid arthritis and multiple sclerosis. Stress can also exacerbate many other physical problems by weakening your body's immune system.

Some of these problems are quite severe, and they don't set in the first time someone is stressed. Instead, they occur after long periods of unmanaged stress, making it important to be able to recognize some of the more common signs and symptoms of stress before significant problems set in. The following list is from the American Institute of Stress (http://www.stress.org/), which lists over 50 common signs and symptoms of stress. If you're experiencing any of these signs and symptoms, it might be an indication of stress and some simple stress management techniques might relieve the symptoms:

- Frequent headaches, jaw clenching, or pain
- Gritting, grinding teeth
- Neck ache, back pain, muscle spasms
- Light headedness, faintness, dizziness
- Ringing, buzzing, or "popping" sounds
- Frequent colds and infections
- Heartburn, stomach pain, nausea
- Difficulty breathing, frequent sighing
- Chest pain, palpitations, rapid pulse
- Diminished sexual desire or performance

- Excess anxiety, worry, guilt, nervousness
- Increased anger, frustration, hostility
- Depression, frequent or wild mood swings
- Increased or decreased appetite
- Insomnia, nightmares, disturbing dreams
- Difficulty concentrating, racing thoughts
- Trouble learning new information
- Forgetfulness, disorganization, confusion
- Difficulty in making decisions
- Feeling overloaded or overwhelmed
- Frequent crying spells or suicidal thoughts
- Increased frustration, irritability, edginess
- Overreaction to petty annoyances
- Obsessive or compulsive behavior
- Reduced work efficiency or productivity
- Lies or excuses to cover up poor work
- Problems in communication, sharing
- Social withdrawal and isolation
- Constant tiredness, weakness, fatigue
- Increased smoking, alcohol, or drug use

It's important to realize that many of these symptoms can be a result of other issues. When these symptoms appear, it's certainly possible that they are the result of unmanaged stress, but just calling something stress isn't a reason not to seek a doctor's advice for physical problems.

Recognizing Burnout

Burnout is a state of mental, emotional, or physical exhaustion. It is often combined with cynicism, depression, and/or lethargy, and job burnout affects a person's ability to get simple tasks done both on and off the job. People in any type of job, including those working in a demanding help desk position, can experience burnout. Ideally, individuals will take steps to prevent burnout by managing stress. If it's too late for prevention, the next best thing is to recognize the symptoms and take steps to turn it around.

Burnout Causes

There are many reasons why individuals experience burnout. Dr. Paula Davis-Laack, author of *10 Things Happy People Do Differently*, defines burnout as "the chronic state of being out of sync with one or more aspects of your life." Most individuals can handle living out of sync for a period of time, but if life, or the work environment, never returns to a balance, it can cause burnout.

Some of the common causes of job burnout are:

- **Lack of control.** When individuals are unable to influence decisions at work such as their schedule, workload, or assignments, it can lead to burnout. Many help desk jobs provide some flexibility in scheduling to give workers some control over their schedule. They define scheduling guidelines such as the minimum number of workers for a shift, but allow workers to pick some of their shifts and trade shifts with other workers.

- **Work overload.** Work overload can be an extension of lack of control at work if individuals are required to do more work than is possible in the time they have. Additionally, work overload can occur if people are tasked with work without having adequate resources to complete the work. For example, imagine a help desk with an inadequate number of technicians and a growing backlog of unresolved incidents. Management might put pressure on the supervisor to reduce the backlog and the supervisor might put pressure on the workers to reduce the backlog. However, if the backlog is due to not enough technicians on the help desk, increased pressure is more likely to increase stress and potentially cause burnout among the workers. Ironically, this actually increases the backlog instead of reducing it.

- **Values conflict.** If individuals are forced to take actions that are against their values, this can cause problems. An individual might be able to do this once or twice, but if forced to do so continually, it will take a toll. For example, if workers are told to lie to customers about problems, it can cause internal conflicts for the workers.

- **Dysfunctional workplace.** Many different situations cause a dysfunctional workplace, including capricious supervisors or managers, harassment of any kind including sexual harassment and racial harassment, and bullying.

- **Too easy or too difficult.** When work is consistently too easy or consistently too difficult, it becomes challenging for most people to tolerate for very long. If it's too easy, it becomes monotonous and takes extra energy to remain focused on the job. If it's consistently overly difficult for an individual, it can become a constant stress resulting in burnout. The Yerkes-Dodson Curve shown previously in this chapter showed the relationship between high and low stress levels and performance. One way help professionals are prone to burnout due to work being too easy is when they are hearing the exact same problem from customers. They might listen to customers repeat the same symptoms and then give the same answers dozens of times a day, causing the job to become monotonous and stressful.

- **Work-life imbalance.** When people do not have a balance between the time they spend at work and outside of work, it can also result in problems. "Balance" is relative, with some people able to spend more time at work than other people are. However, the key is that there are some outside interests, such as time with family, hobbies, and so on.

Burnout Symptoms

People experiencing or approaching burnout typically have multiple symptoms. It's important for individuals to recognize burnout symptoms so that they can change their situation before it reaches a critical stage. Similarly, it's important for managers and supervisors to recognize burnout symptoms so that they can help the employee before the burnout symptoms affect customers, other employees, and the work environment.

Some of the common signs of burnout are:

- **Fatigue and lethargy.** Individuals may feel tired most days with a lack of energy or desire to do things. They might feel physical or emotional exhaustion, combined with trepidation when thinking of what lies ahead.

- **Sleep problems.** This might be insomnia where an individual has trouble falling asleep or staying asleep, despite feeling exhausted. In some individuals, it can be an inability to stay awake during normal waking hours.

- **Physical illness or symptoms.** Due to the exhaustion, the immune system is often weakened, making people more susceptible to common illnesses such as colds or the flu. Additionally, people often have other physical symptoms, such as headaches, chest pain, shortness of breath, dizziness, and fainting. Many of these symptoms can indicate a much more serious problem and should be assessed by a doctor.

- **Eating disorders.** Some people might skip meals due to a lack of appetite while others might turn to emotional overeating. The biggest indicator of a problem in this area is if the individual is noticing a change in their eating habits compared to before the job stress began causing problems.

- **Emotional swings.** This includes anxiety, depression, and anger. Individuals experiencing mild burnout typically experience some tension and worry, and might experience feelings of sadness and hopelessness. Irritability results in angry outbursts, either at home or in the workplace, for some people. Extreme anger has often resulted in violence in the workplace against supervisors and other employees. Extreme depression has resulted in suicide.

> **ON THE SIDE:**   Many workers in the United States Postal Service (USPS) have reported a stressful work environment, and the term "going postal" is linked to many of the incidents since 1983 where USPS workers shot and killed managers, fellow workers, and others. Patrick Sherrill killed 14 USPS employees and wounded six more on August 20, 1986 before committing suicide by shooting himself in the head; this was the first incident where the term "going postal" was used. Several other incidents prompted the USPS to create specific job positions directly related to improving the workplace and preventing workplace violence.

In any high-stress job, workers, supervisors, and managers should be on the lookout for symptoms of burnout. Obvious signs of a potential problem are a change in behavior of a worker. For example, if a worker is typically easy-going but has become more cynical and argumentative, begins to display a general sense of apathy, or productivity and job performance begins to decline, it might be due to burnout. Caring managers and supervisors know their people, recognize these symptoms, and begin to ask questions to identify the problem. In contrast, managers and supervisors working in a toxic work environment don't necessarily know their people, but when problems begin to appear, they often blame the worker without looking for the source of the problem and a solution.

While a help desk job isn't necessarily a high-stress job, it can be if the workload is high, the labor force is relatively low, and/or workers are regularly tasked with solving difficult problems without adequate resources. If people within the organization ignore the symptoms, it can adversely affect the health of the workers. In extreme cases, it can result in workplace violence and/or suicide.

Recovering from Burnout

Burnout won't just go away, so once individuals reach job burnout, they need to take steps to recover. There are different methods that people can use to recover, but the key point is that they can't just push through it. Ignoring burnout symptoms and attempting to just work harder typically results in increasingly more serious symptoms. In contrast, when people are forced to examine what caused the burnout, it typically provides the motivation to make changes that can significantly improve their lives.

One of the key burnout recovery strategies is to take a break. Ideally, individuals will be able to take a vacation where they stay completely away from work for a while. Recreation literally means to re-create, and that's exactly how people should approach a break, taking time to enjoy—to re-create—life with family and friends, and to so recover away from work.

If a vacation or a break away from the job isn't possible, an alternative is to just slow down. Within the IT environment, managers might have the ability to move individuals to a less stressful area of the organization. Employees can make a concerted effort to find a healthier balance between their work and non-work time. For some people, it might mean spending more time with family or friends, taking up a hobby, learning a new sport, starting to play a sport they stopped, starting a new exercise regimen, or joining a gym. There's a lot to be said for banging a little ball around a racquetball court to release some pent-up energy.

> **ON THE SIDE:** Supervisors that notice burnout symptoms in their employees have several options to help them. One tactic many successful supervisors use is to identify a less stressful job that can give the employee a break, and ask the employee for help solving a problem within this less stressful job. This tactic gives the employee a break to recover, without adding additional stress by pointing out employee performance problems caused by the burnout.

Reaching out to family and friends for support can be very helpful for someone experiencing job burnout. Family and friends might not have all the answers, but often all an individual needs is someone willing to listen.

An extreme method of dealing with job burnout is to quit the job causing burnout. However, if this is the only source of an income for an individual, this option can evoke a significant amount of fear. The combination of burnout and fear can cause a downward spiral, causing the individual to feel trapped with no way out. This trapped feeling causes people to turn to suicide, sometimes combined with violence.

On the other hand, many people approaching job burnout realize that their current job isn't what they want to do for their rest of their lives. Instead of staying in a job they hate, they begin looking for what they really want to do and start taking action to move in that direction. It can still be scary, but by facing the fear and taking action, they can take their career to a new level. Fear is natural but it doesn't have to be a roadblock.

Identifying Stressors

Before you can effectively manage stress, it's important to identify what's causing it. Medical professionals identify stress as acute or chronic, and stressors as external or internal.

Acute stress is short-term stress caused by your body's immediate reaction to a stressor. This can be a major event, causing your body to pump enough adrenaline into your system that you can lift a car, or it can be something relatively minor, such as handling a single incident with a difficult customer.

> **ON THE SIDE:**   Most people can quickly recover from acute stress events. However, some significant events can cause long-term problems. For example, many soldiers suffer from post-traumatic stress disorder (PTSD) after living through one or more major battles where they witnessed friends and fellow soldiers die or suffer serious injury.

Chronic stress is long-term and is caused by one or more stressors that persist without being managed. When faced with acute stress from a major event, most people will react immediately to manage the stress. One of the challenges with chronic stressors is that people begin to accept them instead of learning to manage them. They persist and the effects of the stress build, causing physical problems.

External stressors can be from the workplace, the environment, surprises, major life events, and even some social events. As mentioned previously in this chapter, the workplace can be stressful if the workload is too great for the available time or their aren't enough resources to accomplish the job. Demanding or capricious supervisors can cause stress in the workplace. Some environments are stressful when they are too noisy, too dim, or too crowded. While some surprises are enjoyable, a surprise visit from a mother-in-law or other relative is not necessarily enjoyable. Marriage, sickness, or death of a loved one are examples of some major life events that are external stressors.

Internal stressors are self-imposed. For example, one of the top fears is the fear of speaking before a group, and when tasked with doing a presentation, it can cause a significant amount of internal stress. It's common for many people to begin to sweat, get short of breath, and even experience a faster heartbeat. In extreme cases, people break out into hives. All of this is because of a fear of what might happen during or after the talk, but even despite the fear, the presentation might go perfectly. Other internal stressors come from beliefs, attitudes, opinions, and expectations. When events don't match up to what someone expects them to be, the conflict can cause stress. As an example, perfectionists become stressed when they encounter errors because these errors don't match up to their expectation of perfection. In contrast, recovering perfectionists might see the same errors and not give them a second thought.

The list of stressors could go on and on, but the most important thing is for people to recognize when they are stressed and then take the time to identify why. Sometimes, the reasons are obvious, but other times identifying the stressors can be elusive.

One method of identifying stressors is to keep a stress diary. When using a stress diary, you periodically write down how stressed you feel along with any notes. For example, you could use a range of 1 to 10 where 1 is very calm and 10 is the most stressed you've ever felt. Once an hour, you write the time, your perceived stress level, and notes about what you're doing at the time. You can later look at the diary from an objective level to help understand when and why you're stressed.

Managing Stress

Stress management is a combination of techniques and practices that people use to reduce the negative effects of stress. There isn't any single technique that everyone can do to reduce stress; instead, different people use different techniques. From a general perspective, there are three primary methods of managing or reducing stress. They are:

- **Releasing stress.** Immediately after a stressful incident, some people might feel like punching a wall (or punching their boss) and while that would release some of the chemicals, simple exercise would be much better. Any type of physical exertion can help release the stress. For example, running up and down a flight of stairs, doing five minutes of "bounce and shake," pushups, jumping jacks, or sit-ups can all metabolize the excessive chemicals caused by the fight or flight response. You can exercise immediately after a stressful incident for a short time. Also, a regular exercise regimen is helpful in preventing stress-related chemicals from building up in your body. Executive coach Jennifer Cohen wrote a Forbes article titled "5 Things Super Successful People Do Before 8 AM" and at the top of the list is exercise. Other ways you can release stress include meditation, tai chi, yoga, taking a walk, taking a bath, and adopting a different routine such as using different time management practices.

> **AUTHOR'S NOTE:** "Bounce and shake" is a simple exercise where you simply bounce on the heels of your feet and bounce your body by nodding your head slightly and shaking your hands in front of you. John Gray, author of the *Men Are from Mars, Women Are from Venus* series of books, shows how to do the "bounce and shake" in this video: http://www.youtube.com/watch?v=rbnjvAHsxUk. You can use it as a quick 5-minute stress reducer or as part of an exercise regimen.

- **Changing your environment.** If the environment you're working in is too stressful, the simple answer is to change it. You might be able to move to a job more suited to your personality elsewhere in the organization, or even to a different organization. While it sometimes seems to be impossible to change the environment, a person in full-blown burnout will find a way. Instead of waiting for burnout, your long-term health will benefit by changing your environment earlier.

- **Changing your perception.** One of the ways that people manage stress is simply by looking at things differently. Some technicians might perceive every help desk call as a problem that will challenge and stress them, while other technicians might perceive every help desk call as a puzzle to be solved. While solving a puzzle can be challenging, it isn't overly stressful. This doesn't mean that technicians should view every call as a puzzle, but they don't need to view every call as a stressful problem either.

Managing Your Time

A help desk professional's job can be intense on some days, so effective time management skills are important to master. The goal is to manage your time effectively so that you can accomplish everything you're expected to accomplish.

In some jobs, help desk professionals don't have much control over their time. For example, in one high-paced Internet service provider (ISP) company, employees are expected to be at their seat ready to answer phone calls at a certain time. Employees have two 15-minute breaks and one 60-minute meal break during their shift. All other time is spent answering phones to assist customers and documenting these calls in an incident management application. Time management here primarily entails ensuring that the call is being documented while they are helping the customer. Otherwise, the documentation builds up and they are constantly trying to catch up.

However, in most jobs, help desk professionals have the ability to manage their own time. In these jobs, and in other jobs with increasing responsibility, it is useful to have some time management techniques you can utilize.

Document, Document, Document

Almost all help desks use some type of incident management system to document each help desk call. This system tracks all of the work done by help desk professionals, and managers frequently mine the data to get answers to many different questions. For example, if there is a large backlog of open incidents, it might indicate additional help desk professionals are needed. On the other hand, if there aren't many incidents closed during any given time period, it might indicate that work isn't being accomplished.

Incident management systems can also identify trends and common problems, and managers can use this information to justify implementing other IT solutions to reduce the help desk workload. For example, if technicians are spending a lot of time and energy on resetting user passwords, the cost of an automated password reset system might be justified.

None of this is possible if help desk professionals do not consistently document their work assisting customers. Technicians providing assistance need to know what needs to be documented, and supervisors need to ensure technicians are given enough time to complete the documentation.

Whenever possible, technicians should be able to log this information as they're working with customers. This is easier when technicians are helping customers over the phone, via instant message, or chat windows, but if technicians are helping users at the user's desk, it isn't as easy. Instead, the technician needs to take notes and then log the incident later.

Manage Priorities

Frequently, people are stressed because they have too many tasks for the amount of time they have to perform them. However, it's also true that many people waste a lot of time and effort on small, tedious tasks and find that they don't have enough time for the major tasks. In other words, their perception is that they don't have enough time, but by changing their priorities to do the important things first, they end up accomplishing more in the same amount of time. Admittedly, they don't gain any more hours in the day with this process, they just find that they don't need to spend as much time on the smaller tasks.

One effective time management skill is to identify what's important. Some people use lists to remember what they need to do, and this is certainly effective for many people. However, in addition to the list, it's worthwhile to add priorities. For example, you can label items on your list with numbers 1 through 4, using 1 for high priority tasks and 5 for low priority tasks:

- **1—High Priority.** This includes tasks that must be done today.
- **2—Medium-High Priority.** These are important tasks that have a deadline coming up in the next few days.

- **3—Medium Priority.** These are less important tasks that you can work on after completing other more important tasks.
- **4—Low Priority.** These tasks are the least important. In some situations, you might be able to delegate these tasks.

The book *First Things First* by the late Stephen Covey, A. Roger Merrill, and Rebecca R. Merrill is a successful follow-up to Covey's book *The 7 Habits of Highly Effective People* and provides great insight into how to prioritize. It teaches a method that allows you to focus on what is important, not merely what is urgent, by dividing tasks into four quadrants:

- 1—Important and Urgent (crises, deadline-driven projects)
- 2—Important, Not Urgent (preparation, prevention, planning, relationships)
- 3—Urgent, Not Important (interruptions, many pressing matters)
- 4—Not Urgent, Not Important (trivia, time wasters)

On the surface, you might think that the tasks in quadrant 1 are the most important. However, the work you do in quadrant 2 is often much more valuable because it allows you to plan and prepare for upcoming matters, and prevent some crises. Also, the most valuable experiences in most people's lives isn't derived from the work that they do, but instead it's from their relationships and interactions with others. When people let their lives be driven by crises and interruptions (quadrants 1 and 3), they often aren't able to complete quality work through preparation and planning or create long-lasting relationships (quadrant 2).

For most people, it's obvious that quadrant 4 is the least important, but that doesn't stop many people from wasting a lot of time on trivial matters. As an example, Facebook is a great way to interact with friends and family and see what they're up to, even if they're in another city, state, or country. However, most people remember at least one time when they realized they just wasted an hour or more watching videos of dogs attacking their reflection in the mirror, cats dressed up as Puss in Boots, or kids singing, laughing, or crying. This is certainly OK if you intend to spend an hour with this as entertainment, but it becomes a problem when you have important things to do but instead spend it with trivia.

> **AUTHOR'S NOTE:**   Author David Allen has written an excellent book titled *Getting Things Done: The Art of Stress-Free Productivity* which provides practical ideas on organizational efficiency to unclog your brain and focus on what's important. If you don't have time to read the full book, check out *Getting Things Done: A Summary of David Allen's Book on Productivity*.

Give Yourself More Time

Another way of managing your time and simultaneously decreasing your stress level is to give yourself more time to do certain things. As a simple example, imagine two people, Sally and Bob, who have to be at work at 8:00 AM.

Sally chooses to plan her morning so that she can normally arrive ten minutes early, at 7:50 AM. She normally arrives at 7:50 but occasionally, something happens that causes her to be a little later—she's delayed at home and leaves a little later, she forgets something and has to go back to get it, she finds herself caught behind a school bus, an accident slows traffic down, or just about anything that happens in day-to-day life. However, with the extra buffer, these events are just minor inconveniences. She still gets to work by 8:00 AM and is rarely stressed that she'll be late.

In contrast, Bob plans to be at work at 8:00 AM, not earlier. Normally, he makes it there on time, but occasionally those same types of events slow him down and, knowing he doesn't have a moment to spare, he realizes he'll be late. Bob is conscientious about work and being on time, and his supervisor has talked to him about being late, so he tries to make up the time. He tries to go a little faster, and is sometimes a little more aggressive in his driving. He zips through yellow lights as they turn red, beeps his horn, and tailgates slow-moving drivers to encourage them to go faster, all the while worrying if he'll be able to make it to work on time. This worry, combined with all the actions to go a little quicker, add a significant amount of stress to Bob's day.

Ten minutes might not seem like much, but this ten minutes can go a long way toward reducing stress from unexpected events at the start of the day. You can use this same concept for just about any tasks. For example, if you have a looming deadline, give yourself an earlier deadline. If something comes up that prevents you from meeting your deadline, you still have some extra time to complete it and still be on time.

Managing Your Career

A position as a help desk professional can be very rewarding, but for most people it isn't a career. For many people, it's a stepping stone on the path to jobs with increasingly more responsibilities and variety. These other jobs typically provide increased pay too.

It's never too early to begin managing your career. Some people think that they must fully master their current job before they can ever move up, but this is rarely true. Also, you're rarely fully prepared for the job at the next level in your career path. Instead, when you get that new job, the path to succeed in it begins opening up. It's similar to driving a car down the road at night. Your headlights illuminate part of the road in front of you but you never know what's on the road up ahead. Instead, you focus on the road illuminated by your headlights, and as you drive, the rest of the road gradually opens up to you.

Here's what you can do to prepare for the next job: the absolute best you can in your current job. When you put all you have into whatever job you have, you'll learn valuable skills and knowledge that will help you in your career. You rarely know which skills and knowledge will be most valuable, but when you apply yourself fully, you will leave each job with something that will help you at least a little more along the way.

Career Paths

Some of the likely career paths for people beyond the help desk include help desk management, advanced tier 2 and tier 3 jobs, and other advanced IT jobs within the organization. Some of the common IT jobs beyond the help desk include:

- **Network Administration.** Network administrators maintain the network. This typically entails troubleshooting and maintaining network hardware such as routers and switches.

- **Network Architect or Network Engineer.** Beyond administration, network architects or engineers design new networks and/or plan for the expansion of existing networks. For example, if the existing network is slowing down due to excessive traffic, this group will identify changes to improve the network performance.

- **System Administrator.** System administrators maintain and troubleshoot IT systems. An IT system can be a single server such as an email server, or a group of devices that combine to provide an overall service. As an example, a group of web servers in a web farm that interact with multiple database servers is a web site system. System administrators might be responsible for any single server or for groups of servers within this system.

- **System Architect or System Engineer.** The system architects or engineers evaluate and plan the implementation of new systems, or the expansion of existing systems. For example, if an organization is hosting a web site that has performance problems, this group might plan for the implementation of a web farm to spread the load across multiple servers.

- **Web Administration and Development.** Web site developers create web sites and web site administrators maintain them. While there are many tools that streamline this process for basic websites, high volume websites require advanced skills. Administrators and developers often need to have a combination of graphics knowledge and experience combined with programming skills in at least a few programming languages, such as hypertext markup language (HTML), PHP hypertext preprocessor (PHP), and JavaScript.

- **Application Development.** While few organizations have in-house application developers, there are some. Developers understand how to program using two or more programming languages such as Java, JavaScript, C, C#, C++, Python, Ruby, Perl, and Visual Basic. A musician can play more than just a single instrument. Similarly, a programmer must be able to program in more than just a single language; the list of popular languages in use today is much different than the list was ten years ago, and it'll be different ten years in the future.

- **Database Development and Administration.** Database developers design and create databases used for different applications. Once designed, database administrators maintain these databases and servers hosting the databases. Database development requires some specialized knowledge of application development, but database administration is similar to the administration of any server—it just requires completing certain administrative tasks to maintain the databases.

- **Security Specialist.** Attackers continue to launch sophisticated attacks against organizations, making security increasingly important. Security specialists can be focused on individual host systems, ensuring that they all have adequate antivirus software and data is backed up. Security administrators ensure that an organization has adequate physical security. Network security specialists focus on network defense, ensuring that a network has properly operating hardware such as firewalls, intrusion detection systems, and intrusion prevention systems. Some specialists focus on assessing security by performing vulnerability and penetration testing. Forensics specialists investigate incidents to determine the cause and identify what an organization can to prevent other security incidents. Chapter 5, "Security Skills," covers some of the security skills needed by a help desk professional.

- **Trainer.** Technical trainers provide training to IT workers at all levels. They typically have a high aptitude for learning new material and use a variety of techniques to share this information with others. Chapter 8, "Training Skills," covers training in more depth.

- **Technical Writer.** Technical writers are able to break down complex concepts into easy to understand topics. They might write small snippets of information for websites providing instructions for products, or even full-blown technical manuals. Chapter 7, "Writing Skills," covers writing skills in more depth.

Help desk professionals are often exposed to many of these jobs and have an opportunity to utilize skills needed in many of these positions while working in a help desk position. For example, technicians on the help desk might provide training to other technicians or write technical instructions for customers and post them on web sites. Similarly, they might gain a better understanding of the network and servers used within the organization. This can help them get a better idea of what they enjoy and what career path they might want to pursue.

Certifications

Technical certifications help distinguish individuals as having specific knowledge and skills. They are very similar to certifications and accreditations used in other professions. One of the challenges with certifications is identifying which ones will be valuable for your chosen career path. For example, a Linux-related certification won't help much if you're trying to land a job in an organization that doesn't use Linux at all.

AUTHOR'S NOTE: A question I'm frequently asked is, "What is better? A degree or a certification?" In general, a degree is better. Once you have a degree, you have it for the rest of your life. Certifications typically expire after three to five years and even when they don't, their relevancy fades. For example, hiring managers don't care if you have a certification in Windows 2000 because they don't use Windows 2000 anymore. A current certification might land you an immediate job, but if that job disappears, the certification might not be relevant for other jobs, and without a degree, your upward mobility within an organization is often limited. I've worked in an organization where two people were doing similar work, working in similar positions, but the person with a degree was earning $10,000 more than the person without a degree. The best combination is a degree for longevity, and current certifications for positions you're seeking.

Another consideration is the organization that manages the certifications and validates individuals as being certified. Imagine you get sick while on an international cruise and you have a choice between two doctors. One graduated from a Liaison Committee on Medical Education (LCME) accredited school and completed an American Medical Association (AMA) approved residency before entering private practice. The second completed an online training program through the Gibson School of Medicine. Which doctor would you prefer? While this is an extreme example (and there's no indication a Gibson School of Medicine actually exists), it does give you some insight into what employers might look for in a certification.

Some reputable organizations that have well-respected certifications are CompTIA, HDI, Microsoft, Apple, Cisco, and International Information Systems Security Certification Consortium (ISC)[2]. While there are many other certifications available, these are some of the top certification organizations.

- **CompTIA.** CompTIA certifications are vendor neutral and provide a solid foundation for an Information Technology (IT) worker. Vendor neutral indicates that they are not focused on products for any specific company such as Microsoft or Cisco. The A+ certification covers fundamental hardware and software topics for personal computers. Network+ builds on the A+ certification and focuses on networking topics. Security+ builds on the A+ and Network+ certifications with a focus on security topics. You can read more at http://certification.comptia.org/getCertified/steps_to_certification.aspx.

- **HDI.** HDI provides a wide variety of courses for help desk professionals, and most of these courses include certifications exams. Some of their certifications are HDI Customer Service Representative, HDI Support Center Analyst, HDI Desktop Support Technician, Knowledge-Centered Support Fundamentals, and Knowledge-Centered Support Principles. You can read more about these at http://www.thinkhdi.com/certification/professional/testing.aspx.

ON THE SIDE: HDI was previously known as the Help Desk Institute. They rebranded the company in 2005 as HDI (no longer an acronym for Help Desk Institute) to acknowledge the expanding role of the support center beyond the help desk.

- **Apple.** Some organizations that rely on Apple products require technicians to have Apple certifications to validate their knowledge and skills. A basic certification is the Apple Certified Technical Coordinator (ACTC). Advanced certifications include the Apple Certified System Administrator (ASCA) and the Apple Certified Media Administrator (ACMA). You can read more at http://training.apple.com/certification.

- **Microsoft.** Microsoft certifications focus on Microsoft products such as Windows operating systems for desktops and servers. More advanced certifications focus on specific applications such as Microsoft Exchange for email and Microsoft SQL Server for databases. Microsoft certification names have been changing about every three to five years. At this writing, current certification categories are Microsoft Technology Associate (MTA) covering IT fundamentals, Microsoft Certified Solutions Associate (MCSA), Microsoft Certified Solutions Expert (MCSE), and Microsoft Certified Solutions Developer (MCSD). You can read more at http://www.microsoft.com/learning/en-us/mta-certification.aspx and http://www.microsoft.com/learning/en-us/certification-overview.aspx.

- **Cisco.** Cisco certifications focus on Cisco networking products such as routers and switches. Basic certifications include Cisco Certified Entry Networking Technician (CCENT) and Cisco Certified Network Associate (CCNA). Advanced certifications include specialized CCNA certifications and several Cisco Certified Networking Professional (CCNP) certifications. You can read more at http://www.cisco.com/web/learning/certifications/index.html.

- **(ISC)².** Two (ISC)² certifications that are often sought by IT professionals are the basic Systems Security Certified Practitioner (SSCP) and the advanced Certified Information Systems Security Professional (CISSP). Both are focused on IT security and are valuable for individuals in a security-based IT path. You can read more at https://www.isc2.org/credentials/default.aspx.

ON THE SIDE:
Many colleges and universities include continuing education courses designed to help degreed individuals gain knowledge about current technologies. It's common to see them offer courses covering CompTIA, Microsoft, and Cisco certifications.

Most technical certifications require individuals to take and pass one or more proctored certification exams. Exams are typically computer-based, but some still use the old-fashioned pencil and paper. These exams cost money but after paying the fee, just about anyone can take the exams and earn the certifications.

A common question many people ask is, "Will this certification get me a job?" The answer is "No." However, certifications do make you more marketable for job opportunities and increase your chances at getting interviews for many jobs. So, while the certification can help you get the interview, how you perform at the interview really determines if you'll get the job.

Technology changes quickly and to ensure these certifications remain relevant, they are updated every three years or so. Similarly, individuals with certifications are required to update their certifications by either passing new certification exams or completing continuing education requirements.

Chapter Review Activities

Use the features in this section to study and review the topics in this chapter.

Answer These Questions

1. Which of the following statements is FALSE?

   a. A positive attitude can convert irate customers into happy customers.

   b. A positive attitude can convert the customer experience from a negative one to a positive one.

   c. A positive attitude indicates the technician is constantly cheerful toward the customer.

   d. A positive attitude can convert buyers into loyal customers that keep coming back.

2. Of the following choices, what is the BEST definition of self-talk?

   a. A sign of serious mental instability

   b. A stream of negative thoughts that affects a person's self-image

   c. A stream of positive thoughts that affects a person's person

   d. A stream of positive or negative thoughts that can affect self-image and performance

3. Of the following choices, what BEST describes most organizations' view of a potential help desk professional's attitude and aptitude?

   a. Most organizations value attitude more than aptitude

   b. Most organizations value aptitude more than attitude

   c. Most organizations only test for aptitude

   d. Most organizations only test for attitude

4. Of the following choices, what BEST defines a service attitude?

   a. A positive attitude

   b. A caring attitude

   c. An attitude maintained by a service technician

   d. An aptitude for technical services

5. What is meant by "problem ownership"?

   a. Customers recognize problems are their own and they only call for help as a last resort.

   b. Customers work with multiple technicians until a technician takes ownership of the problem.

   c. Technicians take on ownership of a problem and work with it until it is resolved.

   d. Technicians transfer the problem to a department that can take ownership of it.

6. Which of the following is the BEST definition of stress?

   a. A negative force that can result in physical ailments

   b. A positive force that can bring joy and happiness

   c. A state of mind that should be avoided

   d. A state of mental tension and worry caused by problems in life or work

7. Which of the following is the BEST definition of eustress?

   a. A positive form of stress

   b. A negative form of stress

   c. The optimum level of stress

   d. A level of stress causing physical symptoms

8. Which of the following is the BEST definition of distress?

   a. The level of stress that releases adrenaline resulting in super human strength

   b. When the body attempts to adapt to a stressor in the resistance phase of the GAS model

   c. A positive form of stress

   d. A negative form of stress

9. Of the following choices, what are some that are recognized as common signs and symptoms of stress? (Choose all that apply.)

   a. Hair loss

   b. Frequent headaches

   c. Increased or decreased appetite

   d. Frequent colds or infections

10. Of the following choices, what are some common causes of job burnout? (Choose all that apply.)

    a. Lack of control

    b. Work overload

    c. New baby in the household

    d. Dysfunctional workplace

11. Of the following choices, what are some common symptoms of burnout? (Choose all that apply.)

    a. Sleep problems

    b. Eating disorders

    c. Emotional swings

    d. Gun purchases

12. Of the following choices, what are some common methods of releasing stress? (Choose all that apply.)

   a. Leaving the job

   b. Meditation

   c. Exercise

   d. Changing perceptions

13. Help desk workers are typically expected to document actions in an incident management system. Of the following choices, what is the LEAST likely use of this data?

   a. Identify incident backlogs

   b. Identify how many incidents are being closed regularly

   c. Identify trends

   d. Identify English skills

14. You have created a list of items that you know need to be done in the next week or so. From a time management perspective, what else should you do?

   a. Complete the first item on the list as soon as possible

   b. Divide the tasks into a different lists for the number of days you have to accomplish them

   c. Prioritize the tasks in the list

   d. Divide the tasks between work items and personal items

15. Which of the following techniques would be MOST useful to help someone prioritize their tasks?

   a. Write the tasks in a list

   b. Label tasks as either work-based or personal

   c. Identify tasks based on who assigned them

   d. Assign tasks to one of four quadrants

16. Which of the following provides the BEST reason individuals earn certifications?

   a. They show that they have money for the exams.

   b. They show that they have specific knowledge and skills.

   c. They show that they can work well with people.

   d. They show that they are trainable.

17. Which organization manages primarily foundation-level certifications?

   a. Cisco

   b. CompTIA

   c. (ISC)2

   d. Microsoft

18. Which organization manages vendor-neutral certifications?

    a. Apple

    b. Cisco

    c. CompTIA

    d. Microsoft

19. Which organization focuses on certifications related to network devices such as routers and switches?

    a. Cisco

    b. CompTIA

    c. (ISC)2

    d. Microsoft

20. Of the following choices, what combination of education and certifications are BEST for an IT career?

    a. Neither

    b. Degree

    c. Certification

    d. Both

Answers and Explanations

1. **c.** A positive attitude doesn't mean the technician is constantly or overly cheerful, but it does mean that they are able to look at the positive aspects of an issue, rather than focusing on the negative aspects. The other statements are true.

2. **d.** Self-talk is the stream of thoughts that runs through your mind, and it can be positive or negative. Self-talk forms and reinforces a person's self-image, which determines their performance and stimulates similar self-talk. It is not indicative of a mental disorder.

3. **a.** Most organizations value attitude more than aptitude in potential help desk professionals primarily because they recognize that skills can be taught, but it is extremely difficult to teach someone to have a positive attitude. While aptitude and skills testing might be the only apparent testing, most organizations are also evaluating potential employee's attitude.

4. **b.** A service attitude is similar to a caring attitude. It goes beyond just a positive attitude and includes a sense of caring for the customer. The word "service" in this context isn't related to technicians or technical services.

5. **c.** Problem ownership refers to a mindset where a technician takes ownership of a problem and works with it until it is resolved. Problem ownership doesn't refer to customers, and technicians that own a problem do not transfer it.

6. **d.** Stress is a state of mental tension and worry caused by problems in life, work, and relationships. Stress isn't necessarily bad, but when it is excessive as in distress, it can cause physical ailments. Eustress is a form of stress that can be positive. Stress cannot be avoided, but it should be managed to avoid stress becoming long-term distress.

7. **a.** Eustress is positive form of stress that comes from positive events. Distress is a negative form of stress that causes physical and psychological problems if not managed. Eustress can cause problems if a person isn't able to manage it, so by itself it isn't necessarily an optimum level of stress or an excessive level that causes problems.

8. **d.** Distress is a negative form of stress that causes physical and psychological problems if not managed. Super human strength is typically a short-term event, while distress is typically excessive stress over a period of time. In the general adaptation syndrome (GAS) model, distress occurs in the exhaustion phase, not the resistance phase. Eustress is a positive form of stress that comes from positive events.

9. **b, c, d.** Some common signs and symptoms of stress include frequent headaches, changes in appetite, and frequent colds or infections. Hair loss can be a genetic trait or is indicative of a more serious physical ailment and is not a common sign or symptom of stress.

10. **a, b, d.** Some common causes of job burnout include lack of control, work overload, and a dysfunctional workplace. While a new baby in the household can cause a lot of stress and a lack of sleep, the baby does not cause job burnout.

11. **a, b, c.** Some common symptoms of burnout include sleep problems, eating disorders, and emotional swings. Someone purchasing a gun is not a symptom of burnout by itself because there are many reasons a healthy person might purchase a gun.

12. **b, c.** Meditation and exercise are two common methods of releasing stress. Leaving the job is one way to manage stress by changing the environment. Another stress management method is to change the perception of an event by looking at it differently.

13. **d.** Of the given choices, the least likely use of this data is to identify English skills of technicians entering data. The other examples are common uses of the data.

14. **c.** When creating lists, it's important to also prioritize the items on the list. This ensures you complete the important items first.

15. **d.** Assigning tasks to one of four quadrants is an effective method documented in Covey's book *First Things First*. A list isn't prioritized. There are times when personal tasks are more important than work tasks, so this wouldn't prioritize them. Who assigned the task rarely identifies their true priority.

16. **b.** Certifications show that individuals have specific knowledge and skills related to the certification. While they do cost money, that's not why people take them. Also, the certifications do not indicate how well a person will interact with others. Certifications do indicate that someone can learn objectives and indicate they are trainable, but this isn't the best reason to get the certification.

17. **b.** CompTIA manages many foundation-level certifications including A+, Network+, and Security+.

18. **c.** CompTIA certifications are vendor neutral. They do not focus on any individual organization such as Apple, Cisco, or Microsoft.

19. **a.** Cisco certifications such as the CCNA focus on Cisco hardware such as routers and switches.

20. **d.** The best combination is both a degree and certifications for IT careers. The degree is good for long-term employability and upward mobility, and the certification(s) show current knowledge.

Define the Key Terms

The following key terms include the ideas most important to the big ideas in this chapter. To review, without looking at the book or your notes, write a definition for each term, focusing on the meaning, not the wording. Then review your definition compared to your notes, this chapter, and the glossary.

Key Terms for Chapter 1

aptitude	eustress	service attitude
attitude	general adaptation	stress
burnout	syndrome	stress management
distress	self-talk	

Create Mind Maps

For this chapter, create mind maps as follows:

1. Recreate a modified Yerkes-Dodson curve to show the relationship between performance and increased stress. Label the area where performance is at the peak and list some of the problems that can occur when stress is at its highest.

2. Recreate the general adaptation syndrome model and list the three phases of resistance. Draw the graph to show the body's resistance levels to a stressor in each of the three phases.

3. List as many symptoms of stress as you can remember.

4. List as many symptoms of burnout as you can remember.

Case Studies

Case Study 1

Perform an Internet search on "superhuman strength" or "superhuman strength during a crisis" and identify at least one instance where a person demonstrated superhuman strength.

Case Study 2

Do this five-minute practice as a relaxation technique. Sit somewhere that is relatively quiet with your back straight if possible. Count from 50 down to 0 while focusing on your breath. For example, breathe in as you silently say 50, breathe out as you silently say 49, and so on. If you're like most people, your mind will wander and you'll lose count. This is expected. When you realize it happened, continue from the last number you remember. This short five-minute exercise is effective at reducing stress and often provides other side effects, such as proving relief from headache pain.

Case Study 3

Perform an Internet search to identify how many tests an individual must pass to earn each of the following certifications: CompTIA A+, Network+, and Security+; Cisco CCENT and CCNA.

Chapter 4

Technical Skills

Successful help desk specialists have a core set of technical skills, which helps them support the customers. The specific skills vary from one organization to another based on the type of support technicians need to provide. For example, technicians working at an Internet service provider (ISP) might only help users configure their systems for Internet connectivity, but nothing else. Technicians working in another company might only provide support to remote users on how to use one or two applications. Technicians in some companies provide support to users for almost anything, including hardware failures, operating system and application problems, network connectivity, and mobile device configuration. Many topics introduced in this chapter could easily fill a book. The intent isn't to provide you with all the information you need to know regarding technical skills. Instead, the goal of this chapter is to provide an overview of key technical skills needed by successful help desk specialists.

This chapter covers technical skills in four major sections:

- The first section, "Working with Personal Computers," provides an overview of personal computer (PC) hardware, firmware, operating systems, and applications.

- Next, "Working with Networks" provides an introduction into the components found on most networks. This includes a short introduction about protocols and an explanation of the different types of hardware used on networks.

- The "Working with Mobile Devices" section introduces relevant concepts related to smartphones and tablets. It includes information on their operating systems, the different app stores, how to configure email, and important security features of mobile devices.

- Last, "Understanding the Product" stresses the importance for help desk specialists to focus on the product they will support. It also provides information on some common certifications and the importance of continuous learning.

Chapter Outline

Objectives

- Explain basic security precautions related to working with PCs
- List and describe common PC hardware components
- Explain the purpose of a computer's firmware
- Describe the purpose of a PC's operating system
- Describe the purpose of protocols
- Compare and contrast network devices such as hubs, switches, and routers
- Describe the primary purpose of a network firewall
- Explain the differences between a wireless router and a wireless access point

- Compare and contrast different mobile device operating systems
- List the common elements needed to configure email on a mobile device
- Describe a key security benefit related to app stores
- List and summarize security features available on mobile devices
- Summarize common certifications held by help desk specialists
- Define the purpose of continuing education

Key Terms

central processing units (CPUs)

continuing education (CE)

electrostatic discharge (ESD)

firewall

firmware

hub

protocol analyzer

random access memory (RAM)

router

switch

Transmission Control Protocol/Internet Protocol (TCP/IP)

wireless access point (WAP)

wireless router

Working with Personal Computers

Personal computers (PCs) are one of the primary technical tools used by workers. Help desk specialists need to have a good understanding of PCs and how workers use them. It's very common for a help desk to support user PCs. However, even when the help desk doesn't support the PCs, help desk personnel will typically use one when logging incidents, so they need to be familiar with how to use a PC.

The CompTIA A+ certification provides a good outline related to what help desk technicians need to know about PCs. It includes objectives related to PC hardware, operating systems, and troubleshooting. Beyond these objectives, technicians should also understand software applications they are required to support. The following sections provide an overview of these topics.

> **ON THE SIDE:**   Many study guides for the A+ certification are 1000 pages or longer. Obviously, this chapter section cannot include all of the same details that you'll find in a 1000-page study guide—and that isn't the goal. Instead, the goal is to give you an overview of some key topics that many help desk specialists are expected to know.

Reviewing PC Hardware

PCs are modular, allowing technicians to replace the failed parts instead of replacing the entire computer. For example, if a PC power supply fails, a technician replaces the power supply. The process of replacing the failed parts varies from one computer to another, but the key is that technicians can, and do, replace many components. This section introduces some of the common components that PC technicians replace. In some cases, technicians replace these after the components fail. In other cases, technicians replace the components to upgrade the computer.

Both desktop PCs and laptop computers are modular, though desktop PCs are generally much easier to maintain. Experienced technicians can often replace components in a desktop PC without needing detailed instructions. In contrast, you often need to follow specific directions when replacing components in laptop computers. Some components are easily accessible via panels on the back of the laptop. Figure 4-1 shows the back of a laptop with a panel removed. This panel provides access to memory cards and the disk drives, and the figure shows one memory card removed. It's important to realize that all laptops aren't the same. Some have separate panels for memory and hard drives. Some memory cards aren't accessible unless you completely disassemble the laptop.

FIGURE 4-1

Back of a laptop with a panel removed.

A Few Words About Safety

It's important to pay attention to basic safety precautions when working on computers. Safety precautions protect technicians from harm such as electrical shock, and it protects the computers from potential damage.

First, it's important to remove power from a computer prior to replacing most computer components. Technicians turn the system off and remove the power cord from the power source. For laptops, they also remove the battery. An exception is hot-swappable components such as Universal Serial Bus (USB) flash drives, which can be plugged in and removed from a computer while it is powered on.

Static electricity is a significant concern when working with small computer components such as RAM. If you've ever walked across a carpeted floor in the winter, you've probably gotten shocked when you touched a door knob. If you felt it, it was at least 3,000 volts. If you saw the spark, it was at least 8,000 volts. That sounds like a lot, but without electrical current, it can't hurt you. However, static electricity with as little as 250 volts can damage computer components.

Electrostatic discharge (ESD) is a significant concern when working with small computer components such as memory and processors. Technicians wear ESD wrist straps to prevent static from building up, along with other ESD damage prevention methods such as ESD mats. The wrist step provides a connection between the technician and ground. Without ESD protection, a technician can easily ruin a computer component just by touching it.

The technician won't see the damage or feel a shock. However, the damage is real. In many cases, the damage isn't apparent right away. Instead, it weakens the component, making it more susceptible to heat fluctuations. The computer displays intermittent symptoms after it's been running for a while, but these intermittent symptoms can be extremely difficult to troubleshoot. Technicians responsible for replacing computer components should understand ESD and have tools available to prevent ESD damage.

Motherboards

One of the primary components in a computer is the motherboard.

It has several components soldered in place and includes slots for other hardware, as shown in Figure 4-2. The figure shows the processor, memory, external connections, and expansion slots. Additionally, it shows the chipset on this motherboard. The chipset is one or more additional chips, which provides additional features for the computer such as audio, graphics, and network support. The processor and the chipset both generate a significant amount of heat, and heat sinks help dissipate this heat. The motherboard also includes several connections for other components. For example, the six blue connectors next to the chipset provide data connections for hard drives.

> **ON THE SIDE:**   Laptops also have motherboards, but they look significantly different from Figure 4-2. They are smaller, have fewer available slots, and often differ from one manufacturer to another.

Processor with Fan and Heat Sink

Memory Installed in Slots

Chipset with Heat Sink

Connections Available at Back of Computer

Seven Expansion Slots (Three Different Sizes)

FIGURE 4-2

Computer motherboard.

One of the benefits of desktop computer motherboards is that manufacturers follow form factor standards when creating them. Form factor standards dictate specific sizes and mounting holes used to attach the motherboard within the computer. They also provide additional standards related to power and connections. The primary standard in use today is Advanced Technology Extended (ATX). Intel released the original ATX specifications in 1995 and has released several updates to it since then. Beyond ATX, there are several other variants such as Micro-ATX, which is smaller and has fewer expansion slots.

Hard Drives

Hard drives provide long-term storage for data and applications. They include multiple platters that spin, and actuator arms that move read/write heads to different locations on the platters. While hard drives have significantly improved over the years, these moving components result in more hard drive failures than failures with other components in a system. Additionally, it's very common to upgrade a computer by adding an additional hard drive.

When a user first buys a computer, the amount of hard drive space seems astronomical. However, users add files such as documents, pictures, videos, and more, filling up the hard drive over time. The primary issue is that the user runs out of storage space. However, if the hard drive becomes too full, it can significantly degrade the overall performance of the computer.

New systems typically include one internal hard drive, but have room and connections for at least one more. However, before purchasing a new hard drive, it's important to verify the computer has room and connections for another hard drive.

Older computers used parallel Advanced Technology Attachment (PATA)-based hard drives, but most of today's computers use serial ATA (SATA)-based hard drives. There are significant differences between the two related to performance and their power and data connections.

SATA drives support much faster transfer speeds increasing the overall performance of the computer. The three generations of SATA are SATA 1 (supporting transfer speeds up to 1.50 gigabits per second), SATA 2 (supporting transfer speeds up to 3 gigabits per second), and SATA 3 (supporting transfer speeds up to 6 gigabits per second).

> **ON THE SIDE:** Manufacturers often use different names for SATA drives, which confuses even the best technicians. For example, other names used for SATA 2 drives (second generation) are SATA 3G, SATA 3Gb/s, and SATA 3Gbit/s. Unless you remembered that SATA 2 supports transfer speeds up to 3 gigabits per second, you might think that these names were referring to a SATA 3 drive.

If the system supports PATA drives only and can accommodate another hard drive, you need to purchase a PATA drive. If the system supports SATA drives and can accommodate another hard drive, you should purchase a SATA drive. As an alternative, you can purchase and install a SATA expansion card and connect new SATA drives to it.

Most desktop PCs use 3.5-inch wide hard drives while laptops use 2.5-inch wide hard drives. These standard sizes ensure the drives can fit in computer drive bays. The performance is similar between the two. The only difference is that the laptop drives are smaller to accommodate the smaller size of laptops.

A newer trend is the use of solid state drives (SSDs). SSDs don't have any moving parts (such as spinning platters). Instead, they use a special type of flash memory to store data. This is similar to memory used in USB flash drives, and the data stays on the drive even after the computer is turned off.

SSDs are super fast, and because they don't have any moving parts, they use less power. Their prices continue to drop, making them more affordable. They are commonly used in tablets and have been appearing in more laptop computers. Lately, many users have been adding them to desktop PCs.

Memory

Computers use random access memory (RAM) for the majority of their processing. Hard drives provide long-term storage of information and when the computer needs to use it, it transfers data to RAM. Most of today's operating systems crave memory, and upgrading or replacing memory often provides significant performance gains for PCs. However, memory technology increases rapidly, making it a challenge to identify compatible RAM with many computers.

Technicians need to understand the different types of RAM and ensure that new RAM is compatible with the system before replacing it. There are a dizzying array of different types of RAM and RAM specifications. However, there are also applications that technicians can use to identify compatible RAM before purchasing it. For example, Crucial.com sells RAM and other computer components, and they provide free access to two tools: The Crucial Memory Advisor Tool and the Crucial System Scanner Tool. Anyone can use these tools to identify their computer specifications and locate compatible hardware for upgrades.

Most of today's RAM is installed on circuit cards called dual inline memory modules (DIMMs), commonly called memory sticks. Laptops use smaller sized RAM sticks called small outline dual-inline memory modules (SO DIMMs). SO DIMMs provide similar performance as DIMMs used in desktop systems—they are just smaller to accommodate the smaller size of laptop computers.

When you purchase RAM from reputable sources, it will arrive in special antistatic bags. These ensure that static electricity cannot build up and damage the RAM during shipment. Technicians should only remove the RAM from the antistatic bag when they are properly connected with an ESD wrist strap and they are ready to install it. Also, remember to ensure that all power is off before starting.

Figure 4-3 shows a DIMM stick with some construction workers installing it into a memory slot. If you don't have any inch-sized construction workers at your organization, you'll be happy to know it isn't very difficult to replace RAM sticks. If a stick is currently installed, you can press down on the white tabs on both sides of the stick to loosen and remove it. You then install the new RAM into the empty slot. When you push it into place, the white tabs automatically lock it into place.

ON THE SIDE: Most computer components and connections are keyed. This ensures that the component or connection can only be connected in one way. For example, the memory card in Figure 4-3 has notches in it where it plugs into the slot. These notches ensure that the memory card is plugged in correctly. If a technician accidentally tried to plug it in backwards, these notches prevent the card from fitting into the slot.

FIGURE 4-3

Installing memory.

Optical Media Drives

Optical media includes compact discs (CDs), digital versatile discs (DVDs), and Blu-Ray discs (BDs). Optical media drives use lasers to read and write data to and from these discs. Computers commonly include one or more optical media drives to support reading and writing to optical media discs. Technicians and users commonly refer to writing data to a disc as "burning a disc."

ON THE SIDE: Hard disk drives use a "k" in the word disk. Optical media discs use a "c" in the word disc.

Many optical drives are combo drives that support multiple types of optical discs. For example, it's common to have a drive that can read and write to both CDs and DVDs. As the popularity of Blu-Ray discs grows, you can expect to see more combo drives that support them, too.

These drives can fail, requiring replacement, and sometimes users just want to replace them to improve the performance of the existing drive or add additional capabilities to their system. With this in mind, technicians often need to replace the drives. Just as hard disk drives come in both SATA and PATA versions, optical drives also come in both SATA and PATA versions. SATA drives are more common today, but again, if you're replacing an existing drive, you first need to identify if it is a SATA or PATA drive and then replace it with the same technology.

Discs have one and two-letter codes that describe their use, and these often confuse people. Common letter codes are:

- **R.** This indicates the disc is recordable, but data can only be recorded once. It is useful for backups and archives. Technicians refer to it as write once read many (WORM). CDs, DVDs, and Blu-Ray discs uses this code as CD-R, DVD-R, and BD-R.

- **RW.** This indicates the disc is rewritable, allowing users to modify the contents of the disc multiple times. CDs and DVDs use this code as CD-RW and DVD-RW.

- **RE.** This indicates the disc is recordable and erasable similar to how CDs and DVDs are rewritable. Only Blu-Ray discs use this code as BD-RE.

Also, many discs use a + or - to identify different versions. For example, you might see DVD-R and DVD+R discs. Most optical media drives can read both versions. However, some DVD movie players only support one version or the other.

Video Cards

Most motherboards include video capabilities built into the chipset. However, many users choose to upgrade the video capabilities by adding an additional video card. For example, motherboards don't always support High-Definition Multimedia Interface (HDMI) display monitors, so users that want to use these monitors can add an HDMI-capable video card. Also, many of today's games provide astounding graphics, but they require a significant amount of memory on the video card, which isn't typically available from the motherboard video capabilities.

Video cards are relatively easy to replace or upgrade in desktop systems. They plug into a slot in the motherboard. As with other components, a primary consideration is ensuring the system supports the new motherboard. The primary slot type used with video cards is Peripheral Component Interconnect Express (PCIe). However, the slots and video cards come in multiple versions such as PCIe x1, x2, x4, x8, x16, and x32. Higher numbers like x16 and x32 identify larger slots and they provide higher data transfer rates and overall better performance than slots with the lower numbers. Video cards typically use PCIe x16 or PCIe x32 slots.

As with any expansion card that you plan to add to a computer, it's important to ensure the motherboard supports the new video card. It's not very useful to buy a PCIe x32 video card only to find out that the system will only support a PCIe x16 video card.

Power Supplies

Power supplies within a computer convert alternating current (AC) from a power outlet such as a surge protector to direct current (DC) needed by internal components. The ATX standard that defines motherboard specifications also defines power supply requirements, such as the types of connectors required and the specific voltages required on different pins.

Laptops don't have a separate power supply. However, they do use rechargeable and replaceable batteries, which provide DC voltage. Laptops use DC power adapters to convert AC to DC. One end plugs into a power outlet, providing AC power, and the end plugs into the DC jack on the laptop. Most power adapters have an LED, indicating they are plugged in and working, which is very useful since these power adapters often fail. If a laptop battery stops charging, check the adapter and replace it if necessary.

> **ON THE SIDE:** When purchasing replacement batteries for laptop computers, it's extremely important to ensure the replacement is compatible. Many laptops have erupted in flames after people installed incompatible batteries.

Computer power supplies sometimes fail, but they are relatively easy to replace. Power supplies following the ATX standard are the same physical size but they can have different capabilities. For example, some power supplies include connections for both PATA and SATA drives, while others have connections for only one or the other.

A significant characteristic of a power supply is its power rating. Power is computed as a watt (W) and power supplies with higher wattage ratings can support more hardware. With this in mind, you need to ensure the replacement power supply meets or exceeds the wattage of the failed power supply. For example, if the system currently has a 600 W power supply, the replacement power supply should be rated as 600 W or more. Also, if the 600 W power supply failed, it's very possible that it was underrated for the computer load. As an example, hard drives consume a lot of power, and if someone added additional hard drives to a system, it's possible this additional load was too much for the original power supply, causing it to fail. You would need to replace it with a higher wattage power supply.

Another characteristic of power supplies is the number of rails it supports. Each rail provides power to dedicated components such as the processor, disk drives, and case fans. However, a single rail cannot power all these components in most desktop computers. Instead, power supplies have two or more rails, with each rail supporting specific components. For example, one rail can power the processor, another rail can power the hard drives, and a third rail can power the case fans. With this in mind, you need to ensure that the replacement power supply has at least as many rails as the original power supply.

Something else to consider when replacing a failed power supply is the possibility that too many components were plugged into a single rail. For example, if someone added additional hard drives and plugged all the hard drives into the same rail, this extra load might have overloaded the power supply, causing it to fail. Worse, an overloaded rail can provide inconsistent power to hard drives before it actually fails, resulting in hard drive failures or corrupt data.

Processors

Computers include one or more **central processing units (CPUs)** that handle the majority of the systems computer processing. The two primary manufacturers of CPUs are Intel and Advanced Micro Devices (AMD). They manufacture and sell the CPUs used in most computers. CPUs plug into the motherboard and are often removable and replaceable.

As with other components, it's important to verify compatibility of a replacement CPU in a current system. Intel and AMD processors are not interchangeable, meaning you cannot plug in an Intel processor into a motherboard built for an AMD processor. More, most processors are not compatible with other processors from the same manufacturer. In other words, just because you have an Intel motherboard, it doesn't mean that you can plug in any Intel processor.

A CPU generates quite a bit of heat that can damage the CPU if steps aren't taken to protect it. Two common methods to protect CPUs are heat sinks and fans. As an example, Figure 4-4 shows a heat sink attached to a CPU. The CPU is the thin part at the bottom with the pins pointing down. Heat sinks are composed of composite metals that quickly dissipate heat and include a design providing the maximum surface area. The design allows air to easily flow through the heat sink.

FIGURE 4-4

Installing memory.

Additionally, technicians place thermal paste between the bottom of the heat sink and the top of the CPU. Thermal paste fills in microscopic gaps, ensuring the best possible connection between the two and helping the heat sink draw more heat away from the CPU. While Figure 4-2 doesn't show a fan, the fan is placed on top of the heat sink to draw more air flow through it.

Technicians take several precautions when replacing CPUs. First, they follow ESD prevention practices to avoid ESD damage. They also ensure they have new thermal paste they can apply between the heat sink and the CPU. Last, when installing the CPU into the motherboard, they pay attention to the keying of the pins to ensure they plug it in properly. If the CPU is plugged into the motherboard incorrectly, it can easily damage the CPU pins and destroy it.

Other Expansion Cards

The Video Cards section mentioned that video cards plug into expansion slots to provide increased video capabilities for a system. However, these expansion slots can support many more expansion cards beyond just video cards. This includes sound cards, SATA drive cards, network interface cards (NICs), and TV tuner cards.

There are two primary reasons why you'd install a card into an expansion slot: first, if you want to improve a capability from the original system, such as improved graphics; and second, if you want to add a capability to a system. For example, if a system doesn't have any spare SATA connections but you want to add a SATA hard drive, you can install a SATA expansion card to support the new SATA hard drive.

As with other hardware modifications, you need to ensure your system supports the new expansion card. Primarily, you do this by ensuring that the system has a compatible slot for the expansion card. For example, if you plan to add a PCIe x8 10 GB NIC, you need to ensure the system has an empty PCIe x8 slot.

Additionally, you need to ensure the system has enough space to accommodate the new card. This normally isn't a problem, but it can be if any of the installed cards are too wide. As an example, consider Figure 4-5. This is a video card with two graphics processing units (GPUs) and two fans. It plugs into one slot but is two slots wide. Depending on where this is installed in a computer, it's possible for it to cover up another slot. In this scenario, you might have an open slot that isn't usable unless you can move other expansion cards. Unfortunately, it isn't always possible to move the expansion cards to accommodate the new card. The only way you know for sure is to open the computer and look.

FIGURE 4-5

Video card.

Video Monitors

Video monitors are external to computers, but they can sometimes fail and need replacement. Additionally, many users enjoy having two monitors connected to their system. They can perform primary work using one monitor and configure the second monitor to show alerts or other data they observe throughout the day.

If you're adding or replacing a monitor, the most important consideration is ensuring that the video card has the connection to support it. The video card shown in Figure 4-5 includes four common connections: a DisplayPort connection on the far left, an HDMI connection in the middle, and two Digital Visual Interface (DVI) connections. Imagine an existing system has a video card with an available DisplayPort connection. You won't be able to connect a monitor that requires a DVI connection. Thankfully, some adapters allow you to mix and match the connections. For example, if the video card has a DVI connection, but the video monitor uses HDMI, you can use an HDMI to DVI adapter to connect the two. However, there aren't adapters available for all connections.

Most sellers advertise today's monitors as either LCD or LED monitors. LCD is short for liquid crystal display and LED is short for light emitting diode, but this is misleading. Both types are flat panel displays that are thin and light. Additionally, both types use a backlight to shine light through the liquid crystals. Internal electronics change the way the crystals are oriented so that they refract the light differently for the display.

The difference between the two is that traditional LCD monitors use a cold cathode fluorescent lamp (CCFL) as a backlight. LED monitors use LED lights as the backlight. In practice, CCFL backlights fail more often than LEDs. If the backlight fails, the display becomes extremely dim. Another difference is that LED monitors are often brighter than LCD monitors.

Understanding Firmware

Desktop PCs include firmware formally known as Basic Input/Output System (BIOS). **Firmware** is a combination of software and hardware with the software code embedded within a hardware device.

A computer's BIOS includes software code that provides basic instructions for a computer to start, or boot. When you turn the computer on, it reads the code from BIOS, performs a power on self test (POST), and then loads the operating system from the disk. If the POST checks fail, it displays a message indicating the problem. If POST passes, it continues to boot and loads the operating system from the hard drive.

Storing Settings

Older computers commonly included a separate complementary metal oxide semiconductor (CMOS) chip that included user configurable settings for the computer, such as the date and time. The CMOS chip required a battery to retain the settings while the computer powered down. The battery is typically a circular battery located on the computer's motherboard.

Most current computers do not have a CMOS chip. Instead, the user configurable settings for the computer are stored elsewhere. In some systems, these settings are stored in the same chip as the real-time clock, which keeps the system time. Other systems store these settings in a flash-type memory similar to the memory USB flash drives use. Even when the settings are stored in flash memory, you'll still find a battery on the motherboard to power the real-time clock.

> **ON THE SIDE:** Even though most computers do not have a CMOS chip and the battery doesn't power the CMOS chip, many technicians still refer to the location of the settings as CMOS, and the battery as a CMOS battery.

Accessing the Setup Utility

In addition to providing code to start the computer, the BIOS also includes a setup utility program to view and modify the settings. You can access the BIOS program by pressing certain keys when you first turn the computer on. However, these keys are not the same on all computers. The BIOS briefly displays a message indicating what keys to press to access the setup utility. For example, the BIOS might display a message saying "Press the <F2> key to enter the setup utility." If you press the F2 key in time, the BIOS interrupts the computer startup process and instead starts the setup utility. If you don't press it in time, just restart the computer and try again. Some other keys used to start the setup utility on other computers are F1, F10, and Del (the delete key).

> **ON THE SIDE:**   The important thing to remember if you want to access the setup utility is to read the screen just after turning it on. A message will appear indicating what key or key combination to press, though it is typically displayed for a very short time.

One of the most common reasons technicians need to access the BIOS setup utility is to modify the boot sequence. This tells the computer what devices to check when booting. Computers typically boot from the hard drive, but they can also boot from optical devices such as a CD or DVD, and USB devices. As an example, when installing an operating system from a DVD, you need to ensure the system is configured to look for a bootable operating system from the DVD. You might need to ensure the system looks at the DVD first.

Figure 4-6 shows a sample BIOS setup utility with the Boot menu selected. It is currently set to boot from the hard drive first and a CDROM drive second. If the computer has an operating system on the hard drive, it will never boot from the CDROM (or DVD drive) with this configuration. Instead, you need to change it so that the CDROM drive is in the 1st Boot Device column.

FIGURE 4-6

Using BIOS to configure the boot sequence.

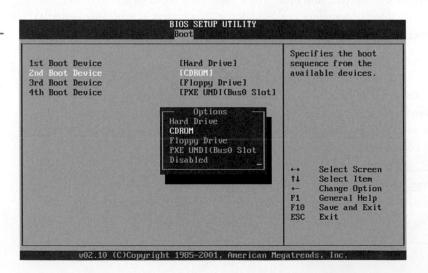

If the system is configured with the hard drive in the last boot device slot, the system will scan all other devices, looking for a bootable operating system. This slows down the boot process. Worse, if it finds a device but the device doesn't have a bootable operating system, the computer typically stops, giving an error such as "Invalid boot disk."

As an example, imagine a computer is configured to boot to a USB device first and a hard drive next. As long as a USB flash drive isn't plugged in, the computer skips the USB drive and boots from the hard drive. If a user plugs a bootable USB flash drive into the system and reboots it, the system will boot to the USB flash drive. However, most flash drives do not include a bootable operating system. If a user leaves a non-bootable flash drive plugged in and reboots the system, it will give an "Invalid boot disk" error. This can be scary for a user because it implies they have a problem with their hard disk. However, the easy solution is to just to remove the USB flash drive and reboot the system. With the flash drive removed, the computer boots normally using the hard disk. A more permanent fix is to modify the boot sequence order in the BIOS.

> **AUTHOR'S NOTE:** The BIOS Setup Utility shown in Figure 4-6 is a screenshot from a virtual PC image. The virtual PC runs as an application within the operating system, making it easy to create a clear image. This BIOS is very basic and your BIOS will probably look very different. For example, it doesn't show USB devices that are included in many current setup utilities. Additionally, most current systems do not have floppy drives, so this setting is missing in many current utilities. The PXE setting allows the device to boot from the network card using a Preboot eXecution Environment (PXE). PXE-compliant computers are able to download software from a network server, and administrators use this to automate the installation of operating systems onto computers.

Understanding PC Operating Systems

An operating system provides the interface between the computer hardware and the applications. Without an operating system, you cannot run the applications. As an example, if you have a computer running Windows 8, you can run applications such as the Google Chrome web browser. However, if your computer does not have an operating system, you cannot run Google Chrome (or any other applications) on the computer.

The primary operating system used on PCs is Windows. Microsoft releases new versions of Windows periodically, and it's important for technicians to be familiar with the version they are expected to support. For example, if an internal help desk provides support to employees and they use Windows 7 and Windows 8, the technicians need to know both of these operating systems. The depth of knowledge needed varies depending on the level of support technicians provide.

ON THE SIDE: Net Applications, a web analytics firm, periodically publishes statistics on in-use desktop operating systems. They reported the following usage statistics for February 2014: Windows 7, 47.31 percent; Windows XP, 29.53 percent; Windows 8, 10.68 percent; OS X, 7.69 percent; Windows Vista, 3.1 percent; Linux, 1.48 percent; and Other, 4.43 percent. You can view up-to-date statistics here: http://www.netmarketshare.com/.

Some help desk specialists do not provide direct support for the operating system, but they still need to understand it. As an example, many ISPs don't provide direct support for the user's computers. However, help desk technicians do assist customers in the process of configuring their computers to access the Internet, and they need to understand various settings in different operating systems.

Additionally, technicians commonly use operating system tools when trouble-shooting and maintaining computers. For example, Windows systems include a Control Panel with several mini-applications or applets. Figure 4-7 shows the Control Panel in a Windows 7 system. It's beyond the scope of this book to cover all these applets, but technicians should be aware of the tools they can use when troubleshooting systems, and the Control Panel includes many useful tools.

FIGURE 4-7

Windows 7 Control Panel.

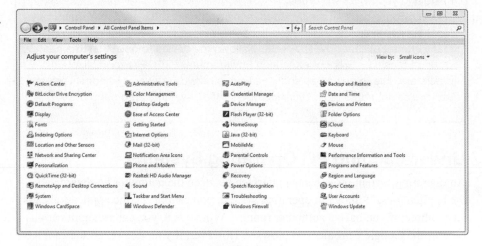

Additional tools are available through the Run Line or Command Prompt. Technicians use these tools in many different scenarios. For example, technicians can start the System Configuration tool with the *msconfig* command and then use it to modify which services and applications run when a system first starts. They can also use the System Configuration tool to force a system to start in Safe Mode instead of booting normally. Similarly, the System Information tool (started with the *msinfo32* command) provides a ready summary of hardware and software installed on a system with the capability to drill down to any component to get more information.

Obviously, this doesn't cover everything about all the current operating systems and all the available tools—that's impossible in this small space. Instead, the goal is to remind you that some help desk technicians provide direct support for operating systems and others don't. However, even when technicians do not support the operating system directly, they often use various operating system tools to help troubleshoot and resolve problems. Successful technicians are educated users themselves. They typically use the product they support, and the more they use it, the more they learn. This in turn helps them quickly resolve many problems for users.

Supporting Software Applications

Many help desk specialists support specific software applications. For example, in one organization, they might be required to support the full suite of Microsoft Office applications in addition to all the other applications employees commonly use. Another organization might have an accounting application that in-house developers created and help desk technicians might need to support it, but they aren't expected to support any other applications.

These two examples provide two extreme points on the application support spectrum, with technicians at one organization supporting all applications, and technicians at another organization supporting only a single application. However, there are many examples between these two extremes. A large number of software developers and organizations have created applications for specific markets or industries. For example, SAP AG has created a line of applications used to manage business operations and customer relations that are very popular in the business world. Help desk personnel at many different organizations provide support for these applications.

The good news is that if an organization requires help desk technicians to support specific applications, they will ensure the technicians are trained to do so. In other words, technicians rarely start a job with all the requisite knowledge for supported applications. Instead, if they have the right technical and personal skills, the organization hires them and then trains them.

Working with Networks

Most computers in use today are connected to a network. Some networks are relatively small and used in homes and small businesses. Others networks used in medium and large businesses can be quite large. However, there are many similarities between these networks, and it's important for technicians to understand some basic networking concepts.

First, networks connect computing devices together so that users can share resources. For example, a simple local area network (LAN) can have two computers and a printer. Users connected to the LAN can access shared files and folders on each of the computers, and print documents through the networked printer. This is significantly easier than using something like USB flash drives to hand-carry files between each computer. It also saves money because only one printer is needed instead of one computer for each user.

> **ON THE SIDE:** The purpose of this section isn't intended to teach you everything you need to know about networks. That amount of knowledge would fill multiple books, and a single section within this chapter just doesn't provide enough space to give you all that information. Instead, this section provides an overview of networks, giving you an idea of some common components.

Introducing Protocols

In the physical world, protocols provide the rules for events, such as when dignitaries meet each other. For example, there are specific guidelines for greeting dignitaries such as the President of the United States (and presidents of other countries), members of congress, members of the U.K. Royal Family, and the Catholic Pope. Similarly, there are specific guidelines when communicating to dignitaries in written communications. While it is possible to ignore these protocols, you'll typically find that it hampers communication. For example, if you greet the Queen of England with "Hey Lady" or the U.S. President with "Yo, Dude," you might find the conversation abruptly ended.

Similarly, protocols provide the rules needed for hosts to communicate with each other on a network. If the protocols aren't followed exactly as specified, it often stops the network communication.

Transmission Control Protocol/Internet Protocol (TCP/IP) is a full suite of protocols used on the Internet and most internal networks. As with other topics in this chapter, it's impossible to cover all the details of the TCP/IP suite in this short section. As an example, RFC 793 (http://www.ietf.org/rfc/rfc793.txt) provides the specifications for Transmission Control Protocol (TCP) and it is 85 pages long.

> **ON THE SIDE:**
> RFC is short for Request For Comments. Protocols are originally released as a draft and based on comments from engineers; they are either updated in a new RFC or ultimately approved as a final RFC.

TCP and User Datagram Protocol (UDP) are two common protocols used for basic connectivity. Almost all data transmissions in a network use one of these.

The Internet Protocol (IP) provides addressing so that data is able to reach its destination. IPv4 has been the primary addressing protocol on the Internet since 1981. It uses 32 bits and addresses are commonly expressed in dotted decimal format such as 192.168.1.5. Each of the decimal numbers represents eight binary bits, and the decimal numbers are separated by dots. Expressed in binary, the IP address of 192.168.1.5 is 1100 0000 . 1010 1000 . 0000 0001 . 0000 0101.

Authorities recognized that the Internet would eventually run out of IPv4 addresses so the Internet Engineering Task Force (IETF) began working on a solution. They eventually developed IPv6. IPv6 uses 128-bit addresses and they are commonly expressed as eight groups of four hexadecimal numbers, separated by colons. Hexadecimal numbers include the numbers 0 through 9 and the letters a through f.

Here's an example of an IPv6 address: fe80:0000:0000:0000:20d4:00f7:003f:0e62. You can simplify this address by eliminating leading zeroes in individual groups like this: fe80:0:0:0:20d4:f7:3f:e62. Since you know that each group has four hexadecimal numbers, you can tell that groups with less than four numbers need leading zeroes. You can simplify the address further by replacing one long group of zeroes with two colons like this: fe80::20d4:f7:3f:e62.

IPv6 addresses will eventually replace IPv4 addresses. Currently, both IPv4 and IPv6 addresses are working side-by-side on the Internet and on many internal networks.

Many protocols allow applications to transfer data over networks. For example, the Hypertext Transfer Protocol (HTTP) is the primary protocol used to transmit web pages over the Internet. HTTP Secure (HTTPS) is the primary protocol used to encrypt sensitive data such as credit card information before sending it over the Internet.

Several protocols support sending and receiving email. Simple Mail Transfer Protocol (SMTP) is the primary protocol used to send email and Post Office Protocol (POP) is the primary protocol used to receive email. Many organizations use Internet Message Access Protocol (IMAP), which allows users to store email messages on a server and organize them in folders.

> **ON THE SIDE:**
> While you can express hexadecimal letters in both upper case and lower case, IETF recommends using lower case only. This avoids complications with applications that examine and analyze IPv6 addresses.

Understanding Common Network Components

Anything connected to a network is commonly called a device, and desktop PCs are the most common type of devices on many networks. However, networks include many types of devices such as servers, printers, laptop computers, smartphones, and tablets. You'll often see a computing device on a network generically referred to as a host, client, or node.

Network devices such as hubs or switches connect these hosts together within a network. Routers connect multiple networks together to create larger and larger networks. The Internet is a massive network, with networks from around the world connected together. Just as in smaller networks, routers connect these Internet networks together.

> **ON THE SIDE:**
> Within this section, computing devices connected to a network are called hosts.

Using Hubs

A **hub** is a very basic network device and it has multiple physical ports used to provide connectivity to network hosts. You can get hubs with as many as 32 physical ports. You connect each host to the hub with a cable such as a twisted pair cable. Twisted pair cables have multiple pairs of wires that carry data signals between the network host and the hub.

As an example, Figure 4-8 shows three computers and a printer connected together using a hub. Computer 1 is connected to port 1 of the hub, Computer 2 is connected to port 2, the printer is connected to hub port 3, and Computer 4 is connected to port 4. This configuration allows computer users to share files with each other and they can all send print jobs to the printer.

FIGURE 4-8

Network using a hub to connect hosts.

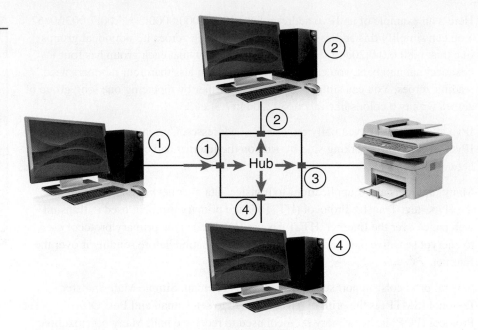

A distinguishing characteristic of a hub is that all data sent into one port goes out all other ports. For example, when Computer 1 sends a print job to the printer on port 3, the data also goes to Computers 2 and 4. The other two computers look at the traffic and recognize it is not addressed to them, so they don't process it. However, this extra traffic does add to the workload of the network and these computers.

Another way of saying this is that a hub has no intelligence. It cannot analyze traffic but instead just forwards all the traffic it receives on one port to all the other ports. In contrast, switches can analyze the traffic.

Using Switches to Connect Computers

A **switch** connects hosts together on the network similar to a hub. However, a switch provides better performance for the network and an added layer of security when compared to a hub, and most of today's networks use switches instead of hubs. A switch has the capability of learning what devices are connected to each physical port and it stores this information in the switch's memory. It uses this information to send data transmissions to only to the intended host device. Just as you can get hubs with a different number of ports, you can also get switches with more ports. Switches with 32 to 64 ports are common in larger networks.

As an example, consider Figure 4-9, which shows a network connected with a switch. In this figure, Computer 1 is sending a print job to the printer connected to port 3. This is similar to Figure 4-8 showing a hub, but a significant difference is that the switch sends the print job to only port 3 for the printer. Computers 2 and 4 never receive this traffic, so the print job doesn't add to their workload or the traffic on their connections.

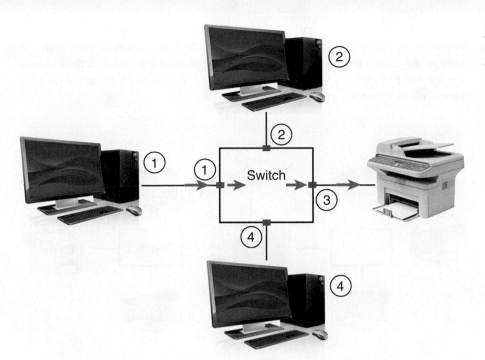

FIGURE 4-9

Network using a switch to connect hosts.

The switch also provides a security benefit by preventing the traffic from going to the other ports. A **protocol analyzer** (also called a sniffer) is software that allows a system to capture traffic. Attackers use sniffers to capture and analyze traffic that they might not otherwise be able to see. Imagine the systems are connected with a hub as shown in Figure 4-8. A malicious user on Computer 2 could use a sniffer to capture the print job sent by Computer 1, along with any other data sent over the network. With a little analysis, this user could read all the data sent over the network to any other system. In contrast, a switch is selective. When Computer 1 sends the print job to the printer, the print job never reaches Computer 2. A malicious user running a sniffer on Computer 2 never has the opportunity to capture it.

> **ON THE SIDE:**   Switches have many more capabilities beyond what's described here. Some are unmanaged switches and simply work when you plug them in. Others are managed switches, providing administrators with the ability to program them with additional features.

Using Routers to Connect Networks

After connecting hosts together into networks, you can then connect these networks together using a **router**. Routers analyze traffic and use routing protocols to identify the best path for data to get to a destination.

Figure 4-10 shows a router configured to connect two networks to the Internet. Switch 1 connects some hosts on one network and Switch 2 connects additional hosts on the second network. If Computer 1 needs to send a print job to the printer, it sends it to Switch 1. Switch 1 sends it to Router 1 and Router 1 sends the print job to Switch, which then sends it to the printer.

FIGURE 4-10

A router connecting networks.

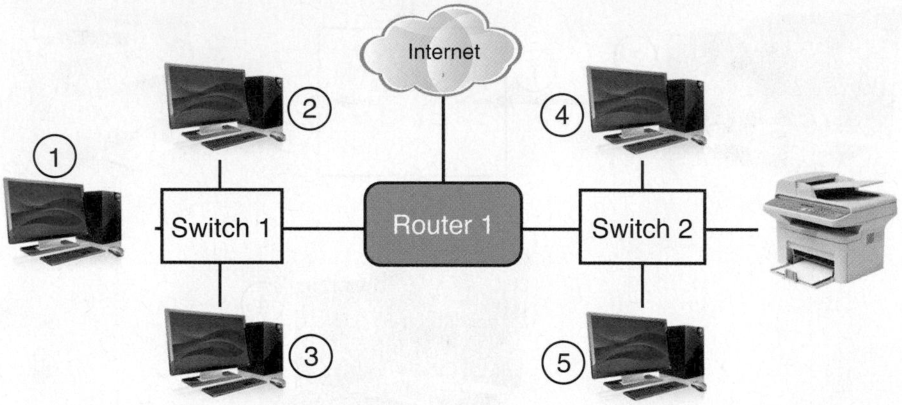

Router 1 provides access to the Internet for all the systems on the two internal networks. For example, if Computer 4 needs to access a web page on the Internet, it sends the request to Switch 2. Switch 2 sends the request to Router 1 and Router 1 routes the request to the Internet. When the Internet web server receives the request, it responds with the web page, which is routed back to Router 1, through Switch 2, and back to Computer 4.

Figure 4-10 shows a relatively small network. However, business networks commonly have many more hosts connected to each switch, and many more routers connecting all of the networks together. For comparison, Figure 4-11 shows a larger network with three routers connecting seven different networks, through seven switches. While individual hosts aren't shown, each switch has multiple hosts connected to them. These hosts include desktop PCs, printers, and servers. Additionally, any of the hosts on this network can access the Internet through Router 1. For example, a computer connected to Switch 7 can access the Internet through Router 3, Router 2, and then Router 1.

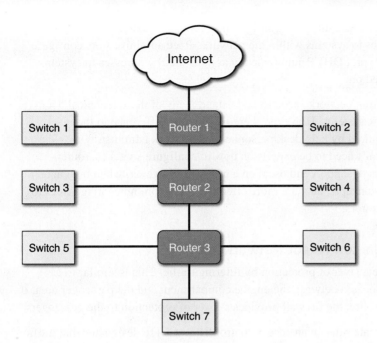

FIGURE 4-11

Multiple routers connecting networks

Underlying this process is a significant amount of technical details. For example, each host on the network has a 48-bit Media Access Control (MAC) address. Additionally, each host has an IPv4 and/or an IPv6 address.

MAC addresses are semi-permanently assigned to network interface cards (NICs) without any additional action required by administrators. While administrators can change the MAC addresses, that is rarely required.

> **ON THE SIDE:** A relatively new type of disk drive, called a solid state disk (SSD), has begun to compete with hard disk drives. These drives use flash memory instead of platters and actuator arms. But they connect over the same buses, and play the same role, as traditional internal hard disk drives (HDD).
>
> The advantages and disadvantages of SSDs, at least around publication time for this book? SSD drives read data much faster than HDDs. I did a brief informal experiment with two Macs, running the same version of the OS, one with an HDD and one with an SSD. The Mac with the SSD actually had a slower processor. (Note that one of the most time-consuming tasks that occur when you turn on a computer is the reading of OS files to load into RAM.) In this informal test, the Mac with the SSD booted in 15 seconds; the one with the HDD, 135 seconds.

ON THE SIDE:
Most NICs have MAC addresses permanently assigned to them from the manufacturer. However, it's relatively easy to modify this address using software within an operating system. The NIC still retains the permanent MAC address, but if operating system settings override it, the original MAC address is ignored.

Most networks use Dynamic Host Configuration Protocol (DHCP) to automatically assign IP addresses to systems within the network. Once administrators configure DHCP on the network, DHCP automatically assigns the IP addresses to systems after they're turned on.

Personnel supporting networks need to understand many of these technical details to support network systems. However, there is a distinct difference in the level of knowledge required by help desk personnel and network administrators. Help desk personnel don't need to be experts on how to configure switches, routers, and DHCP servers to support end users on a network. However, when they understand the overall concepts, they are more effective when communicating issues to network administrators.

Using Firewalls to Protect Networks

Firewalls provide a layer of protection by filtering traffic. This is similar to a firewall in a car, located between the engine compartment and the passenger area. If the engine catches fire, the firewall provides a layer of protection to the passengers.

Administrators create rules in an access control list (ACL) to designate what traffic is allowed or blocked, and the firewall enforces these rules. Most firewalls use an implicit deny policy. An implicit deny policy includes explicit rules to define allowed traffic. The firewall then blocks all other traffic, even though the ACL doesn't include explicit rules for all blocked traffic.

Network firewalls protect a network and host-based firewalls protect individual systems. As an example, consider Figure 4-12. The network firewall is located between the Internet and Router 1. Firewall rules filter traffic in and out of the network, and help protect the network from Internet attacks. Without a firewall, attackers on the Internet from anywhere in the world might be able to access all the computers within the internal network.

FIGURE 4-12

Multiple routers connecting networks.

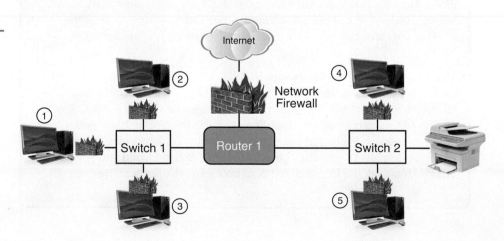

Figure 4-12 also shows host-based firewalls on each computer. A host-based firewall is software running on a system designed to provide an additional layer of protection. If an attack gets past the network firewall, or bypasses it through an internal source, these host-based firewalls help protect the internal systems.

Firewalls have significantly improved over the years. Three iterations of firewalls are:

- **First generation.** Packet filtering firewalls were the first generation. Data sent through a network is formatted in packets, which include information such as the source and destination IP addresses, and the protocol used in the packet. Packets also include logical port numbers used to identify specific protocols. A packet filtering firewall allows or blocks traffic based on the IP addresses and/or port numbers.

- **Second generation.** Systems commonly communicate together by transmitting multiple packets back and forth in a conversation. Second generation firewalls are able to examine all the packets within the conversation instead of just relying on data in each individual packet. These are called stateful firewalls because they can examine the packets within the state of an ongoing conversation or session. The firewall then chooses to allow or block the traffic based on the context of the session.

- **Third generation.** Application layer firewalls are the third generation. These firewalls understand specific commands in various application protocols and can block malicious commands. As an example, web servers use the Hypertext Transfer Protocol (HTTP) to serve web pages. The GET command requests web pages but HTTP supports many more commands. For example, the DELETE command will delete data. A third generation firewall can block malicious commands such as the DELETE command, but allow the GET command.

> **ON THE SIDE:**
> Defense-in-depth is a security strategy using multiple layers of defense. Using both network-based firewalls and host-based firewalls is an example of defense-in-depth.

Firewalls continue to advance, and many technicians have adopted terms such as fourth generation and next generation firewalls, though these terms aren't universally embraced. Other systems such as an intrusion detection system (IDS), an intrusion prevention system (IPS), and a unified threat management (UTM) device provide advanced capabilities that can enhance or supplement traditional firewalls.

Using Wireless Devices in Networks

Wireless networks have become quite common. A significant benefit is that it is relatively easy to set up a network connecting multiple devices together without the cost of running cables to all the hosts. While early iterations of wireless networks had significant security issues, current wireless protocols provide much more security. For example, Wired Equivalent Privacy (WEP) was the primary security mechanism recommended with early wireless networks. However, WEP is flawed and should not be used. Wi-Fi Protected Access II (WPA2) is the permanent replacement for WEP and provides a high level of security for networks.

Many small wireless networks, such as those in homes and small businesses, use wireless routers. In addition to eliminating the need for cables, wireless routers include several additional components that make them easy to use. Some of the additional components are:

- **Wireless transceiver.** The wireless transceiver transmits and receives wireless signals to and from wireless devices. It can provide connectivity to wireless devices such as tablets, smartphones, wireless laptops, wireless printers, and any other device that has compatible wireless capabilities.

- **Switch.** The switch component of the wireless router connects devices together in the network, similar to how a regular switch connects devices together in a network. A difference is that it connects both wired and wireless devices via the switch.

- **Router.** This works similar to how any router works, as described previously in this chapter. A difference is that wireless routers used in small networks typically only connect one internal network to the Internet, while routers in larger networks connect multiple networks together.

- **Protocols and services such as DHCP.** Wireless routers include several services to support protocols such as DHCP. DHCP provides automatic IP addressing to internal systems. When included on a wireless router, it allows systems to work without manually configuring IP addresses.

- **Firewall.** Most wireless routers include basic firewall capabilities, providing a layer of protection for the internal network.

Figure 4-13 shows an outline of a wireless router along with a diagram of a network that includes both wired and wireless hosts. The two computers are wired and would be connected to the wireless routers via cables to the connections for wired hosts. The tablet, smartphone, and wireless printer connect to the wireless router wirelessly. However, all of these devices are logically connected within the network via the switching component of the wireless router. The wireless router provides a path to the Internet for all internal clients and it also includes a firewall, which provides a layer of protection for this connection.

Larger organizations often use **wireless access points (WAPs)** instead of wireless routers. A WAP provides network connectivity for wireless devices but it does not include a routing component. Wireless devices connect to the network via the WAP and the WAP connects to the network via a wired switch.

ON THE SIDE: Wireless routers always include a WAP, which provides the wireless transceiver component. However, WAPs do not have routing capabilities.

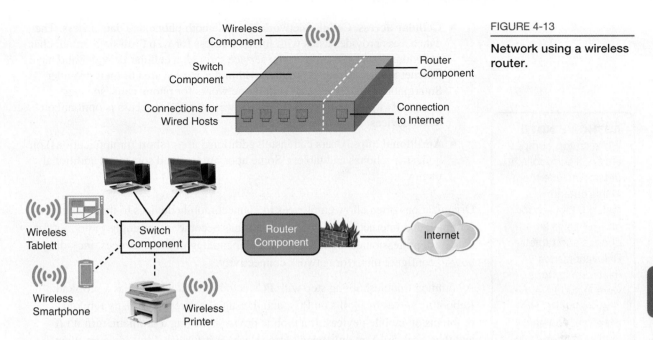

FIGURE 4-13

Network using a wireless router.

4

Working with Mobile Devices

More and more employees are using mobile devices such as smartphones and tablets. Smartphones combine several features in a cellular phone such as a camera, web browser, email application, personal data assistant (PDA), and much more. Tablets include many of these abilities but without a cellular phone.

Some common features of smartphones and tablets are:

- **Handheld and battery operated.** Batteries are lightweight and when charged, allow people to use the device without a direct power connection.

- **Solid state drives (SSDs).** These are lightweight and do not have any moving parts. In addition to consuming very little power, they are less susceptible to damage if a user drops the device.

- **Touch screens.** Users interact with the device with touch gestures instead of a mouse and keyboard, though some of the touch gestures mimic mouse actions. For example, a finger tap works like a mouse click and a double finger tap works like a double tap. Many devices support the use of a stylus (which works like a pen), though a stylus isn't required for most current mobile devices.

- **Wireless capability.** Most devices can connect to wireless networks through a WAP or wireless router. This typically provides them with Internet access.

- **Cellular access.** Cellular networks provide both phone and data access. The data access provides users with Internet access for web browsing, email, chat, and more. Users subscribe to the service through a cellular provider and have Internet access as long as they are within the service area of their provider. Smartphones use these same cellular networks for phone calls, so smartphones always have this capability. However, cellular access is optional on tablet devices.
- **Additional apps.** Users can install additional apps (short for applications) on both smartphones and tablets. Some apps are free and some cost additional money.

AUTHOR'S NOTE:
While laptop computers are also mobile, I did not include them in this category. Instead, this section only refers to smartphones and tablets. Relevant issues related to laptops were included in the "Reviewing PC Hardware" section earlier in this chapter.

Organizations often allow employees to connect mobile devices to their network for email and Internet access. As a result, it has become increasingly important for help desk professionals to have a basic understanding of these devices, including how to configure them for network connectivity.

A common troubleshooting step with PCs is to reboot it when it has a problem. Rebooting solves many ills on PCs, and the same step resolves many random problems on mobile devices. If a mobile device is having a problem, turn it off and then back on. You only need to troubleshoot it further if the same problem reappears.

Comparing Operating Systems

Smartphones have an operating system, which runs the device. This is similar to an operating system used on desktop PCs in that it provides an interface between the device's hardware and the apps you run on the device. Without an operating system, the devices are nothing more than expensive paperweights.

The three popular mobile device operating systems are Apple's iOS, Google's Android, and Microsoft's Windows Phone. The Apple iOS is proprietary, owned by Apple. You will only see it on Apple devices such as iPhones and iPads. Microsoft owns Microsoft's Windows Phone operating system, but they do license its use for non-Microsoft phones. Android is based on the Linux operating system and Google released it as open source. In other words, anyone can modify and distribute the Android operating system. Google has released many smartphones and tablets using the Android operating system. Additionally, many other manufacturers have adapted the Android operating system to their devices and sold it under their brand. For example, Samsung sells several different mobile devices under their Samsung Galaxy brand.

Android-based devices are the most popular, according to a survey released by Kantar Worldpanel ComTech in early 2014. It shows that overall people are buying more Android devices than devices running Apple or Microsoft operating systems, but the figures vary in different countries. For example, Android had a slim lead in the U.S. with 50.6 percent versus 43.9 percent for iOS devices, and 4.3 percent for Windows Phone. In Europe, Android was on top with 68.6 percent market share, compared to 18.5 percent for iOS and 10.3 percent for Windows Phone. Other mobile devices such as BlackBerry barely compare.

This is relevant because it gives insight into the devices technicians are likely to support. In the early 2000's, the primary smartphone technicians supported were Blackberrys. Today, technicians primarily support iOS and Android devices.

Comparing App Stores

With PCs, you can purchase applications almost anywhere and install them on your computer. However, mobile device apps are not available anywhere. Instead, you need to purchase them from online sources. The three primary online sources are:

- **Apple's App Store.** This is easily accessible via the App Store app included with the mobile device. Apple controls this store and all products sold in the store. Additionally, this is the only location where you can purchase apps for Apple devices.
- **Google Play.** The primary location where you can purchase Android apps is through the Google Play store, controlled by Google. The Google Play store is accessible through an app on Android devices, and through the web browser. Unlike iOS-based apps, you can purchase some Android apps through other sources. For example, you can purchase Android apps in Amazon's Apps for Android store. Many of Amazon's Kindle versions use the Android operating system.
- **Windows Phone Store and Windows Store.** Microsoft sells Windows smartphone apps through the Windows Phone Store, and Windows tablet apps through the Windows Store. Similar to the Apple devices, you can purchase Microsoft-based apps only through Microsoft controlled stores.

One of the great benefits of these app stores is that it makes it more difficult for attackers to infect the apps. As an example, an app developer must register with Apple before uploading an app. Apple performs checks on the app before making it available for sale. Even if Apple doesn't catch an infected app before it goes on sale, they can easily remove it once they discover a problem. Additionally, Apple flags the developer and blocks them from posting any more apps. All of this discourages attackers from trying to post infected apps and reduces the incidence of malicious software (malware).

Configuring Email

One of the primary benefits many users enjoy with mobile devices is the ability to access their email. Some email accounts are very simple to configure, but some others require a little more work.

Google's Gmail is an example of an email account that is relatively easy to configure. You can configure a Gmail account on most mobile devices by just entering the email address and password. Software within the device handles many of the underlying details without requiring users to enter anything else.

Of course, employees of an organization typically want to access their work email with their device. This requires a little more information, such as the username and password of an authorized user, the user's email address, and the name of the email server. Many organizations use Microsoft Exchange for email services so the name of the server is the name of the Microsoft Exchange server.

Users often want to access their home email through these devices too. This often requires you to configure email protocol settings. The "Introducing Protocols" section earlier in this chapter mentioned SMTP, POP3, and IMAP. Devices send email with SMTP and receive email with POP3. Some ISPs also support IMAP, which allows users to access and manage email stored on an email server. The specific configuration steps depend on the ISP. For example, you typically need to enter the name of the SMTP server and the name of the POP3 server. Additionally, you might need to enter the logical port numbers for the protocols. Table 4-1 lists common port numbers needed to configure emails.

TABLE 4-1
Default Ports for Email

Protocol	Default Port
SMTP	25
POP3	110
IMAP	143
Secure SMTP (SMTPS)	465
Secure POP3 (POP3S)	995
Secure IMAP (IMAPS)	993

Also, some ISPs require you to configure SMTP and POP3 separately, entering the username and password twice. A common problem that occurs here is a typo in one of the entries. If the user can send email but not receive it, verify the POP3 settings. If the user can receive email but not send it, verify the SMTP settings.

Implementing Security on Mobile Devices

Most mobile devices support several common security mechanisms that technicians should understand. The following list summarizes some of them:

- **Passcode or screen locks.** These lock the screen, preventing use of the device after the device is idle for a period of time, such as after ten minutes. When the device is locked, the user must enter the passcode to unlock it. The passcode is often just a set of digits, but some devices support finger gestures to unlock the device. A screen lock makes it more difficult for a thief to access data on the device.

- **Login attempt restriction.** If the device has valuable data, you can enable this feature as an extra precaution in addition to a screen lock. If a thief enters the incorrect pass code too many times, the device will erase all data on the device. This prevents a thief from guessing all the possible digit combinations.

- **Remote wipe.** When this feature is enabled, it allows a user to send a signal to a lost or stolen device that erases all data on the system, effectively wiping it clean.

- **GPS locator.** Most mobile devices include access to a Global Positioning System (GPS), which shows the location of the device. GPS is useful for many apps, but it can also help you locate a lost or stolen device. When the GPS locator feature is enabled, it allows you to identify the location of a lost or stolen device, and even send messages to the device.

Comparing Landscape Modes to Portrait Modes

One of the common complaints with these devices is related to landscape and portrait display modes. Most people are familiar with landscape and portrait modes from printing. If you want a normal printed page, you use portrait mode. When you hold the page to read it, it is taller than it is wide. In contrast, landscape mode prints the page so that it is wider than it is tall.

Similarly, most mobile devices allow you to view the display in portrait or landscape mode. A difference is that mobile devices can detect how you're holding the device, and they will automatically adjust the orientation of the display. When this doesn't work, users often ask for help.

Accelerometers and gyroscopes within mobile devices detect the movement and orientation of the device, and they are constantly sending data to the device. However, not all apps use this data. If users complain that devices are not changing orientation when they move the device, one of the first steps is to verify that the app supports this feature. You can exit the app and see if the device changes modes from within its operating system. If it automatically changes in the operating system but not the app, it indicates that either the app doesn't support the feature or the feature is disabled in the app.

Another check is to see if the feature is disabled in the operating system. This setting varies between devices and sometimes varies in different versions of similar devices. Figure 4-14 shows the setting on an iPad Air running iOS 7. The Control Center is accessible from just about any screen by swiping up from the bottom—it causes the screen to dim. The arrow in the figure points to the orientation lock; you select it to toggle the lock on or off.

> **ON THE SIDE:** The display shows the iPad General Settings with the Control Center settings selected. The device is currently configured to allow users to access the Control Center from both the Lock Screen and within Apps.

FIGURE 4-14

Modifying the orientation lock on an iPad.

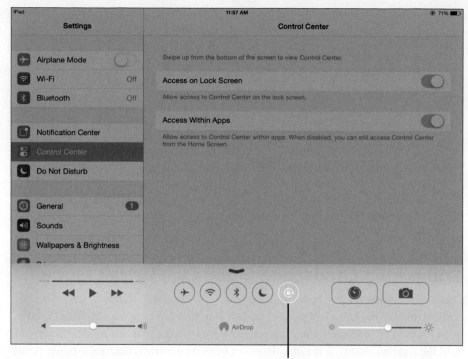

iPad Orientation Lock

Understanding the Product

The majority of this chapter introduced concepts related to personal computers, networks, and mobile devices. Help desk professionals might support all of these or have a very narrow focus and support only a single application for end users. You often don't know all the products you'll support until you start the job.

Most organizations don't expect new help desk specialists to be experts on these products when they start. Instead, many organizations provide help desk professionals with product specific training after hiring them. Additionally, once they get on the job, successful technicians learn as much about the products they support as they can.

A help desk professional is expected to have some level of technical knowledge and expertise before they're hired. However, it is sometimes difficult for prospective employees to convince prospective employers that they have the relevant knowledge. Technical certifications help many people get past this hurdle.

Getting Certified

Professional certifications validate a level of knowledge or expertise in a specific topic or field. These certifications provide several benefits, both for individuals and organizations.

If you've flown anywhere using a known airline, you can bet the pilots were certi-fied. They held a valid pilot license at the time, were certified to fly that aircraft, and passed a relatively recent medical exam. This is very comforting to know as a customer, especially when the plane runs into some turbulence. Since external organizations certify the pilots, airlines don't need to manage the specifics related to the certification requirements. Instead, they just ensure their pilots hold valid certifications.

Similarly, many organizations appreciate the value of IT certifications because they validate the knowledge and skills of employees, or potential employees. Organiza-tions don't need to manage the specifics related to the certification requirements such as updating the certifications as technology changes. However, when individ-uals hold certain certifications, organizations have a level of confidence related to their technical expertise.

Job seekers often find that certifications provide them with more opportunities. Many times a job requires employees to have a specific certification and those without the certification on their resume don't get a second look. As an example, the Department of Defense (DoD) directive 8570.1 requires anyone with admin-istrative privileges on a DoD system to have a certification such as the CompTIA Security+ certification. Hiring managers, unless they get desperate, simply look past job applicants without the certification.

Reviewing Common Certifications

Some of the common certifications that apply to help desk specialists include:

- **CompTIA A+.** Many people consider the A+ certification as the starting point of an IT career. It validates an understanding of basic computer and operating system concepts for IT professionals with at least 12 months of hands-on lab or field experience. This includes PCs, laptops, and other mobile devices such as smartphones. Close to one million people have earned the A+ certification.

- **CompTIA Network+.** The Network+ certification builds on A+ knowledge and focuses on networking concepts. It validates an individual's under-standing of networking features and functions, including virtual networking, and networking security. It covers hardware such as cables, routers, and switches. It also covers many of the protocols used on networks including the TCP/IP suite of protocols. More than 350,000 people worldwide have become Network+ certified.

- **CompTIA Security+.** The Security+ certification builds on the Network+ certification and focuses on IT security concepts. It validates an individual's knowledge of security concepts, tools, and procedures to guard against security risks and how to react to security breaches. It includes concepts related to risk and risk mitigation using various security controls. Some jobs related to Security+ include Network Security Administrator and Systems Security Administrator. More than 300,000 people worldwide have become Security+ certified.

ON THE SIDE: The combination of the CompTIA A+, Net-work+, and Secu-rity+ certifications provide individuals with a solid founda-tion of relevant IT knowledge. Many IT professionals started with these three cer-tifications and moved on to more advanced certifications as they progressed in their IT careers.

- **Microsoft operating system certifications.** The majority of desktop computers used in organizations run a Windows operating system. The flavor of Windows changes over time and in different organizations. However, Microsoft typically has one or more certifications targeted at specific operating systems. At this writing, Microsoft has certifications for Windows 7 and Windows 8 operating systems, along with certifications for more advanced topics, such as Windows server operating systems.

- **HDI certifications.** HDI sponsors several certifications for personnel working in or managing help desk and service desk centers. HDI changed its name in 2004 from Help Desk Institute to simply HDI.

It's important to remember that none of these certifications will guarantee a job. However, they will often increase your chances of landing a job interview. With certain certifications on your resume, you can attract the attention of hiring managers. Once you get to the interview, it's up to you to demonstrate that you have the knowledge related to the underlying certification, and that your personality is a good fit for the company and the job.

Comparing Certifications to Degrees

Many job seekers ask "What's better—a degree or a certification?" Individuals with both find the most success, so the simple answer is "both." Of course, that doesn't really answer the question.

In general, a degree makes it easier to find employment even when the economy is depressed. When jobs are scarce, hiring managers value degrees much more than they value certifications. In contrast, when the economy is booming and jobs are plentiful, certifications alone will often get you a good job. In some cases during a booming economy, you can get a good IT job without a degree or a certification. However, the job may not last if the company starts to have money problems during an economic downturn.

Also, those with a degree typically earn more money for the same work as someone without a degree, and someone with a degree has more career advancement opportunities. Organizations are more likely to promote degreed individuals into managerial and executive positions. Without a degree, career opportunities are limited. In short, a degree provides significant long-term benefits.

> **AUTHOR'S NOTE:**   While working in some technical jobs, I frequently saw examples where degreed personnel were making $10 to $15 thousand more annually than non-degreed personnel performing the same job. This isn't always the case, but it is true often enough to stress the value of finishing a degree.

It's worth mentioning that some positions require specific certifications. For example, many DoD contractor jobs require contractors to have at least a Security+ certification. It doesn't matter what level of knowledge job applicants have or how many degrees they possess. Without the Security+ certification, they won't be granted any privileges needed for the job, so they will not be hired.

Continuous Learning

Almost all professional fields require individuals to continue their learning. If you think about it, it makes a lot sense. For example, you probably wouldn't want to go to a doctor who earned a medical degree 20 years ago but never learned anything new since. The medical field is constantly changing as medical professionals learn more and more information about the human body. Similarly, technology is constantly changing. A technology expert 20 years ago would be lost in today's technology without learning new material.

Many professions require individuals to earn **continuing education (CE)** credits. These ensure that individuals continue their learning even after becoming certified. For example, pharmacists are required to earn at least 30 CE credits a year in many states. They can only earn these credits through approved sources.

Similarly, many technical certifications require individuals to earn CE credits to maintain their certifications. As an example, individuals with a CompTIA A+ certification must earn at least 20 continuing education units (CEUs) within three years after earning the certification. The CompTIA Network+ certification requires 30 CEUs, and the Security+ requires 50 CEUs. If you meet the requirements for higher-level certifications, it covers the lower-level certifications. For example, if someone has A+, Network+, and Security+ certifications and completes the 50 CEUs for Security+, it covers the requirements for A+ and Network+.

ON THE SIDE: The CompTIA CE program also gives credit for passing higher-level certifications. For example, if someone has an A+ and then earns a Network+, they have met the A+ CEU requirement. For more information on the CompTIA CE program, check out this page: http://certification.comptia.org/stayCertified.aspx.

Many IT professionals get into IT careers starting with something like an A+ certification but build on that knowledge with progressively more challenging and technical certifications. Also, many professionals continue their learning but forgo certifications when they aren't needed. However, they still continue to learn. As an example, administrators working in an IT department might become experts in managing and maintaining Microsoft Exchange servers used for email. Their company might not care about certifications, but they do want to ensure that these administrators are trained on new versions of Exchange. Companies frequently send technicians and administrators to training at outside training companies.

Chapter Review Activities

Use the features in this section to study and review the topics in this chapter.

Answer These Questions

1. What should a technician use to prevent ESD damage when replacing RAM on a laptop?

   a. ATX

   b. Wrist strap

   c. Ensure the battery is in place

   d. Ensure all power is removed

2. Where will you find expansion card slots on a PC?

   a. In the power supply

   b. In the SATA

   c. Within the PCIe connections

   d. On the motherboard

3. What type of memory is installed in laptops?

   a. DIMM

   b. SO DIMM

   c. PATA

   d. SATA

4. Of the following choices, what BEST identifies the fastest disk drive interface?

   a. SSD

   b. PATA

   c. SATA

   d. DIMM

5. What provides the basic instructions for a computer to start?

   a. BIOS

   b. Operating system

   c. Hard disk

   d. POST

6. What is the standard used for power supplies?

   a. SATA

   b. PATA

   c. ATX

   d. PCIe

7. What provides the primary interface between the computer's hardware and the software applications?

   a. BIOS

   b. Hard drives

   c. Memory

   d. Operating system

8. What is the primary protocol suite used on the Internet and in internal networks?

   a. TCP

   b. IP

   c. TCP/IP

   d. IETF

9. Which of the following devices connects devices together in a network?

   a. Switch

   b. Router

   c. Firewall

   d. IPS

10. Which of the following statements is TRUE?

    a. Hubs are used instead of switches due to increased network performance and better security.

    b. Switches are used instead of hubs due to increased network performance and better security.

    c. Hubs are used instead of routers due to increased network performance and better security.

    d. Routers are used instead of hubs due to increased network performance and better security.

11. Which of the following devices connects networks together?

    a. Switch

    b. Router

    c. Firewall

    d. IDS

12. What is the primary purpose of a firewall?

    a. Block traffic going into a network

    b. Block traffic going out of a network

    c. Control traffic going in and out of a network

    d. Filter traffic based on IP addresses and/or port numbers

13. Which of the following statements is TRUE?

    a. A WAP always includes a routing component

    b. A wireless router always includes a WAP component

    c. WAPs and wireless routers do not have any similarities

    d. WAPS typically include multiple services while wireless routers do not include additional services.

14. What operating system will you find on an Apple smartphone?

    a. Android

    b. iOS

    c. Linux

    d. Windows

15. Which of the following is one of the primary benefits to users of app stores such as Google Play and the Apple App Store?

    a. Allows them to buy any apps

    b. Requires the users to register

    c. Only high-quality apps are available

    d. Reduces the risk of malware

16. What security feature allows you to erase all data on a lost or stolen device?

    a. Screen lock

    b. Remote wipe

    c. GPS locator

    d. Accelerometer

17. When configuring email settings for a mobile device, what port should you use for sending email?

    a. 25

    b. 110

    c. 143

    d. 995

18. What mobile device hardware allows it to switch automatically between landscape and portrait display modes? (Select TWO.)

   a. Accelerometer

   b. GPS

   c. Gyroscope

   d. Android

19. Which of the following certifications validates a person's knowledge of basic computer concepts?

   a. A+

   b. Network+

   c. Security+

   d. HDI

20. Which of the following BEST describes the purpose of IT-related continuing education?

   a. It ensures that technicians continue to learn new material.

   b. It ensures that technicians keep up-to-date with current technology.

   c. It provides certification vendors with an additional stream of revenue.

   d. It ensures that the technical field isn't flooded with technicians.

Answers and Explanations

1. b. An electrostatic discharge (ESD) wrist strap helps prevent ESD damage from static buildup. ATX is a motherboard form factor. All power should be removed prior to replacing sensitive components such as random access memory (RAM). This includes removing the battery.

2. d. PC expansion card slots are located on the motherboard. They aren't in the power supply. SATA is an interface for hard drives, and PCIe is a standard for expansion cards.

3. b. Laptops use small outline dual inline memory modules (SO DIMMS). DIMMS are installed in desktop computers. PATA and SATA are disk drive interfaces.

4. c. Serial ATA (SATA) is the fastest disk drive interface of the given choices. PATA is an older interface and slower. Solid state drives (SSDs) are faster than traditional hard disk drives, but SSD refers to the type of drive, not the interface.

5. a. The Basic Input/Output System (BIOS) is firmware on a computer and it includes the basic instructions for a computer to start. It performs a power on self test (POST) and if POST passes, it retrieves the operating system from the hard disk.

6. c. The ATX standard provides specifications for both motherboards and power supplies. SATA and PATA are hard drive standards. PCIe is an expansion slot standard.

7. d. The operating system provides the primary interface between the computer's hardware and the applications. The BIOS provides the initial code to start the computer, which then locates the operating system on the hard drive, and loads it into memory. Once the operating system is loaded into memory, users can start applications.

8. **c.** TCP/IP is the primary protocol suite used on the Internet and in internal networks. TCP is one protocol in the suite and IP is another, but TCP/IP includes many more protocols. The IETF oversees development of protocols.

9. **a.** Switches connect devices together in a network and routers connect networks together. Firewalls control traffic going in and out of a network. An intrusion prevention system (IPS) helps prevent attacks from reaching a network.

10. **b.** Switches are used instead of hubs due to increased network performance and better security. Hubs provide less features and security. Hubs and routers and not interchangeable.

11. **b.** Routers connect networks together and switches connect devices together in a network. Firewalls control traffic going in and out of a network. An intrusion detection system (IDS) detects network attacks.

12. **c.** The primary purpose of a firewall is to control traffic going in and out of a network. Firewalls don't look exclusively at either incoming or outgoing traffic. First-generation firewalls filter traffic based on IP addresses and port numbers, but more advanced firewalls are also available.

13. **b.** A wireless router always includes a wireless access point (WAP) component to provide connectivity for wireless hosts. WAPs do not include a routing component. Wireless routers typically include multiple services, but these aren't common on WAPs.

14. **b.** Apple smartphones and other mobile devices run the iOS operating system. Android is a Linux-based operating system running on Google Android devices and other devices that use this open source software. Windows smartphones run a Windows operating system.

15. **d.** Vendors such as Apple and Google control what apps are available for sale at these app stores, which makes it harder for attackers to upload malicious software (malware). The vendors can restrict what apps are for sale, so users aren't necessarily able to buy any apps. Many users do not consider registration to be a benefit. While many high-quality apps are available, you can also buy some junk.

16. **b.** Remote wipe is a security feature that allows the owner to send a signal to a device and erase all its data. Screen lock locks the device but doesn't erase data unless it is configured with the login attempt restriction. A GPS locator helps you find a lost or stolen device. An accelerometer isn't a security feature.

17. **a.** Mobile devices use SMTP for sending email and SMTP uses port 25. POP3 uses port 110 when receiving email. IMAP uses port 143 and secure POP3 uses port 995.

18. **a, c.** Accelerometers and gyroscopes detect movement of a device and allow it to automatically switch modes depending on how the user is holding the device. GPS provides location services. Android is an operating system.

19. **a.** The A+ certification validates a person's understanding of basic computer and operating system concepts. Network+ validates an individual's understanding of networking features and functions. Security+ validates an individual's knowledge of security concepts. HDI certifications focus on skills needed by service desk personnel.

20. **b.** Continuing education ensures that technicians keep up-to-date with current technology. Just learning new material isn't enough; it needs to be related to current technology. Many people accuse certification vendors of using continuing education as an additional stream of revenue, but that isn't the purpose any more than the medical certification authorities only do it for money.

Define the Key Terms

The following key terms include the ideas most important to the big ideas in this chapter. To review, without looking at the book or your notes, write a definition for each term, focusing on the meaning, not the wording. Then review your definition compared to your notes, this chapter, and the glossary.

Key Terms for Chapter 4

central processing units (CPUs)	hub	Transmission Control Protocol/Internet Protocol (TCP/IP)
continuing education (CE)	protocol analyzer	
electrostatic discharge (ESD)	random access memory (RAM)	wireless access point (WAP)
firewall	router	wireless router
firmware	switch	

List the Words Inside Acronyms

The following are the most common acronyms discussed in this chapter. As a way to review those terms, simply write down the words that each letter represents in each acronym.

Acronyms for Chapter 4

AC	GPS	PATA
ACL	GPUs	PC
AMD	HDMI	PCIe
ATX	HTTP	PDA
BD	HTTPS	POP
BIOS	IDS	POP3S
CCFL	IETF	POST
CD	IMAP	PXE
CE	IMAPS	RAM
CEUs	IP	SATA
CMOS	IPS	SMTP
CPUs	IPv4	SMTPS
DC	IPv6	SO DIMM
DHCP	ISP	SSDs
DIMM	LAN	TCP
DoD	LCD	TCP/IP
DVD	LED	UDP
DVI	MAC	USB
ESD	NICs	UTM

W	WEP	WORM
WAP	WPA2	

Create Mind Maps

For this chapter, create mind maps as follows:

1. Create a mind map listing the different components commonly found on a motherboard. Start with a rectangle labeled motherboard. Next, draw outlines of the common components found on a motherboard and label them.

2. Create a mind map listing the different types of networking devices and their usage. Start with a circle labeled network. Draw lines out from this with the names of known networking devices and their primary purpose.

Define Other Terms

Define the following additional terms from this chapter, and check your answers in the glossary:

CompTIA A+   CompTIA Network+   CompTIA Security+

Case Studies

Case Study 1

Launch the BIOS setup utility on your computer and look at the various screens. Locate the screen that allows you to view the boot sequence order. Don't change anything, just look. As a reminder, the computer will display the key or key sequence used to access this utility during the boot-up cycle.

Case Study 2

Use the Crucial Memory Advisor Tool (at crucial.com) to identify the type of RAM your system uses. If desired, download and install the Crucial System Scanner Tool to identify additional components in your system.

Case Study 3

Look at the back of your computer and locate the video cable. See if you can identify the type of connection used by your system (such as HDMI, DVI, or DisplayPort). Alternately, you can look at the connection on your monitor.

Chapter 5

Security Skills

Help desk specialists need to have a good understanding of security concepts to be effective on the job. While they don't need to be security specialists, they do need a deeper understanding of security concepts than typical users. Many users are unaware of security risks and ignore recommendations related to security. For example, the most common password in use on IT systems is "123456" and attackers know this. Uneducated users continue to use the password because it's easy to remember, while security-conscious users create strong, complex passwords.

When help desk specialists understand many of the common threats and risks to information technology (IT), they are more likely to follow the rules and guidelines put in place to thwart attackers. They are better prepared to explain these issues to users to help them understand. Additionally, they are better prepared to recognize attacks when they are occurring and help users resolve problems due to security compromises. Help desk specialists aren't expected to be security specialists. However, management within most organizations understands cyber security threats and places a high value on employees that have IT security skills.

This chapter covers IT security concepts in three major sections:

- The first section, "Protecting IT Resources," introduces the security triad of confidentiality, integrity, and availability; it then explains how the majority of security goals and rules focus on protecting this triad.

- Next, "Understanding Malware" focuses on malicious software such as viruses and worms. It provides information on how malware replicates, common symptoms, and how an organization protects against malware attacks.

- Last, "Managing Risk" defines risk, threats, and vulnerabilities. It also covers some basic security controls that organizations implement to mitigate their risk and reduce their IT losses in risk management programs.

Chapter Outline

Objectives

- List and define the three elements of the security triad

- Describe the principle of least privilege

- Summarize the goal of encryption

- Explain the purpose of fault tolerance techniques

- List and compare three different types of malware

- Describe at least three of the common objectives of malware

- List and explain common ways viruses replicate from system to system

- Describe the primary tool used to protect against malware

- Define risk, residual risk, threats, and vulnerabilities

- Compare and contrast different threat categories

- Describe the purpose or risk management

- List and describe at least three security controls designed to reduce risk

Key Terms

adware	drive-by download	rogueware
availability	fault tolerance	spam
botnet	integrity	spyware
confidentiality	keylogger	threat
cyber theft	malware	Trojan (or Trojan horse)
cyber vandalism	phishing	virus
cyber-attacks	principle of least privilege	vulnerability
cyber-criminal	residual risk	worm
cybercrime	risk	
cyberspace	risk management	

Protecting IT Resources

Information technology (IT) Security has become increasingly important to organizations due to the increasing number of criminals attempting to exploit weaknesses in IT systems. In addition to devoting a significant amount of resources to protect against threats, organizations also value employees that understand basic security issues.

Employees that understand some of the threats against an organization are much more likely to follow the rules put in place to mitigate these threats. In contrast, employees that don't understand the threats sometimes ignore and even circumvent the rules. Also, attackers have a better chance at tricking uneducated employees.

As a simple example, most organizations tell users they should not ever give out the account passwords. Imagine if an employee doesn't understand the importance of security and gets this email that looks like it is from an executive within the company.

> Subj: SSO Project
>
> As you probably know, we are in the middle of a single sign-on (SSO) project designed to make it easier for employees to sign in once and access all resources without having to sign on again. This should streamline everyone's work.
>
> Unfortunately, the project is behind due to a problem related to passwords. The project lead suspects this is due to special characters used in some passwords.
>
> I need everyone to reply to this e-mail with your user name and password so that we can determine what needs to be changed to accommodate all passwords. We must complete this test as soon as possible so please respond as soon as you receive this e-mail.

> **ON THE SIDE:**   Security professionals use emails like this as vulnerability tests. It's relatively easy for security professionals (and attackers) to modify the From line to impersonate any user, including high-level executives. Additionally, they modify the Reply To line so that the response goes to the security professionals (or attackers). The security company KnowBe4 (http://www.knowbe4.com/) uses similar tests to help an organization detect their security posture.

This email is an example of a spear-phishing test but could also be a spear-phishing attack. Phishing uses email to try to trick users into giving up information such as passwords. A phishing email might go out to tens of thousands of unrelated users. Spear-phishing is a phishing attack targeting people within a single organization.

Security company KnowBe4 reports that as many as 91 percent of successful data breaches start with a spear-phishing attack. This is a malicious email similar to the example, which targets employees within a company. Once a single user's system is compromised, the attackers now have an inside source they can use to launch additional attacks and gain progressively more and more information.

When users aren't trained, as many as 70 percent of them respond with their password to an email like the example. Attackers can still trick trained users, but the percentage is much lower.

Introducing the Security Triad

The primary focus of IT security is to protect the confidentiality, integrity, and availability of IT systems and data. Together, these three are known as the security triad, as shown in Figure 5-1. You might see them listed as the AIC security triad or the CIA security triad. Understanding each of these elements goes a long way to helping you understand the goals of many security programs and security controls.

FIGURE 5-1

The security triad.

The following sections explore these concepts in greater depth, but the following bullets provide an introduction:

- **Confidentiality** prevents the unauthorized disclosure of data.
- **Integrity** provides assurances that data and IT systems are not modified.
- **Availability** ensures that IT systems and data are available when needed.

Protecting Confidentiality

Confidentiality prevents the unauthorized disclosure of data. An organization will use a wide variety of methods to ensure the confidentiality of data, including implementing the principle of least privilege and encrypting data based on its importance.

The **principle of least privilege** ensures that users have access to what they need for their job, but no more. Users might only need read access to some files, but need full control access to other files. Similarly, someone in the payroll department might need access to salary data while people in the sales department should not have access to this data at all.

ON THE SIDE:
Privileges include
both rights and per-
missions. Rights indi-
cate what a person
can do with a system,
such as changing the
system time. Permis-
sions refer to access
granted to files such
as the ability to read,
modify, or delete a
file.

ON THE SIDE: A
smart card is typically
the size of a credit
card and it includes
security certificates
and other information
to identify the holder
of the card.

While it is much simpler to just give all users the same access to all data, it doesn't provide any security. Users might accidentally delete files if they have full control access. Happy employees that find out other employees are making more money for the same job might become disgruntled workers and intentionally delete files.

Using the principle of least privilege, administrators ensure that users have the appropriate permissions to perform their job, and no more. Without implementing the principle of least privilege, users might have unlimited access to all organizational data, increasing the possibility of unauthorized disclosure. Information such as salary data and company secrets can remain confidential.

One of the first steps when implementing the principle of least privilege is to ensure that secure identification and authentication controls are in place. IT systems identify users based on a username or account number. Users prove their identity using an authentication mechanism such as a password. There are three primary methods of authentication known as authentication factors:

- Something you know, such as a password or personal identification number (PIN).
- Something you have, such as a smart card.
- Something you are using, or biometrics, such as a fingerprint.

Multifactor authentication combines two or more of the authentication factors. For example, many authentication systems require users to use both a smart card and a PIN to identify themselves. In this example, the authentication combines the something you know factor (using a PIN) with the something you have factor (a smart card).

With secure identification and authentication mechanisms in place, administrators assign appropriate permissions to users so that the users can access data they need for their job. They typically use methods such as roles to streamline this process. For example, everyone in the payroll department can be in the payroll role. Administrators then assign permissions to this role.

Note that this process is dependent on secure identification and authentication methods. If everyone uses the same account to log on, the system cannot identify individuals. Similarly, if authentication mechanisms are not secure, it becomes easy for attackers to impersonate users and compromise the confidentiality of data. Users must use strong passwords and not give them out to others.

Another way to protect confidentiality of data is with encryption. Encryption methods scramble data so that it is unreadable. Figure 5-2 shows the general process used for encryption and decryption. In the figure, "Secret to Success" is readable as plain text. An encryption method scrambles the plain text, resulting in unrecognizable cipher text. Unauthorized users are not able to read this cipher text, protecting its confidentiality. Authorized users have access to the decryption method for this cipher text, and after decrypting it, they can see the data as plain text.

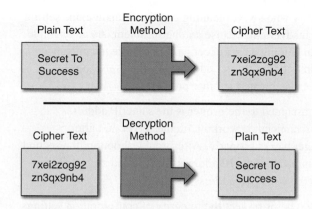

FIGURE 5-2

Encrypting and decrypting data.

Ideally, unauthorized individuals cannot decrypt encrypted data. In reality, given enough time and resources, attackers can eventually decrypt most encrypted data. The goal of many encryption methods is to make it sufficiently difficult so that it isn't worth the attacker's time. For example, some encryption methods suggest it will take 50 years or more for an attacker to decrypt the data. If this data is credit card data, the credit cards will have expired by the time the attacker decrypted the data.

Protecting Integrity

Integrity provides assurances that data and IT systems are not modified. While users regularly modify some data files, there are many files, such as operating system files, that should not change. Similarly, administrators configure IT systems and networks, but unauthorized changes can cause significant problems.

In many situations, some of the same principles used to provide confidentiality also contribute to integrity. For example, enforcing the principle of least privilege reduces access to IT systems and data. If users don't have the appropriate privileges to modify files or configuration settings, it reduces the possibility of accidental changes. Of course, it also reduces the possibility of a disgruntled employee from purposely making changes to cause problems.

Viruses often attempt to modify operating system files. Integrity methods attempt to protect these files and verify that that they haven't been modified. Specifically, antivirus software uses cryptographic techniques to record characteristics of these files. Later, they verify the file has not changed by verifying the characteristics have not changed. Ensuring that systems have up-to-date antivirus software installed goes a long way toward protecting the integrity of these system files. The "Understanding Malware" section covers more information on antivirus software.

Sometimes users need assurances that a message they received has not lost integrity. Senders can use sophisticated methods such as digital signatures. A digital signature uses cryptographic methods to verify the received message is the same as the sent message. If the message lost integrity, the recipient is alerted.

Many outages occur accidentally when well-meaning personnel change one setting to resolve a problem but then inadvertently cause another problem. As an example, imagine a help desk technician helping a user access a printer. The technician ultimately changes the IP address of the printer and verifies the user can print. Problem solved. However, this also created another problem.

The IP address the technician assigned to the printer is the same IP address assigned to a server. Another technician is working on the server and after restarting the server, it no longer works properly. After troubleshooting, the second technician realizes the problem is due to an IP address conflict and an hour or two later discovers the printer has the wrong IP address assigned.

A change management program helps protect the integrity of configuration settings and helps prevent these types of outages. When used, technicians do not make any changes without going through a change management process. Changes are proposed, analyzed, and approved or denied. While a change management program does slow down the process of getting some changes completed, it reduces many outages caused by well-meaning technicians.

> **ON THE SIDE:**   Technicians often don't understand the underlying purpose of change management programs. They view these programs as a hindrance to their ability to do their jobs and often circumvent the process. While their heart might be in the right place—thinking about providing quick service to a customer—circumventing the change management process often puts them in a different place—looking for another job.

Protecting Availability

Availability ensures that IT systems and data are available when needed. This varies based on the needs of the organization. For example, some IT systems, such as web servers, need to be operational 24 hours a day, 365 days a year. Other IT systems might only need to be available during a typical workweek, Monday through Friday.

Further, the importance of systems might dictate that additional steps are needed to ensure systems stay operational even if a fault occurs. **Fault tolerance** techniques typically use additional hardware to ensure that systems can tolerate faults and continue to operate. For example, an uninterruptible power supply (UPS) uses battery power to keep systems operational during short-term power outages and generators keep systems operational during long-term power outages.

Fault tolerance techniques implement redundant hardware or systems. For example, a server can use a redundant array of independent disks (RAID) to protect against disk failures. Failover clusters include redundant servers that can automatically switch to a different server if one fails. Some organizations even have redundant locations so that they can continue to operate during and after disasters such as fires, floods, or earthquakes.

Organizations cannot afford to add redundancies to every single system. Instead, they put a lot of effort into analyzing their organization and identifying where redundant systems provide cost benefits. **Business continuity planning (BCP)** is an overall planning lifecycle dedicated to analysis, design, implementation, testing, and maintenance of various elements designed to keep the organization operating even after a significant outage.

For example, a **business impact analysis (BIA)** helps identify critical functions and services and helps the organization determine the cost impact if critical functions and services are not restored within a given period. Management uses this data to determine the maximum allowable downtime for systems, commonly called a **recovery time objective (RTO)**.

IT administrators use the RTO to determine what redundancies to add. They will often look for a **single point of failure (SPOF)** within a system and add redundancies to protect it. An SPOF is any component that can cause the entire system or service to fail if it fails. For example, imagine a website hosted by a single server. If this server fails, the website is no longer available, so this web server is an SPOF. Administrators can add multiple servers in a web farm so the website will continue to operate even if one of the servers fails. This eliminates individual servers as SPOFs.

> **ON THE SIDE:**   As a help desk specialist, you probably won't be involved in the creation of the BIA and RTOs. However, it's important to realize that organizations don't just haphazardly add in redundant systems. They do so after analyzing the systems and the impact of outages related to these systems.

Another important element of availability is data. The most common way to protect the data is to ensure that reliable backups are created and available when needed. There is a wide variety of different backup techniques, but the method used isn't as important as ensuring that reliable backups exist.

One of the key questions organizations ask related to data is, "What data can we afford to lose?" Interestingly, if you ask many managers this question, they say, "None." However, when they realize the cost of performing backups, testing them, and storing them, they change their answer. The key is that there isn't a simple answer. It takes some thought to balance the cost of backups with the potential loss of data and the cost of this loss.

Understanding Malware

One of the most important concepts that help desk professionals should be aware of is malicious software (malware). Users will often call for help when their systems are infected with malware, though they don't always recognize that malware is the problem. When help desk professionals understand malware and can recognize common symptoms, they are better prepared to help users resolve these problems.

Many people consider all malware to be a virus. However, malware includes several different types of malicious software such as viruses, worms, Trojans, rogueware, and more. Figure 5-3 indicates some of the malicious uses of malware such as fraud, spammers, and attacks. It's important to realize that existing legislation outlaws the deliberate use and distribution of malware. However, laws rarely stop dedicated criminals, so organizations need to be aware of malware and actively work to combat it.

FIGURE 5-3

Malware.

A **virus** includes malicious code embedded in an application, which runs when the user starts or runs the infected application. For example, imagine that the acme.exe application is infected on a user's computer. As long as the user never launches this application, it will not cause any damage. However, when the user does launch the application, the malicious code also runs.

In contrast, a **worm** is self-replicating. It includes code that allows it to replicate over a network without user intervention. Worms typically look for services running on a network that they can exploit. For example, File Transfer Protocol (FTP) and Trivial FTP (TFTP) are useful for transferring files over a network. Some worms look for these services and use them to find and infect other computers on a network.

A **Trojan** (or Trojan Horse) appears to be a useful application but it includes a malicious component. Trojans get their name from the famous Trojan horse from Greek mythology. Attackers were unable to win their battles against the city of Troy, so they tried a different tactic: they offered a gift of a large wooden horse. The people of Troy happily rolled it inside the city walls, unaware that soldiers were hiding inside the horse. That night, the soldiers got out of the horse and launched an attack. Similarly, Trojan malware often appears as something useful, such as games, utilities, and even some free antivirus programs. However, when users install these applications, they are also installing malicious components.

Rogueware is a type of Trojan that masks itself as free antivirus software. Attackers first try to trick users into thinking that their computer is infected with malware, and then encourage the users to download and install free antivirus software. After running the application, the rogueware reports serious infections and then lets the user know that the free version does not remove the malware. However, they can update to the paid version and quickly remove all the malware. In reality, the rogueware reports bogus infections and the entire goal is to get the user to pay for the full version. Worse, the full version doesn't include any actual antivirus protection and many times includes additional malware.

In recent years, rogueware has expanded, and attackers have become more malicious. They often take over the systems and block user's access to their data—or even to use the system at all. Users face the prospect of losing all their data or paying a ransom to gain access to their system. Criminals have been successful with this ransom method, and many security professionals now refer to this as ransomware.

> **ON THE SIDE:** In past years, criminals have been defrauding users out of as much as $34 million per month with ransomware. A benefit for them is that they don't need to steal banking credentials and risk being caught using them. Uneducated users willingly give their money to these criminals.

Spyware collects information on users without their knowledge or consent. Extreme versions of spyware capture a user's keystrokes and periodically send this data to criminals.

Some parents install spyware on their children's computers to monitor activity and help protect their children from Internet-based threats. Also, many websites capture user information and use it for marketing and sales purposes. However, legitimate websites include a privacy policy, which explains exactly what information they collect, and how they use it.

Adware displays unwanted advertisements to users. Some adware installs itself as additional toolbars in the user's browser and changes the user's home page. Some adware uses pop-up windows to show advertisements. Adware will typically monitor the user's activity and behavior to determine what advertisements to show the user and then uses methods such as pop-up windows to show advertisements. Adware is often difficult to remove.

Malware includes an activation mechanism where they perform one or more dedicated tasks or objectives. Some objectives are relatively harmless while others cause a significant amount of damage. Here are some common objectives of malware:

- **Display a message.** Some early viruses displayed harmless messages such as "Legalize Marijuana."
- **Corrupt, delete, or destroy files.** The goal is often to disable a computer, or cause a user to lose access to data. In some cases, malware will attempt to destroy files to hide its tracks. For example, log files might record the malware activity, so by deleting or modifying log files, the malware can avoid detection.

- **Modify files.** Some malware modifies files to modify the behavior of a computer. For example, by modifying some system files, the malware can redirect Internet requests. If a user tries to go to http://www.mcafee.com/, the system redirects it to another site. This makes some websites inaccessible and often sends users to malicious websites. Also, malware replicates itself by modifying files, and embedding malicious code within these files.

- **Give an attacker remote access.** Malware can give an attacker full control of a computer via a remote location. Remote access Trojans or remote access tools (RATs) give attackers full control over systems using the Internet, while the attackers remain relatively safe in another country.

- **Join a botnet.** A botnet is a network of computers on the Internet. After malware joins the computer to a botnet, criminals control them and have these computers do their bidding. Many botnets include tens of thousands of computers (called zombies), which routinely send out spam and launch attacks on other Internet-based computers.

- **Install a keylogger.** A **keylogger** captures all keystrokes and can then send the captured data to a criminal. For example, some keyloggers wait for users to access specific websites such as banking websites, and then capture username and password information.

- **Steal money.** The methods malware use to steal varies, but this is often a primary goal. Installing a keylogger is one way criminals can get user's information. Rogueware tricks users in paying a ransom to get their computers back to normal.

> **ON THE SIDE:**   Keyloggers can be software or hardware based. Malware might install a software-based keylogger but not a hardware-based keylogger. Hardware-based keyloggers are physically located between the keyboard and the computer and they typically look like plugs. The keyboard connection plugs into keylogger instead of the computer, and the keylogger plugs into the computer.

Figure 5-4 gives an idea of how botnets work, though botnets will have many more little bots, or zombies. A bot herder (the criminal controlling the botnet) manages a command and control server and the zombies periodically check in with this server for instructions. Bot herders often rent access to their botnet to other criminals. For example, a criminal might want to launch a phishing attack by sending out malicious spam to hundreds of thousands of email address. The criminal rents access to the botnet and loads the instructions on the command and control server. The zombies check in, download the email and some of the email addresses, and begin sending out the malicious spam.

FIGURE 5-4
_____

Botnet.

Replicating Malware

Malware is only useful to criminals when it infects user computers, so replicating the malware is an important goal. It's important for users and help desk professionals to understand how malware is replicated so they can prevent the replication when possible.

Since worms self-replicate without any user interaction, there typically isn't anything users can do to prevent them from replicating. Administrators implement network security to thwart worms. Help desk technicians just need to ensure they do not make any unauthorized changes to the network, which might reduce network security.

One of the classic ways users install viruses is by starting an infected application on their system. Many times users download infected applications from the Internet. These might be Trojans with the primary purpose of including malicious code; or, they might have started out as legitimate applications and are now infected applications.

As an example, download.cnet.com includes more than 150,000 free downloads. If an attacker is able to infect one of these applications, users can unknowingly download it and install on their system. Further, even CNET has knowingly added spyware and adware to many of the software packages they distribute. Sometime in 2011 or 2012, they began bundling toolbars and other unwanted apps into the installer they provided with Nmap Security Scanner. When Insecure.org realized what CNET was doing, they complained. Eventually CNET removed the malware from the Nmap Security Scanner tool, but it remains on many downloads hosted by CNET (http://insecure.org/news/download-com-fiasco.html).

Ideally, users should view every application from an unverified source with suspicion. Unfortunately, most users don't recognize the risk and routinely download and install applications without giving it much thought.

Unsuspecting users also install viruses through other actions. For example, a **drive-by download** attempts to infect any user that visits a specific website. Criminals sometimes create websites embedded with malicious drive-by download files. Other websites start out as legitimate websites, but criminals hack into them and add their drive-by download files. For example, criminals modified the Dolphins Stadium website prior to the 2007 Super Bowl. Unprotected systems downloaded code from a server in China and then automatically installed a program designed to steal passwords.

Many documents include the ability to run sophisticated scripts. These are designed to add value and usability to these documents. For example, Portable Document Files (PDFs) can be interactive, allowing users to click within them, starting animation, audio, video, and taking users to websites. Unfortunately, criminals have discovered how to exploit these scripts for malicious reasons. Because of this, documents can include malware. PDFs have been popular with criminals, but criminals have also infected other file types such as Microsoft Word. Just as users should view applications from unverified sources suspiciously, they should also view files from unverified sources suspiciously.

Spam is unwanted email and the source of a lot of malware. In many cases, the spam is a simple one-liner with a link. It might appear to come from a friend with a note like, "You have to check this out." However, the link takes you to a malicious website, which often includes drive-by downloads. Botnets send much of this spam.

Phishing is a specialized type of spam, which tries to trick users into giving up information such as passwords. It will typically include the following elements:

- A warning about suspicious activity on an account.
- A request to validate the account by clicking on a link and providing credentials.
- A sense of urgency, such as locking your account if you don't act quickly.

For example, you might get a message that looks like it's from PayPal saying there is suspicious activity on your account. Unless you validate your credentials immediately, your account will be locked. These emails often look like they are valid with the same graphics of the live site. If users click to the site, it even looks real. If the user enters a valid username and password, the attacker captures it and can then use the credentials to impersonate the user.

Some attackers target certain groups or individuals with phishing attacks. For example, spear-phishing targets people within a single organization as mentioned in the phishing test at the beginning of this chapter. Whaling targets high-level executives or "big phish."

One whaling attack sent bogus subpoenas via email to many corporate executives. The email included an infected PDF that supposedly included details on the subpoena. When the recipient opened the PDF file, the malware ran and infected the user's system.

Another way users help to replicate malware is with Universal Serial Bus (USB) flash drives. Here is one way malware replicates between systems with a USB flash drive:

- A user inserts an uninfected USB flash drive into an infected system.
- The system recognizes the drive and then infects it with malware. The user can copy files to and from this drive without noticing the malware.
- Later, the user plugs the USB flash drive into another system. When the system accesses the flash drive, it activates the malware, and the malware infects the system.

Note that the user isn't actually executing an application in this example. Instead, the user's action of plugging in the USB flash drive causes the system to execute code to read the USB flash drive. Normally, this is helpful but not when the USB flash drive is infected.

Malware commonly has multiple components within it. As an example, many viruses include a worm component that they use to replicate across a network. First, the virus infects a single computer. This might be from a USB drive, after a user clicked on malicious link, or installed as a Trojan. Once the virus is installed, it launches the worm component to search the network for other systems. When the worm component finds vulnerable systems, it installs the virus component onto these systems by modifying one or more files, and then repeats the process of looking for more systems to infect.

While this section covered many of the common ways malware is replicated, it didn't cover every possibility. Additionally, criminals are constantly updating their tactics to circumvent methods designed to block the malware. Security professionals wage an almost constant battle as they try to thwart the criminal's attempts.

> **ON THE SIDE:**
> Many organizations restrict the use of USB flash drives to thwart these types of infections. In some cases, organizations prohibit the use of USB flash drives. In other cases, technical controls restrict how a system accesses a flash drive.

Recognizing Malware Symptoms

There isn't a single symptom that indicates a system is infected, but there are several symptoms that give you some clues. It's important to note that these symptoms might indicate another issue, so seeing one of these symptoms doesn't indicate a system is definitely infected. However, it does provide a hint that it might be. Help desk specialists should consider the possibility of infection when users report any of these symptoms:

- **Reduced performance.** Some malware consumes a lot of processing power. This can slow down the overall performance of the computer. Users often complain about a distinct difference in performance, rather than a gradual slowing down of the system. Over time, a computer can slow down just because more and more legitimate applications are installed and running. In contrast, a recent infection causes a dramatic change.

- **Slow network performance.** Some malware consumes network bandwidth, resulting in network access for the user appearing slower. As an example, malware that joins a computer to a botnet might get the computer to start sending spam to thousands of other computers. While the computer is sending the spam, network bandwidth is limited for other work.
- **Random crashes and restarts.** Malware often corrupts key files and causes computers to stop or restart. They might stop with a blue screen displaying a stop error. Or they might just periodically restart on their own.
- **Unexplained behavior.** Some malware causes random symptoms that just aren't normal, such as modifying the look of an application. As an example, some malware modifies web browsers by adding toolbars, modifying the home page, or preventing users from accessing specific websites.
- **Random pop-ups.** Some malware causes pop-up windows to appear randomly. These often include unwanted ads. Some companies still use web browser pop-ups for legitimate reasons, such as logging on. However, if the pop-ups aren't connected to a specific website, they are probably malware.

It's worth noting that one of the goals of criminals is often to ensure that the malware is not detected. The longer the malware can operate undetected, the longer it can pursue its objective. If the goal is to steal user passwords and it's detected as soon as it's installed, it might not capture any passwords. However, if it remains undetected for 30 days or more, there is a good chance it will capture some passwords. With this in mind, many criminals go to great lengths to hide the malware.

Protecting Against Malware

The best protection against malware is up-to-date antivirus software. Antivirus software attempts to block the installation of malware on a system, and periodically scans a system to verify it hasn't been infected.

Malware displays specific attributes that antivirus software detects. For example, a known virus might have a specific name and be stored in a specific folder on a computer. Similarly, it might have a specific string of text embedded within it such as "this is a malicious virus," though the strings are rarely that clear and direct.

These attributes make up the malware signature. Antivirus software includes a database of known viruses, which include signature definitions. When a new virus emerges, security experts identify the signature and add it to the database. Just as criminals are constantly updating malware, antivirus companies are constantly updating the signature definitions.

Most antivirus software includes the ability to automatically determine if the signatures it has are up-to-date, and download new signatures when they are available. When installed and up-to-date, antivirus software can detect known malware before a user installs it, and, using periodic antivirus scans, detect malware that was previously installed.

Heuristic analysis is another method of detecting malware. Antivirus software with heuristic capabilities can detect malware based on attributes that are more generic, or when the malware displays suspicious activity. The goal of heuristic analysis is to detect new malware, though this is much more difficult than detecting previously known malware with signature definitions.

Organizations also protect access to their network to block malware. Firewalls help to block some malware. Sophisticated intrusion detection systems (IDSs) and intrusion prevention systems (IPSs) are more effective at detecting and blocking malware. These devices and systems attempt to block malware at the boundary of the organization is between the private network and the public Internet.

Removing Malware

Most malware is relatively is easy to remove if you have a good antivirus application. You start an antivirus scan of the system, and when the antivirus program detects malware, it asks you if you want to remove or quarantine the virus. If you want to remove it, the antivirus program deletes it. If you quarantine it, the antivirus program isolates it so that it cannot cause damage but keeps it so that forensic experts can examine the file.

However, some malware extends its malicious tentacles throughout systems and networks and can be extremely challenging to remove. For example, malware that includes both virus and worm components can infect every system in a network. If you clean one system but leave it connected to an infected network, it will just be a matter of time before it's infected again. In this case, you might need to isolate all the systems, clean them individually, and bring them back online one-by-one.

Most antivirus companies provide detailed instructions for many viruses that are difficult to remove. Check with the antivirus vendor if you run across a virus that is difficult to remove. Sometimes you need to start systems in safe mode and delete all temporary files before running the antivirus software. Other times you need to start the system with a bootable CD containing antivirus software and run the software in a mini-operating system.

Malware is one threat to an organization and most systems are vulnerable to malware infection. It is possible to reduce these vulnerabilities by implementing security controls, such as up-to-date antivirus software. However, antivirus software only mitigates threats related to malware, and organizations need to consider many more types of threats. The next section discusses other risks to an organization, including some of the common threats and vulnerabilities.

Managing Risk

Risk is the likelihood that a threat will exploit a vulnerability resulting in a loss, as shown in Figure 5-5. In this context, a threat is anything or anyone that represents a possible danger to an organization's information technology (IT) resources. This

AUTHOR'S NOTE:
Years ago, security experts recommended updating signature definitions at least once a week. However, virus authors have become adept at releasing hundreds of slightly modified versions of malware a day. Updating the definitions once a week isn't enough. Instead, many antivirus software programs will automatically check for new definitions several times a day.

5

includes attackers but there are other potential threats. Another way of thinking of this is that a threat is anything that can compromise the confidentiality, integrity, or availability of an organization's resources.

FIGURE 5-5

Risk.

Threat	Exploits	Vulnerability	Resulting in Loss
Attacker		Vulnerable IT Resources	Money Losses

Vulnerabilities are weaknesses and include weaknesses in IT systems, networks, configuration settings, users, and data. As an example, from the "Understanding Malware" section, IT resources without up-to-date antivirus software are vulnerable to malware attacks. If an attacker successfully installs a RAT or a keylogger, he might be able to access a user's bank account and empty it.

Note a key point here: Not every vulnerability results in a loss. It's only when a threat exploits a vulnerability that a loss occurs. Organizations spend a lot of time and energy evaluating various threats and vulnerabilities to determine the likelihood that a threat will exploit a vulnerability, and only address risks that have a high likelihood to occur and/or can result in a substantial loss.

Malware is an example of a threat that has a high likelihood of occurring. Any computer with Internet access will likely be infected unless it has up-to-date antivirus software installed. If an unsuspecting user visits a malicious website, that website can use a drive-by download to infect the user's system. The malware can monitor the user's activity to capture usernames, passwords, and credit card information. Attackers can then impersonate the user, charge the credit cards, and empty bank accounts. Most people recognize this threat, and take steps to prevent it by installing antivirus software and keeping it up to date.

Fire is an example of a threat that has a low likelihood to occur, but can result in a substantial loss. Organizations reduce the risk of fire with fire alarm and fire suppression systems. The alarms detect fire or smoke and alert occupants of the threat. Many also tie into the fire department, helping fire fighters arrive at potential fires quicker. Fire extinguishers and more sophisticated fire suppression systems help to extinguish fires before excessive damage occurs. The fire detection and suppression systems cost money, but it is money well spent because they help reduce the losses if a fire occurs. Additionally, organizations purchase fire insurance to reduce this risk even further. If a fire does occur and causes damage, the insurance reduces the impact of this damage to the organization.

ON THE SIDE:
Risk management focuses on threat pairs of both a threat and a vulnerability. Threats that cannot be matched to vulnerabilities are not a risk. For example, attackers that specialize in exploiting web servers do not represent a risk to a company that does not have any web servers.

It's impossible to eliminate risk, but organizations can manage it. **Risk management** is the process of evaluating risks and reducing them to an acceptable level using various security controls. Risk assessments help an organization identify risks, the potential losses, and possible controls they can implement to mitigate the risk. Management compares the potential losses against the cost of the controls to determine what controls to implement.

An important point here is that senior management decides the level of risk they are willing to accept and what security controls to eliminate. **Residual risk** is the amount of risk that remains after implementing security controls to mitigate the risk. Because senior personnel are responsible for deciding the level of risk to accept, they are also responsible for any losses resulting from residual risk.

The overall methods used for risk management are:

- **Risk mitigation.** An organization implements controls to reduce the risk with the goal of reducing the risk to an acceptable level. For example, an organization can reduce the risk of virus infections by installing and updating antivirus software on systems. The risk of these systems becoming infected is substantially reduced.

- **Risk transference.** Risk transference shifts the risk entirely onto a third party. For example, some forms of insurance, such as fire insurance, transfer the risk to the insurance company. If a fire occurs, the insurance company pays for the losses.

- **Risk sharing.** In some cases, it isn't possible or desirable to shift the entire risk onto a third party, but the risk can be shared. This allows an organization to share some of the responsibility or liability with another entity. Organizations typically share risk in this way when the other organization is more qualified to address the risk. For example, an organization might not have the technical expertise to manage large databases such as email lists, so it might partner with another organization to share the risk of maintaining the data. If the database is compromised, both organizations will share some of the responsibility and liability.

- **Risk avoidance.** An organization can avoid the risk completely by not engaging in a risky activity. For example, a small company might consider expanding by getting involved in e-commerce and selling products over the Internet. After evaluating the potential risks and potential gains, they might decide to avoid the risks completely by not expanding into e-commerce.

- **Risk acceptance.** After reducing risk to an acceptable level by implementing various security controls, an organization chooses to accept the remaining risk, known as residual risk. For example, consider an organization that has installed antivirus software and implemented methods to keep it up-to-date. New malware might still infect these systems, but most organizations accept this risk. In contrast, if you want to eliminate any risk of a computer infection, you can keep it unplugged and buried in your back yard. It's secure, but not very useful.

> **ON THE SIDE:** The United States National Institute of Standards and Technology (NIST) has published many Special Publications (SP) on IT security. SP 800-39 is titled "Managing Information Security Risk" and includes a wealth of information on risk and risk mitigation techniques, including more information on mitigating, transferring, sharing, avoiding, and accepting risk. You can access it and other SP 800 series documents here: http://csrc.nist.gov/publications/PubsSPs.html.

Recognizing Threats

If you pay attention to the news at all, you've probably heard about a cyber-attack against an organization. Some are huge and covered in the news for weeks or months. Others are never covered in the media but still result in significant losses to individuals and organizations.

As an example of a large cyber-attack, attackers stole credit card and personal data on over 110 million consumers in November and December of 2013. Evidence indicates this started as malware written by a Russian programmer. Criminals bought the malware via an international black market and after some modifications began infecting point-of-sale (POS) terminals, where consumers complete their purchases using credit or debit cards. At one point, experts estimated the malware had infected the majority of POS terminals in all 1,800 Target Corp stores, along with POS terminals at Neiman Marcus and other unnamed stores. When customers swiped their credit and debit cards, the malware captured their information and sent it to the criminals. Criminals then began selling the data to other criminals who began making fraudulent charges against these cards.

> **ON THE SIDE:** Target Corp initially announced that attackers stole credit card data from 40 million consumers. Later, they announced that attackers also stole names, mailing addresses, and phone numbers or email addresses on an additional 70 million individuals.

It's worth noting that this was successful despite a large professional IT security team working at Target Corp. Some experts indicate this attack targeted stores in the United States because credit cards used in the states use less secure magnetic strips. In contrast, credit cards in Europe use embedded security chips in their credit cards, which encrypt all data sent to POS machines and would have foiled this attack. Chip-based credit cards are more expensive than magnetic strip-based credit cards, which has slowed their adoption.

When discussing various threats, it's valuable to understand some of the terminology. The following list includes some common terms:

- **Cyberspace** refers to the online world of computer networks where people can interact with other people and things without physically being with them. People commonly interact with cyberspace via the Internet. For example, a website exists in cyberspace, and people can access the website through the Internet.

- **Cyber vandalism** refers to any attacks by vandals with the intent to destroy, deface, or spoil IT resources without permission. For example, attackers that deface an organization's website are cyber vandals engaged in cyber vandalism.

- **Cyber-attacks** are any attacks on an organization's IT resources. The purpose of the attacks might be for monetary gain, intelligence gathering, or vandalism. For example, denial of service (DoS) attacks prevent legitimate users from accessing the IT resources. Other attacks, such as the attack on Target Corp, attempt to go unnoticed for as long as possible.

- **Cyber theft** is the theft of financial or other personal information through cyberspace. As an example, criminals used a computer virus named Coreflood to infect more than 2 million PCs. Coreflood gave the criminals remote control over these PCs. The virus captured banking credentials and sent them to the criminals who used this to steal funds. When U.S. authorities shut it down in 2011, they estimated the criminals behind it had stolen as much as $100 million. You can think of these criminals as expert pickpockets (see Figure 5-6)—with the help of technology, they can steal from thousands of people at a time.

- **Cybercrime** is any type of computer crime that targets computers or uses computer networks or devices, and violates existing laws. It includes cyber vandalism, cyber theft, and cyber-attacks. **Cyber-criminals** break into computer systems for malicious reasons and often for personal gain.

FIGURE 5-6

Cybercriminals and cyber theft.

ON THE SIDE: The United States Department of Homeland Security (DHS) maintains a section of their website devoted to cybersecurity and methods to combat cyber crime. You can access it here: http://www.dhs.gov/cybersecurity-overview.

Governments and anti-government entities engage in cyber espionage, cyber warfare, and cyber terrorism. For example, China's government entities have reportedly launched many attacks on both public and private targets in the United States, Russia, Canada, and France, though the Chinese often say that outsiders hijacked their systems and used them in the attacks. The United States government has stepped up efforts to detect and deter attacks on US IT resources, and many federal agencies are involved in cybersecurity. This includes the United States Cyber Command, the Department of Homeland Security (DHS), the Central Intelligence Agency (CIA), and the National Security Agency (NSA).

An **advanced persistent threat (APT)** is a group or entity that has the capability and intent to persistently target a specific organization. They often have the backing of a government, giving them access to a significant number of resources. Many security experts suspect that organized crime gangs might also fund some APTs. They have specific goals, such as breaking into a government network or installing malware on POS systems. They will continue working on the project until they reach their goals.

As an example of an APT, Dmitri Alperovitch, Vice President at McAfee, wrote an intriguing white paper titled "Revealed: Operation Shady RAT," which is an ongoing series of cyber-attacks that have targeted dozens of organizations worldwide. Some of the targets were government entities, defense contractors, organizations associated with the Olympics, and news media companies. It included attacks on targets in 14 different countries. Alperovitch reports this as a "targeted operation by one specific actor." In other words, one entity, such as a government, funded and directed these attacks against specific targets. While the report does shed some light on attacks, Alperovitch stresses that these attacks aren't new, and he suggests that the entire set of Fortune Global 2,000 firms can be divided into two categories: "Those that know they've been compromised, and those that don't yet know."

ON THE SIDE: You can access the full white paper titled "Revealed: Operation Shady RAT" here: http://www.mcafee.com/us/resources/white-papers/wp-operation-shady-rat.pdf.

Common Threats

While it's impossible to list all the possible threats that organizations consider, it is important to understand some of the common threats. The following section mentions some of the common threats with a focus on what help desk professionals should understand. It includes malware, social engineers, phishing, attacks, and some environmental threats.

As mentioned in the "Understanding Malware" section, malware includes viruses, worms, Trojans, spyware, and other forms of malicious software. Malware presents a significant threat and causes damage to individuals and organizations daily. The importance of having up-to-date antivirus software and recognizing malware symptoms cannot be overstated.

Social engineers use trickery, flattery, and other tactics to get users to give up information they wouldn't normally give up or perform an action they wouldn't normally perform. For example, a criminal might dress up as a pest control technician and trick a front desk receptionist into giving him access to restricted spaces.

Tailgating is the practice of closely following behind someone else without using credentials. For example, imagine employees must enter a code into a cypher lock and open a door. A criminal can follow closely behind an employee that opens the door, and gain access without the code. The employee might notice and look back, but a skilled social engineer would flash a warm disarming smile with a cheerful "hello" and might still get inside.

Most social engineering attempts simply trick others by talking. However, social engineering has extended into the technical arena. For example, rogueware attempts to trick users into thinking their systems are infected with malware, and then they install the malicious rogueware.

Some phishing emails use social engineering tactics to trick users into giving up information, such as their banking credentials. Other phishing emails try to trick users into clicking on a malicious link where a drive-by download is ready to infect their systems with malware. Similarly, spear-phishing (targeting people within the same organization) and whaling (targeting high-level executives) attacks use social engineering tactics to trick people.

Training personnel about social engineering tactics goes a long way toward thwarting their attacks. This includes training regular users and help desk specialists. When the help desk specialists understand the attacks, they are less likely to be fooled. Similarly, when users report issues, trained help desk specialists are able to identify when a social engineer might have victimized the user.

Attackers also have a wide assortment of tools that they are constantly updating. Some tools launch denial of service (DoS) attacks designed to disrupt or disable the services provided by an IT system. If attackers control multiple systems, such as in a botnet, they launch distributed DoS (DDoS) attacks from multiple systems at a time. Many botnets include tens of thousands of computers, and criminals have used them to launch massive attacks on many organizations. Organizations use a variety of different network devices to thwart these attacks. Some devices mentioned in this chapter include firewalls, IDSs, and IPSs.

> **ON THE SIDE:** DoS attacks come from a single source, while DDoS attacks come from multiple sources at the same time. DDoS attacks often come from computers in a botnet. Criminals controlling a botnet can launch an attack from tens of thousands of computers at the same time and easily overload many legitimate systems that are not prepared to handle these types of attacks.

Environmental threats include power losses and losses to heating, ventilation, and air conditioning (HVAC) systems. Organizations often implement redundant power sources such as UPS or generators for critical systems. Additionally, organizations ensure they have adequate HVAC systems for their equipment. Other environmental threats include floods, tornadoes, earthquakes, hurricanes, or any other natural event.

While this section included many common threats, it certainly didn't include all possible threats. Risk management specialists put a lot of time and effort into analyzing an organization and identifying potential threats. This includes detailed business continuity planning and business impact analysis studies. When identifying threats, these specialists look at threats in many different categories, such as intentional or accidental, internal or external, and natural or man-made.

Comparing Accidental Threats to Intentional Threats

Not all threats are intentional attacks; instead, they are accidents or mistakes. As a simple example, if someone accidentally spills a cup of coffee in a server, they can damage the server, affecting the availability of resources the server provides. To combat this, many organizations have simple rules in place prohibiting food and beverages within a server room.

Similarly, if a user accidentally deletes data, it results in a loss of data. As mentioned previously, the principle of least privilege goes a long way toward preventing these types of mistakes or errors. If a user doesn't have access to data, the user cannot accidentally delete it.

Many policies and procedures help prevent accidental threats, too. For example, the change management policy mentioned in the "Protecting Integrity" section helps prevent accidental outages due to unauthorized changes. When technicians follow established procedures before making changes, they are less likely to accidentally cause an outage.

Of course, many attackers are very deliberate in their attacks. An attacker that launches a DoS attack on an organization's website does so with a specific goal in mind, such as ensuring that legitimate users cannot access the website.

Comparing Internal Threats to External Threats

Threats can come from within an organization or outside of it. Internal threats are within the boundary of the organization and are most commonly employees. Contractors or others that have access to internal resources are also internal threats. External threats come from outside the organization.

The infamous disgruntled worker or malicious insider is an internal threat and can cause a significant amount of damage. As an example, a disgruntled UNIX engineer at Fannie Mae wrote a malicious script designed to delete data and backups for several thousand servers and shut them down. Employers fired him for making unrelated, unauthorized changes violating their change management policy, but he retained access to his account for the remainder of the workday. He installed the script and scheduled it to run on a different day. Thankfully, another administrator discovered the script and disabled it before it ran.

Untrained employees or employees granted too much access to IT resources are also internal threats. Even if they are happy in the job, they could cause accidental damage to IT resources.

External threats typically attack an organization's resources through the Internet. If an organization has any servers with public IP addresses on the Internet, attackers can attack them directly. However, with the use of malware, external attackers can also attack internal IT resources without direct access. For example, imagine that an employee visits a malicious website and inadvertently installs a malicious remote access tool. The attacker remains external to the organization but now has access to internal resources through this user's computer.

Not all external threats are technical in nature. For example, dumpster divers simply look through an organization's trash looking for valuable information. Many organizations have specific rules in place specifying what employees can throw away, and what must be shredded or burned.

Comparing Natural Threats to Man-Made Threats

Mother Nature can cause a significant amount of danger through events such as floods, hurricanes, tornadoes, and earthquakes. These natural events can compromise the confidentiality, integrity, and availability of resources, so organizations consider them when performing risk assessments.

One benefit when examining natural threats is that some events are highly unlikely at certain areas. For example, organizations in San Francisco, California don't worry much about hurricanes because hurricanes are not a threat in northern California. San Francisco organizations do consider the possibility of earthquakes, though. Similarly, people in Miami, Florida don't worry too much about earthquakes, but they do plan for hurricanes.

Any threats by an individual are man-made. Man-made threats can be intentional or accidental, and can come from within the organization or be external.

Comparing Hackers to Attackers

The term **hacker** has morphed over the years due to how the media uses it. Currently, the media refers to a hacker as someone who breaks into IT systems illegally, for personal gain or malicious purposes. However, the term hacker originally referred to a highly skilled and knowledgeable individual that used these skills and knowledge to gain and spread knowledge, but not for malicious purposes. For example, Steve Wozniak helped Steve Jobs build the first Apple computer and IT professionals widely regarded him as a hacker (in a good way). In this context, it was a compliment to call him a hacker because it indicated others recognized his expertise.

However, due to how the media refers to individuals involved in cyber-crime as hackers, people do not consider it a compliment today. Instead, it indicates the individual is a criminal.

> **AUTHOR'S NOTE:**   Many people in the technical community insist that a hacker is not malicious. They introduced the term cracker to indicate a criminal, trying to protect the good-guy image of hackers. However, *cracker* is a racial slur and the media did not adopt it. Instead, when discussing cyber-crimes, the media refers to the cyber-criminals as hackers. In this book, I attempted to bypass the debate of hackers and crackers. Instead, I simply use the term attacker.

A common way that talented, law-abiding IT professionals are differentiated from cyber-criminals is by calling them white-hats and black-hats, or white-hat hackers and black-hat hackers. If you think of a typical western movie or TV show, the good guys wore white hats and the bad guys wore black hats. Similarly, a **white-hat** hacker is a professional that uses his or her talents for positive law-abiding purposes. IT security professionals working within an organization to protect it from malicious attacks are white-hats. They have a good understanding of common attacks, methods to protect against them, and how to use forensic procedures to investigate evidence after an attack.

> **ON THE SIDE:**   The International Council of Electronic Commerce Consultants (EC-Council) provides training and certifications to IT professionals with a focus on IT security. A popular certification of theirs is the Certified Ethical Hacker (C|EH) certification. Some other certifications focus on forensic investigations, penetration testing, security analysis, security administration, and incident handling.

In contrast, a **black-hat** hacker breaks into computer systems for malicious reasons or personal gain. A black-hat hacker is a criminal, or more specifically, a cyber-criminal. When you hear the media referring to hackers, they are implying black-hat hackers.

Gray-hat hackers are somewhere between the white-hat and black-hat hackers. They are not deliberately malicious in their actions and don't break into systems for monetary gain, but their actions do break laws. For example, an individual might surf the Internet looking for vulnerable systems and attempt to break into these systems. After breaking in, the gray-hat doesn't attempt to cause damage. Typically, the gray-hat individual will notify the organization of their vulnerability.

A key with gray-hat hackers is that they are often breaking laws by breaking into these systems, but not for malicious reasons or for personal gain. Note that law-enforcement personnel can prosecute a gray-hat hacker for breaking into systems, as if they were a black-hat hacker. A shoplifter, caught as he walks out of a store without paying, can say he meant to pay, but the police probably won't believe him. Similarly, a gray-hat hacker caught trying to break into a system can say he wasn't going to do any damage, but the police probably won't believe him.

Calculating Losses

Some losses from attacks result in tangible losses, making them easy to calculate. For example, if someone stole your banking credentials and transferred $500 from your bank account, you lost $500.

Other losses have an intangible value, which can be more difficult to calculate. Successful attacks can damage a brand and affect customer confidence. This results in lost customers and makes it more difficult to attract new customers. Companies refer to this as the loss of goodwill and often have to invest more money in advertising and public relations efforts to regain the trust of the customers.

As an example, consider the attack on Target Corp in November and December 2013 mentioned earlier in this section. Once the attack was public, Target reduced their sales projections, indicating they would be down 2.5 percent from their previous projections. Additionally, their stock quickly dropped 2.2 percent. These represent tangible losses.

Angry customers then flooded Target's Facebook page with comments such as "Shop at Target, become a target" and "Thank you Target for nearly costing me and my wife our identities, we will never shop or purchase anything in your store again." While these comments were highly visible, many more customers didn't take the time to post comments, but instead just stopped going to the store. These lost customers are intangible losses that are difficult to calculate.

Will customers continue to tell their friends and family to avoid Target? Or will Target be able to regain their trust? In some cases, consumers have short memories and forget about these events quickly. However, in other cases, customers react and permanently change their shopping behaviors. Customers might only associate the risk with Target and think that Target is not a safe place to use a credit card. Many experts agree that Target needs to invest in advertising and public relations efforts to ensure that the long-term impact is minimized.

Several lawyers indicated class action lawsuits against Target are certain. This will result in additional costs that are difficult to predict. Target will likely have to pay for any fraud on the compromised cards, and depending on the results of investigations, credit card issuers may fine them for non-compliance with security standards.

> **ON THE SIDE:**   It's entirely possible that Target was in full compliance with security standards and might not be fined for non-compliance. The Payment Card Industry Data Security Standard (PCI DSS) is one of the primary standards companies follow when using credit cards. Security experts indicate that due to how attackers quickly adapt new tactics, adhering to PCI DSS may not be enough to stop some attacks. Companies can do everything required by PCI DSS and more, yet still suffer losses from attacks.

Target offered customers one year of free credit monitoring and identity theft protection to all customers who shopped in US stores. Of course, Target is paying for this protection.

> **ON THE SIDE:**
> KnowBe4 reports that 91 percent of successful data breaches start with a spear-phishing attack.

In January 2014, Target announced that they were investing $5 million in cybersecurity as part of a coalition of several organizations focusing on cybersecurity. About the same time, they announced that they were closing eight stores in the US. While these closures aren't a direct result of the attack, the attack probably did impact these stores' sales during the last two weeks of the Christmas buying season. Despite improved sales performance before the attack became public, Target reported sales declined by 2 percentage points (to 6 percent) after customers heard about the attack. These losses might have been the last straw that forced the decision to close these stores.

While many customers were victimized by this attack, the losses suffered by Target Corp were clearly much greater. Years from now, forensic experts might determine this attack was successful because one untrained employee responded to a phishing attack and infected his computer. This malware then spread through the company, ultimately giving the attackers access to the POS terminals. It might have been avoided by spending a few thousand dollars on training.

Identifying Vulnerabilities

Organizations mitigate risks by reducing vulnerabilities. They complete risk assessments to identify the risks, and then look for ways to reduce them. It's not always easy to identify all the existing risks and keep up with emerging threats, which is why many organizations employ IT security professionals that understand the current risks.

During a risk assessment, IT security professionals look at a variety of different sources to identify existing vulnerabilities. For example, they look at prior events such as successful attacks. They examine these events to determine how it succeeded, and what vulnerabilities can be reduced to prevent them from succeeding again. They also examine existing policies and procedures to determine if the organization has security policies in place and whether employees are following the policies. Audits (internal or external) are useful at determining if people within an organization follow the existing guidelines, rules, and laws.

> **ON THE SIDE:** Some organizations are very effective at documenting security policies, but not so effective at following them. These policies identify secure procedures and guidelines. However, supervisors and management personnel do not enforce them. When employees see the policies aren't enforced, they do not follow them.

Other methods used to detect vulnerabilities include logs and trouble events. Many attacks are recorded in logs but aren't necessarily detected unless someone examines the logs. Similarly, many attacks result in outages and result in help desk calls. If the attacks aren't recognized as attacks right away, they can be overlooked. By examining the help desk reports and looking for trends and anomalies, security experts often identify overlooked attacks. For example, imagine an attacker launches a DoS attack on a server. Users call the help desk to report it, and an administrator restarts the server. With the server restarted, the problem disappears. Help desk personnel close the incident and move on to the next problem. However, by analyzing the incidents during a risk assessment, a security professional is able to note recurring and often predictable patterns in outages related to attacks.

After identifying the vulnerabilities, the next step is to identify ways to reduce them. An organization often reduces vulnerabilities by implementing security controls.

Implementing Security Controls

Organizations implement a variety of different security controls to protect their assets. Security controls can be technical controls, operational controls, and management controls. They are further defined as preventive, detective, or corrective.

Administrators implement technical controls using technology. For example, antivirus software is an application that administrators install on systems. Once installed, the software protects the systems without any other intervention needed.

Operational controls provide guidelines or rules on how personnel should perform certain operational duties. For example, a change management policy instructs personnel on how to request configuration changes. This written policy only succeeds when personnel understand it and follow it. Another operational control is training for personnel at all levels of an organization. The training helps people understand security issues, the security policies designed to reduce vulnerabilities, and how to follow and enforce these policies.

Management controls refer to assessments and tests ordered by management personnel. For example, management can fund a business impact analysis and a risk assessment. These tools help management understand the risks and how to mitigate them. Reports from these assessments might recommend implementing specific security controls.

Preventive controls attempt to prevent losses before they occur. For example, many organizations implement acceptable usage policies (AUPs) that define acceptable usage of IT resources. The AUP also defines unauthorized activities, such as sending spam to coworkers. Users read and acknowledge the AUP when they start the job and periodically afterwards, such as during annual security training. By educating users with the AUP and reminding them of the policies, an organization can prevent many losses due to user accidents. Note that an AUP is an operational control but is preventive in nature.

Detective controls attempt to detect when a threat exploits a vulnerability. Some detective controls can detect the events in real time. For example, a closed circuit television (CCTV) system monitored by a security guard can detect illegal activity. Other detective controls detect the events after they've occurred. For example, security personnel can use CCTV recordings to detect events that happened in the past.

Corrective controls attempt to reverse the impact of a loss. For example, if an organization has reliable data backups, it can use these backups to recover from data losses.

Several security controls were listed throughout this chapter but they weren't necessarily defined as security controls. To put them into context, many of these security controls are listed here:

- Basic security principles such as the principle of least privilege to limit access
- Encryption techniques to enforce confidentiality
- Simple rules such as prohibiting food and beverages in certain areas to protect hardware such as servers in a server room
- Policies such as change management policies to prevent losses due to unauthorized changes
- Fault-tolerant techniques to prevent losses related to SPOFs
- Up-to-date antivirus software to protect against malware
- Risk management programs including risk assessments and BIA studies to help identify threats and vulnerabilities
- Network devices such as firewalls, IDSs, and IPSs to protect networks
- Training to help educate employees about risks and organizational policies designed to reduce risk
- Audits to help an organization discover lapses in security procedures
- AUPs to help educate and remind employees of acceptable usage policies

Chapter Review Activities

Use the features in this section to study and review the topics in this chapter.

Answer These Questions

1. Which of the following items is NOT one of the three primary elements of the security triad?

   a. Availability

   b. Confidentiality

   c. Integrity

   d. Least privilege

2. What principle enforces the concept of giving users the rights and permissions they need for their job, but no more?

   a. Principle of something you know

   b. Authentication

   c. Encryption

   d. Principle of least privilege

3. What is the goal of encrypting data?

   a. Availability

   b. Confidentiality

   c. Integrity

   d. Least privilege

4. What is the primary purpose of a change management program?

   a. Prevent unauthorized disclosure of data

   b. Protect confidentiality

   c. Prevent outages

   d. Enforce least privilege

5. What would an organization use to eliminate an SPOF?

   a. Fault tolerance

   b. BIA

   c. RTO

   d. RAID

6. How does an organization identify critical functions and services that it needs to protect with redundancy techniques?

    a. BCP

    b. BIA

    c. SPOF

    d. RTO

7. What security goal provides assurances that data and IT systems are not modified?

    a. Availability

    b. Confidentiality

    c. Integrity

    d. Least privilege

8. Which of the following types of malware installs itself without user intervention?

    a. Virus

    b. Worm

    c. Rogueware

    d. Trojan

9. Which of the following types of malware looks beneficial to the user but includes a malicious component?

    a. Virus

    b. Worm

    c. Antivirus software

    d. Trojan

10. Which of the following masks itself as free antivirus software?

    a. Trojan

    b. Virus

    c. Rogueware

    d. Worm

11. What is a zombie?

    a. A botnet

    b. A criminal launching attacks

    c. A criminal controlling a botnet

    d. A computer joined to a botnet

12. Which of the following is NOT one of the common objectives of malware?

    a. Detect attacks

    b. Steal money

    c. Join a botnet

    d. Install a keylogger

13. A user clicks a link in an email. Afterwards, installed malware reports suspicious activity. What is the MOST likely cause of this?

    a. Spam

    b. Whaling

    c. Drive-by download

    d. Rogueware

14. Of the following choices, what provides the BEST protection against malware?

    a. Rogueware

    b. The newest version of antivirus software

    c. Antivirus software with up-to-date definitions

    d. Antispyware software

15. Of the following choices, what provides the BEST protection against malware?

    a. Rogueware

    b. The newest version of antivirus software

    c. Antivirus software with up-to-date definitions

    d. Antispyware software

16. Which of the following MOST accurately defines a threat?

    a. Any entity that supports confidentiality, integrity, or availability

    b. Social engineering

    c. A weakness in an IT resource

    d. Any entity that represents danger to an organization's IT resources

17. Which of the following MOST accurately defines a vulnerability?

    a. The likelihood that an organization will suffer a loss

    b. A potential danger to an organization's IT resources

    c. A weakness

    d. Malware

18. Which of the following is NOT an example of contrasting threat categories?

    a. Intentional and accidental

    b. Internal and external

    c. Natural and man-made

    d. White-hat and black-hat

19. What is the primary purpose of risk management?

    a. Eliminate risk

    b. Reduce risk

    c. Reduce threats

    d. Eliminate vulnerabilities

20. What type of security control is antivirus software?

    a. Operational

    b. Technical

    c. Management

    d. Corrective

Answers and Explanations

1. **d.** The security triad includes confidentiality, integrity, and availability. The principle of least privilege helps prevent compromises of each, but is not one of the three elements of the security triad.

2. **d.** The principle of least privilege ensures that users have access to what they need for their job, but no more. Authentication includes three factors including something you know (such as passwords). Encryption helps enforce confidentiality.

3. **b.** Encryption helps ensure the confidentiality of data. Confidentiality is one of the three primary security principles, and it prevents the unauthorized disclosure of data. Availability ensures systems are available when needed. Integrity provides assurances that data and systems have not been modified. The principle of least privilege ensures that users have access to what they need for their job, but no more.

4. **c.** Change management programs help prevent outages by preventing unauthorized changes. They do not prevent the unauthorized disclosure of data, protect confidentiality, or enforce the principle of least privilege.

5. **a.** An organization would use a fault tolerance technique to eliminate a single point of failure (SPOF). A business impact analysis (BIA) helps identify critical functions and services, and also helps identify SPOFs. A recovery time objective (RTO) identifies maximum allowable downtime for systems. A redundant array of independent disks (RAID) is a fault tolerant method for hard drives, but not all SPOFs are hard drive related.

6. b. A business impact analysis (BIA) helps identify critical functions and services. This helps where fault tolerance or redundancy techniques can eliminate single points of failure (SPOF). Business continuity planning (BCP) is a continuous process used to identify how an organization can continue to operate after a significant outage. A recovery time objective (RTO) identifies maximum allowable downtime for systems.

7. c. Integrity provides assurances that data and systems have not been modified. Availability ensures systems are available when needed. Confidentiality prevents the unauthorized disclosure of data. The principle of least privilege ensures that users have access to what they need for their job, but no more.

8. b. Worms are self-replicating and install themselves on computers without any user interaction. Viruses, rogueware, and Trojans all require user interaction.

9. d. A Trojan (or Trojan Horse) looks beneficial to the user, such as a useful utility, but includes malicious code. Viruses and worms do not look useful to users. Antivirus software blocks and detects malware. It is not malicious.

10. c. Rogueware masks itself as free antivirus software. If users download and install it, it inaccurately reports infections and attempts to trick users into paying to remove them. Rogueware is a type of Trojan, but not all Trojans are rogueware. Viruses and worms do not mask themselves as free antivirus software.

11. d. Computers joined to a botnet are zombies. Some malware joins computers to botnets, and criminals controlling the botnet direct these zombies to launch attacks.

12. a. Malware does not detect attacks, but it might be involved in launching attacks. Attackers often use malware to steal money from users by installing software-based keyloggers and capturing credentials. Some malware joins computers to botnets.

13. c. This describes a drive-by download where the email link took the user to a malicious website, which attempted to install malicious code. The email was spam, but not all spam is malicious. Whaling is targeted phishing sent to high-level executives. Rogueware is fake antivirus software that attempts to trick users into paying for it.

14. c. Antivirus software with up-to-date definitions provides the best protection against malware. Rogueware is fake antivirus software and doesn't protect against malware. New versions of antivirus software might be good, but they also need up-to-date definitions. Antispyware software targets spyware, not all malware.

15. c. Antivirus software with up-to-date definitions provides the best protection against malware. Rogueware is fake antivirus software and doesn't protect against malware. New versions of antivirus software might be good, but they also need up-to-date definitions. Antispyware software targets spyware, not all malware.

16. d. A threat is anyone or anything that represents a possible danger to an organization's IT resources. Threats can compromise the confidentiality, integrity, or availability of these resources. Social engineering is an example of a threat, but it does not define a threat. Vulnerabilities are weaknesses.

17. c. Vulnerabilities are weaknesses. Risk is the likelihood that a threat will exploit a vulnerability, but not all vulnerabilities result in losses. Threats represent potential danger. Malware is a threat.

18. d. White-hat (or white-hat hackers) are not threats, so white-hat and black-hat are not contrasting threat categories. The other examples are valid threat categories.

19. b. The primary purpose of risk management is to reduce risk to an acceptable level. It is not possible eliminate risk or eliminate vulnerabilities; they can be reduced. While it is possible to reduce the effectiveness of threats and reduce the impact when a threat exploits a vulnerability, it is not possible to reduce actual threats.

20. b. Antivirus software is a technical control because it uses technology to provide protection. Operational controls are guidelines or rules. Management controls are assessments and tests ordered by management. Corrective controls attempt to reverse the impact of a loss.

Define the Key Terms

The following key terms include the ideas most important to the big ideas in this chapter. To review, without looking at the book or your notes, write a definition for each term, focusing on the meaning, not the wording. Then review your definition compared to your notes, this chapter, and the glossary.

Key Terms for Chapter 5

adware	drive-by download	risk management
availability	fault tolerance	rogueware
botnet	integrity	spam
confidentiality	keylogger	spyware
cyber theft	malware	threat
cyber vandalism	phishing	Trojan (or Trojan horse)
cyber-attacks	principle of least privilege	virus
cyber-criminal	residual risk	vulnerability
cybercrime	risk	worm
cyberspace		

List the Words Inside Acronyms

The following are the most common acronyms discussed in this chapter. As a way to review those terms, simply write down the words that each letter represents in each acronym.

Acronyms for Chapter 5

APT	HVAC	RAID
AUP	IDS	RAT
BCP	IPS	RTO
BIA	NIST	SPOF
BSOD	PCI DSS	SSO
CCTV	PDF	TFTP
DDoS	PIN	UPS
DoS	POS	USB
FTP		

Create Mind Maps

For this chapter, create mind maps as follows:

1. Create a mind map to list different types of malware. Start with a circle labeled "malware," draw lines outward from the circle, and label these lines with malware types you know about. Next, add notes identifying how to reduce the success of the different types of malware.

2. Create a mind map to list some common security controls implemented by an organization. Start with a circle labeled "security controls," draw lines outward from the circle, and label these lines with different security controls. Next, add notes describing the purpose of these security controls and the related threats and vulnerabilities.

Define Other Terms

Define the following additional terms from this chapter, and check your answers in the glossary:

advanced persistent threat (APT)

black-hat

business impact analysis (BIA)

business continuity planning (BCP)

denial of service (DoS)

distributed denial of service (DDoS)

gray-hat

single point of failure (SPOF)

white-hat

Case Studies

Case Study 1

Use the Internet to search on "rogueware images." Review the images for common rogueware currently in use and compare these images to valid antivirus software.

Case Study 2

Perform a risk analysis on your system and Internet behavior to determine potential vulnerabilities to known threats. You can use the Internet Crime Schemes page hosted by the Internet Crime Complaint Center (IC3) to review some current and ongoing Internet schemes (http://www.ic3.gov/crimeschemes.aspx).

Chapter | 6

Troubleshooting Skills

Troubleshooting is the process of defining, diagnosing, and solving problems. Within Information Technology (IT), the problems are related to the computing device (such as a computer or tablet), or connectivity on a network. On computing devices, the problem might be hardware, operating system, or application related. Network connectivity might be on a local network or connectivity to the Internet. However, no matter where the problem is located, successful technicians need effective troubleshooting skills to resolve the problems.

This chapter covers troubleshooting skills in three major sections:

- The first section, "Recognizing Key Troubleshooting Steps," covers some common steps used when troubleshooting IT issues. This section leads you through seven steps in a known troubleshooting model. While this model isn't the only one used by technicians, it does provide you with insight into common troubleshooting techniques.

- "Following Standard Operating Procedures" is the next section, and it presents information on troubleshooting guides that many organizations use. Troubleshooting guides are typically written documents but they may include flow charts. They provide technicians with key checks they can perform when troubleshooting various symptoms. Additionally, organizations often have software available to help technicians solve problems. This section covers some of the commonly available software.

- All problems aren't documented in troubleshooting guides. Instead, technicians often need to use some of the key skills discussed in the "Understanding Problem-Solving Skills" section. One of the key skills discussed in this section is critical thinking, which is important to understand for almost all professionals.

Chapter Outline

Objectives

- Summarize common troubleshooting steps used in IT

- Describe the instances when technicians escalate problems

- Discuss the challenges of escalating a problem too quickly or too late

- Summarize the benefits of performing root cause analysis

- Describe the purpose of a troubleshooting guide

- Identify the common elements used in a flow chart

- Explain the benefits of remote access applications

- Summarize the connection between a knowledge base and incident documentation

- Summarize the pros and cons of expert systems

- Describe critical thinking

- Compare linear thinking with critical thinking

Key Terms

content management system (CMS)

critical thinking

flow chart

knowledge base

Patch Tuesday

Recognizing Key Troubleshooting Steps

Troubleshooting is one of the core tasks for help desk professionals. When customers and users have problems that they can't solve, they go to the help desk for assistance. Some problems might be extremely simple to solve, such as showing the user how to turn on the power for the monitor. However, most problems will be more difficult and require the technician to use a process to troubleshoot systems and return them to full operation.

Technicians working on the help desk build up knowledge and experience. Over time, they typically see the same problems, so they are able to help users solve them relatively quickly. However, there will still be problems that are new to them and not documented anywhere else. When this occurs, it's important to have an understanding of some basic troubleshooting methods they can use to resolve the issue. These methods are the same methods new technicians can use when they lack the extensive knowledge of experienced technicians.

Technicians typically use basic troubleshooting steps when troubleshooting most technical problems. By following these steps, technicians are able to resolve problems as quickly as possible. Additionally, these steps help ensure technicians don't create new problems in the process.

CompTIA has published a list of troubleshooting steps in some of their certifications such as CompTIA A+ and CompTIA Network+ certifications. CompTIA has changed these steps slightly over time, but overall the steps maintain the same concepts. The following list of troubleshooting steps is derived from the CompTIA Network+ objectives:

1. Identify the problem.
2. Establish a theory of probable cause.
3. Test the theory to determine the cause.
4. Establish a plan of action to resolve the problem.
5. Implement the solution or escalate if necessary.
6. Verify full system functionality.
7. Document findings, actions, and outcomes.

> **ON THE SIDE:**   This list of troubleshooting steps isn't the only possible list you might see or use. Any organization might document them differently based on the processes used within the organization. However, this list does allow you to see some of the basic steps used in troubleshooting and how troubleshooting is a process.

These steps are numbered, indicating you'd start at step 1 and end on step 7. However, it's important to realize that many of the steps are repeated while troubleshooting any individual problem. For example, technicians typically repeat steps 2 and 3 multiples times until they have verified that a theory is the likely cause of a problem. Only then would they move on to establish a plan of action to resolve the problem.

A dangerous approach to troubleshooting is known as the Easter egg approach, or the trial and error approach. Instead of approaching a problem with a logical troubleshooting model, technicians instead just randomly try different things to see if they can fix the problem. Admittedly, technicians can sometimes solve problems this way. However, it takes them much longer and in the process, they sometimes make changes that cause additional problems. Overall, it's best to approach troubleshooting with an analytic mind, combining basic troubleshooting steps with critical thinking skills.

Identifying the Problem

In this first step, your goal is to gather information about the issue. Normally, this starts by a user reporting a problem to the help desk. Users don't always recognize what symptoms are relevant or know how to communicate the problems they see. For example, if a user is unable to access a specific website, the user might say, "The Internet is down." It's highly unlikely the entire Internet has failed, so this is where the technician's communication skills become important to understand the real issue.

This step includes the following four items:

- Gathering information
- Identifying symptoms
- Determining if anything has changed
- Questioning users

These items aren't necessarily done in order and are often combined with each other. For example, you might question a user to gather more information.

Gathering Information

Within this step, you gather information on the problem from all available sources. If a user reports the problem, you start by documenting what the user reports. If it's a network problem, you might verify that there aren't other known network issues causing the problem for everyone.

Identifying Symptoms

A key step when identifying a problem is identifying the symptoms. The goal is to ensure that you can repeat the symptom so that you're able to verify later that the problem is solved. For example, if a user states that he can't open an application, you would identify what happens when the user tries to open the application. Sometimes users start applications with shortcuts, so you might try to start the application via the shortcut and via other methods. If the application starts with other methods, but not with the shortcut, this helps you identify that the problem is with the shortcut.

Determining if Anything Has Changed

Many problems are caused by changes, so it's important to determine if there have been any recent changes to the system. For example, a system might start having problems right after a user responded to a spam email by inadvertently clicking on a malicious link. Similarly, a system might have problems starting after an update.

Many updates are sent to systems automatically, so the user might not be aware of the update. However, updates are often predictable. For example, Microsoft sends out patches to systems on **Patch Tuesday** in North America. Patch Tuesday is the second Tuesday of every month. Technicians should be aware of when updates are sent to systems so that they can easily determine if systems have recently been updated.

> **ON THE SIDE:**   Many organizations control the deployment of patches to systems. They often test patches before deploying them, so they might use a different schedule than the second Tuesday of every month. Also, Microsoft sometimes releases out-of-band patches on days other the second Tuesday of the month when they determine that a critical patch needs to be released sooner.

Questioning Users

Questioning users is an extremely important skill for help desk professionals. The goal is to ask questions so that you can get more information on the problem and effective questioning skills are essential. Chapter 2, "Communication Skills," presented information on open-ended questions. As a reminder, an open-ended question is any question that cannot be answered with just a one- or two-word response such as "Yes" or "No."

Some technicians view users as adversaries rather than as collaborators. They expect problems when working with users and this often comes out in their questions. Other times, technicians use poor questioning techniques, creating an adversarial relationship, but they're unaware they've caused the problems. However, when technicians view the relationship with the user as a collaboration where both parties want to solve the problem, the process is normally much easier.

As an example, a user might have made a change to the system but might not recognize this change caused the problem. If a technician asks something like, "What have you changed recently?" or "What have you done to the system?," it can easily put the user on the defensive. On the other hand, using open-ended questions such as, "What symptoms are you seeing?" and, "Can you explain the problem?" gives the user an opportunity to explain the problem without feeling attacked.

Establishing a Theory of Probable Cause

Once you've identified relevant symptoms, the next step is to establish a theory of what caused these symptoms. This is simply making an educated guess. For example, if a user is unable to access a specific website, it could be due to one of the following issues:

- Website is down
- Computer doesn't have Internet access

Either one of these theories could be causing the problem based on the symptom. However, if you have additional information, such as what the user can do, it narrows down the possibilities.

It's important at this point to question the obvious possibilities. Many problems are due to simple issues that can easily be solved, and by verifying these first, technicians help the users get their problem resolved quicker. As an example, if the monitor isn't displaying anything, the obvious reason is that it doesn't have power. If a user complains that a printer isn't working, it's worth asking if it ever worked. The problem might be that it was never installed correctly.

Testing the Theory to Determine the Cause

In this step, you check your theory to see if it is accurate. For example, if you suspect the user doesn't have Internet access, you can see if the user can access any websites. If the user cannot access any websites, it indicates your theory is correct. If the user can access other websites but is unable to access only one, it could be that there is an issue with that website.

Note that the process of establishing and testing a theory isn't complete at this point. Instead, you typically need to go through these two steps several times until you have sufficient information to resolve the problem. For example, if you determine that the user doesn't have any Internet access, you need to identify why. It might be that everyone in the organization has lost Internet access, and you might need to go back to the first step to gather more information and identify additional symptoms. It might be that only this user is affected because this user doesn't have any network connectivity.

Figure 6-1 shows a **flow chart** of the process. A flow chart is a diagram that represents an algorithm or process. You go through these steps until you can establish a plan of action to resolve the problem. For example, you could ultimately determine

ON THE SIDE:
Flow charts identify steps in a process. The diamond or rhombus-shaped symbols represent a decision point where the path varies based on the result.

that only the user's system has a problem and then discover that the user's network connection is disconnected. At that point, you can move on to establish a plan of action to resolve it.

FIGURE 6-1

Flow chart to identify the probable cause.

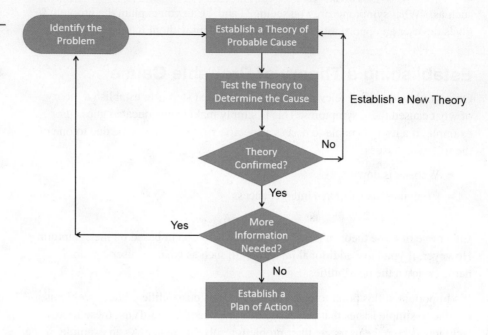

As an example, a technician might go through these steps before identifying the actual cause of the problem:

- **Theory: This user lost all Internet access.**
  Result after testing theory: True, the problem isn't related to a single website. The technician then attempts to establish a theory related to why the user lost all Internet access.

- **Theory: No one has Internet access.**
  Result after testing theory: False, other users have Internet access. The technician then attempts to establish a theory related to why only this user lost all Internet access.

- **Theory: This user doesn't have network access.**
  Result after testing theory: True, the user's system has no network access. The technician then attempts to establish a theory related to why the system doesn't have any network access.

- **Theory: Network interface card (NIC) disconnected.**
  Result after testing theory: True, the network cable is not connected to user's system. The technician can now establish a plan of action to solve the problem. In this case, the plan might be to plug the cable into the NIC.

For any single problem, it's common for technicians to go through these steps multiple times. Some theories might lead the technician to a dead end while others provide the technician with more information to continue troubleshooting. It's important to realize that even though a theory proves to be false, that doesn't mean the effort was wasted. The knowledge you gain through the process still brings you closer to identifying the cause.

> **ON THE SIDE:** Documentation is also important during these steps. As technicians verify what works and what doesn't, they add this to the ticket. This is useful if another technician might need to take over the problem later. It's also useful to determine if the symptoms change while troubleshooting the problem.

Understanding the Escalation Process

Chapter 1, "Introduction to Help Desk Support Roles," introduced IT tiers used within an organization. When technicians at tier 1 have run out of ideas and cannot come up with another theory of probable cause, they escalate the issue. This passes the problem to tier 2. If tier 2 technicians cannot resolve it, they escalate it to tier 3, and so on.

Figure 6-2 shows where escalation occurs when a technician has run out of new theories. Technicians would complete this loop of establishing and testing a theory multiple times until they either establish a plan of action or escalate the issue.

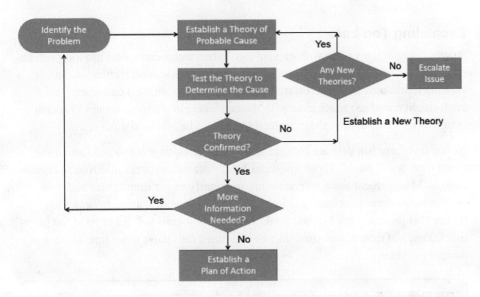

FIGURE 6-2

Flow chart showing escalation step.

Escalating Too Quickly

One of the help desk challenges occurs when technicians escalate the problem too quickly. For example, some lower-tier technicians get into the habit of escalating issues rather than trying to resolve them. This overloads upper-tier technicians with relatively simple problems.

One of the best ways to avoid this is to ensure help desk technicians have adequate training. This includes training them on basic troubleshooting steps along with training on the product(s) the technicians support. If technicians don't have the knowledge and expertise to resolve problems, they will escalate issues rather quickly.

Many organizations have specific procedures in place on what to do prior to escalating an issue. For example, they might have a checklist of potential failure points to check along with possible solutions. They require technicians to complete this checklist prior to escalating an issue.

One of the metrics organizations monitor when evaluating help desk performance is the number of escalations in relation to the number of received incidents. There isn't a perfect percentage that fits all organizations, but managers are aware of a target percentage. For example, one organization might have a target of 10 percent. In other words, if the help desk receives 100 incidents in a week, they will escalate 10 of them. If the percentage begins to trend higher, it indicates a problem that management needs to investigate.

In addition to monitoring the overall number of escalations, managers often monitor who is escalating incidents. On average, technicians would escalate approximately the same number of tickets. However, if a single technician is escalating most of the incidents, it indicates this technician might need additional training or guidance on when to escalate an issue.

Escalating Too Late

Another potential problem with escalation is when technicians wait too long before escalating an incident. If management puts a lot of pressure on technicians to escalate issues only as a last resort, it can result in a dissatisfied customer. Technicians might spend too much time with the customer. In contrast, if the technician escalates the issue earlier, the customer's issue can be resolved quicker.

Notice that there is a delicate balance here. How much time is too little and how much time is too much? Those questions have different answers in different organizations. Management has a responsibility to identify target timeframes and then communicate these timeframes to help desk technicians. It's also important to realize that these are just targets. Some complex problems will go beyond the target timeframe, and technicians shouldn't be penalized for taking more time on new or complex problems.

> **ON THE SIDE:** An organization often has specific guidelines on escalation based on how many users are affected. For example, if an outage is preventing 10 users from accessing Internet resources, technicians would escalate this rather quickly. The outage might be affecting more than these 10 users. However, technicians wouldn't need to spend time identifying everyone that is affected. When technicians notice the outage reaches a specific threshold, they escalate the issue.

It's important to realize that technicians working at the higher tiers have a significant amount of knowledge and expertise. In addition to solving problems quicker, they can also use escalated incidents as teaching opportunities for the tier 1 help desk technicians. Effective help desk managers strive to build a collaborative working relationships between the help desk technicians and technicians working at higher tiers.

Establishing a Plan of Action to Resolve the Problem

Once you have a clear idea of the probable cause, you can establish a plan of action to resolve it. This can be relatively simple or complex based on the problem. If the problem is that the network cable isn't connected, the plan of action is to connect it.

If everyone in the organization lost Internet access due to a failed router, the solution becomes more complex. If help desk personnel were responsible for the router, they would need to replace it and configure the new router with the same settings as the original.

Implementing the Solution or Escalating if Necessary

In this step, you implement the solution based on your plan of action. If your plan is to connect the network cable, that's what you do. When you've identified the problem and can resolve it, this step becomes rather simple. You implement your solution and verify it solved the problem.

As an example, if the problem was no network access, and you determined the solution was to plug in the network cable, you would verify the user had network access after you plugged the cable into the system. You could do this by verifying the user could access the website mentioned in the original report.

In many environments, simply plugging in the cable wouldn't resolve the problem immediately. Instead, the system might take as long as five minutes to obtain appropriate Internet Protocol (IP) addressing information from a Dynamic Host Configuration Protocol (DHCP) server within the network. This typically occurs automatically without anyone additional steps, but it does take time. Technicians can force this to happen immediately with specific commands, if they know what commands to enter. Similarly, a system restart would force the system to configure itself properly as part of the startup process.

However, the problem might still remain even after plugging the cable in. The cable could have a break in it. It might not be connected at the wall plug. Most networks include switches and the cable might not be connected at the switch, the physical port where the cable goes might be disabled, or the switch might have a fault. The key is that if the solution didn't resolve the problem, the technician needs to go back to establish a new theory.

ON THE SIDE:
Technicians familiar with NICs know that they have link lights. If the link lights are lit and blinking, it indicates the system is connected to the network and transmitting traffic. However, if the link lights are not lit, it indicates a fault.

Figure 6-3 shows a partial flow chart at this point. It's entirely possible that you might repeat these steps multiple times before the problem is completely resolved. For example, you might plug in the cable but realize the problem isn't resolved. Next, you realize the other end of the cable isn't plugged into the wall so you plug it in there, but it still doesn't resolve the problem. You might theorize the cable has a break in it so you replace it, and realize it has resolved the problem.

FIGURE 6-3

Flow chart after implementing solution.

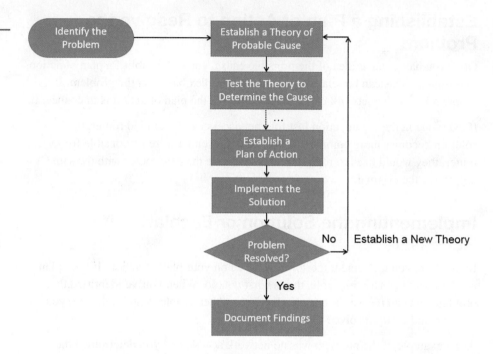

An important troubleshooting step that technicians need to consider is related to configuration changes they make while troubleshooting. If the change didn't resolve the problem, they should return the configuration setting to its original setting. If a technician goes through a system making a dozen different changes, it's highly likely that one or more of these changes will cause more problems. Even if they successfully solved the original problem, the system won't work properly due to the other changes they entered. On the other hand, if the technician consistently returns the configuration to its original setting, it is less likely that they'll cause problems.

> **ON THE SIDE:**   If you are absolutely sure a setting should be changed, then by all means change it even if it doesn't solve the current problem. Experienced technicians sometimes find that inexperienced technicians inserted problems into the system while troubleshooting, and they end up undoing these changes.

There may be times when you are unable to implement the solution. If that's the case, you escalate the issue. One of the primary reasons technicians escalate an issue at this level is due to a lack of privileges to resolve a problem. For example, if an authorized user is unable to access files on a server, the solution might be to change the file permissions. However, the help desk technician might not have elevated privileges to change the permissions. In this case, it's appropriate to escalate the issue.

> **ON THE SIDE:**   A challenge within organizations is the amount of privileges to give level I technicians. If these technicians have too many privileges, they can inadvertently cause damage and might be able to access sensitive data. Some organizations err on the side of security and significantly limit the privileges of help desk personnel. This forces these technicians to escalate almost all of the trouble calls. Over time, technicians recognize there are very few problems they can solve and they get into the habit of just documenting the ticket and then escalating it. This can negatively affect their motivation and desire to learn more.

Verifying Full System Functionality

In addition to verifying that the original problem is resolved, technicians should verify full system functionality. A key point is to ensure that the solution you implemented didn't cause another problem. As an obvious example, imagine that two computers were side by side and one had a problem with a network connection. You could remove the network cable from one computer and plug it into the other computer. While this might solve the problem in one computer, it creates a problem in the other computer. This isn't an acceptable solution.

Last, this step includes implementing preventive measures if necessary. This includes any type of preventive maintenance designed to help ensure the system operates properly. For example, if the original cables were laying on the floor, you might use cable ties or some other method to protect them. Similarly, if you were troubleshooting a computer and noticed that it had excessive dust inside it, you would clean it out to prevent heat damage.

As you read this, you can see that the steps are distinguishable from each other. However, in practice, experienced technicians often zip through these steps without giving them much thought. For example, a technician might come upon the problem, suspect the cable is disconnected, and plug it in. After plugging it in, the technician might notice the link lights on the NIC aren't displaying correctly and trace the cable to the wall noticing the other end isn't plugged in. While doing this, the technician isn't consciously thinking, "I need to establish a new theory." However, that is effectively what the technician is doing. The difference is that the technician has gone through these steps so many times that they are automatic.

You can compare this to driving a car. When you first learn to drive, you are very conscious of all the steps. You carefully put on your seat belt, ensure the mirrors are set correctly, check the seat adjustment, place your foot on the brake, start the car, and put it into gear. Each one of these steps is separate and distinct from the others. However, after driving for several years, you get into the car and are on your way in a flash. You still do all the steps, you just don't need to give them all your attention because they are automatic.

If you established good habits when you started to drive, these habits became ingrained in you and you continue to use them. Similarly, if technicians establish good habits when they start troubleshooting systems, these habits became a natural part of their troubleshooting skills. The key is to start with good troubleshooting habits rather than getting into the habit of trial and error troubleshooting without any real focus.

Documenting Findings, Actions, and Outcomes

After verifying the system is operating, you need to document the solution. Typically, you do this with an incident management system. You or someone else created a ticket when the user first reported the problem. At this point, you ensure the ticket accurately reflects the symptoms, and you add in what you found and how you solved the problem. For example, you might mention that the user lost network access due to a faulty cable. You replaced the cable and verified the system was now operating correctly.

The process you use is dependent on your organization and the incident management system in use. For example, one organization might want technicians to close the ticket immediately after documenting their findings. Another organization might want technicians to document their findings but not close the ticket; instead, supervisors close tickets after reviewing them.

Identifying the Root Cause

An important consideration when documenting an incident is to consider the root cause. In other words, the goal isn't to just resolve the problem but also to understand what caused it. Root cause analysis is the process of analyzing problems to determine the root cause.

Admittedly, this isn't possible for every single problem. There are times when software gremlins cause applications to misbehave and a quick reboot solves the problem. If this is the only time the user has experienced the problem, and a reboot resolved it, it is not necessary to spend an additional 30 minutes to analyze it. Trying to identify the root cause of every one of these problems is a sure path to insanity.

However, if a problem repeats, it is important to identify the root cause. For example, if a reboot solved a problem for a user before, but the user is reporting the same symptoms the next day, the technician should do more than just reboot the system—they should attempt to identify the root cause and implement a more permanent solution.

Preventing Future Problems

One of the primary reasons for identifying the root cause is to prevent future problems. If a problem repeats for the user, it takes up the user's time and energy and then results in a help desk call. Of course, an additional help desk call takes up more time and energy from help desk technicians.

Supervisors often initiate root cause analysis steps when they notice trends in the help desk incidents. They look for situations such as a string of incidents with the same symptoms. For example, imagine that the help desk is suddenly flooded with help desk calls saying that the audio on desktop systems stopped. Individual technicians might not notice this as a trend, but when supervisors review the incident logs, the trend might be readily apparent. The supervisor might assign a technician to investigate what changed just before these calls started. It could be that a recent Microsoft Windows update caused the problems. A temporary solution would be to remove the update and report the problem to Microsoft to identify why the update is breaking the audio. It could be the systems need an updated audio driver. More importantly, by identifying the root cause and taking action to resolve it, it eliminates help desk calls for the problem.

Once technicians identify the root cause, they can add the issue to the organization's knowledge base along with key symptoms. Now, when any technician recognizes these key symptoms, they'll be able to quickly resolve the problem.

Following Standard Operating Procedures (SOPs)

Organizations commonly have a set of rules or guidelines known as standard operating procedures (SOPs). SOPs are used for many purposes, including providing help desk personnel with information they can use to answer trouble calls. This includes scripts that technicians should use when talking to customers, such as how to greet the customer and what to say when ending the conversation. It can also include specific procedures to use when troubleshooting various problems.

Chapter 1 covered the steps in a typical incident process. Figure 6-4 shows these steps as a reminder. However, it's important to realize that these steps are not universal. Any organization might have a slightly different process based on their needs. An SOP manual would indicate specifically how the process works within an organization.

FIGURE 6-4

Typical steps in an incident process.

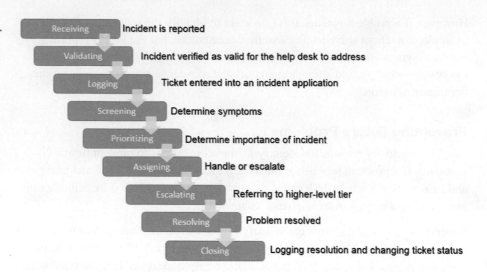

Receiving — Incident is reported

Validating — Incident verified as valid for the help desk to address

Logging — Ticket entered into an incident application

Screening — Determine symptoms

Prioritizing — Determine importance of incident

Assigning — Handle or escalate

Escalating — Referring to higher-level tier

Resolving — Problem resolved

Closing — Logging resolution and changing ticket status

Most organizations use some type of incident-tracking application. The SOP would include information on the application used within the organization. More specifically, it would give technicians guidance on what to do at each of these steps, including how to enter information into the application.

Using Troubleshooting Guides

Troubleshooting guides can be very valuable to technicians when troubleshooting problems. A troubleshooting guide documents the specific steps technicians should take to diagnose and resolve problems. Some organizations use a written document to create these guides and others use flow charts. The key is that technicians can use these guides to identify and resolve problems.

Using Written Guides

Written guides provide technicians with an informal description of the process and include key items to check. Based on the results of the checks, the guide then directs technicians on what action to take next. As an example, the following is an example of a written guide when an employee complains of an Internet connectivity problem:

1. **Can the system access any websites?**
   If no, go to step 2.
   If yes, go to step 100.

2. **Can the system access any internal network resources such as email?**
   If no, go to step 3.
   If yes, go to step 200.

3. **Is the LED light on the NIC lit?**
   If no, go to step 4.
   If yes, go to step 300.

4. **Is the NIC cable plugged in?**
   If no, plug it in and see if problem is resolved. If the problem is not resolved, go to step 5.

5. **Verify the cable doesn't have any breaks. If necessary, replace the cable. Did this resolve the problem?**
   If no, go to step 6.

> **ON THE SIDE:** This is only a partial example. A full guide would have more steps to complete this process, but all of the steps are omitted here for brevity. Many times the checks for troubleshooting are common, even when the symptoms are slightly different. In this example, the steps starting at 100, 200, and 300 could be the same steps used to troubleshoot different problems.

These steps lead the technician through the process of identifying symptoms and taking specific actions based on the findings. The actual steps in any troubleshooting guide can be quite extensive and specific, but do help the technician focus on relevant issues.

In some cases, there are very specific errors caused by known issues. For example, an application might consistently crash logging error code 0x5B4D due to a corrupt file. When a technician verifies the application is giving this error code, they can then use the troubleshooting guide to determine what to do. If the error code is documented in the troubleshooting guide, it can lead the technician through the steps to resolve the problem.

Using Flow Charts

Some troubleshooting guides use flow charts to identify symptoms and troubleshoot problems. They provide a graphical representation of the issue and lead the technician through a series of steps. These steps can be exactly the same steps mentioned in the written guides, but flow charts are sometimes easier to follow.

Figure 6-5 shows some of the common symbols used in a flow chart. Arrows show the direction of the flow chart.

FIGURE 6-5

Flow chart symbols.

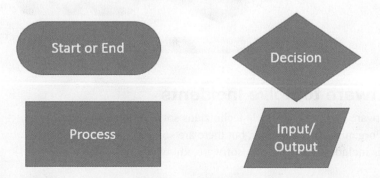

- An oval represents a start or end point
- A rectangle represents a process
- A diamond or rhombus represents a decision
- A parallelogram represents input and output

As an example, Figure 6-6 partially represents some of the same steps mentioned in the written troubleshooting guide. One obvious difference is that flow charts take up much more paper space. Troubleshooting guides can be quite extensive, and a guide using flow charts can be quite large.

> **ON THE SIDE:**   In addition to taking up a lot of space, flow charts are also very time consuming to create. From a business perspective, time is money, so they aren't used that often. When technology stands still, it sometimes makes sense to use them because they are very useful tools for technicians. However, when the technology changes, the flow charts often need to be changed too. Many organizations simply don't consider them worth investing in only to have them out of date when another change occurs. In contrast, a written guide is much easier to update.

FIGURE 6-6

Flow chart troubleshooting guide.

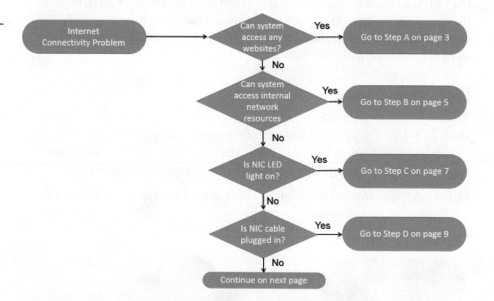

Using Software to Solve Incidents

Many times software is available to help technicians solve problems. The software varies from one organization to another, but there are some common categories of software. This includes remote access software, knowledge bases, and expert systems.

Accessing Systems Remotely

Remote access software allows technicians to remotely connect to systems and configure the operating system and applications. Many times, the technicians can control the remote system while the user observes the technician's actions. This allows technicians to provide training to the user on how the problem is resolved.

Imagine an employee at Home Depot is assisting a customer ordering kitchen cabinets. The employee uses an application to order them but the application is not allowing him to complete the order. The solution might be something as simple as ensuring a checkbox is checked early in the ordering process, but the employee is unaware of this requirement. Instead, the employee calls the Home Depot help desk and asks for assistance. The help desk technician can remotely connect to the employee's computer. Once connected, the technician can ask the employee to show him the steps and talk to him while the employee completes the process. When the technician notices that the appropriate box isn't being checked, he can let the employee know to check it. Alternately, the technician can take control of the employee's computer and lead him through the steps to complete the order.

Windows Remote Assistance is an available option on Microsoft systems. Users can request assistance using Windows Remote Assistance using an invitation. Once invited, technicians can connect to the user's system. This allows the technician to view the user's desktop. If the user grants permission, the technician can take control of the mouse and keyboard to configure the system or show the user how to complete an action. Windows Remote Assistance includes a chat window so that the two people can communicate via chat if they aren't connected over the phone. Also, the technician can transfer files to the user's computer, as long as the user approves the transfer.

Microsoft's Remote Desktop also supports remote connections. Technicians with appropriate permissions are able to use the Remote Desktop Connection application to connect to the user's system. This is useful when connecting to remote systems to configure them. Once connected, the technician has full control over the computer and can do almost anything as if the technician was sitting in front of the computer. A drawback with this is that when the technician connects, the user is not able to see what the technician is doing. However, this tool is very useful if the user doesn't need to see the activity.

ON THE SIDE:
Systems must be properly configured to allow remote desktop connections. These connection settings are disabled by default.

There are dozens of applications that support remote connections. Virtual Network Computing (VNC) includes a full family of remote access applications. UltraVNC is one of the most popular of these. It is an open source application so it is freely available. The technician can take control of the user's computer similar to how technicians can do so with Windows Remote Assistance. It also includes a chat window and the ability to transfer files.

One of the benefits of the non-Microsoft versions is that systems can be configured to support remote connections without the user initiating invitations. The process of sending a Windows Remote Assistance invitation is challenging for some users, especially when they are already frustrated with another problem. However, with some of the non-Microsoft versions, the technician can connect to the user's system remotely, without any action from the user. This also presents some security issues. Organizations do not want unauthorized users remotely connecting to computers.

Troubleshooting with Knowledge Bases

One of the key pieces of software that most help desks have available to them is a **knowledge base**. A knowledge base is a store of information that is readily available for technicians. IT-based knowledge bases often include information technicians use when troubleshooting. It would typically include symptoms and solutions for various problems, along with any related tutorials or procedures.

Most incident-tracking applications include a searchable database. Technicians can enter in keywords based on the symptoms or error codes they see. The application searches the database and returns a listing of relevant items. In many cases, the application can provide the technician with a listing of specific incidents that had similar symptoms or error codes. By browsing through these incidents, the technician can learn how other technicians solved similar problems.

The value of these applications is directly proportional to how accurately technicians enter data into them. When technicians enter clear symptoms and solutions, it is very useful to other technicians. However, if technicians don't take the time to adequately document the problem, or the steps they used to resolve it, the entries aren't valuable. Instead, future technicians must go through the troubleshooting process as if the entry didn't exist at all.

Using Expert Systems

An expert system attempts to emulate the decision-making skills of a human expert. They are sometimes referred to as artificial intelligence (AI) because the software appears to have a level of intelligence derived from a computer system. The goal for an expert system is to be able to solve one or more complex problems using a knowledge base and a group of rules.

Expert systems can be used to solve some computer problems and many are in use today. Some expert systems used within support centers are accessible online. Users can access a web page over the Internet and then answer a series of questions. These questions are similar to the yes and no questions in a flow chart. The difference is that the customer is doing all of the interaction to answer these questions. The web page displays a question, and waits for the customer to enter the answer. Another web page appears based on the customer's answer.

As an example, Vanguard Software Corporation has been selling decision support analysis systems since 1995. They currently sell the Vanguard Knowledge Automation System, which can be adapted to help desks. Some of the capabilities include:

ON THE SIDE:
It's also possible to create these systems so that they are accessible only within an intranet. Employees can access the system, but it is not accessible from the Internet.

- **Call center support.** Technicians can use this when assisting customers. It helps the technicians know what to ask the customer and what to do next based on the answer.
- **Web self-service.** Customers are able to use these for guided troubleshooting, diagnosis assistance, and debugging. The benefit is that the customers are able to do all the work on their own.

This system combines the strengths of a **content management system (CMS)** with rules that experts can easily enter into the system. The system guides users through a series of questions, applies the rules based on their answers, and provides the users with relevant content.

A CMS is an application used to manage the content on a website. For example, many blogs use WordPress as a CMS. For most activities, WordPress is as easy to use as Microsoft Word. Content managers can post the content through WordPress and WordPress handles the delivery of the content to users. It also includes a search engine so that users can search for specific content.

Within the Vanguard Knowledge Automation System, experts are able to collaborate to add content into the CMS. Additionally, experts are able to use the Vanguard Studio to create the rules used within the expert system. One of the benefits of this system is that it is relatively easy to manipulate. If an organization has either written troubleshooting guides or flow charts, that information can easily be entered into the system. However, if the organization doesn't have trouble-shooting guides available, it can be difficult to enter all the rules into the system from scratch. These are the same benefits and challenges with any expert systems.

As an example, consider computer-based chess games. It's estimated that chess originated in the 6th century, so there is a wealth of information on it. However, it wasn't a simple matter to enter all this information into computer applications that could play chess. The first game was created in 1978. It was enjoyable for amateurs but no match for experts. It took almost 20 years for enough information to be entered into computer applications for a computer to be able to beat a master. IBM developed a chess-playing computer named Deep Blue, which won one game in a tournament against chess master Garry Kasparov in 1996. The next year, Deep Blue won the match against master Garry Kasparov.

Most expert systems don't have the benefit of addressing a single challenge such as winning chess games. Additionally, they don't have centuries of accumulated knowledge on the systems they need to support. While they can be useful in many situations, they can't be depended on to solve all of the problems that technicians and users face. Just as some of the early computer-based chess games sometimes led the computer into unwinnable situations, expert systems can sometimes lead technicians to the wrong conclusions. Technicians need to have additional skills they can use when troubleshooting and not depend on expert systems to give them all the answers.

Understanding Problem-Solving Skills

Problem-solving skills include a group of different types of thinking to resolve issues. It's impossible to document all possible problems before they appear. In many situations, technicians have only minimal external resources they can use when troubleshooting. Instead, successful technicians need to utilize a variety of skills to resolve problems as they appear. These include critical thinking skills, the ability to employ different thinking methods, and the ability to make decisions.

Critical Thinking Skills

When new or different problems appear, successful technicians use critical thinking skills to identify the symptoms and resolve the problem. **Critical thinking** is a broad topic that applies to several disciplines such as science, mathematics, history, economics, and philosophy, and many colleges and universities include critical thinking courses to help students develop these skills. It includes the ability to use your personal experience, logical thought processes, and creativity to analyze and evaluate situations. Further, critical thinking allows you to use the information gathered to reach a conclusion or answer.

As a simple example, consider this statement: Joe is over 60 inches tall so he is tall. In this example, the fact indicates that Joe is 60 inches tall and the conclusion is that he is tall. However, is this accurate?

By evaluating the sentence critically, you realize you need to identify the definition of *tall*. If Joe lives in a jungle with a group of short pygmies, than yes, 60 inches is tall. However, the statement is false if Joe lives in an area where most men are 68 inches or taller. Of course, this also depends on Joe's age. It's easy to assume Joe is a man, but what if he is a child of six years. A six-year old child over 60 inches tall is indeed tall anywhere in the world.

As a technical example, consider this statement related to a computer: The computer is plugged in so it has power. In this example, the fact indicates that the computer is plugged in and the conclusion is that it has power. Is this true?

Clearly, there isn't enough information. Simply stating that the computer is plugged in doesn't give enough information to conclude that the system has power. It might be plugged into a surge protector that is not connected to a power outlet. Also, the surge protector might be turned off or faulty. The computer might be plugged into a wall outlet that is faulty. The computer might be plugged in to a good power source, but the power switch might be off.

In contrast, consider this statement: The computer power LED is lit so the computer has power. In this example, the fact indicates that the power LED is lit and the conclusion is that it has power. Is this true?

You can logically think about all the elements needed to illuminate the power LED. The computer needs to be plugged into a live power outlet and turned on. In this example, it is logical to conclude that the computer has power.

Critical thinking typically includes the following activities:

- **Actively thinking about the issue.** In each of the previous examples, it takes some thought to evaluate the statement and the conclusion. Similarly, technicians using critical thinking skills take the time to think about the problem to explore all of the symptoms and identify possible solutions.

- **Asking questions.** Philosophers and scholars since Euripides at around 480 BC have been advising people to question everything—not to be argumentative but instead to understand. When troubleshooting a problem, successful technicians often ask themselves questions about the problem and then seek the answer.

- **Analyzing and evaluating evidence and symptoms.** As you troubleshoot a problem, you will gather facts related to the symptoms. Technicians need to evaluate each of these symptoms in the context of the problem at hand.

- **Seeking different perspectives.** Many times, you can easily solve a problem just by looking at it from a different perspective. This requires the ability to step back from the problem and look at it in a different way. Another way of thinking about this is to use creativity to find a different solution.

> **ON THE SIDE:** Critical thinking is a skill and as with other skills, you can improve it. This page outlines nine strategies to improve your critical thinking abilities in everyday life: https://www.criticalthinking.org/pages/critical-thinking-in-everyday-life-9-strategies/512. As a simple example, you can end every day with a short review by asking and answering some simple questions such as: "If I had to repeat today, what would I do differently?" and, "Is there something that I could have done differently today to be more productive, more creative, or a better friend?"

Critical thinking is one of the skills that will help you succeed as a help desk specialist and in many other career paths. Some basics related to critical thinking that are especially useful when troubleshooting problems are:

- **Be open-minded and aware of alternatives.** There is often more than one way to solve a problem. Similarly, there is often more than one way to troubleshoot any given problem. Successful technicians often learn different methods of troubleshooting and adopt their knowledge to the problem at hand.

- **Constantly learn.** IT is constantly changing so IT professionals need to take time to learn about new products and services. Many professions require professionals to earn continuing education credits by attending classes or seminars. Similarly, many technical certifications require certified individuals to earn continuing education credits to maintain their certification.

- **Weigh the credibility of sources.** Not all information sources have the same credibility. For example, just because something is published on the Internet doesn't mean it's true. It doesn't take very long to find examples of web pages that include obvious factual errors. One method that investigative reporters often use is to verify facts from multiple sources they know to be reliable. Technicians can use the same procedure. They should attempt to verify stated facts from little known sources with reliable sources. There are multiple reliable sources on the Internet and elsewhere. For example, the Microsoft Knowledge Base is a reliable source when troubleshooting Microsoft issues. Similarly, an in-house troubleshooting guide is likely to be highly reliable.

- **Ask clarifying questions.** If something isn't clear, ask appropriate questions to clarify the issue. You might ask these questions to a user. In other situations, they might be questions that come to mind for yourself and you realize the answer will clarify the problem or the solution. If the questions come to mind for yourself, you can often investigate on your own to get the answers. If the answer still isn't clear, you can often get clarifying answers from experienced technicians.

- **Establish realistic theories and test them.** Theories are based on evidence and when troubleshooting, your available evidence is the problem symptoms. In other words, theories should be based on the symptoms. By testing the theory, you confirm or deny its validity. You do not want to implement a solution for a false theory because the problem will remain. Remember, you bring yourself closer to a solution each time you confirm or deny a theory. Do not consider it a failure when you prove a theory to be false.

- **Identify your conclusions, reasons, and assumptions.** When you make a conclusion, be aware of what led you to it. If your reasons and assumptions for the conclusion are faulty, your conclusion is likely to be faulty too. For example, the earlier example "Joe is over 60 inches tall so he is tall" came to a conclusion based on an unclear statement. If your conclusion is based on inaccurate or incomplete statements, you can't depend on the conclusion.

Types of Thinking

When troubleshooting, it's often valuable to use different types of thinking based on the problem at hand. In some situations, it's best to approach a problem from a linear perspective, following steps in order. However, in other situations, it's better to employ creative thinking skills to solve a problem.

An effective aptitude test for a potential IT professional is to see if the person can follow directions. Following directions using linear thinking is an on-the-job skill needed in many different situations, such as when installing or upgrading software applications. However, it can be extremely challenging for some people. They skip steps and get frustrated when things don't work. They combine steps in their mind and then have problems completing them, without understanding why. Successful technicians are able to follow the directions exactly.

> **AUTHOR'S NOTE:** When teaching IT classes, I have frequently come across students that have problems following lab directions. For example, they complain that step 5 isn't working. After checking, it becomes obvious they haven't completed step 4. I often give them an index card to cover up future steps until they complete the current step and this helps. These people have a high level of intelligence. They just have some trouble with tasks requiring linear thinking, and there are ways to overcome it if they decide to pursue a career in IT. On the other hand, they might find it easier to excel in another job that requires creative skills.

Even if you can easily follow the directions, you'll find that many troubleshooting problems require thought beyond what the directions provide. In these cases, it's important for technicians to identify a creative solution that isn't readily apparent. This is part of the critical thinking process where the technician attempts to look at the problem from a different perspective.

As an example of using a different perspective, consider Figure 6-7. Imagine that each of these 24 lines are toothpicks. Remove eight toothpicks to leave exactly two squares. Many times people want more information, but this is all you need: remove eight toothpicks to leave exactly two squares.

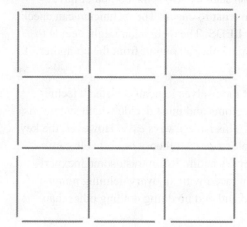

FIGURE 6-7

Toothpick challenge.

The natural inclination is to view this as nine squares all of the same size. However, if you keep that perspective, it is not possible to solve this challenge. Instead, you need to look at it from a different perspective.

Here's a hint. How many total squares do you see in Figure 6-7? The answer is 14.

Figure 6-8 shows that there are nine 1x1 squares, one 3x3 square, and four 2x2 squares. Once you look at this as more than just nine 1x1 squares, it becomes simpler to solve the challenge.

FIGURE 6-8

Counting the squares.

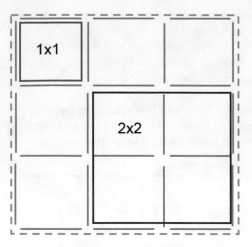

If the solution to this challenge still isn't clear, check out Figure 6-9 at the end of this chapter for two possible solutions.

Making Decisions

The ability to make decisions is a key part of troubleshooting. While troubleshooting any single problem, a technician often needs to make multiple decisions based on the symptoms. A simple question such as "Does the computer have power?" requires the technician to decide what to check. The technician can check power plugs, power switches, and power LEDS. The technician might decide to first verify the monitor has power and can display an output from the computer. If it does, none of the other checks are necessary.

Computer problems don't always present themselves logically. Instead, technicians often see a barrage of different symptoms and must decide which symptoms are most relevant to the problem at hand. This isn't always easy. However, the key is that technicians use all of their skills to decide on a theory of probable cause and then test it. If that theory is false, they try again. In contrast, some inexperienced technicians sometimes freeze when faced with an overwhelming number of symptoms. They are unsure what to do and end up doing nothing other than continue to collect more symptoms.

Chapter 2 devoted a full chapter on communication skills. These are instrumental when talking to users to get the most information. However, the user perspective isn't always the most important, so technicians must evaluate the information they receive to identify what is most relevant. As a simple example, a user might complain that he is unable to access email. When the technician looks at the computer, he sees that the computer doesn't appear to have power. What is the most relevant symptom? The user might use his computer only to access email. From his perspective, this was the most important symptom. He can no longer use it to do so. However, from a troubleshooting perspective, the most important symptom is a lack of power.

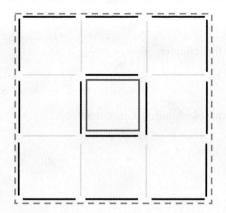 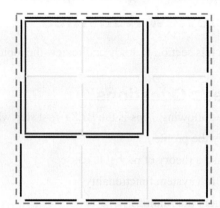

FIGURE 6-9

Toothpick challenge solution.

Chapter Review Activities

Use the features in this section to study and review the topics in this chapter.

Answer These Questions

1. Which of the following steps is the BEST first step when troubleshooting a problem?

    a. Identify the problem

    b. Establish a theory of probable cause

    c. Verify full system functionality

    d. Document the findings

2. Which of the following actions is NOT a typical step when identifying a problem?

    a. Identifying symptoms

    b. Determining if anything has changed

    c. Questioning users

    d. Checking the knowledge base for tickets from this user

3. Which of the following questions would be BEST when questioning users to gather information on a problem?

    a. What did you do?

    b. Can you explain the problem?

    c. Is it working now?

    d. What have you changed recently?

4. What should a technician do after establishing a theory of probable cause for a problem?

    a. Identify the problem

    b. Test the theory

    c. Establish a plan of action

    d. Document the findings

5. Which of the following are valid reasons to escalate an issue? (Choose TWO.)

    a. The technician has spent more than 30 minutes with the customer.

    b. The technician has run out of ideas of possible causes.

    c. The technician doesn't have adequate permissions to resolve the problem.

    d. The technician's shift is ending.

6. Of the following choices, what is the PRIMARY drawback from escalating an issue too quickly?

   a. Overloads level I technicians

   b. Overloads level II technicians

   c. Adds to the overall help desk workload

   d. Is a disservice to the customer

7. Of the following choices, what is the PRIMARY drawback from escalating an issue too slowly?

   a. Overloads level I technicians

   b. Overloads level II technicians

   c. Reduces costs

   d. Is a disservice to the customer

8. A technician implemented a solution but found that it didn't resolve the problem. What should the technician do next?

   a. Escalate the issue

   b. Test another theory

   c. Establish another theory

   d. Document findings

9. When verifying full system functionality, what else should a technician do?

   a. Perform preventive maintenance measures, if necessary

   b. Gather information

   c. Cancel the escalation

   d. Update the troubleshooting guide

10. Of the following choices, what is the PRIMARY benefit of identifying the root cause of a problem?

   a. It increases the help desk workload

   b. It helps technicians resolve more tickets

   c. It helps prevent future problems

   d. It helps very full system functionality

11. What is the primary purpose of a troubleshooting guide included within an SOP document?

   a. Give technicians the scripts to use when talking to customers

   b. Help technicians resolve problems

   c. Help technicians identify symptoms

   d. Provide a listing of all known problems

12. How is a decision represented in a flow chart?

    a. Parallelogram

    b. Oval

    c. Rectangle

    d. Diamond

13. What are the primary drawbacks of using flow charts for troubleshooting guides? (Choose TWO.)

    a. Too time consuming to follow

    b. Too time consuming to create

    c. Takes up a lot of paper space

    d. Difficult to create from a written troubleshooting guide

14. What can a technician use to show a remote user how to perform a task?

    a. Knowledge base

    b. Expert system

    c. Troubleshooting guide

    d. Remote access software

15. What is a PRIMARY benefit of documenting findings when closing an incident?

    a. The information is available in the knowledge base.

    b. Supervisors can verify the work.

    c. It shows the writing skills of the technician.

    d. It identifies the root cause of a problem.

16. Of the following choices, what is a user most likely to see within an expert system?

    a. A CMS

    b. Flow charts

    c. Directions on documenting an incident

    d. A listing a new problems

17. Which of the following is NOT one of the primary drawbacks of expert systems?

    a. Difficult to enter all the rules

    b. Can sometimes lead technicians to the wrong conclusions

    c. They can only focus on a single problem

    d. Time consuming to create the content for the CMS

18. Which of the following is not part of critical thinking skills?

    a. Asking questions

    b. Analyzing and evaluating symptoms

    c. Seeking different perspectives

    d. Accepting conclusions

19. Individuals use a variety of different actions when using and improving critical thinking skills. Which of the following is NOT one of those actions?

    a. Be open-minded and aware of alternatives

    b. Weigh the credibility of sources

    c. Avoid reevaluating facts after you have come to a conclusion

    d. Ask clarifying questions

20. What type of thinking is most useful when troubleshooting problems?

    a. Linear thinking

    b. Creative thinking

    c. Logical thinking

    d. A combination of the different thinking styles

Answers and Explanations

1. **a.** The first step when troubleshooting is to identify the problem. Once you identify the problem, you can establish a theory of probable cause. After implementing a solution, you would verify full system functionality. The last step is to document the findings.

2. **d.** It is not necessary to check a knowledge base for previous tickets from a particular user when identifying a problem. The other answers are common actions to take when identifying a problem.

3. **b.** Open-ended questions such as "Can you explain the problem?" are useful, especially when they are asked in a non-threatening manner. Asking the user what they did or what they changed implies they caused the problem and can discourage them from being collaborators. Closed-ended questions such as, "Is it working now?" allows the user to answer the question with a yes or no and doesn't give much information.

4. **b.** The technician should test the theory after establishing it. The first step is to identify the problem. Technicians establish a plan of action after testing a theory. The last step is to document the findings.

5. **b, c.** The two valid reasons to escalate an issue is when the technician has run out of ideas of possible causes or the technician doesn't have adequate permissions to resolve a problem. The acceptable amount of time to spend with a customer varies in different organizations. Most organizations have procedures to handle what technicians should do when their shift ends. The technician might work overtime, another technician might take over the problem, or the problem might be left alone until the next day.

6. **b.** A primary drawback of escalating issues too quickly is that it overloads upper-level technicians, and the first level beyond the help desk is level II. The help desk is primarily level I so escalating the issue to does not add to the help desk workload. The customer will likely be helped quickly when an issue is escalated so this does not indicate a disservice to the customer.

7. **d.** The primary drawback of taking too much time before escalating an issue is that it is a disservice to the customer. Technicians should be willing and able to escalate the issue when the problem exceeds their expertise. Taking a long time before escalating the issue reduces level II workload. This does not reduce costs and if it did, it wouldn't be a drawback.

8. **c.** If the implemented solution didn't resolve the problem, the technician should establish another theory and go through the steps again. The technician should not escalate the issue until they run out of theories. You can't test another theory until you establish a new one. Documenting findings is the last step.

9. **a.** Many times while troubleshooting a system, it becomes obvious that preventative maintenance measures are needed and these should be done before returning the system to the user. Gathering information is done first. There isn't any indication the incident was escalated so you wouldn't cancel the escalation. Also, there isn't any indication existing troubleshooting guides need to be updated.

10. **c.** You can help prevent future problems by identifying the root cause of a problem. This does not increase the help desk workload or help technicians resolve more tickets, but it can reduce the workload and help technicians resolve tickets related to the problem quicker. It is not associated with verifying full system functionality.

11. **b.** The primary purpose of a troubleshooting guide is to help technicians resolve problems. An SOP will often include scripts such as how to greet a customer or what to say when ending the conversation, but that isn't the primary purpose of the SOP. Technicians need to identify symptoms on their own. A troubleshooting guide will rarely be able to list all known problems.

12. **d.** Diamonds are used to represent decision points in flow charts. An oval represents a start or end point. A rectangle represents a process. A parallelogram represents input and output.

13. **b, c.** The two primary drawbacks of troubleshooting guide flow charts is that they are time consuming to follow and they take up a lot of paper space. When created, they are rather easy to follow. Flow charts are relatively easy to create if a written troubleshooting guide is available.

14. **d.** Technicians can use remote access software to show users how to perform a task from a remote location. Technicians connect into the user's system and take control of it to demonstrate actions. Knowledge bases, expert systems, and troubleshooting guides do not include remote connectivity software.

15. **a.** Most incident-tracking applications include a search ability so documentation is included in the knowledge base. Technicians can search the knowledge base to get information on previously solved problems. Supervisors can use this to verify the work, but that isn't a requirement. Also, the documentation can demonstrate the writing skills of a technician but that isn't the purpose. The documentation doesn't always identify the root cause of a problem.

16. **a.** A content management system (CMS) is included within many expert systems and it allows users and technicians to search for solutions. Expert systems might be developed with flow charts, but these are not apparent to the users. A CMS will often include incident documentation, but the expert system wouldn't typically include directions on how to document an incident. Expert systems are often difficult to update, so new problems wouldn't be included right away.

17. **c.** Expert systems can focus on more than one problems. All of the other answers do correctly identify the primary drawbacks of expert systems.

18. **d.** Accepting conclusions without analyzing the facts is not a part of critical thinking. Actively thinking about an issue to draw a conclusion is part of critical thinking as are the other distractors.

19. **c.** You should identify the reasons and assumptions that brought you to a conclusion, and if you determine that these are faulty, you should reevaluate your conclusion. The other statements are common activities associated with using and improving critical thinking skills.

20. **d.** A combination of different thinking styles is needed when troubleshooting problems. Critical thinking might be considered the most important, but it wasn't listed. Any individual problem might need linear thinking, creative thinking, or logical thinking styles.

Define the Key Terms

The following key terms include the ideas most important to the big ideas in this chapter. To review, without looking at the book or your notes, write a definition for each term, focusing on the meaning, not the wording. Then review your definition compared to your notes, this chapter, and the glossary.

Key Terms for Chapter 6

content management system (CMS)	critical thinking	knowledge base
	flow chart	Patch Tuesday

List the Words Inside Acronyms

The following are the most common acronyms discussed in this chapter. As a way to review those terms, simply write down the words that each letter represents in each acronym.

Acronyms for Chapter 6

AI	CMS

Create Mind Maps

For this chapter, create a mind map as follows:

1. Create a mind map to list different the steps in a typical troubleshooting process. Attempt to list the steps in order and add notes on each step.

Case Studies

Case Study 1

Create a flow chart to verify a computer and monitor both have power. The symptom is that nothing is displayed on the screen. The flow chart should lead the technician through the process of verifying all sources of power for both.

Case Study 2

Use Figure 6-7 in this chapter to arrange 24 toothpicks. Remove four toothpicks to leave exactly five squares. Reassemble the toothpicks and remove four toothpicks to leave nine squares.

Chapter 7

Writing Skills

Effective writing is an important skill for help desk specialists. At the very least, they need to enter information into an incident-tracking application when documenting help desk incidents. Beyond basic incident management, they will often create documents for customers and other help desk specialists. Additionally, with so many technology-based support capabilities such as email, instant messaging, and chat windows, they will often communicate with customers using text. Technicians that can't write effectively find it more difficult to help customers. Worse, when technicians can't communicate with customers using text, it reflects poorly on the overall organizations.

This chapter includes four major sections:

- The first section, "Comparing Writing Styles," introduces the four primary writing styles: expository, persuasive, descriptive, and narrative. It describes some of the formal style sheets that writers need to follow for different types of documents. This section also includes some general tips and hints on writing effective documents.

- Next, the "Understanding Technical Writing" section focuses on writing technical documents. In this section, you'll learn the process many technical documents go through from initial idea to a completed document.

- The "Writing for Customers" section covers many of the specific types of documents that you might create when writing for customers. This includes web pages, frequently asked questions, tutorials, white papers, and more. You'll also learn about a basic rule called 3-30-3 you can use to help ensure these documents are effective.

- Last, the "Writing for Internal Personnel" section covers some of the documents you might create for internal employees. This section also discusses how organizations use information entered into incident management systems as a knowledge base.

Chapter Outline

Objectives

- List and compare the four primary writing styles
- Describe the differences between technical writing and persuasive writing
- Compare and contrast the differences between active and passive writing
- Describe the differences between similes and metaphors used in analogies
- Discuss an alternative to using the phrase he/she in writing
- Summarize the writing process for a white paper from beginning to end
- Describe the primary purpose of technical editing
- List the five C's of copy editing

- Explain the benefits of listing prerequisites in a technical document
- Summarize the meaning of the 3-30-3 rule
- Describe one of the primary benefits of a FAQ page
- Discuss one or more common mistakes to avoid when writing tutorials
- Summarize techniques you can use to create useful white papers
- Discuss the similarities between writing for customers and writing for internal users
- Describe how people within an organization use a knowledge base
- Explain how technical writing applies to documenting incidents

Key Terms

active writing

analogy

expository writing

frequently asked questions (FAQs)

knowledge base

passive writing

persuasive writing

technical writing

white paper

Comparing Writing Styles

There are many different writing styles. The four most often cited are expository, persuasive, descriptive, and narrative styles. Additionally, there are many styles within these.

Expository writing focuses on a topic or subject and omits the opinions of the author. Academic papers such as essays and research papers use this style. Organizations follow this style in memorandums and other official communications between employees. It focuses on facts and often attempts to provide the reader with a conclusion based on these facts.

Technical writing is a form of expository writing. It's used to inform or teach the reader about a subject. It typically includes facts and will often explain how to perform tasks and procedures.

Persuasive writing is similar to technical writing in that it includes facts. However, it also includes opinions and justifications from the author. It attempts to convince the reader of a specific point of view. Authors often use the persuasive writing style in marketing materials, including many white papers. Skilled authors include subtle marketing within white papers, guiding the reader to a conclusion related to a company product or service, without making it obvious.

Descriptive and narrative writing are used in fiction and can be poetic in nature. Descriptive writing describes people, places, and events. Authors often attempt to appeal to your senses in descriptive writing. Authors put themselves into the story with narrative writing as they describe people and events from the perspective of a character.

While these give you some generic ideas of different styles, it certainly doesn't cover all of them. Many documents combine different styles. For example, historical novels intertwine fictional characters with facts from historical events. They entertain and teach at the same time.

> **ON THE SIDE:**
> *Path of a Patriot: The Die is Now Cast, 1772-1774* by Selena Joy Layden is an example of a historical novel. The main character is fictional but interacts with many well-known historical figures in Colonial America.

If you've read any technical documents, you might have noticed that some have different styles than others. They are still technical in nature, but they are approached from a slightly different perspective. For example, some documents such as white papers take on a very serious tone. In contrast, the *For Dummies* series of books uses humor with a goal of being irreverent without distracting readers from primary teaching points. Some books use high-level language appropriate for graduate students. Other books use language written at the 10th-grade level. None of these styles is wrong. The point is that even within the technical writing style, there are many possible variations.

Official style documents for technical writing include the *Chicago Manual of Style* (CMS), the *AP Stylebook*, and the *MLA Style Manual*. These guides provide standardized rules and guidelines for different types of documents, such as how to use citations, footnotes, and endnotes. They show consistent ways to present numbers, such as 9, nine, 10, or ten.

Notice that these styles omit the American Psychological Association (APA) style guide taught and used in academic institutions. Technical documents rarely use the APA style. However, if you learn it, you will easily be able to adopt this knowledge to match one of the other guides.

If you don't write professionally, you might be a little surprised at how many rules, guidelines, and exceptions apply just to numbers. As an example, AP says to spell out whole numbers up to nine, so you would represent them as nine and 10. CMS has a rule and an alternate rule. The rule says to spell out whole numbers up to one hundred, so you would use nine and ten. The alternate rule says to spell out whole numbers up to nine, so you could use nine and 10, similar to the AP rule.

Many times, an organization will give you a separate style sheet to follow. This guide might indicate the use of CMS or another official style manual. It might also include comments on the tone of the book. For example, the style sheet might indicate you should write the text as if you were writing it for a friend. In this example, you'd write the text as if you were guiding your friend about the important concepts, going in-depth when necessary to ensure your friend could understand it.

A company style sheet might include details on fonts to use for different headings and the main text. It could define the use of bullets and tables. It would typically describe what types of figures you can add, how to refer to figures in the text, and how to create figure captions. Many documents have additional features such as notes in the margins. For example, this book includes two margin elements: ON THE SIDE and AUTHOR'S NOTE. The publisher provided specific instructions on when to use these and how to format them.

Not all organizations have detailed style sheets, though. Instead, they might just give you a sample document and ask you to follow it as a template. When you have questions, you ask your contact what to do. With or without a style sheet, you can still follow some common guidelines when writing technical documents. These include:

- **Use plain language.** While you might have an assortment of tools to help you find different words to say the same thing, the simplest words are often the best. Authors that try to pump up their writing with complex words often plug in words that muddy the message.

- **Stick to English.** You might know French, Latin, Spanish, or some other language, but everyone doesn't know these languages. When you use foreign phrases in your writing, it often confuses readers that don't know these phrases. You could take the time to explain the foreign phrase, but when you do, you end up putting many more words to a concept that you could have simply explained in English.

- **Avoid industry jargon.** Ensure your audience knows the terms and phrases you use. If they don't understand the jargon, don't use it. The exception is when you need to teach it. For example, you might need to teach someone how to handle stop errors in Windows systems. In this case, they need to know that many technicians call these a Blue Screen of Death or BSOD error.

ON THE SIDE:
AP is an acronym for Associated Press and MLA is an acronym for the Modern Language Association of America. Writers and editors commonly refer to the style guides with the acronyms instead of spelling them out.

ON THE SIDE:
When writing sidebar and other elements, they will look different in your draft document than they do in the final document. For example, this ON THE SIDE element is under the preceding paragraph in Microsoft Word. Later, a compositor placed it beside the paragraph.

7

- **Spell out acronyms.** Anytime you use an acronym, ensure you spell it out the first time you use it. For example, if you mention a denial of service attack, you would spell it the first time and then add the acronym in parentheses like this: denial of service (DoS). You can then use the DoS acronym without spelling it out.

- **Avoid repeated words.** This includes repeated words in paragraphs and sentences. For example, don't start two paragraphs in a row with the word "The." Also, avoid starting subsequent sentences in a paragraph with the same word. It becomes monotonous to read a paragraph that starts every sentence with the word "The." Last, avoid repeating the same word in a sentence. This repetition is distracting and often makes it difficult for readers to understand. Worse, it might give the reader the impression you have a limited vocabulary or imagination.

ON THE SIDE:
Occasionally, it's appropriate to ignore a guideline. However, if you do ignore it, do so consciously. For example, you might choose to repeat the same word in consecutive sentences to create a cadence or add emphasis.

If you notice repetition in your writing, take the time to rewrite it. For example, the following bullet provides the same information as the preceding one. It has all the information, but the repetition makes it harder to read and understand. It isn't as clear:

- **Avoid repeated words.** Avoid starting consecutive paragraphs with the same word. Avoid starting consecutive sentences in the same paragraph with the same word. Avoid repeating the same word in the same sentence. It can become monotonous for the reader. It becomes distracting, and in general, it's best to avoid anything that detracts from the message.

Comparing Active Writing to Passive Writing

Active and passive writing (also called active and passive voice) are two styles you should understand as a technical writer. In general, active writing uses fewer words, provides better clarity, and is easier to read and understand. Passive writing typically uses more words, lacks clarity, and is often difficult to comprehend.

Technically, **active writing** follows the order of subject, verb, and object. In simpler terms, you can think of this as *A does B*. Consider the following active voice statement:

- Technicians reset user passwords.

In this example, the subject is *technicians*, the verb is *reset*, and the object is *user passwords*. It's clear, direct, and easy to understand.

In contrast, **passive writing** modifies the object as the subject. It's often written as *B was done* or *B was done by A*. Here are two examples using the passive voice:

- User passwords are reset.
- User passwords are reset by technicians.

Notice that in the first example, it isn't clear who resets the passwords because the subject (technicians in this example) is removed. Even if you add *technicians* back in as "User passwords are reset by technicians," the sentence is still passive and clunky compared to the more direct "Technicians reset user passwords."

ON THE SIDE: Politicians are famous for using the passive voice to muddle issues. One of the most popular, non-apology apologies is "mistakes were made." Many U.S. presidents uttered this phrase while engulfed in a scandal. This includes Presidents Grant, Nixon, Reagan, and Clinton. Most people recognize it as an attempt to acknowledge the mistake without taking or assigning responsibility. If you watch the news, it won't take long for you to hear a current politician (of any political party) use this phrase, or a derivative.

Here is a method you can use to convert a passive sentence into an active sentence, and make your writing easier to understand. First, identify the action. Next, identify who or what is performing the action. Last, reorder the sentence so that it follows the format of *doer* and *action*. In our previous passive example of "User passwords are reset by technicians," the action is *passwords are reset* and technicians are performing this action. "Technicians reset user passwords" follows the format of *doer* and *action*.

While active writing is preferable, there are exceptions where you need to use it. You can use the passive voice when you don't know who performed an action, or you don't want to identify who performed it. For example, imagine an unknown technician completed an unauthorized change on a server, causing the server to crash, and resulting in a three-hour outage. When documenting this, you might write, "The server crashed at 10:30 AM after a configuration change was made."

Similarly, when a writing style prohibits the use of "I", you might need to use a passive voice. For example, if you took pictures to show damage in a server room, you might write, "Photos of the server room were taken to document the damage," instead of, "I took photos of the server room to document the damage."

Using Short Sections

Technical documents can be complex. One way to make them easier to understand is to divide the topics into simpler concepts and present the simpler concepts in short sections. This is especially useful when writing for end users, but many technical workers appreciate this method too.

In addition to dividing the topics, it also adds more white space to a page. A page with one long paragraph looks daunting. A page with multiple paragraphs and possibly one or more section titles is pleasing to the eye and easier to read for many people.

As an example, consider the two pages in Figure 7-1 using placeholder text. The page on the left uses headings and paragraph breaks to add white space to the page. The page on the right is just a long stream of text and looks intimidating. The page on the right might be appropriate for a doctoral thesis, but will intimidate most readers.

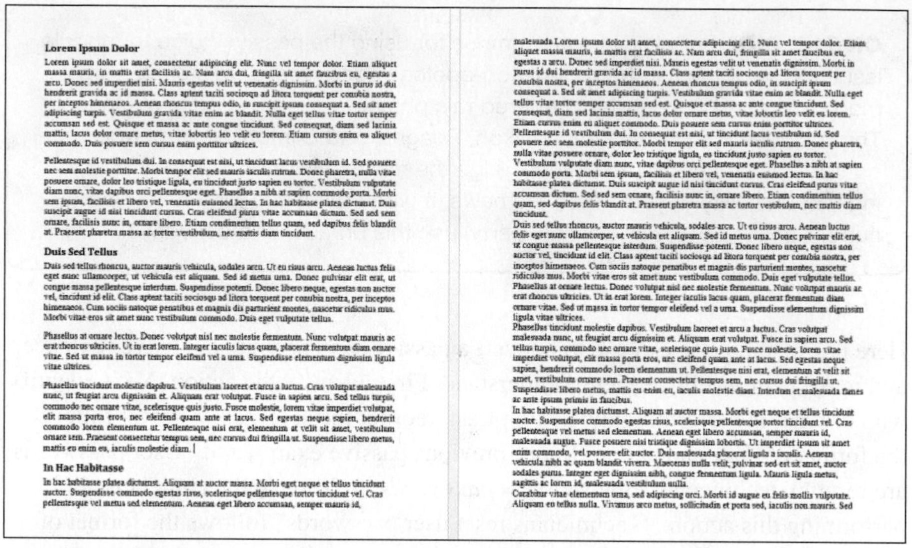

FIGURE 7-1

Using short sections for white space.

Using Stories and Analogies

Analogies help people understand topics. Chapter 8, "Training Skills," discusses the power of telling stories and analogies in the classroom. These can ignite the imagination of students in the classroom, and you can also use them to engage readers.

As an example, Chapter 5, "Security Skills," discusses threats and stresses that criminals are attacking organizations regularly. It includes a story about an actual attack on Target Corp, and intertwines this story to stress additional points such as the costs related to an attack.

You don't need to have detailed stories to make points. Often, just a simple analogy suffices. An **analogy** is a comparison between two things and can help people connect known concepts with unfamiliar concepts. Some analogies are similes and some are metaphors. A simile compares two things using the word *like* or *as*. For example, "being a technical author can be as rewarding as being a help desk specialist." A metaphor also compares two things but it does not use the words *like* or *as*. For example, "when it came to helping users, Joe was a rock star."

Of course, you can also use examples to stress your points. The previous paragraph didn't just explain similes and metaphors, it also gave examples to help clarify them.

Avoiding Absolutes

When writing, avoid using absolutes such as all, always, none, and never. With few exceptions, these are not accurate. If you do use an absolute such as "all," a reader might think of an exception, realize the statement is incorrect, and then question the accuracy of other statements in your document.

There are times when you should use absolutes. For example, users should understand they should *never* give out their password. As soon as a user begins making exceptions to this guideline, they risk giving their password out to a social engineer or other attacker. However, if they understand never means never, it's less likely they'll be tricked.

Using Pronouns

One of the challenges with technical writing is the use of pronouns. For example, if you want to indicate a help desk specialist needs to be an effective writer, you could write, "Effective writing skills will help him advance in his career." Of course, women can also be help desk specialists, so this statement seems to exclude women. You could write it as, "Effective writing skills will help her advance in her career," but this seems to exclude men.

Some writing styles allow you to mix up pronouns within the book, including both genders at different times. Authors often indicate this style in the introduction.

One recommendation is to use him or her like this: "Effective writing skills will help him or her advance in his or her career." However, this *him or her* approach often slows readers down. It becomes harder to read and comprehend the content. You can use this if you must, but think of this as a last resort.

Some writers, publishers, and editors accept the use of the *singular they* (including *them* or *their*). In other words, "Effective writing skills will help a technician advance in their career" is acceptable to some people. However, not everyone accepts it and some people look at it as sloppy writing. If your reader is one of these people, it can be distracting and detract from the primary point.

A better approach is to use plural pronouns such as *they*, *them*, or *their* along with plural nouns. For example, you can write, "Effective writing skills will help technicians advance in their career." Notice that technicians is plural and matches the plural pronoun *their*. This method avoids the challenge of using *his or her* and slowing the reader down. Also, the sentence remains clear and direct.

AUTHOR'S NOTE:
In a Security+ book that I self-published, I followed a simple pronoun style rule throughout the book: I mixed up the use of male and female pronouns, but I ensured that I never used female pronouns to refer to a criminal or attacker.

Understanding Technical Writing

Technical writing provides readers with technical information. Successful technical writers are able to explain complex concepts, breaking them down into easy to understand topics. They might write small snippets of information for websites such as product instructions or answers to frequently asked questions (FAQs). Many technical writers create extensive technical manuals.

As mentioned previously, technical writing is a form of expository writing. Its goal is to create useful documents that educate and inform the reader. As a help desk specialist, you might engage in technical writing to help people understand concepts related to computing hardware, software, or configuration settings.

Knowing Your Audience

Before you start writing, you should know your audience. In other words, you should have a good idea of who will be reading your text. When you can accurately identify your audience, you have a much better chance at creating a document that will be useful.

One technique that many non-fiction writers use when writing books is to write as much as you can about your target reader. This includes age, gender, education level, background, skills, likes, dislikes, goals, and dreams. It could be someone you know or a fictional person. Coach Sean Smith (http://coachseansmith.com/) refers to this process as identifying your seeker. You have information to provide and someone is seeking it. When you can accurately identify your seeker, you have a much better chance at creating a highly useful document.

> **AUTHOR'S NOTE:**   When writing, I often envision a student in a class I've taught. I think about how I can make the topic clear for that student just as if I was sitting next to them. For large projects such as a book, visions of different students come to mind in different chapters. I remember questions they asked and take the time to ensure I explain these concepts so the student that asked the question can understand the topic.

Many books have a section in the introduction titled something like "Assumptions" or "Who This Book is For." This section identifies the target reader, including assumed background knowledge and skill level. However, you don't always have this information available when you're tasked with writing a topic for a website or for internal personnel. If it's not clear, it's worth your time to ask questions such as "Who is this for?" or "Who will be reading this?"

If you're writing content for other help desk specialists, you can assume a certain level of technical knowledge. Regular users won't have the same level of technical knowledge. If you're writing content for basic users, you might need to ensure the content includes the basics before it gets into anything too technical.

Planning

Before actually starting to write, you should do some planning. Planning includes ensuring you understand the objectives of the writing project. The objectives might be general or very specific, but the importance of starting with objectives cannot be overemphasized. Starting to write without knowing the goal is a surefire way to ensure that a lot of your writing ends up on the editing room floor.

As an example, your supervisor might ask you to write a short tutorial to teach users how to configure a specific application setting. When users have access to this tutorial and can follow it, they can do so on their own without calling into the help desk. This lets you know the target audience is regular users and they should be able to use your document to configure the setting. As a similar example, your supervisor might ask you to write a tutorial for other help desk users. They should be able to use your document to configure the setting themselves, or guide users through the steps.

It's also a good idea to have a target length of the document. You can typically answer FAQs in a paragraph or two. White papers are normally two or more pages. Technical manuals can be anywhere from a few pages to hundreds of pages. Clearly, these require different levels of planning.

Outlines help you organize the topics before you start. These are most useful when working on large projects such as technical manuals, but can also be valuable when working on smaller projects such as white papers. The outline includes headings and subheadings but rarely needs much more. Many authors also use a working outline where they include notes within different sections.

Following the Process

The process of any technical document typically goes through several stages. If you are about to take on a writing project, it's valuable to have an idea of this process before you start. The details of the process will be different in different organizations, and sometimes even when working with different individuals. However, there are some general processes that you can expect with just about any technical document, and these include several stages of editing and reviews.

The following bullets introduce some of the processes to expect while technical writing, and the following sections explain them in more depth:

- **Developmental review.** This review occurs at the beginning of a project but can occur again at any time afterwards. During this review, someone such as a supervisor or a developmental editor will help you define the project. If some cases, you might need to provide an outline or a summary of the final product.

- **Technical editing.** After you submit your first draft, a technical editor reviews the document. The technical editor's goal is to ensure that the document is technically accurate and covers the technical aspects adequately. In some cases, the document might go back and forth between the author and the technical editor to clarify certain topics.

- **Copy editing.** A copy editor reviews the document to ensure it is clear, correct, concise, comprehensible, and consistent. When a style sheet is available, the copy editor verifies the document follows the guidelines outlined in the style sheet.

- **Typesetting.** At this stage, a compositor or web design specialist creates the document in the final format. This might be as a Portable Document Format (PDF) file, a web page, or some other format. This person does not modify the content. Instead, the goal is only to make it look graphically appealing.

- **Proofing.** When the final document is complete, different people proof it. One of the goals here is to verify errors weren't inserted during the layout phase. The author reviews it to ensure all requested changes were applied correctly. Sometimes, a separate proofer, someone that has never seen the document before, reviews the document, looking for any errors in the document.

Not every technical document you write will necessarily go through all these stages. For example, if you're tasked with posting an answer to a FAQ, you don't need to worry about the layout or proofing. However, it's important to ensure you include editing whenever possible. Errors creep in and authors can easily overlook them because they are so close to the content.

Completing Your First Draft

Once you know what to write and how to format it, you complete your first draft. "First draft" is a little bit of a misnomer, though—it is rarely *your* first draft, but is instead the first draft that you turn in.

> **AUTHOR'S NOTE:**   The procedure I describe here to create a first draft isn't necessarily what every technical author follows, and I'm not suggesting this is the only process. However, I have found that this process has proven to be successful for me. If you create any technical documents, consider trying it.

Ernest Hemingway once said that the secret to writing is rewriting. This certainly worked well for him with novels. It also applies to just about any writing that you can do. With this in mind, the first goal is simply to get the concepts down on paper. As mentioned earlier, you don't have to get it perfect, you just have to get it started. You can improve it later when you rewrite and edit the document. Also, editors will provide you with feedback.

Imagine you're tasked with writing a two-page white paper. One way to do this is to write the entire white paper without focusing too much on perfection. The goal at this point is to ensure you cover the objectives for the white paper and you get the technical details correct. If specific graphics come to mind while writing this pass, add them. If you have an idea of a graphic, you can just write in a note such as "add chart here." Many times, the graphic idea will morph in your mind and when you come back to it later, it will be easier to create or find it.

After completing this first pass, you can go through the document a second time with the goal of ensuring the topics are clear. During this second pass, you might add analogies and examples to clarify some topics that are complex or unclear. These also help make the document a little more interesting. Also, during this pass, you can add in any graphics that didn't come to mind during the first pass.

Next, do one more pass through your document. At this point, the content should be clear and cover the objectives. Your goal is to look for any typos and obvious issues related to spelling, grammar, and punctuation.

> **ON THE SIDE:**   Word processors such as Microsoft Word include sophisticated spelling and grammar checkers that are valuable to use. However, these don't catch everything. A phrase like "We must untie this company" might look perfect to the spelling and grammar checkers, but you might have meant to write *unite* instead of *untie*. When doing your final pass through the document, it's best to read every word yourself.

Once you've completed the third pass, you now have your first draft. This is the document you turn in for the next phase—technical editing.

Technical Editing

The technical editor helps ensure the document is technically accurate and adequately covers the technical concepts. A technical editor provides feedback to the author with the goal of helping the author identify any potential technical issues or errors.

Successful technical editors are those that have a keen eye for noticing technical errors and can tactfully point them out. Their goal isn't to show how smart they are, but instead their goal is to help the author create the best document possible.

> **AUTHOR'S NOTE:** If you have an interest in technical writing as a career, technical editing is a great way to get started. You have an opportunity to see the process and provide input for a technical project. When technical editors take the time and effort to provide useful, detailed feedback, publishers call them back for additional projects. They often ask quality technical editors to contribute chapters to books.

Also, technical editors do not address grammatical and spelling errors unless something is very obvious. Many publishers don't want them to spend any time or effort with grammar or spelling but instead only focus on the technical aspects of the document. When technical editors start focusing on grammar and spelling, they often overlook the technical issues.

As a writer, it's important that you do not take editing feedback personally. Instead, simply look at the feedback, determine if it is valid, make a change if necessary, and then move on. While most technical editors are tactful and respectful when providing feedback, readers can be rather harsh if a document is technically inaccurate. By evaluating all the feedback objectively, you have a better chance of eliminating the errors.

Many technical people have opportunities to be technical editors. If you have the knowledge, it's a relatively simple matter to read a document for accuracy and provide thoughtful feedback.

Copy Editing

Copy editors are often the unsung heroes behind many successful technical documents. The five C's summarize the core of their job: clear, correct, concise, comprehensible, and consistent.

- **Clear.** They help ensure that the document says what the author intended. Many times a subtle change of words or punctuations gives a completely different message. For example, look at Figure 7-2. "Let's eat, Grandma" means something completely different from "Let's eat Grandma." Copy editors try to spot and correct these types of mistakes.

- **Correct.** Correctness refers to the spelling and grammar. It also includes ensuring that the document follows the style sheet rules. For example, they ensure numbers are spelled out when they should be.

- **Concise.** Editors can help eliminate unneeded words and phrases. Sometimes they do this by converting passive writing to active writing. Other times, they recognize redundancies and edit them or point them out to the author.

- **Comprehensible.** Editors help ensure that the words form understandable sentences.

- **Consistent.** Editors help ensure the author used certain styles and spellings consistently. For example, both web site and website are acceptable spellings to different publishers. However, a single document should use only one spelling.

FIGURE 7-2

"Let's eat, Grandma" or "Let's eat Grandma."

ON THE SIDE: The author is ultimately responsible for all errors within a document. Technical editors and copy editors help authors improve the document, but it's important for an author to start with the best possible product and verify corrections are accurate. Also, if a first draft includes nine errors, it makes it more likely that one will be missed during the editing process. In contrast, if the first draft includes only one error, editors are more likely to catch it.

Typesetting

Books and many documents are laid out using sophisticated desktop publishing applications such as Adobe InDesign and QuarkXPress. These tools help ensure that the final printed document appears exactly as desired. They use a WYSIWYG (What You See Is What You Get) interface.

Designers use these applications to lay out the text and graphics on the pages and ensure that the text and graphics appear consistently when printed. WYSIWYG tools are used to create many PDF documents. However, it's also possible to create PDF files using standard word processors such as Microsoft Word.

In contrast, web pages can look different from one computer to another. For example, one computer might not have the same fonts as another, causing the text on each to look different. Similarly, users can change default settings for text sizes, causing the text and paragraphs on one computer to be larger than they are on the other computer.

Proofing

Proofing is the process of reviewing the final product and verifying it doesn't have any errors. Errors have a habit of creeping into documents during the editing and typesetting process. Proofing helps people find and fix them before publishing the document.

If the document has gone through the typesetting phase, a proof is created. The proof might be a digital file that proofers can review. In some cases, the proof is a physical document. Either way, the proof provides people with an opportunity to verify the final product is acceptable.

Even when a document doesn't go through the typesetting phase, it is still possible to proof it. For example, you can proof a blog post or FAQ entry before it goes live. This is just a matter of someone giving it one more look to ensure it doesn't have any errors.

Spelling Out Prerequisites

When writing technical topics, it's important to spell out the prerequisites. Many times procedures will only work when certain conditions are met. If users don't know what these conditions are, they might try to complete a procedure only to have it fail without knowing why. This can be frustrating for the reader and cause them to suspect the accuracy of the entire text.

As an example, many applications show context-sensitive menus based on user permissions. Administrators see some menus, but the application hides these menus from regular users. If you are describing menus that only administrators see, ensure you tell the reader they need to access the application with administrative permissions. Otherwise, you're describing menus that are invisible to the reader.

Similarly, some applications require additional components before they work. For example, one company sells website applications to customers and posts online tutorials customers can use to enhance these applications. One tutorial provided specific directions on how to add a feature to the application. The directions were simple and clear. Unfortunately, they didn't work.

Many customers complained in online comments. Other customers posted comments saying the procedures worked for them, but it was not clear why the instructions weren't working for everyone. Eventually the company realized that some customers had certain required software components installed while other customers didn't have these installed. The website included tutorials on how to install these components, but customers didn't know they were needed so they didn't look for them. Instead, customers became frustrated with the product. The company later added two sentences to the beginning of the tutorial. They stated the prerequisites and included links to tutorials on how to meet them. What had been an extremely frustrating issue for customers suddenly disappeared.

Writing for Customers

A significant amount of technical writing supports users or customers. This is especially true of any writing you might complete as a help desk specialist. In some cases, you might be writing directly to a user via instant message (IM) or chat windows. Other times you might exchange emails with users. Additionally, many other methods allow an organization to provide support to users indirectly. For example, web pages, blog posts, and FAQs can all provide information to users without talking directly to a user. A single FAQ can help hundreds of users resolve a problem without ever calling the company.

> **ON THE SIDE:**   Chapter 2, "Communication Skills," discusses different communication methods including text-only methods such as email, IM, and chat windows. As a reminder, text-only communication methods don't support non-verbal communication methods. This makes it very important to ensure that written communications are clear.

All of this stresses the importance of effective technical writing, especially for any topics posted on web pages for users. If you can write the topics clearly, users can understand and use them. In contrast, when topics are not clear, it confuses and frustrates the users.

One of the primary benefits of writing for customers is that you can avoid many help desk calls with well-written and accessible documentation. If clear help is readily available, many people will use it. More, if they can find the information they need one time, they are more likely to use the same source for help again. Used effectively, websites can become self-service conduits for users.

In contrast, if they can't get the answer through the website, they'll call the help desk, taking up the time of help desk employees. Worse, if they can't get the answer through the website one time, they are much less likely to try to find an answer through the website the next time they have a problem.

This section covers many of the common documents help desk specialists might write for customers. It also includes information on a basic rule you can use—the 3-30-3 rule.

Following the 3-30-30 Rule

The 3-30-3 rule is a marketing rule, but is important to understand when writing content for customers. It is especially useful to use this rule when creating web pages, brochures, newsletters, and white papers.

- **3.** You have three seconds to grab your reader's attention. If you don't get the reader's attention within three seconds, they are likely to leave and unlikely to return. Some techniques that help grab the reader's attention are engaging headlines and section headers, and ensuring the content is visually appealing. You can make the content visually appealing with appropriate graphics and effective use of white space on the page.

- **30.** You have 30 seconds to engage the reader. Many times, you can do this with an overview or summary of the topic. This should describe the content in such a way that it appeals to the reader, but be short enough that the reader can read it in 30 seconds or less.

- **3.** You have three minutes to get your message across. The reader should be able to get to the point within three minutes or less. This doesn't mean that the entire content must be consumed within three minutes. If you get to the primary point within three minutes, readers are more likely to continue reading to get additional information. Many people skim content, especially if it is long. However, when you present it in such a way that the reader can quickly read it, they are more likely to do so.

> **ON THE SIDE:** The average speed of readers when reading paper documents ranges between 250 and 400 words per minute. It is slower when reading topics on a computer screen, ranging between 200 and 300 words per minute. You can use these word counts to calculate the ideal size of your document based on your audience. Many websites break up large topics into two or more web pages.

Contributing to Web Pages

Organizations commonly host websites. They use them to promote the organization, communicate with customers, and advertise their products or services. Many times, these websites have help pages and/or a list of frequently asked questions with appropriate answers. As a help desk specialist, supervisors might ask you to contribute content to the site.

> **ON THE SIDE:** Admittedly, not everyone will use documentation, no matter how well you write it and how accessible it is. Some people find it easier to ask and prefer to call someone else for help. Still, well-written and accessible documentation will reduce help desk calls for many issues.

7

When doing any single page, consider the 3-30-3 rule. Use titles and headings to grab the reader's attention within three seconds. Include an engaging summary or overview at the very beginning to let the reader know what the page covers. This summary can be just a sentence or two on many pages, but should not take a reader longer than 30 seconds to read. Last, the page should get to the main point within three minutes.

A common recommended word count of many blog posts is between 600 and 800 words. Some people recommend short posts of 250 to 500 words, and others recommend long posts of up to 2000 words. However, posts between 600 and 800 words meet the three-minute rule for average readers, and you can apply the rule for just about any web page.

One of the great benefits of web pages is that you can easily expand the topics into more pages. For example, if the topic is too complex to present in 800 words, divide it into two or more pages. When readers are interested, they are certainly willing to click to another page. In contrast, a single large page often looks daunting. When readers realize how long a single page is, they often lose interest and leave.

As a technical writer, you probably won't be asked to design the entire website. However, if someone does task you with designing the organization's website, be aware that this is no simple task. A lot of detailed consideration goes into designing a website to ensure that the content is graphically pleasing and easy to find; it's easy to make common mistakes that chase the readers away.

> **ON THE SIDE:** Vincent Flander's website Web Pages That Suck (http://www.webpagesthatsuck.com/) includes resources that you can use to create useful websites and avoid some common mistakes. They also publish an annual list of websites they consider the worst websites of the year.

Creating FAQs

Frequently asked questions (FAQs) can be very valuable for help desk professionals. FAQs help users solve their own problems by listing a frequently asked question and the answer. If you can communicate to the user how to solve their own problems with a FAQ, they won't be calling the help desk. This reduces costs by reducing calls. Many organizations have a web page dedicated to FAQs used to answer common user queries. Here's an important point about FAQs, though: Make sure the organization is clear on why they are using them. Some companies create FAQs that really aren't questions that anyone asks frequently. As an example, customers rarely ask questions like, "Why is your service so awesome?"

This doesn't mean that organizations cannot or should not include marketing concepts within a FAQ—they can. However, individual questions should focus on meeting the needs of the customers, not the organization. For example, customers might often ask about shipping methods. In addition to providing the basic details, the answer can include information on how customers can upgrade to premium shipping. Similarly, they might ask about refund policies. You can include information on past performance and guarantees.

There are many different tools available to help you create visually appealing FAQs. In general, it's best to show the full list of questions so that the user can easily scan them. If you have a large number of FAQs, you can organize them by category. When users find questions they're interested in, they should be able to click it to see the answer.

Figure 7-3 shows an example of a few questions on a FAQ page. This page has a down arrow at the right of each question. Users can click on it to expand it, as shown in the figure for the first question. Notice the down arrow changes to an up arrow so the user can click to close it if desired.

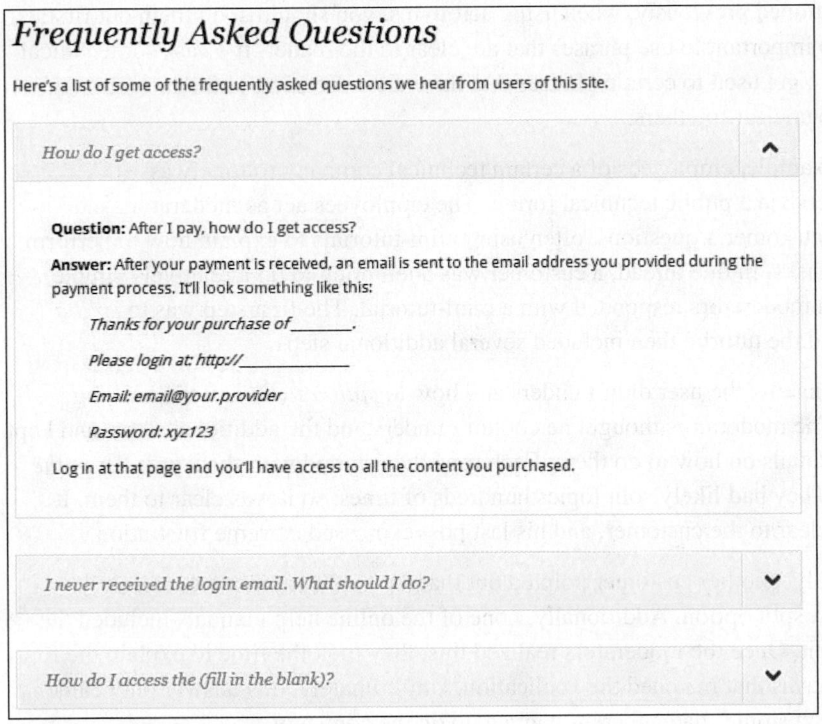

FIGURE 7-3

FAQ page.

Writing Tutorials

A tutorial is a self-guided document that a reader can use to learn new material. The tutorial might teach about a topic such as features in an application, or teach how to perform certain tasks such as how to install and configure an application. A benefit of a tutorial is that readers can use them at their own pace.

Technical tutorials commonly include step-by-step instructions. These are sometimes called exercises or labs. A common mistake when creating these exercises is assuming readers know more than they do. The individual steps should be clear and easy to follow.

Additionally, it's important to ensure it's clear to the reader how to start the tutorial. As an example, imagine someone is telling you how to get to a business location and gives you these instructions: "Take a left on Main Street. Follow it for three miles and turn right on First Street. The business is the first building on the left." This might work if you're heading toward Main Street. However, if you aren't starting close to Main Street and you don't have a clue where Main Street is, these directions aren't very useful. Worse, if you approach Main Street from the opposite direction and turn left, you'll be going in the wrong direction.

Compare this analogy to your tutorial. If it shows a user how to configure a setting in an application, ensure the user knows how to start the application and get to the configuration page. Instructions that start on a configuration page without showing the reader how to get there are confusing and frustrating.

As mentioned previously, when using acronyms, you should spell them out first. It's also important to use phrases that are clear to the reader. It's easy for technical people to get used to certain phrases that have clear meaning to them, forgetting they are unclear to others.

As an example, employees of a certain technical company routinely assist customers via a public technical forum. The employees act as moderators and answer customer's questions, often using mini-tutorials to explain how to perform certain tasks. In one thread, a customer was attempting to do a relatively simple task and moderators responded with a mini-tutorial. The first step was to *split a topic* and the tutorial then included several additional steps.

Unfortunately, the user didn't understand how to *split a topic* and tried asking again. The moderators thought he couldn't understand the additional steps, and kept giving details on how to do them. Each time they started with the words "*split the topic.*" They had likely split topics hundreds of times, so it was clear to them. It wasn't clear to the customer, and his last post expressed extreme frustration.

Ultimately, another customer pointed out that the application interface didn't include a split option. Additionally, none of the online help manuals included the word split. Once the moderators realized this, they took the time to explain the first step in terms that matched the application. Unfortunately, this answer only came after the customer had apparently given up on the company.

An effective way of creating tutorials is to go through the process yourself, documenting each step as you go. This can take some time, but the finished product is more accurate than if you just write the steps from memory. It can also help ensure you give the reader all the information needed to accomplish the task.

When writing tutorials, it's important to be consistent when describing what a user sees on the screen. A style sheet might identify how to do this, but if you don't have one, you need to think about how you'll describe it. For example, Figure 7-4 shows the Options page for Microsoft Word. Imagine you want the user to deselect the option to show the Start screen when the application starts. This is the last option on the page.

> **ON THE SIDE:**
> Many applications show users context-sensitive menus that change when the application displays different screens or pages. When writing tutorials for these types of applications, it's best to start the tutorial by launching the application. This ensures that the reader will see the same menus you're describing.

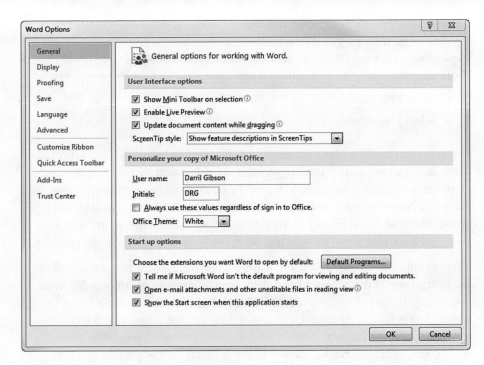

FIGURE 7-4

Microsoft Word Options page.

Here are five possible ways to do this:

- Deselect the checkbox for Show the Start screen when this application starts.
- Deselect the checkbox for Show The Start Screen When This Application Starts.
- Deselect the checkbox for *Show the Start screen when this application starts*.
- Deselect the checkbox for **Show the Start screen when this application starts**.
- Deselect the checkbox for "Show the Start screen when this application starts."

The style you use is often just a matter of preference. The first example is sometimes confusing because it isn't always easy to differentiate the words in the sentence with the words on the screen. Using capitalization differentiates the screen text from the rest of the text, but can confuse some people because it's not exactly how it shows on the screen. Bolding or italicizing the text makes it stand out, but this might conflict with other styles in your document. For example, you might be using bold or italics to show key terms. Similarly, quote marks make it stand out, but might conflict with other styles. The key here is to pick a style for the document and stick with it. If something is unclear to readers, they often compare it to similar instructions. When you are consistent with the style, it makes it easier for the reader.

It also important to give users instructions sequentially in the order the user will see them. When you want a user to select the File menu after opening the Options menu, say so in this order. In this example, you could write, "Select the File menu and then select the Options menu." In contrast, if this is written as "Select the Options menu from the File menu," users often hunt for the Options menu first. Depending on the knowledge level of your readers, you might be able to use a shortcut option. Two shortcut options many writers and publishers prefer are:

- Select File > Start
- Select File | Start

If you need to give the user a warning, give the warning before the instruction that needs it. For example, if a user can accidentally delete data by selecting the wrong response in a step, say so before you give the instruction. Instructions that lead users to a dangerous page without a clear warning can cause them to select the wrong response. It can be very frustrating to follow a step, cause a problem, and then read a warning about the step that would've helped you prevent the problem.

After writing the tutorial, it's best to leave it alone for a day or two. Later, follow the instructions in the tutorial to complete the task. After a one- or two-day break, you're able to look at the instructions with a fresh perspective and it's easier to identify areas that aren't clear. Of course, during this second pass, you would take the time to edit the instructions as needed. After tweaking it yourself, it's also a good idea to have someone else follow the instructions and provide you with feedback.

Contributing to Brochures

A brochure is a flyer or small pamphlet. A common format uses a standard 8" x 10" piece of paper with text and graphics on both sides, and a tri-fold design. This results in six individual panels (three on each side) with more information available to the reader as they unfold the paper.

Organizations typically use brochures for marketing. They might use sophisticated desktop publishing applications to create them. However, simpler tools such as Microsoft Publisher are available. It's even possible to create some simple brochures using Microsoft Word.

As a help desk specialist, you probably won't create the entire brochure on your own. However, you might be asked to provide technical text used within the brochure. Similarly, you might be asked to edit or proof the brochure. If so, ensure you have a clear understanding of what's desired.

For example, if you're asked to write some text for the copy, ask what topics they want to cover and how many words they expect you to write. Brochures typically have a limited amount of space for text, and marketing people normally don't want to fill this with technical details. If you're asked to edit or proof it, ask if you're expected to focus on the technical details as a technical editor, or if they want other feedback.

Figures 7-5 and 7-6 show the front and back pages of a brochure template from Microsoft Publisher. The designer simply needs to fill in the blocks with the appropriate text and graphics and it's ready to go. The size of the paper is typically 8.5 x 11 inches with text and/or graphics on both sides. However, you can see that the amount of text is limited due to how the panels are laid out.

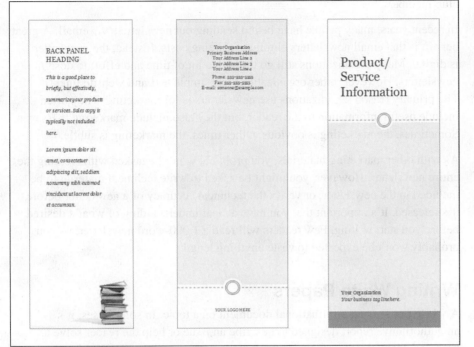

FIGURE 7-5

Brochure front page.

FIGURE 7-6

Brochure back page.

Contributing to Newsletters

A newsletter is a regularly distributed document sent to subscribers. Historically, a newsletter refers to a leaflet that a group might periodically send to members. For example, a soccer club might hand out newsletters during a soccer season for the club members.

In recent years, many people have begun sending out newsletters via email. A great benefit is that email newsletters eliminate printing costs. Instead, the newsletter is digital. Many organizations still go through a lot of time and effort to design newsletters. However, other organizations use simple text and website links. The primary reason organizations use newsletters is for marketing. They often include useful information to the reader, but they also include marketing messages. Sometimes, the marketing is obvious. Other times, the marketing is subtle.

As with other marketing materials, you probably won't be tasked with creating the entire newsletter. However, you might be asked to write technical material to be included in the newsletter, or verify the technical accuracy of a newsletter before it's released. It's important that you have a clear understanding of what's desired before you start writing. Few readers will read a 1,000-word newsletter, so you probably won't be expected to write anything lengthy.

Writing White Papers

A **white paper** is an informational document on a topic. In some cases, it's an authoritative report designed to describe an issue or help the reader solve a problem. Many times, companies use white papers as sales tools. Within the government, white papers typically provide information on a policy, which might become a law.

The best use of a white paper is to provide useful, meaningful information to the reader. If the information isn't useful, readers aren't going to read it. Many companies use them to describe a problem or issue and then use persuasive writing methods to indicate their products or services are the ideal solution. As a reminder, persuasive writing methods attempt to sway the opinion of the reader.

Some people consider white papers to be technical papers simply designed to explain a topic. However, most companies can't afford to invest in publishing technical papers without a return on their investment. Instead, they use white papers as marketing tools. They still provide useful, meaningful information, but they also help influence buyer decisions. It's important to include valuable information for the reader. Otherwise, the white paper becomes a sales brochure.

The following bullets describe some techniques you can use to create useful, effective white papers:

- **Identify the audience.** White papers written for *everyone* fail to attract the right reader. By identifying the audience, you can ensure the language and technical level matches the expectations of the reader.

- **Create an engaging title.** Think about your readers and create a title that describes a benefit for them. Also, use words that indicate the topic will be an easy read rather than a long, dry document. "How to Stop Thieves from Stealing Your Identity" and "Five Simple Steps to Prevent Malware Infections" are appealing titles to many users. In contrast, "Information Technology Security" and "Using Antivirus Software" won't engage many readers.

- **Inform and convince.** Ensure the white paper presents useful information to inform the reader of an issue or a problem. Then use persuasive writing methods to convince the reader. The goal might be to get the reader to visit a website, buy a product, or request more information.

- **Follow the 3-30-3 rule.** Ensure you use the 3-30-3 rule described earlier to grab their attention in 3 seconds, give them a 30-second summary, and make your point within 3 minutes of reading time. Remember, the entire length of the document doesn't need to be limited to three minutes of reading time, but you should make your point within that time. Use charts, graphs, or other graphics to present detailed information. Use bullets to list facts that the reader can easily scan.

> **AUTHOR'S NOTE:**   Many organizations realize the value of hiring professional writers to create their white papers. Instead of doing these in-house, they frequently hire writers that know how to communicate complex topics and understand persuasive writing. These organizations often pay outside writers generously to create the white papers, so employees that have this skill can provide a lot of value to the organization and help them save the cost of outsourcing these projects.

Writing Technical Manuals

Technical manuals are full texts focused on a specific technical topic. The manual might be on a specific piece of hardware or a software application sold or serviced by the organization. An organization might choose to create the technical manual in-house or hire someone else to write it. Even if they do outsource the writing, they will typically ask someone within the organization to review it for technical accuracy.

Many publishers publish technical manuals on a wide assortment of technical topics. This includes certification exams, programming languages, and much more.

However, non-publisher organizations sometimes create these types of technical manuals, too. You can think of them as a large white paper. These books inform the reader, but also include references to the publishing organization as a logical source to solve various problems.

For example, KnowBe4 gives away a free e-book titled Cyberheist. The author wrote it for IT personnel in small and medium enterprises and talks about "the biggest financial threat facing American businesses since the meltdown of 2008."

ON THE SIDE:
Cyberheist's e-book
is available as a
free download here:
http://www.knowbe4.
com/free-e-book/.

It is a well-written book and paints a good picture of many of the threats facing businesses. It also guides the reader toward looking at many of the solutions to these threats provided by KnowBe4.

Your organization probably won't ask a help desk specialist to write a book over 200 pages like this. However, they might ask you to contribute to it by writing some sections or to review it as a technical editor. As with other technical documents, ensure you know what is desired before you start.

Writing for Internal Personnel

If you can communicate effectively with customers using text, you can use the same skills to communicate with internal personnel. The same rules and guidelines apply.

The biggest difference is the target audience. You might be writing for internal users or technical people such as other help desk specialists. If you're writing for internal users, the same guidelines for customers apply. Internal users are the customers for a help desk. If you're writing for technicians, you can assume a higher level of knowledge and expertise. Careful, though—you don't want to assume too much and leave out key information.

Comparing Internal Documents to External Documents

You'll find that most of the document types provided for customers are also provided for internal users. The following bullets show many of the similarities:

- **Web pages.** Many organizations host an internal website for employees only and you might contribute to the website with web pages or blog posts. The same elements that make these engaging for customers also apply to internal employees. Again though, make sure you understand the target audience. Some web pages might be only for help desk specialists, while others might be for all personnel.

- **FAQs.** These provide answers for internal personnel just as they can for external customers. If these can help a user solve a problem without involving the help desk, it results in one less help desk call.

- **Tutorials.** Help desk personnel commonly use tutorials when helping users. These provide step-by-step instructions but instead of the user reading them, the help desk technician guides the user through the steps. These should be clear and easy to follow just as they should be for customers.

- **Newsletters.** Some organizations use an internal newsletter to share information. These might occasionally include technical information, so you might be asked to contribute to them.

- **White papers.** White papers written for internal employees often still use persuasive writing styles. However, instead of trying to sell a product, they often try to persuade the user into following a policy or procedure. For example, a security-based white paper might document IT-based losses to the organization. It would then explain the policies designed to thwart these losses. When employees understand the reasoning behind security policies, they are more likely to follow them.

Using a Knowledge Base

Many organizations provide searchable knowledge bases to help people resolve problems. In some cases, only in-house personnel can use these knowledge bases. In other cases, these knowledge bases are freely available for anyone to use.

A **knowledge base** stores information in such a way that users can retrieve and use it. An IT-based knowledge base often includes information that technicians can use to identify problems and solutions. It might include symptoms, symptom causes, problem resolutions, tutorials, and procedures. As an example, imagine a technician is helping a customer troubleshoot a problem. If another technician troubleshot a similar problem and documented it in the knowledge base, the solution is available. The first technician can search the knowledge base, find the knowledge base entry, and quickly resolve the problem.

Strictly speaking, a knowledge base isn't a database. Databases are highly structured using specific rules. In contrast, a knowledge base often includes unstructured data. Some data from the knowledge base might be stored in a back-end database, but due to how the data can be loosely structured, it isn't necessarily in a database. For example, a knowledge base might include searchable web pages.

Microsoft maintains a knowledge base (KB) of more than 150,000 articles that are accessible to anyone. Microsoft personnel follow specific procedures documenting these KB articles after resolving customer issues. These are online and searchable from here: http://support.microsoft.com/search/. If you see a specific error, you can often do an Internet search with the error and locate the KB article that shows how to resolve it.

> **ON THE SIDE:**   KB article 242450 provides information on how to search this knowledgebase using keywords and query words. As with other Microsoft KB articles, if you know the number, you can use it in the URL like this: http://support.microsoft.com/kb/242450.

Documenting Incidents

Technicians log incidents and record activity on the incident in a help desk application. Normally, only other help desk personnel, supervisors, and managers will see these, so you don't have to worry about making things clear for customers.

However, it's still important to write clearly because this information is often available in a knowledge base.

As a reminder, a typical incident process includes logging information in a ticket. This ticket tracks the incident from the initial report until the ticket is resolved and closed. Technicians log activity in the ticket throughout its lifetime.

What isn't always apparent is that data entered into these tickets is also available in the knowledge base. As an example, BMC Software sells many tools, including some for problem management and incident management. Organizations use the BMC Remedy Incident Management application to log and track incidents. This tool includes a search feature that technicians can use to search for similar problems and possible solutions.

In order for the search feature to be useful, the knowledge base needs to have valuable information. This means that technicians need to enter appropriate information when they are logging incidents. Consider these two examples logged by technicians after solving the same problem. One technician resolved the problem and then entered this into the company's knowledge base: "broke… fixed it." A second technician resolved a similar problem and logged this entry: "System was manually configured with incorrect IP address. Reconfigured to use DHCP. Verified problem was resolved."

The first one is cute; it might even get some chuckles from other technicians. However, the second one provides valuable information for a knowledge base. Someone searching the knowledge base to help them resolve a problem can use this information to solve it quickly. There's another benefit of the second entry too. When it's time for the company to promote from within, the second technician is much more likely to be promoted than the first technician.

As another example of an external knowledge base, BMC Software hosts an online knowledge base that anyone can search (http://www.bmc.com/support). Users of their applications can search the knowledge base for problems they are experiencing and possible solutions.

More and more organizations are using similar online knowledge bases for their products. They can be as useful as FAQs. If customers can search the knowledge base and get the answers they need, they are less likely to ask for help from a help desk.

Chapter Review Activities

Use the features in this section to study and review the topics in this chapter.

Answer These Questions

1. Of the following choices, what type of writing is MOST closely associated with technical writing?
   a. Expository
   b. Persuasive
   c. Descriptive
   d. Narrative

2. Of the following choices, which one BEST describes the primary difference between technical writing and persuasive writing?
   a. Technical writing includes facts and opinions while persuasive writing only includes facts.
   b. Persuasive writing includes facts and opinions while technical writing only includes facts.
   c. Technical writing is used primarily in fiction while persuasive is used primarily in non-fiction.
   d. Technical writing is used primarily in non-fiction while persuasive is used primarily in fiction.

3. What is a primary benefit of using active writing in technical documents?
   a. It avoids placing blame or responsibility.
   b. It adds bulk to the documents with the additional words.
   c. It eliminates the use of first person writing.
   d. It is easier to read and understand.

4. Of the following sentences, which one is the BEST example of active writing?
   a. User passwords are reset.
   b. User passwords are reset by technicians.
   c. Technicians reset user passwords.
   d. None. Each of these examples uses passive writing.

5. Which of the following is an example of a simile used in an analogy?
   a. He could troubleshoot systems better than any other technicians could.
   b. He could troubleshoot systems as well as an Olympic skater could skate.
   c. He was a rock star when it came to troubleshooting systems.
   d. No one could troubleshoot systems as effectively as he could.

6. Which of the following sentences reflects the best use of pronouns in a technical document?

    a. Effective writing skills will help him advance in his career.

    b. Effective writing skills will help a technician advance in their career.

    c. Effective writing skills will help a technician advance in her career.

    d. Effective writing skills will help technicians advance in their careers.

7. Of the following choices, what is the BEST choice of what you should identify before starting a writing project?

    a. Technical editor

    b. Copy editor

    c. Audience

    d. Editing process

8. Which of the following is MOST commonly used as a planning tool for technical documents?

    a. Needs assessment

    b. Tasking document

    c. Audience profile

    d. Outline

9. Of the following choices, what BEST represents the primary goal of a technical editor?

    a. Provide feedback on the document.

    b. Provide feedback on the grammar and spelling of a document.

    c. Provide feedback on the grammar, spelling, and technical accuracy of a document.

    d. Provide feedback on the technical accuracy of a document.

10. Of the following choices, what BEST represents the goal of a copy editor?

    a. Ensure a document is clear, correct, concise, comprehensible, and consistent.

    b. Ensure the document is understandable and does not have any grammar or spelling errors.

    c. Ensure a document follows the appropriate style guide.

    d. Ensure the grammar and spelling of a document is accurate.

11. Who is primarily responsible for ensuring a technical document is clear, correct, and comprehensible?

    a. Author

    b. Copy editor

    c. Publisher

    d. Technical editor

12. What is the purpose of identifying the prerequisites in a tutorial?

    a. To ensure the document is written for the appropriate audience

    b. To ensure the reader understands requirements to complete the tutorial

    c. To ensure all customers can complete the tutorial

    d. To help the author identify the reader

13. You are tasked with writing a technical white paper using the 3-30-3 rule. What does the 3-30-3 rule indicate?

    a. The document should be no more than 3 pages, readable in 30 minutes and make at least 3 points.

    b. Technical documents should engage the reader within 3 seconds, be readable in 30 minutes or less, and include at least 3 main points.

    c. Technical documents should grab the reader's attention within 3 seconds, engage the reader within 30 seconds, and get the message across within 3 minutes.

    d. Technical documents should be readable in 3 minutes, include no more than 30 pages, and include a summary within 3 minutes.

14. Of the following choices, what is the BEST word count for a blog post when following the 3-30-3 rule?

    a. 30 words

    b. 90 words

    c. 600 words

    d. 3,000 words

15. Which of the following MOST accurately reflects a primary organizational benefit of a FAQ page?

    a. It reduces help desk calls.

    b. It shows the company helps users.

    c. It provides answers to common problems.

    d. It provides the company with an additional marketing tool.

16. Which of the following reflects a common problem related to tutorials?

    a. Assuming readers have access to the tutorial

    b. Talking down to the reader

    c. Not using the 3-30-3 rule

    d. Assuming readers knows more than they do

17. Which of the following is NOT a method used to create an effective white paper?

    a. Identify the audience

    b. Create an engaging title

    c. Use the 3-30-3 rule

    d. Ensure opinions are omitted

18. What is the difference between writing for external customers and internal users?

    a. Internal users are more knowledgeable.

    b. External customers are more knowledgeable.

    c. You can assume a higher level of expertise from internal users.

    d. None of the above.

19. Which of the following statements BEST describes an IT-based knowledge base?

    a. A structured database

    b. A group of retrievable information

    c. A data store available to internal personnel only

    d. A data store available to external personnel only

20. Why is it important for technicians to log incident data clearly and accurately?

    a. So customers can understand them

    b. So supervisors and managers can understand them

    c. So their time is accurately logged

    d. So it can be located via a knowledge base search

Answers and Explanations

1. a. Technical writing is an example of expository writing. Persuasive writing is similar, but it includes opinions. Descriptive and narrative writing styles are used in fiction.

2. b. Persuasive writing includes opinions and attempts to convince the reader. Technical writing focuses on facts and omits opinions. Both technical writing and persuasive writing are primarily used in non-fiction.

3. d. One of the primary benefits of active writing is that it is easier to read and understand for the reader. Passive writing avoids placing blame or responsibility. Passive writing typically uses fewer words. It is possible to use the first person with active writing.

4. c. Active writing typically takes the form of subject, verb, object. In this example, the subject is technicians, the verb is reset, and the object is user passwords. The other two examples are passive.

5. **b.** A simile compares two things using the words like or as and the example that compares the technician to an Olympic skater uses the word as. The first and last answers are neither similes nor metaphors. Referring to him as a rock star is a metaphor.

6. **d.** The use of plural technicians matches the plural their and is the best use of pronouns. Some readers view using only him or only her as excluding members of the opposite sex. Mixing the singular technician and the plural word their is a mismatch.

7. **c.** One of the first things an author should do before starting a project is to identify the audience. Knowing the editing process and the specific editors isn't as critical when starting a project.

8. **d.** Authors commonly use an outline as a planning tool for technical documents. The other answers might be used, but they are not planning tools used by the author.

9. **d.** Technical editors should focus on the technical accuracy of a document. Generic feedback might be useful, but not if the technical details are omitted. Copy editors focus on grammar and spelling. When a technical editor focuses on grammar and spelling, they often lose sight of the technical details.

10. **a.** The five C's of copy editing help ensure a document is clear, correct, concise, comprehensible, and consistent. The other answers describe part of the copy editor's job, but not all of it.

11. **a.** The author is primarily responsible for ensuring a technical document is clear, correct, and comprehensible. A publisher (or company sponsoring the project) normally ensures that copy editors and technical editors assist the author, but the author is primarily responsible for the content.

12. **b.** Identifying the prerequisites ensures readers understand the requirements to complete the tutorial. This is separate from identifying the audience and instead identifies specific conditions that need to be met for the tutorial to work. Tutorials aren't necessarily meant for all customers, and prerequisites might identify conditions (such as administrative privileges) that a customer cannot meet.

13. **c.** The 3-30-3 rule states you should grab the reader's attention within 3 seconds, engage the reader within 30 seconds, and get your primary message across within 3 minutes.

14. **c.** An average reader can read a blog post between 600 and 800 words in three minutes, so this is the best choice. Posts of 30 words or 90 words are extremely short and won't have much content. Posts of 3,000 words are extremely long and will take much longer than three minutes to read.

15. **a.** A primary benefit of a frequently asked question (FAQ) page is that it can reduce help desk calls. If users can resolve their problems without, it ultimately saves money for the organization. The other answers are also true but they do not reflect primary benefits for the organization.

16. **d.** A common problem related to tutorials is assuming readers know more than they do. If readers don't have access to the tutorial, they won't be able to read it. Talking down to the reader is rarely a problem. The 3-30-3 rule doesn't apply to tutorials.

17. **d.** Organizations often publish white papers as marketing tools and use persuasive writing methods to sway the opinion of the reader so opinions are included. The other answers are methods used to create an effective white paper.

18. **d.** External customers and internal users have the same characteristics, and you would use the same writing styles for each. Internal users are customers of the help desk. Neither group is more knowledgeable nor has a higher level of expertise.

19. **b.** A knowledge base is a group of retrievable information. A knowledge base is loosely structured. Knowledge bases can be available for both internal and external users.

20. d. Incident applications typically connect to a knowledge base. When data is entered clearly and accurately, other technicians can search the knowledge base and locate the incident data. Customers won't necessarily see the incident data. While clear entries do help supervisors and managers understand them, this isn't the goal. Not all incident applications track time.

Define the Key Terms

The following key terms include the ideas most important to the big ideas in this chapter. To review, without looking at the book or your notes, write a definition for each term, focusing on the meaning, not the wording. Then review your definition compared to your notes, this chapter, and the glossary.

Key Terms for Chapter 7

active writing	frequently asked questions (FAQs)	persuasive writing
analogy		technical writing
expository writing	knowledge base	white paper
	passive writing	

List the Words Inside Acronyms

The following are the most common acronyms discussed in this chapter. As a way to review those terms, simply write down the words that each letter represents in each acronym.

Acronyms for Chapter 7

AP	FAQ	MLA
CMS	KB	PDF
DoS (as in DoS attack)	IM	WYSIWYG

Create Mind Maps

For this chapter, create a mind map as follows:

1. Create a mind map to outline the process of creating a white paper. Start with when a supervisor first assigns the topic to the author. Take it to the final stage when a completed PDF file is available to customers.

Case Studies

Case Study 1

Write a technical description of your alarm clock. Include a description of each of the buttons and/or knobs. Describe how to use these to set the time or alarm.

Case Study 2

Write a tutorial someone can use to set your alarm clock to ring at 7 AM. Ask a classmate to review it as a technical editor.

Case Study 3

Write a two-page white paper documenting a security issue that has caused a problem. For example, you could document the results of not using up-to-date antivirus software. If desired, you can use an issue documented in Chapter 5. Use persuasive writing to indicate the importance of following a procedure or implementing a process to avoid the issue.

Chapter | 8

Training Skills

Help desk specialists frequently need to train customers, users, and other help desk personnel, so a basic understanding of training skills can be very useful. It's not enough to just master the technical knowledge to be a successful trainer. Instead, trainers have a wide variety of skills and techniques that they use to share their knowledge and help others learn. Some of these skills are unique to classroom training, but many of them apply to both classroom training and one-on-one training.

It's important to realize that many of the skills discussed in this chapter can take quite a while for anyone to master. Additionally, the topics in this chapter introduce training, but a single chapter cannot adequately cover all of the possible skills needed to create and deliver successful training courses. Due to space constraints and the goal of this book, these topics are condensed and included in three major sections:

- The first section, "Effective Training Skills," is the largest section and it covers the attitude, skills, and knowledge that trainers need to lead successful classes. A primary point within this chapter is that trainers need much more than knowledge about a topic. To be successful, they need to understand how their attitude affects classroom learning, and also have some basic teaching skills.

- Next, the "Steps Involved in Training" section outlines the steps involved in creating and delivering training. An extremely important step is to identify the needs and objectives of the course and the audience. Once you identify your target audience and what they need to learn, you can create training materials and deliver the training. One of the key steps prior to delivering the training is preparation. This includes preparing the environment, preparing yourself so that you're ready to deliver the training, and preparing the students so that they are ready to learn.

- Last, the "One-on-One vs. Group Training" section compares some of the differences between one-on-one training and classroom or group training. It also discusses some considerations when training customers or end users individually, and training other help desk personnel individually.

Chapter Outline

Effective Training Skills

Steps Involved in Training

One-on-One vs. Group Training

Chapter Review Activities

Objectives

- List the three primary attributes of effective trainers

- Describe at least five skills used by successful trainers

- Differentiate between the different levels of knowledge between a person that understands a group of tasks, performs a group of tasks, and teaches others to perform these tasks

- Discuss at least five assumptions related to adult learners

- Compare the six levels of knowledge identified in Bloom's Taxonomy

- Explain the importance of creating objectives

- Describe the steps involved in creating training materials

- List at least five tips used to create effective PowerPoint presentations

- Discuss techniques trainers can use when delivering the training to help a class run smoothly

- Compare the differences between one-on-one and group training

- Describe the benefits of training customers

- Describe the benefits of using checklists to train other help desk personnel

Key Terms

analogy

andragogy

auditory learner

Bloom's Taxonomy

bridging

eLearning

empowering words

filler words

kinesthetic learner

learning style

on-the-job training

pedagogy

PowerPoint presentations

rapport

reading/writing learner

story

trainer

visual learner

Effective Training Skills

Some people believe that anyone that can perform a specific task or possesses some knowledge can teach that task or knowledge to someone else. They believe that if you know the topic everything else is easy. Don't believe it. Knowledge is important, but knowledge alone simply isn't enough. As an example, some technical managers think that top performers in certain job positions are the best people to train others and they assign them the task of developing and delivering training. While this works adequately sometimes, it can also fail miserably, simply because these top performers don't have the skillset required to pass on their information. Ideally, management will carefully select personnel to train others based on their full skillset, including their training skills.

In reality, there are two additional attributes that you'll find in most effective trainers beyond knowledge. These additional attributes are an appropriate attitude, and the ability to use various skills and techniques to transfer the information. This section describes many of the skills possessed by effective trainers. It can be useful for managers screening workers as potential trainers, and useful to anyone tasked with training others.

Instructor, Teacher, Trainer, or Facilitator

The terms instructor, teacher, trainer, and facilitator are sometimes used interchangeably, but there are differences. This chapter focuses on trainers and training skills, but many of these skills can be used by anyone to share their knowledge and help others learn no matter what job position they hold.

An **instructor** or **teacher** is someone with a wide body of knowledge, concepts, and theories, who passes this on via lecturing or presentations. A **professor** is a faculty member at an institution of higher education, such as a university or college, who instructs and teaches. Within a college or university, an instructor is a person who instructs but hasn't reached the level of a professor.

A **trainer** is someone with a narrow level of knowledge and experience on a topic who transfers this knowledge via training sessions, presentations, exercises, case studies, and examples. Individuals providing technical training on specific technical topics are trainers.

Facilitators moderate sessions to bring out the knowledge of the participants and help them share their knowledge with each other. They provide guidance and supervision to help the group reach a specific outcome, such as learning about a topic or communicate more effectively.

These definitions provide a generic understanding of the roles, but in reality, the roles are rarely that narrow. You'll often see instructors that train students using a lot of interaction beyond just lectures, and you'll see trainers that sometimes instruct others with lectures. Similarly, when interacting with a knowledgeable audience, instructors and trainers will often use facilitation skills to help the students share their knowledge with others.

AUTHOR'S NOTE: Within this chapter, the focus is on trainers and effective training skills they can use to transfer knowledge to their students. These skills are effective when providing technical training and are also used by many professors, teachers, and facilitators. However, these skills are not required in every situation where one person is sharing their knowledge with others. For example, a professor lecturing a hall filled with 100 highly motivated students might not use the same skills that a technical trainer teaching 10 students would use. However, both the professor and the trainer can still be successful at transferring their knowledge.

Attitude

An old saying that many effective trainers know and understand is, "People don't care how much you know until they know how much you care." If you are the smartest person in the room but people perceive you as an arrogant know-it-all, many people simply won't listen to you. However, when you understand how your attitude shapes others perceptions of you, you can use this to become a better trainer.

Effective trainers start their presentations with a positive, upbeat attitude, and they bring enthusiasm and energy to every presentation. Whenever possible, trainers amplify the positive aspects of each presentation and create interest in the topics, along with amplifying the positive aspects of the students.

One simple technique that many effective trainers include in their presentations is the use of **empowering words**. Empowering words are positive words and phrases spoken by the trainer in response to student interaction. These positive words encourage more interaction and positive responses from students.

As an example, when a student answers a question, a simple response such as "excellent" is an empowering word. In contrast, another trainer might realize the student was answering the question correctly, then look down at the trainer manual for a reminder of what comes next, and never acknowledge the student. In the first example, the student is recognized for participating and receives a verbal reward for doing so. In the second example, the student is not recognized and doesn't receive any reward. This student might easily feel ignored and be reluctant to answer a question again. Similarly, other students in the classroom might observe this process and choose not to participate either.

AUTHOR'S NOTE: When students interact in the class, they are much more likely to leave the class with more knowledge. However, encouraging classroom interaction is helpful for a trainer, too. Classes with high levels of student participation make the training more fun and enjoyable for the trainer, and even after teaching for a full day, trainers often feel energized. Classes with low levels of student participation can be extremely painful for the trainer, and they find themselves drained of energy at the end of the day. With this in mind, anything a trainer can do to help the class participate more is often as useful for the students as it is for the trainer.

Some might call this stroking the student's ego and in a sense, that is correct. However, it really is much deeper. Author Steven Covey wrote (and often talked) about the emotional bank account related to relationships. It works similar to an actual bank account, where you can make monetary deposits and withdrawals; if you make more deposits, your account will be richer, but if you make more withdrawals, you end up with financial problems.

Figure 8-1 shows some examples of deposits and withdrawals in an emotional bank account. You make deposits by understanding the individual, keeping commitments, clarifying your expectations, attending to the little things, and showing personal integrity. You make withdrawals by breaking promises, ignoring or not listening to students, being unkind or discourteous, using angry words, and creating false expectations. As a trainer, you typically start with a zero balance in your emotional bank account with each student, so you need to start making deposits as quickly as possible, and empowering words are an easy way to do so. If you later make a mistake recognized as a withdrawal, students are more likely to forgive you if you have a positive balance. Also, if you make a mistake, you can turn this into a deposit by acknowledging it and sincerely apologizing.

FIGURE 8-1

Emotional bank account.

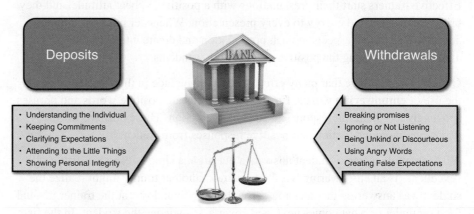

Author and poet Maya Angelou summed it up perfectly in one of her speeches:

- People will forget what you said.
- People will forget what you did.
- But people will never forget how you made them feel.

It doesn't cost anything to make students feel better about themselves, and empowering words go a long way to do so.

Some other examples of empowering words and phrases are: absolutely, awesome, bazinga, bingo, bravo, brilliant, cool, correct, deep question, dynamite answer, excellent, fantastic, good, good question, great, great question, helpful answer, I like you, incredible, ingenious, interesting, intriguing, jackpot, just what I was looking for, magnificent, marvelous, nice idea, never heard it put so well, outstanding, powerful answer, right, sharp answer, super, superb, sure, thank you, undeniable, useful idea, very good question, very much so, victory, way to go, well done, winner, woo hoo, wonderful, X-ray vision, yes, you're right, you're quick, you're very kind, and zinger.

> **AUTHOR'S NOTE:** As a trainer and professor, I frequently used an enthusiastic "Woo Hoo!" as an empowering phrase in the classroom. Many times when walking through a store or mall, I hear someone yell out "Woo Hoo!" when they recognize me and want to say "Hello." You often don't know what you'll do or say that will really stick with people, but if you're going to be remembered for something, I can tell you from experience, it's really a great feeling knowing that you're remembered for some of the positive moments you bring to people.

Skills and Techniques

In addition to a positive, upbeat attitude, an effective trainer needs to include some basic skills and techniques in any training session. Some of these skills, such as a speaking voice, might be obvious to you, but some of the other skills might be new to you.

Using a Trainer's Speaking Voice

Most training events occur within a classroom, and trainers need to have a good speaking voice with the ability to project their voice so that all the students can them. Trainers speak in a way that allows them to be heard by everyone, but not so loud that it sounds like they're yelling. Speaking clearly, at an adequate decibel level, and with a variety of tones and inflections enhances student interest and learning.

If you ever saw a live play, especially one where the actors didn't have microphones, think of how the actors spoke. They don't use a conversational voice but instead talk so that the entire audience can hear them. If the audience can't hear the actors, they'll quickly become bored and might even leave. Similarly, if students can't hear the trainer, they will quickly become bored and disengage from the training.

> **ON THE SIDE:** Trainers need to be conscious of their voice inflections. The wrong inflection can change a statement into a question. For example, the statement "I like you" sounds like a question when said with a rising inflection on *you* ("I like you?"). Chapter 2, "Communication Skills," discussed this in the context of a help desk specialist talking to a customer. If a trainer frequently uses a rising inflection at the end of statements, it comes across as a lack of self-confidence and students might suspect the trainer doesn't know the content.

Effective trainers vary their tone and volume for variety instead of speaking with the same monotonous, monotone voice. Actor Ben Stein in the movie "Ferris Bueller's Day Off" did a great performance as the worst monotone teacher in the world. You might remember him saying "Bueller?... Bueller?... Bueller?" but he also gave a droning lecture on economics that few people remember. The information that anyone hears by someone with a boring monotone voice is also likely to be forgotten soon, though they might never forget the pain as they had to sit through it.

Making Comfortable Eye Contact

While talking to a class of students, make comfortable eye contact with as many participants as possible. The goal is to make a connection, but not stare at the person, making them uncomfortable. It helps establish rapport with the students and lets them know you view them as real people. Toastmasters helps many people improve their communication, public speaking, and leadership skills, and they recommend eye contact for about four to five seconds when speaking.

Not everyone is comfortable with eye contact, so if you notice someone looking uncomfortable or uneasy when you're looking at them, be respectful and look away. Also, if you look for too long, it comes across as a stare and the other person might perceive it in many different ways. Depending on your body language and facial expressions, they might think you're flirting, glaring, or ogling. You can avoid these misperceptions by simply scanning the room and not looking at any one person for too long.

Eye contact lets you keep in touch with what is going on in the classroom. If the students become distracted by something you're doing or saying, or by something else going on in the classroom, you'll notice it right away if you're making eye contact. In contrast, trainers that talk to the white board or PowerPoint display when teaching a topic have their backs (or at least the back of their heads) facing the audience. In addition to disconnecting from the students, their voice doesn't travel as well and students often have trouble hearing and understanding them.

Many successful trainers scan the room from left to right and then back from right to left, occasionally pausing while they make eye contact with a participant. This does need to be somewhat random though, because you don't want to appear as though you're a robot on a swivel.

> **AUTHOR'S NOTE:**   Some people suggest that you do not make eye contact with students but instead look at the top of their heads or their foreheads. However, I've found that this often creates a disconnect between me and the students. When I make comfortable eye contact with students around the room, I'm able to make a connection that isn't possible when eye contact is avoided. Also, when making eye contact, it's much easier to read their body language and recognize when students might be confused or puzzled about a topic.

Moving Away from the Podium

It is common with many new trainers to grab hold of the podium with both hands and never let go. These trainers sometimes hold the podium so tight that blood drains from their knuckles, making them appear white. It also makes the trainers look tense and uptight, and can seriously detract from the topic they're trying to teach.

Whenever possible, it's best to use the front of the classroom as a stage and move around. You might need to refer to your notes on the podium occasionally, but that doesn't mean that you have to stay there throughout the entire presentation.

A common technique used by many speakers and trainers is to move to a different area of the room, face the audience, plant their feet, and continue talking. Depending on the topic, they might continue talking while they are moving, but you won't see them staying in one place constantly, or moving constantly.

When you're moving around, your presentations appear more dynamic and the variety makes it easier for your students to stay engaged. Another benefit of moving around is that it allows you to view the classroom, and the students, from different perspectives.

> **ON THE SIDE:**   If you want to see some effective ways that many talented speakers use the stage, watch some TED talks on ted.com or YouTube.com. Technology, Entertainment, Design (TED) conferences have the slogan of "ideas worth spreading" and speakers can talk for a maximum of 18 minutes. You'll hear some awesome speakers, and if you pay attention to their methods, you can also gain some outstanding insight into how to deliver great presentations.

Using Comfortable Gestures

As you move around the room, you'll be free to make gestures that can connect with the students. The goal is to use natural and non-distracting gestures and movements, while also being conscious of your body language. For example, open-handed gestures are inviting, but using an open palm toward the students is aggressive, giving a message of "talk to the hand!"

One of the challenges with gestures is eliminating unconscious, distracting gestures. For example, trainers might constantly click a pen, or repeatedly remove and replace the top of a whiteboard marker. Some trainers have an unconscious habit of rocking back and forth on their feet. They might even insist they don't do it, until they see a video of themselves. It's also easy to fidget with items in your pocket, such as coins or keys, but by removing them before starting a training session, you eliminate that possible distraction.

Asking people for feedback is an effective way of learning if you have any distracting gestures, and if any of your gestures make your students feel more comfortable. Any training should include a method where students provide feedback, and you add a question related to the trainer's effectiveness in this feedback form. You don't need to specifically mention gestures, but if you have some gestures that are especially welcoming, or especially distracting, the students will mention them. Another method to discover any unconscious gestures you might have is to create videos of your presentations and watch them later.

Asking Questions

Questions are a great way to engage the students. They can help you gauge the students' understanding of topics and give your students an opportunity to get involved with the class. Trainers often use two primary types of questions: canvassing questions and open-ended questions.

Canvassing questions ask students a simple question and encourage them to raise their hands. For example, you can ask, "How many of you have called into a help desk yourself?" You can raise your hand as a clue that you want them to raise their hand if this applies to them. You can build on this with a follow-up question such as, "Does anyone remember a bad experience you're willing to share when you called into a help desk?" This gives people an opportunity to speak up and share their experience. Many times, you can use the students' stories to help you move into the topic or expand it.

Be careful that you do not ambush students when asking canvassing questions. For example, imagine a trainer asking, "Does anyone remember a bad experience when you called into a help desk?" and encouraging the students to raise their hands. Then, he picks one of the students and asks them to tell their story. This can easily make students uncomfortable. It's simple to raise your hand with other people in the class. It's something completely different to be picked out of a crowd to tell a story you might not be comfortable telling. Additionally, other students will recognize what happened and you might suddenly find that no one is responding to your canvassing questions.

One more technique you can use with canvassing questions is to use them to gauge classroom participation. You ask one canvassing question and then ask the opposite question. For example, you can ask, "How many of you have called into a help desk yourself?" and then follow it up with, "How many of you have never called into a help desk?" Ideally, you'll see everyone raise their hands to one of the two questions. If you find that many people are not participating, you can use some humor and ask something like, "How many people are tired of help desk topics and need to take a break?"

Chapter 2 covered open-ended questions. As a reminder, an open-ended question is any question that can't be answered with a simple one- or two-word answer. For example, in the summary of a topic, trainers often use questions to gauge the student's understanding of the topics. Here are two sample questions:

- Do you remember what a canvassing question is?
- What is a canvassing question?

In the first question, students might internalize the question and think "Yes" but not respond. In the second question, students are more likely to go over the description of a canvassing question in their mind. If they have been participating, they are more likely to respond to the second question.

> **ON THE SIDE:** After asking a question, ensure you pause before saying anything. Many new trainers ask the question, become uncomfortable with the silence, and then quickly answer the question. Students quickly learn that the trainer will answer the question, so they don't respond to the questions. In contrast, if you pause and wait for an answer, students become uncomfortable with the silence and will seek to break it by answering.

Last, it's important to reward those that answer. I remember working with one trainer that always had treats like bite-size Halloween candy bars. During the summary, he would ask open-ended questions and throw a piece of candy to the first person that answered correctly. It didn't take long at all for the students to get used to this, and his summary sessions were very lively. You don't have to buy candy to get your students to participate, though—simpler rewards, such as empowering words described earlier, can be effective, too.

Taking and Answering Questions

In addition to asking questions, effective trainers need to know how to take and answer questions. Depending on the size and formality of the class, students might be encouraged to raise their hand to ask a question or just blurt out their question when it comes to mind. Either way, trainers need to respond, and there a few ways to do so.

First, you need to ensure you understand the question. Some questions are clear, but if the question isn't clear, you might need to ask the student for clarification. Next, respond with empowering words to the student saying something like "thanks for asking that" or "good question." Then restate the question so that all the students can hear it. Many times, a student speaks only loud enough for the trainer to hear but other people might not have heard it. If they don't know what the question is, they won't be able to follow the answer. After restating the question, you can answer it in one of the following ways:

- **Answer it directly.** The simplest way to answer the question is to simply state the answer. Many times, students will attempt to answer the question when they ask it and if so, you can affirm their understanding. If possible, reiterate the answer using the same or similar words they used.

- **Postpone the question.** If the answer is too deep but the topic will be covered later, you can ask the student to hold the question because it will be covered in a future topic. It's sometimes useful to give a mini-answer. For example, if you're teaching a topic on risk and a student asks, "What is a vulnerability?," you can mention that a vulnerability is simply a weakness, and the topic will be explored in greater depth in a later topic.

■ **Redirect the question.** In this technique, you restate the question and then redirect the question to the class asking if anyone knows the answer. Many times, a student might ask a question for a topic that you just covered. By redirecting the question to the class, it can be a mini-review of a topic while also letting you gauge other student's understanding of the topic. If no one can answer it, it lets you know you might need to reteach the topic. Ensure you thank or verbally reward anyone that answers. Last, after one or more student's provides the answer, you speak as the authority and give the definitive answer. This is especially true when two or more students answer and their answers seem to conflict with each other. Whenever possible, repeat the words that these students used in their explanation. This helps amplify what was accurate while also validating the student's response.

When taking questions, an important point to remember is that it's OK to say you don't know the answer. Many times students are just curious when they ask a question and it isn't important to them. Other times, they really want the answer. One technique to use if you don't know the answer is to say, "I don't know that answer. If it's important to you I can look it up and get back to you," or simply say, "I don't know that answer. I'm going to have to look it up and get back to you."

If you do say you'll get back to the student, keep your commitment and ensure you do. That student (and all the others) will be expecting the answer. Even if the question and the answer become less important to them, they will remember if you don't answer. This becomes a promise that you've given, and when you never give the answer, it becomes a broken promise.

Many trainers draw a box in the corner of the white board and use it to remind them of questions to research later. When they can't answer a question right away and they promise to research it, they write a note about the question in this box to remind them. Figure 8-2 shows an example, where the topic is on Effective Training but the trainer has written notes based on student questions. One student asked if the organization is currently looking for an in-house trainer and another student asked if the organization's acceptable usage policy (AUP) has been updated recently.

FIGURE 8-2

Questions to research.

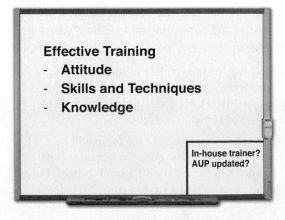

Telling Stories and Analogies

Stories and analogies have the power to ignite people's imagination and move their hearts, minds, and feet into action. A **story** is an account of a real-life event, and when you are able to tell stories that relate to a concept you are teaching, you can make the topics come alive. An analogy provides a comparison between two things and can help people connect a known concept with an unknown concept, making the newer concept easier to understand. Both are very effective at translating abstract or complex ideas into simpler concrete concepts.

> **AUTHOR'S NOTE:** Storytelling is a skill needed by more than just train-ers. Successful leaders in almost any business master the art of storytelling to inspire and motivate others and enlist these people in their vision. Peter Guber's book *Tell to Win: Connect, Persuade, and Triumph with the Hidden Power of Story* provides great insight into the power of stories. It also includes steps you can use to create compelling stories that will help people under-stand and spur them to action. John Chambers, chairman and CEO of Cisco, wrote this about the book: "Guber has it right—effective story telling is one of the most important things leaders can do to drive productive collaboration, especially in today's video-centric and connected world."

If you've ever watched any of the Through The Wormhole TV shows, you've probably seen this done many times. Scientists regularly take simple concepts, such as a bouncing ball, and relate them to much deeper scientific principles, making them much easier to understand.

As an example of using a story, imagine you want to teach students about the impor-tance of backing up data. You could teach this by just stating the facts like this:

> "Backups provide copies of data that can be restored if the original data is lost or corrupted. When updated backups exist, it's relatively easy to restore lost data. However, if the original data is lost or corrupted and backups don't exist, the data is lost forever."

The previous example certainly tells the key points related to backups. However, if someone doesn't already understand the importance of backups, these key points might not stick with them. In contrast, the following example is more likely to reach more students:

> "It's important to have backups and while many people know this, they don't take the time to create them. As an example, in 2009, MegaPetCo owned a small chain of pet stores and they were enjoying some great success. All their company data was stored in a single primary database, and after an adminis-trator incorrectly performed a bulk update, it deleted all the data. If they had backups, this incident would have been merely inconvenient—but they didn't have any backups. Zero. Within months, MegaPetCo filed for bankruptcy, closed all their stores, and laid off several hundred employees. Some people don't recognize the importance of backups until they experience a painful loss. Sometimes they just lose an important file that they have to recreate from scratch, other times they lose their entire organization."

When telling stories, it's important to ensure the story is relevant. The goal isn't to tell stories to entertain the students, but instead tell a story that makes a point. As an example, the story about MegaPetCo is relevant in the topic of backups. However, if you were teaching a topic on documenting help desk calls, it isn't relevant and shouldn't be told.

Stories of your own life experiences are often useful so that it demonstrates this isn't just something that happens to someone else. For example, if you lost a company report that was due the next day and you had to work late into the night to recreate it because you didn't have a backup, that is relevant and useful. It shows some vulnerability and that you can make mistakes just like anyone else. It also makes the point that anyone can lose a file, and without backups, the loss can be painful. Be careful of exaggerations, though. If you start telling exaggerated stories, they often come across as less than accurate and it can affect your credibility. Students might not believe other facts you tell them and suspect that they might be exaggerated too. Many exaggerations include absolutes such as *all*, *always*, *everyone*, *none*, *never*, and *no one*. For example, saying, "Losing data is painful for *everyone*," or, "*All* companies backup their data" include absolute words (everyone and all), but there are likely some exceptions. Many people are tuned into these words and recognize there are almost always exceptions, so these statements using them are often not true.

Last, stay on topic. It's important that you get to the point of your story as soon as possible. As an example, the MegaPetCo story takes about a minute to tell and it stresses the importance of creating backups within that time. Succinct story-telling takes planning and preparation for most people. For example, you might know of a relevant story, but if you don't write it out or practice telling it, you might take five to ten minutes to tell the story. Most of this becomes fluff and filler. Instead of getting your audience's attention to engage them and make a point, you become a long-winded storyteller that loses the students' interest.

Using Training Aids

Training aids are often useful for enhancing instruction topics by engaging additional senses beyond just the sense of hearing. Some examples of training aids include whiteboards, interactive white boards, PowerPoint presentations, video, and equipment or other hardware. One of the primary goals when using training aids is to ensure that the aid enhances the training and does not detract from the learning experience.

When using a white board and PowerPoint presentations, you need to ensure that the display is large enough to see for all the students. For white boards in a typical classroom, one- to two-inch letters are needed to ensure all the students can read what you've written. A one-inch letter is readable from 10 feet away and a two-inch letter is readable from 20 feet away. You can check this by writing something on the board and viewing it from the back of the classroom.

When writing on the white board, use short phrases or key words to emphasize your points—you don't need to write out the full topic. There may be times when you find it best to write topics on the white board before you start. As an example, Figure 8-3 shows text added on a white board before a complex cryptography class. In this case, the trainer has realized that students often forget the basics related to confidentiality, integrity, and non-repudiation during the topic. The trainer plans to teach them early in the topic, and as the topic becomes more complex, the trainer is able to reinforce these key points by referring back to these notes.

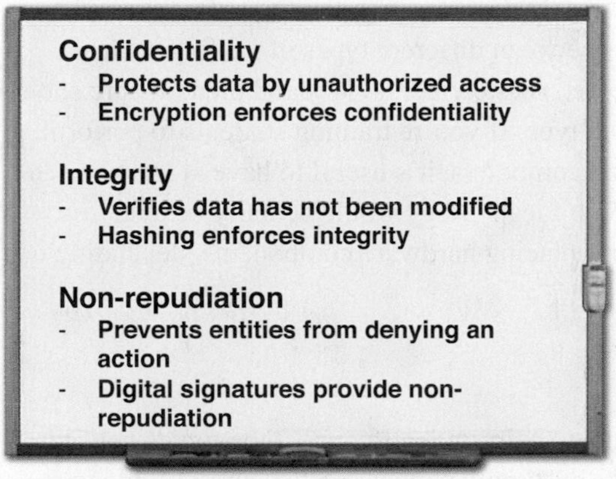

Confidentiality
- **Protects data by unauthorized access**
- **Encryption enforces confidentiality**

Integrity
- **Verifies data has not been modified**
- **Hashing enforces integrity**

Non-repudiation
- **Prevents entities from denying an action**
- **Digital signatures provide non-repudiation**

FIGURE 8-3

Text written before class starts.

ON THE SIDE: Many classes have two white boards mounted side-by-side. This makes it easy to write some notes on one white board before the class starts and use the other white board as needed during the class. Even if you only have a single white board, you can still write some topics on it before the class, but you might need to save some space for other topics.

The "Creating PowerPoint Presentations" section later in this chapter covers PowerPoint in more depth, but as an introduction, neat and simple presentations are much more effective as training aids than busy and complex presentations. A key point is to ensure that these presentations are grammatically correct. If a slide has a grammatical error such as a misspelled word, it can be extremely distracting for some students. The entire time you are talking about the topic, some students will not be able to do anything other than focus on this misspelling. Also, this error can cause some students to question the validity of other information.

When using any type of audio or video presentations, you need to ensure it is loud enough for everyone to hear. Also, you should take time the test these presentations. You might know exactly what video you want to show but be unable to find it. Worse, you might start the wrong presentation and then have to stop it and start again. All of this becomes distracting for the students. One easy way to ensure you can easily start the correct video is to embed the video or video links into your PowerPoint presentation. It takes a few more preparatory steps but ultimately makes it much easier to start during your presentation.

Before showing the video, introduce it with enthusiasm and give the students some key points to look for. This helps create some interest and excitement in the video, and they'll be actively looking for these key points. After the video is over, lead a short discussion about it to ensure the students caught the key points. You can typically show short videos of about five minutes just about any time when they are appropriate. However, it's best to avoid longer videos right after lunch. Digestion tends to make people tired, and a video after lunch might put them to sleep.

Equipment and hardware can vary widely depending on the topic. For example, if you want to stress the differences between different types of cabling such as shielded twisted pair (STP), unshielded twisted pair (UTP), and plenum-safe cable, you can pass around samples of each type. If you're training students to perform hardware maintenance with personal computers, it's useful to have at least one computer that they can touch and feel. Ideally, they would actually be able to practice by removing, installing, or replacing hardware components, depending on the objectives of the class.

Bridging Topics

Bridging topics is a useful technique to help students connect the topics between multiple sessions. You bridge topics by simply connecting the current topic to a past or future topic. It helps the students realize that the course is not just a string of disjointed topics, but instead is a connected group of interrelated topics.

You might have noticed bridging in different areas of this book. As an example, in Chapter 1, "Introduction to Help Desk Support Roles," several different skills were introduced as either hard skills or soft skills. One paragraph mentioned training skills with a short summary and then mentioned that these skills were covered in more depth in Chapter 8. In the section on handling difficult situations in Chapter 2, it warned of the potential for burnout and then mentioned that managing stress and recognizing burnout is covered in Chapter 3, "Personal Skills."

This technique is especially valuable when you are teaching multiple sessions of a class, such as teaching several class periods in a day or week, or even several class sessions taught once or twice a week for a month or two. In addition to helping students understand how the topics are connected, it also helps them mentally prepare for what's coming and remember what they previously learned.

As an example, imagine you're teaching a four-session class on Information Technology (IT) security with the following topics:

- Understanding Risk
- Common Threats
- Common Vulnerabilities
- Mitigating Risk

When bridging topics, you tie them together by reinforcing the importance of past topics and building on future topics. Here's the text of what a trainer might say at some point during the first session:

"Risk is the likelihood that threats will exploit vulnerabilities. That's a short sentence, but it has a lot of depth. Vulnerabilities are simply weaknesses, such as a single user's computer without anti-virus software installed, making it vulnerable to malicious software (malware). Threats are anything or anyone that represent possible danger, such as malware infecting a computer. In this case, the risk is the likelihood that this computer will become infected with malware. You can mitigate (or reduce) risks by reducing or eliminating the vulnerabilities, or reducing the effects of the threat. Malware is almost everywhere, so it's unlikely you'll be able to remove it as a threat, but it is possible to install anti-virus software to reduce the vulnerability.

"Malware is only a single threat to our IT infrastructure, but there are many more that you'll learn about in the second session, Common Threats. In the third session, Common Vulnerabilities, we'll cover many of the common IT vulnerabilities and how threats can exploit them. In the last session, Mitigating Risk, you'll learn about many of the controls implemented in our organization and how they help reduce our risks by addressing vulnerabilities and threats."

In this example, the trainer is able to define risk and introduce threats, vulnerabilities, and mitigation techniques without having to dig into these topics too deep. Instead, the bridging technique simply tells the students they will learn more about these topics in a later session.

Similarly, in subsequent sessions, the trainer can bridge the topic with past sessions by reminding the students of the definition of risk. For example, in the "Common Vulnerabilities" session, the trainer might say this:

"You might remember from the first session that risk is the likelihood that a threat will exploit a vulnerability. You learned about many common threats in the previous session, and in this session, you'll learn about many of the common vulnerabilities or weaknesses."

Being Aware of Filler Words

Beware of using filler words when teaching. **Filler words** are short, meaningless words that many people use when they pause to think, or simply to fill in gaps. Some popular filler words are "uh," "um," "you know," and "like." Consider this example riddled with filler words:

ON THE SIDE:
As a simple exercise, you can pair up and have one person read this paragraph with the filler words, and then read it without them. Give each person an opportunity to talk and an opportunity to listen. Note that this paragraph is similar to the last paragraph in the previous section on Bridging.

"Uh, you might remember from the first session, um, that risk is the likelihood that a threat will, you know, exploit a vulnerability. Like, you learned about many common threats, uh, in the previous session and like, in this session, you'll learn about many of the, you know, common vulnerabilities or weaknesses."

Many people use filler words unconsciously and are unaware how seriously these filler words detract from their message. In some cases, they distract students so much from the message that students make a game out of just counting filler words. If you suspect you are using filler words excessively, do a mini-presentation for a friend or two and ask them to count your filler words. Knowing they are counting the filler words will help you become more conscious of saying them and help you reduce them. Another way you can see if you are using them excessively is to create a video of yourself and then watch it.

Using the Three-Minute Guideline

Another technique many trainers use to keep their students engaged is the three-minute guideline. This guideline encourages trainers to engage the students at least every three minutes. You can do this with a question, an engaging story or analogy, handing out a training aid such as different cables, showing a short video, or doing an exercise. It provides students with a mental break from a long lecture and helps them stay focused while you are providing key information.

Not all topics allow you to do this, so it's best to consider this a guideline rather than a rule. However, when trainers ignore this guideline and instead just talk for an hour without giving their students an opportunity to engage in the topic, students often enter into a different state of consciousness that has nothing to do with what the trainer is saying.

> **ON THE SIDE:**   Different states of consciousness are quite common in many students. This ranges from simple daydreaming to actually falling asleep. Some students vigorously scribble notes throughout a lecture to help themselves stay focused, and this can be quite effective for these students. However, as a trainer, you cannot force students to take notes aggressively, but you can engage them with questions, stories, training aids, and exercises.

Telling and Showing

An old Chinese proverb is, "Tell me and I'll forget; show me and I may remember; involve me and I'll understand." As with many proverbs, it has a lot of wisdom. If your only method of teaching is telling, don't be surprised if your students forget. Showing them will help them learn, but getting them involved helps them understand. With an understanding of a topic, they are more likely to keep the knowledge for a much longer time.

When teaching trainers how to teach and facilitate classes, I often started one session doing everything wrong. I didn't do this at the beginning of a course, but instead did it after I had established rapport with the class and taught some material showing that I did have some teaching skills. I came in late, looked flustered, and muttered something about a phone call. I didn't apologize for being late, but instead started into the topic by first mentioning it wasn't very important but I had to teach it anyway, and I started to read from my notes using a soft monotone voice. Sometimes I dropped the notes, started fumbling with the slide presentation, read from the slides, and/or started scribbling illegible notes on the white board. When someone inevitably suggested we take a break so I could get organized, I gruffly responded saying something along the lines of what a stupid idea that was since we just started. I rarely was able to keep a straight face with this for more than five minutes.

After explaining my intent to do everything wrong, and apologizing to the student I attacked (with my gruff response), we had a lively discussion. I invited the students to point out everything I did wrong and how I might do it differently. I only did this after presenting the correct methods—just telling them what to do isn't as effective of a learning experience as first teaching them what to avoid and then showing them the result of doing things incorrectly. Here are some obvious points that came out:

- **Apologize if you're late:** If you expect students to be on time to class, you should be on time, and if you aren't, you should apologize profusely. If you did have a horrible phone call that made you late and is still on your mind, it's OK to mention it. For example, if your best friend borrowed your car and you just learned he was in auto accident but you don't have details on his health or the condition of your car, it's OK to say so, especially if it's heavy on your mind. Teachers and trainers are human, and it's OK to allow your human traits to come out.

- **Don't talk in a monotone:** Most people understand the importance of varying their voice tone and volume when teaching, but they don't always recognize how painful it can be to listen to until they've experienced it. Similarly, speak clearly and face the students when talking.

- **Don't attack the material:** Telling students that the topic isn't important is sure to turn off their interest; they'll think, "If it's not important, why are we wasting our time?" Instead, generate interest and tell the students what is important about the topic.

- **Don't read to the students:** Many people are offended when a trainer reads from a book. It's one thing when an adult reads a child's story to children, but when one adult reads to another, it comes off as condescending at best. At worst, it makes trainers look as though they don't understand the material enough to talk about it.

- **Don't attack students:** Gruffly telling students that they have stupid ideas comes off as an attack, and it is one way to quickly unite the class against you. When students recognize a trainer verbally attacking another student, they will often rally around that student and against you. When a student suggested taking a break so that I could get organized, a better response might have been, "Thank you, but I'm OK," or even, "Thank you. That's a great idea. Let's take a short break."

Any time you're able to demonstrate either the things to do or the things to avoid, it helps the students gain a deeper understanding of the topic. This exercise has been very effective when helping students learn teaching techniques, but you can also use the same concept with other exercises. For example, when teaching skills for help desk specialists, you could set up a demonstration where you are the help desk specialist helping someone over the phone and you do everything wrong. You could then lead a discussion asking the students to point out everything you did incorrectly, and how you might improve it the next time.

Understanding Your Subject Matter

Any trainer is expected to have an expert level of knowledge of the topic, and this often requires a significant amount of study and preparation before teaching the topic. As an example, consider a certification exam such as the CompTIA Security+ certification discussed in Chapter 3. There are multiple levels of knowledge of this topic:

- **Basic knowledge.** If you read a book on the Security+ certification exam, you will have a basic knowledge of the topic. You will likely be able to talk about different topics related to the exam, but probably won't have enough knowledge to talk about all the topics, pass the exam, or teach a class on it.

- **Certification knowledge.** If you study the objectives with the intent to take and pass the exam, you will have a deeper level of knowledge. While studying for a certification exam, many people recognize gaps in their knowledge, and due to concern that they might not pass the test, they seek out answers to fill in these gaps. While a person with this level of knowledge will earn the certification, this doesn't mean that they have a deep enough knowledge of the topics to teach it to others.

- **Training knowledge.** Trainers that study a topic with the intent of teaching have a much deeper level of knowledge than someone that just read a book or someone that has actually passed the exam. Trainers know that students often ask questions related to topic they don't understand. In order to answer many of these questions and help these students understand, the trainer often has to provide a deeper explanation. As an example, if a Security+ student asks why one protocol uses Transmission Control Protocol (TCP) but another protocol uses User Datagram Protocol (UDP), the trainer can't simply say, "Because I said so." Instead, the trainer needs to understand these protocols, how they work, and why is preferable in certain situations compared to the other.

Additionally, a trainer needs to be able to relate this knowledge in different ways. For example, as stressed in the "Telling Stories" section earlier, simply talking about backups might not be enough to ensure the students understand the topic. However, by bringing in real-life and relevant stories, the trainer is able to help the students learn the information at a deeper level.

ON THE SIDE: Many trainers listen to an inner questioning voice while they are preparing to teach a topic. As they prepare, they come up with possible questions that a student might ask related to the topic. Instead of just letting these questions pass, they take the time to investigate and learn the answers. If they teach the topic once, they might not hear students ask all of these questions, but they are prepared for many of the questions that students do ask. Also, when working with a class that is overly quiet, they can use these questions to engage the audience.

Steps Involved in Training

Successful training doesn't happen by accident, or haphazardly. Instead, there are reproducible patterns involved in both the development of courseware and training delivery. This section discusses some generic information on learning styles and adult learning theories. Next, it covers some of the basics of developing a course, and then on delivering a course.

Understanding How People Learn

Not everyone learns the same way. Instead, many people have a preferred learning style, and when trainers present the material based on the student's preferred learning style, students are often able to learn the material easier. A **learning style** refers to how someone learns, such as by seeing, hearing, reading, or doing. The four learning styles are:

- **Visual learners** learn best by seeing the material. PowerPoint presentations with appropriate charts, graphics, and other types of graphics are useful to these learners.

- **Auditory learners** learn best by hearing the material, or listening. Trainers engage these learners with a comfortable speaking voice, varying their tone and volume, and by adding stories and analogies to their presentations.

- **Reading/writing learners** learn best by reading and sometimes by writing. These learners value the text displayed in PowerPoint presentations along with student handouts or study guides that they can read at their own pace. Beyond technical training, many people regularly write in journals and find that by writing, they are able to gain deeper insights into their experiences.

- **Kinesthetic learners** (also known as experiential or tactile learners) learn best by doing. These learners enjoy labs and exercises where they can perform a task.

8

> **ON THE SIDE:** These learning styles are based on the neuro-linguistic programming (NLP) VARK models, which focus on how the mind processes and stores information. VARK is short for visual, auditory, reading-writing, and kinesthetic. Neil Fleming expanded these models and applied them to learning in the Fleming VARK model. You might see this occasionally listed as VAK, omitting reading/writing, or including reading/writing topics in the visual learning topic.

People can typically learn with any of these styles, but they tend to learn easier with their preferred learning style. Successful trainers attempt to engage students with all of the learning styles when they teach. For example, trainers might give pre-class reading assignments and then during the class, talk through a topic while also showing PowerPoint presentations and using other visual aids. After teaching a topic, they give students an opportunity to perform a task by doing a lab or exercise.

Understanding Why Adults Learn

Pedagogy is the science and art of education, and most courseware follows formal pedagogical principles. More specifically, most technical courseware follows many of the adult learning principles popularized in the United States by Malcolm Knowles. Knowles defined **andragogy**, or adult learning, as the art and science of helping adults learn.

Adult learning theory differs from the pedagogical principles used to teach children, and it is based on six assumptions of adult learners:

- **Adult learners have a need to know why they should learn something.** While it might be enough to tell a child you need to learn this "because I said so," adults need to understand the value of the learning. Whenever possible, the benefits of learning should be clear.

- **Adult learners have a need to be self-directing.** Instead of being told what to do and when to do it, adults want the responsibility of making their own decisions. Adult training includes opportunities for adults to search and discover knowledge and concepts on their own. As an example, labs and exercises might have narrow goals, such as completing specific steps, but they also give adults the opportunity to explore concepts beyond these steps. Similarly, reading assignments give adults an opportunity to dig into the materials as much as they desire, or to simply read it quickly to get the primary topics.

- **Adults draw upon their experiences to aid in their learning.** Adults have a greater volume and different quality of experience than youth, and they can draw on this experience as a resource in learning. Analogies that link topics with what adults already know to new topics helps provide the new topics with a much richer meaning.

- **Adult readiness to learn is tied to their roles and responsibilities.** Adult learners become ready to learn when life events demonstrate a need to learn.

If they don't see a need to learn, they will often consider the training a waste of their time. As an example, if an organization is considering adding new server applications in a year, and they send employees to training now, the employees are unlikely to value the training, and in turn, they are unlikely retain the information. In contrast, these students are more likely to learn the material if the server applications are currently being installed and the employees will be required to use these applications next week.

- **Adults want to be able to apply knowledge as soon as possible.** Adults often enter into a learning experience with a task-centered or problem-centered orientation to learning. In contrast, children experience a subject-centered orientation to learning. For example, children are learning knowledge to pass a test. Adults need to understand the knowledge is useful because it will help them perform a relevant task or solve a problem.

- **Adults are motivated to learn by both internal and external factors.** While adults are motivated to learn by external factors such as job requirements, there is a limit to this motivation. Adult learners are also motivated by internal factors based on their individual goals, values, and beliefs. For example, one person might see the current job as temporary and only be motivated to learn just enough to get by. Another person might see the current job as one step in a very successful career and be motivated to learn as much as possible, understanding that this knowledge might be valuable in a future job. Stories are often useful at helping people tune in to an internal motivating factor and increasing their interest in a topic.

Successful trainers understand that adults are different from children and adults learn differently. Whenever possible, trainers attempt to consider each of these adult learning principles and help adult learners see the value of the training in the different areas.

Developing a Course

Course development typically takes a lot of time and energy, but when course developers follow established procedures and guidelines, they can create outstanding courses. Even when developing a simple one-session class, you can follow some basic procedures to create a great learning experience for your students. As an example, imagine that you plan to teach students the generic troubleshooting steps listed in Chapter 6, "Troubleshooting Skills":

1. Identify the problem.
2. Establish a theory of probable cause.
3. Test the theory to determine the cause.
4. Establish a plan of action to resolve the problem.
5. Implement the solution or escalate if necessary.
6. Verify full system functionality and, if applicable, implement preventative measures.
7. Document findings, actions, and outcomes.

The following bullets outline the basic steps you would take to develop this class, assuming you had to develop the materials yourself:

1. **Identify the objectives.** In this step, you'll write out objectives for each of the troubleshooting steps. If you've been tasked to create the course but you weren't provided any objectives, ensure you verify these objectives meet the expectations of the course. The entire course is based on these objectives, and you don't want to complete the course development only to find that it doesn't teach what was expected or desired.

2. **Identify the audience.** Ensure you understand the students that will attend the course and their current level of expected knowledge. You don't want to talk down to the students by giving them information they already know. Similarly, you don't want to talk over their head so that they leave the course without learning anything.

3. **Create an outline.** Outlines break the course down into individual modules, and individual modules cover several related objectives. While creating the outline, you should order the modules in a logical progression based on what you expect the students to know and what you are teaching them. For example, you wouldn't want to teach them how to establish a plan of action prior to identifying the problem.

4. **Write modules one-by-one in an instructor guide.** Each module should include the module title, the objectives, the topics within the module, and a summary.

5. **Create a PowerPoint template.** This template will include some design elements that complement the topic, but can be used for every module within the course.

6. **Create PowerPoint slides for the modules.** Many times, course developers create the instructor guide and the PowerPoint slides at the same time. Some developers use PowerPoint to list the module contents first, and then add the points into the instructor guide. The order isn't as important as ensuring that the PowerPoint slides cover the relevant content.

7. **Create student handouts if necessary.** Student handouts might be a printout of the slides, a book or booklet that includes information students can use during the class, and any exercises or labs. If a module includes student handouts, you would create these before moving on to the next module.

As you dig into the details of the course, many of the concepts will become clearer to you than they were when you created the outline. When putting a course together, it's entirely possible that you'll end up adding or removing topics, moving topics into different modules, or changing the order. As long as the course meets all of the training objectives, it really doesn't matter if the final product doesn't match your original outline exactly.

Identifying Needs and Objectives

The first step in creating training is to identify what you want to accomplish. The most common way to do this is by first identifying the needs or objectives of the training. With these identified, it becomes much easier to create the training, and also to evaluate the training based on the original goal of what you wanted to accomplish.

Dr. Benjamin Bloom created Bloom's Taxonomy of Learning Domains (commonly called **Bloom's Taxonomy**) in 1956, which provides a classification of learning objectives on six different levels. It has been updated and revised several times over the years. Figure 8-4 shows a diagram of the Bloom's Taxonomy—Learning In Action model, divided into six sections. It shows each of the six levels on the inside, verbs used to describe these objectives in the middle, and methods used to teach these objectives on the outside.

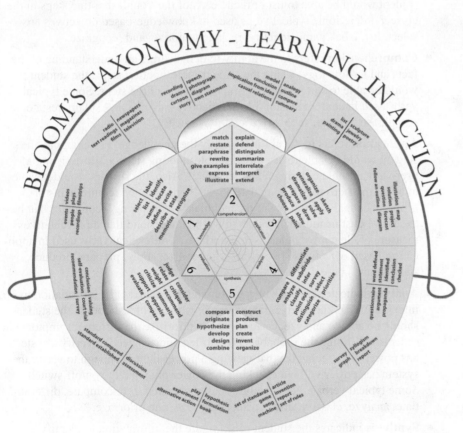

FIGURE 8-4

Bloom's Taxonomy.

If you were tasked with teaching the generic troubleshooting steps mentioned earlier, you could use Bloom's Taxonomy to help develop objectives related to these steps. The following bullets show each of the six levels of knowledge, along with how you could use these levels when creating objectives to teach the troubleshooting steps.

> **ON THE SIDE:**   As a reminder, the seven troubleshooting steps are:
> 1. Identify the problem.
> 2. Establish a theory of probable cause.
> 3. Test the theory to determine the cause.
> 4. Establish a plan of action to resolve the problem.
> 5. Implement the solution or escalate if necessary.
> 6. Verify full system functionality and, if applicable, implement preventative measures.
> 7. Document findings, actions, and outcomes.

- **Knowledge** indicates a basic memorization of facts and terminology. The student would be able to list or recite each of the troubleshooting steps in the correct order. Some typical verbs used in knowledge-based objectives are select, list, label, name, identify, recite, memorize, and recognize.

- **Comprehension** refers to the ability to demonstrate an understanding of the facts and terminology. Using the same troubleshooting steps, the student would be able to summarize or paraphrase each of the steps. Some typical verbs used in comprehension-based objectives are match, explain, restate, paraphrase, rewrite, summarize, and illustrate.

- **Application** refers to the ability to apply the knowledge. For example, the student would be able to use these troubleshooting steps while assisting a user with a problem during a help desk call. Also, the student would be able to adapt the steps to accommodate slight changes in the requirements of different calls. For example, if the technician is repairing a computer that has excessive dust inside, the technician would understand that a preventative measure of cleaning the dust is appropriate. Some typical verbs used in application-based objectives are organize, generalize, apply, prepare, produce, show, draw, choose, or paint.

- **Analysis** indicates the student can examine and analyze the information to infer additional knowledge. For example, while troubleshooting, the student should be able to analyze, categorize, and prioritize the different symptoms in order to determine the probable cause. If technicians need to verify a system has power, they recognize that viewing a power light is enough to verify the system has power without checking the power plug and the on/off switch. Some typical verbs used in analysis-based objectives are compare, differentiate, analyze, classify, distinguish, categorize, and prioritize.

- **Synthesis** indicates the student can compile the information to identify a pattern or a solution. After analyzing the information, the student should identify theories of probable causes and potential solutions. Some typical verbs used in synthesis-based objectives are compose, construct, originate, produce, develop, create, design, invent, and organize.

■ **Evaluation** indicates the student can make judgments about information based on evidence or criteria. For example, if technicians determine they need to escalate a problem because they do not have sufficient permissions to resolve it, they should be able support the decision based on evidence such as an error indicating they do not have sufficient permissions. Some typical verbs used in evaluation-based objectives are judge, consider, relate, critique, appraise, support, and evaluate.

Identifying the Audience

When creating courseware, you need to understand who will be receiving the training. The objectives often help you understand the audience based on what they are expected to learn. However, it is important to spell this out so that there isn't confusion between people teaching the topics, people attending the course, and managers/supervisors sending employees to the course.

As an example, if you are creating a course to teach students basic troubleshooting steps, you would expect these students are technically oriented and working in a job where they need to understand these steps; an accountant might be an outstanding accountant but be totally lost in this course. Sometimes you need to teach similar topics to a high-level audience, such as executives within the organization. Understanding that these executives won't actually be troubleshooting, you would just teach them the information as an overview.

Many courses include a list of prerequisites for a course. This helps potential students understand the knowledge they're expected to have prior to attending the course, and helps prevent unqualified personnel from attending the course. When students don't meet the prerequisites, they are either lost throughout the course, or they ask very basic questions, which slows down the momentum of the course for the other students.

Choosing a Delivery Method

One of the key steps in training development is deciding how you want to deliver the training. For the purpose of this book, it's assumed that the help desk specialist doesn't have a lot of resources to create the training materials, so training will either be in a classroom setting or one-on-one. However, for completeness, it's worthwhile knowing about the different delivery methods available for training:

■ **Classroom learning** refers to instructor-led sessions taught in a classroom. It is useful when you need to teach several students a topic at the same time, and is especially valuable when students will be performing labs or exercises. For example, if students need access to computers to perform labs, a classroom with computers is ideal. Similarly, if students are to perform exercises in pairs or groups, such as practicing communication skills used with customers, the classroom environment works well.

- **eLearning** (short for electronic learning) refers to any method where students learn topics through an electronic source. Users access web pages over the Internet or an internal network to learn topics in some eLearning applications. Other methods include computer-based applications where users can interact with the program to learn material. Many eLearning applications embed audio, video, and animations to teach topics, and require users to click through the application and also answer quiz or test questions before moving onto the next lesson.

- **Lectures** can provide valuable information just through the spoken voice. In some cases, a lecture can be in person, such as a lecture by a professor to a class of 150 students. It can also be through a recording, allowing the student to listen using a device such as an MP3 player. This method is dependent on the students actively listening, but motivated students can often get a lot out of the lecture method. When listening to recordings, students are able to pause and repeat topics based on their needs.

- **Video recordings** include a trainer talking to students through recordings. Currently there are thousands of free training sessions for a wide variety of topics on YouTube (http://www.youtube.com/). Similarly, many training companies host training videos on the Internet and sell them as DVDs.

- **Blended learning** refers to a combination of an instructor-led classroom session in combination with eLearning applications and/or videos. A benefit of blended learning is that students can learn through self-directed learning at their own pace, but also have the benefit of learning topics from an instructor. The instructor teaches some of the more complex topics and is also available to answer any trainee questions related to other self-directed learning.

- **Tutorials** are self-guided materials that a trainee can read and follow to learn new material. Trainees work on their own and at their own pace. Effective technical writing skills (covered in Chapter 7, "Writing Skills") are key to the success of any tutorials.

> **ON THE SIDE:**   After a trainers have delivered the same training to students a few times, they might choose to reproduce the training as a video or audio recording. This allows more students to access the same material at their leisure. While high-quality recording equipment will produce high-quality recordings, trainers can also create useful recordings with simple equipment. For example, it's possible to create both audio and video recordings using a webcam. Additional tools such as TechSmith's Camtasia (http://www.tech-smith.com/camtasia.html) can add some great professional effects without a steep cost.

Creating Training Materials

Once you've identified the training objectives and the delivery method, you can begin creating training materials. Training materials typically consist of PowerPoint presentations, student handouts, and an instructor manual. The instructor manual might just be notes to yourself if you're the only person that will perform the training. However, if others will use your training materials, you'll need to spend more time with the instructor manual to ensure other trainers will understand some of the concepts and how you intend to teach them.

One path is to look for off-the-shelf materials that you can use, and adapt them to the class. As an example, if you planned on teaching security topics to students, you could look for existing training materials covering the topics. The CompTIA Security+ certification is a very popular certification and many training companies have created courseware to teach it. A quick Internet search on "CompTIA Security+ courseware" will show you many options. Even if the courseware doesn't fit your purposes exactly, it will often still be useful if you can pick and choose what topics you plan to teach.

If you can't find a full course you can adapt, you might be able to use an existing textbook to teach your topics. Many publishers such as Pearson ensure that instructor materials are available for many of their textbooks. Some publishers sell these materials separately, but many others give the materials away when you plan to use their textbooks. If there aren't any instructor materials available, you can make some PowerPoint presentations and maybe add some supplementary handouts, but the textbook will still have a lot of content that you don't have to reproduce.

The last option is to create the materials yourself from scratch. This will obviously take the most time. You'll have to create all the handouts, PowerPoint presentations, and any exercises or labs needed for the class.

> **ON THE SIDE:** When creating training materials from scratch, it can take a significant amount of time. Based on a survey by the Chapman Alliance (Chapman, B., 2010, *How Long Does it Take to Create Learning?* http://www.chapmanalliance.com/howlong/), it can take from 22 to 82 hours to develop a single hour of instructor-led training, depending on the level of knowledge and the materials needed to teach the course. For an eLearning course, it can take between 49 and 716 hours to develop a single hour of training, again depending on the level of knowledge and the materials used. eLearning materials can take so much longer due to the time required to create the applications, flash presentations, and professional-quality videos. All of this can be done quicker, but as the old saying goes, you can have it good, quick, or cheap—pick two.

Creating Exercises

Exercises are very effective at helping students learn and are used in many technical training courses. These allow the students to actually perform the steps to complete a task and give the students an opportunity to explore a little on their own.

When creating exercises, it's extremely important to follow effective technical writing guidelines, as described in Chapter 7. Make sure the steps are clear and written in the proper order. As an obvious example, you wouldn't give instructions on how to start an application, and then mention that the system should be powered on before starting. If you need to tell the trainee that the system should be powered on before starting the application, include this information before the instructions on how to start the application.

One of the best ways to create an exercise is to perform the tasks within the exercise and document each step as you're doing it. This helps ensure that the each of the steps are included and the steps are in the proper order. Additionally, it's useful to get someone else to do the exercise to test it. Something that is obvious to you while you're developing the exercise might not be clear at all to the student; this feedback helps you realize additional instructions you might need in the exercise.

Creating PowerPoint Presentations

Microsoft Office suites include the Microsoft **PowerPoint** application, which many trainers use to create training slides. One of the great benefits of PowerPoint is that you can use templates. Templates are applied as master slides and apply to multiple slides within your presentation. After selecting an existing template, or creating your own, it becomes relatively simple to add your content.

As an example, Figure 8-5 shows Microsoft PowerPoint open with the template showing. The first slide in the template is selected and displayed in the primary window. It has a graphic background placed at the top and bottom, a title, five levels of bullets, and footer content. You can modify the position of any of this content on the master slide and modify the font size and style for any of the text. It automatically applies to other slides in your presentation.

FIGURE 8-5

PowerPoint template.

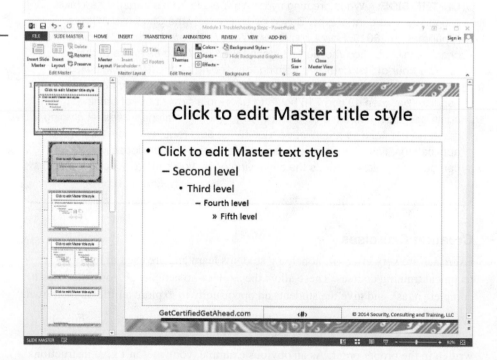

PowerPoint also has several preconfigured slides that you can modify if desired. In the left pane of the figure, you can see four generic slide types as masters. Each of these inherit all of the properties of the primary slide master but can be modified so that they are templates for the other types of slides in your presentation:

- Slide 1 is modified as a module title slide; you could use as the first slide in the presentation.
- Slide 2 is a standard bullet list slide. The only thing different from this and the primary master is that a red bar has been added right below the title.
- Slide 3 is a side-by-side bullet list. You can use this slide type to compare different lists or create a larger two-column bullet list.
- Slide 4 is a blank slide that can be used on any slide where you don't want preconfigured text boxes. For example, you could use this for a slide with charts, graphs, or other graphics.

Your presentations don't need to use all of these slide types. Many effective presentations use a simple bullet template for all their slides.

Beyond the master templates, effective PowerPoint presentations are typically neat and simple. Too much text, grammatical errors, and poor or unrelated graphics can distract from the message and even irritate your students.

One way you can ensure that your PowerPoint slides don't look too "busy" or overwhelming is with the simple rule of six. The rule of six has two components. First, don't include any more than six words in any line or bullet. Second, don't include any more than six lines or six bullets. Along with the rule of six, limit each slide to a single idea. If you find that a slide is too busy, you can often resolve the problem by separating the concepts onto different slides.

Use both upper- and lower-case letters on your slides. Many times a title will have all of the major words capitalized (such as "Tips for Troubleshooting"), but the key is consistency. If you use this format for one slide, ensure you use it for all slides. The content bullets should have the first word of each bullet capitalized, but not the others. Also, you can often omit punctuation such as periods, but again, consistency is key. If one bullet ends with a period but the others don't, it becomes distracting for the students. Also, be consistent with the fonts and font sizes you use. Using a master slide can help you with this—you pick the fonts and sizes once and you're done.

Color can add interest but ensure that you use colors that match; clashing colors can be highly distracting. Most themes come with colors in a matching palette, so you don't need to give this much thought unless you're picking your colors from scratch. If necessary, you can use an online tool to pick your colors. For example, ColorBlender (www.colorblender.com) allows you to create one color and it then creates a pallet of six matching colors.

Animation can be useful to show certain concepts, but a common mistake of many new PowerPoint users is to overdo the animation. Remember, the goal is to use the training aid to enhance the instruction. If the animation is excessive, it takes away from the content and becomes distracting.

Reading Assignments

In addition to the training, directing trainees to read materials before or after the training can help them gain a deeper understanding of topics. For example, if you have students read about a new topic before class, they will gain a basic understanding of the topic. After teaching the topic, their knowledge level will be much deeper than it would be if they were never exposed to the topic before. Additionally, while reading a new topic, they will likely come across concepts that aren't clear and they will come to the class with questions they hope to get answered.

Trainers often mention after-class reading assignments as optional. For example, instead of spending a lot of time on a topic that isn't directly related to the class objectives, a trainer might mention a source that students can look at if they're interested in learning more information. The reading assignment might be a book, a chapter in a study guide, user manual sections, online tutorials, blog posts, or white papers. If the material is relevant and it can help the trainees gain a better understanding of the topic, it is worth mentioning.

Delivering the Training

Courses and modules within courses often follow a simple formula of introduction, content, and summary. Many trainers shorten this to the following three sentences:

- Tell the students what you're going to tell them (introduction)
- Tell them (main topic)
- Tell them what you told them (summary)

The introduction of the module is extremely important to set the tone of the module. One way to start a course or module is to tell the students the objectives. However, even though these are very helpful to create the course and individual modules, they can sometimes come across rather dry when presenting them to students.

Many trainers use the What's In It For Me (WIIFM) technique by identifying why the module is valuable for the student. For example, if you're teaching the "Identify the Problem" topic from the troubleshooting steps, you can stress that technicians that are able to quickly identify problems find it much easier to resolve them, but technicians that have problems identifying the actual problem often experience much more on-the-job stress. Whether you use the WIIFM technique or something else, it's important to add some interest and excitement from the start.

The content of the module includes all the topics. When teaching these, you can use PowerPoint slides, various questioning techniques, relevant stories or analogies, and any other skills, techniques, and training aids you have available.

After teaching the topic, you can summarize it. A summary PowerPoint slide is often valuable. With the summary slide showing the main topics, you can ask open-ended questions to gauge the students' understanding of the topics and determine if you met the topic objectives.

Great trainers make training look effortless, but the truth is that there has been a great deal of preparation done behind the scenes. There are three areas where preparation can help you complete a successful training. They are preparing the environment, preparing yourself, and preparing the students. These topics, along with some other techniques you can use when delivering training, are included in this section.

Preparing the Environment

Before starting a training session, you should prepare the classroom and ensure that it is ready for the class. This includes ensuring that the equipment is operational and you know how to use it, and the classroom is clean and organized based on your needs.

Most classrooms are equipped with an overhead projector, so you should check it out and ensure it works. You might need to bring in a laptop and plug it into the projector, or bring your PowerPoint presentation on a CD, DVD, or USB flash drive. No matter what you'll be using, ensure you check it out and get it working. Once it's displayed, go to the back of the room and ensure it is focused and viewable for all the students. Depending on the equipment, you might need to close window shades or dim lights to ensure the display is bright enough. Some projectors might allow you to adjust the size of the display to ensure it is viewable. If your topic will have users performing labs or exercises on computers, ensure the computers are working.

Many times, you'll want to turn the display off while you expand a topic and talk about something else. You can usually blank the display using PowerPoint by right-clicking within the presentation and selecting Screen > White Screen or Screen > Black Screen. If you need to do this, take the time to determine how to do so before you start teaching the topic.

White boards can get quite dingy after trainers have written and erased multiple colors on them, making any new writing difficult to see, so you should start your class with a clean board. It's best to use a specialized cleaner designed for dry erase boards. Also, before the class starts, test the pens to ensure they haven't dried out.

After you've cleaned the board, write the course title, your name, and contact information on the board, as shown in Figure 8-6. Students that walk into the class want to know they're in the right place, and the course title helps them verify this. Writing your name lets the students remember it easily, and adding contact information lets them know you are available and accessible for additional help.

FIGURE 8-6

Preparing the white board.

**Training Skills
Darril Gibson
darril@darrilgibson.com**

Ideally, the room will be clean and organized, but if not, take the time to put it together for your class. You students' first impression of you will be derived partly from their first impression of the classroom. If the classroom is a mess, they might attribute this partly to you. Along these lines, when you finish your class, think of the next class and put the classroom back together for them.

Preparing Yourself

You prepare yourself by ensuring you know the material and ensuring you have a clear idea of how to present it. This includes being familiar with the training aids, having stories and analogies ready, and having questions you can use to engage the students.

Effective trainers tend to over prepare. They typically have a much deeper level of knowledge than they need to teach it. However, this level of knowledge prepares them to answer just about any questions that students have. In addition to the knowledge, trainers often have additional exercises, stories, and analogies ready to use when needed to help students learn different concepts. However, these extras aren't always needed for each set of students, so they might not use them in each class.

Any class has a beginning, a middle, and an end—no surprise there. However, there are different techniques you might use to prepare for each of these sections.

The most difficult part of a class is typically the beginning. This is the introduction and it might last as long as five to ten minutes. Even the most successful trainers and speakers admit a level of fear or nervousness before the start of a class or talk. They spend a lot of time preparing and practicing their introduction so that they know it inside and out. Once they start the introduction, they are able to go into autopilot for a few minutes, and any lingering fear or nervousness disappears. After the introduction, they are teaching material that they know and understand, and with the potential nervousness of the introduction behind them, they are able to continue the rest of the class. In contrast, a trainer that stumbles, stutters, and stammers through the introduction often has problems throughout the entire presentation.

In the middle, you'll focus on your content. While you won't read the content from your training guide, you will often have many notes in it to personalize it and remind you of what's important. While preparing for the class, you might remember some relevant stories or analogies that will help the students understand the topic. They might be from events that occurred within your organization or events that are completely external to the organization. You can put some notes into your training guide to help you remember these stories. You don't have to fully document these events, but instead just write down a few key words such as "Malware attack in 2013—took down email for five days."

The end can also be challenging if you're not prepared, so it's worthwhile taking time to identify how you'll end the class and preparing for it. For example, if you plan to use questions in a summary, ensure you have the questions ready. If you plan to reinforce one or more key points, you might like to take the time to rehearse how you'll do so.

Preparing the Students

The third area of preparation is the students. You can help prepare the students prior to the class by ensuring they can learn who the class is for, what the class will cover, and what prerequisite knowledge they're expected to have. You can include this information in course descriptions. Students that come to a class and then learn it doesn't apply to them spend a lot of time either trying to figure out how to get out, or distracting others since they aren't interested in the class.

Whenever possible, give students the start and expected end times up front. When providing times, it's best to overestimate the end time. If you tell people that you're expecting a class to run until 5 PM but you finish at 3 PM, they are usually happy. On the other hand, if you tell them the class will probably be over by 3 PM but you keep them until 5 PM, their happiness might begin to fade at 3:30 PM. Worse, many students probably won't be as attentive between 3 PM and 5 PM if they were expecting to leave by 3 PM. Even if you do an outstanding job with the presentation, they might still leave with an overall poor perception of the class if they're kept longer than they anticipated.

At the start of a class, it's best to do some housekeeping and provide students with some basic ground rules and guidelines. During this time, you can let them know about basic facility issues, such as where the restrooms are, where they can find snacks and drinks, any rules about eating or drinking in the classroom, phone usage, and other required topics unique to your environment, such as fire alarm procedures. Many times, trainers give out their phone number or other contact information, so that students can contact them if they anticipate being late. During this time, you can also let them know about expected breaks and expected meal periods, depending on the length of the class.

When letting students know the ground rules or guidelines of the class, you have an opportunity to exercise some control. You don't want to be overly strict with this, but you also don't want to appear lackadaisical. It's always easy to relax control as

AUTHOR'S NOTE: You typically would not start with the housekeeping and ground rules. Instead, it's best to do a positive, upbeat introduction on the topic and give students an idea of what they'll learn. The goal is to get them excited about the topic, and then you can bring up the housekeeping topics. Even the term "housekeeping" helps to remind students these are similar guidelines they'd hear in any class.

the class progresses and both you and the students are enjoying the time. However, if you start the class extremely lax, you'll find it almost impossible to exercise more control later.

Arriving Early

It's best to show up to the classroom early for several reasons. First, you need to ensure that the classroom is properly prepared and the equipment is operational. Even if you were able to check out the classroom on a previous day, things change from day-to-day. Someone else might have used the classroom and you might find things quite differently. By showing up early, you'll have time to put things together if necessary.

You'll also be able to greet the students as they arrive. People follow the same patterns for classes as they do for anything else, so you'll find that some students are early, some are right on time, and some are late. By greeting the early birds, you can start conversations with them, help them get comfortable in the classroom, and ultimately start your class with some friendly faces of people you know.

Building Rapport

As mentioned in the "Attitude" section earlier in this chapter, students don't care how much you know until they know how much you care. With this in mind, it's important to start building rapport as soon as possible. **Rapport** refers to a close and harmonious relationship where people or groups understand each other's feelings or ideas, and are able to communicate effectively based on this mutual understanding.

You don't have to share a lifetime of experience or agree with everything other people say to have rapport with them. However, when people have anything in common and they are able to communicate effectively with each other, they often feel as though they are in sync. With this in mind, you can build rapport with others by greeting them warmly, starting conversations, and listening to them.

Controlling Nervousness

It's perfectly natural to be nervous before doing a presentation. Even professionals who speak, train, and/or teach regularly admit that they are often nervous. This can be good up to a point. The primary reason people are nervous is that they're afraid who they'll look foolish. This provides motivation to ensure they are ready. Here's a list of several things you can do to minimize your nervousness:

- **Prepare, prepare, prepare.** As mentioned previously, it's best to prepare yourself by knowing the material, prepare the environment by ensuring the classroom is ready, and prepare the students so that they know what to expect. Ensuring you know the material is one of the best ways to control your nervousness.
- **Rehearse your introduction.** The time when trainers are most likely to freeze is during the introduction. If you rehearse your introduction and have it down pat, you'll be able to easily launch into it.

ON THE SIDE:
Salespeople attempt to build relationships with others by building rapport. Their goal is gain the trust and confidence of others, making it much easier to finalize sales deals. In contrast, people are less likely to close a sales deal when they don't trust the salesperson. Similarly, students are less likely to accept information provided by a trainer when they don't the trust the trainer.

- **Create a vision.** Prior to your presentation, conduct an imaginary presentation in your mind. In your vision, picture yourself as positive, upbeat, and energized about your material, and your audience as friendly and eager to learn.

- **Make the room yours.** Before you begin the presentation, and ideally before students arrive, spend some time looking around the room to become familiar with it. The goal is to become comfortable with your surroundings.

- **Greet students and start conversations.** As students begin to arrive, greet them, say hello, and start conversations. This helps build rapport with them and increases their comfort level. It also helps you to see them as individuals rather than judges of your performance.

- **Make eye contact.** Before speaking and while you're talking, make eye contact with as many participants as possible. This will help you realize that they are fellow human beings who are not out to see you fail. Most students want you to succeed as a trainer so that they can get good information out of the training and have an enjoyable time doing so.

Demonstrating Tasks

In many technical courses, your goal will be to ensure that the students can perform specific tasks such as configure an application, or open and log information into an incident. If you have your computer connected to an overhead projector for Power-Point presentations, you can use it to show how to perform the task: You simply perform the task on the computer and the students can follow your actions on the display.

A common procedure used in many courses is to talk about the task, demonstrate the steps in the task, and then give the students an opportunity to perform the task themselves. How you demonstrate the task is often dependent on the skill level of the audience.

If the skill level is very low, you can demonstrate each step individually and have the students perform the task with you. For example, if you're trying to get them to configure an application, you show them how to open the application and ask them to open the application on their computer. After all the students have the application open, you then have them select a menu item to configure the settings. After they have the menu item open, you move to the next step. By waiting for everyone to do exactly what you've done, you ensure that all the students are able to perform each step. A drawback is that this can be very time consuming and tedious, especially for more advanced students waiting for the slower students to get to the same spot.

When the students' skill level is higher, you can demonstrate the entire task and then let them do it on their own. For example, after talking about the task, you would open the application, select the menu item, and configure the settings. Students are watching what you're doing, but they aren't doing it themselves at the same time. A benefit is that you can quickly show the steps without needing to wait for every student to get to the same spot.

Engaging Students with Group Discussions

One way to get trainees engaged in a topic is to get them talking about it. For example, after presenting information on a topic, you can invite the participants to share their own experiences and knowledge.

In discussions involving the entire class, you'll often find that the same people are speaking up, while others tend to be quiet. However, if you break the class into smaller groups, some of the quiet students are more likely to participate and get more out of the class.

Assigning Reading

In addition to the training, directing trainees to read materials before or after the training can help them gain a deeper understanding of topics. For example, if you have students read about a new topic before class, they will gain a basic under-standing of the topic. After teaching the topic, their knowledge level will be deeper than it would have been if they never heard about the topic before. Additionally, while reading a new topic, individuals will likely come across concepts that aren't clear and they will come to the class with questions they hope to get answered.

Trainers often mention after-class reading assignments as optional. For example, instead of spending a lot of time on a topic that isn't directly related to the class objectives, a trainer might mention a source that students can look at if they're interested in learning more information. The reading assignment might be a book, a chapter in a study guide, user manual sections, online tutorials, blog posts, or white papers. If the material is relevant and it can help the trainees gain a better under-standing of the topic, it is worth mentioning.

Doing a Daily Review

If you are teaching a class on multiple days, you can use daily reviews to start each class and remind students of previous topics. These reviews are very effective at energizing students at the beginning of a class and reminding students of previously covered topics.

One way of doing a daily review is to ask questions about the previous topics. It's best to start with simple questions so that it is easier for students to answer and get involved. Gradually add in questions that are more difficult during the review, and students will keep up. In contrast, if you start with difficult questions, you probably won't get the same level of interaction.

When doing these reviews, consider rewards for students that answer. Empowering words such as "excellent" or "great answer" are very effective. Or you can use the candy technique mentioned in the "Asking Questions" section earlier.

Another benefit of a daily review is that it often raises questions on previously covered topics. You could start the class with a question such as, "Are there any questions about topics we covered in the last class?" However, unless one or more students really dug into a topic and was stuck with a concept, you're unlikely to get a response. In contrast, if you do a review where you engage their minds, they will remember topics that weren't completely clear, and they are more likely to ask a question.

> **AUTHOR'S NOTE:** I learned this method of a daily review when I attended another trainer's class. He was able to glance at the topics in his instructor guide, and then started asking questions about them. The first time I tried this technique, I had problems coming up with questions, so I wrote questions in my instructor guide before I tried it again. Eventually, I was able to ask questions on the fly, similar to how he did so, but it took time. More importantly, many students told me that these reviews were extremely valuable to them, and they were very conscious of being on time to the class so that they could benefit from the review.

Asking for Feedback

At the end of a course, it's very valuable to ask for feedback. The most common method is by giving the students access to a feedback form and asking them to complete it. These can be printed pages that you hand out or online web pages. Online web forms are usually the best because you can automate the collection of the data and summarize the feedback. However, online feedback forms take time to develop, and due to a variety of technical issues, might not always be available.

You can include anything in a feedback form, using either basic or in-depth questions, and you can make it as short or as long as you like. If it's too long or complex, though, don't be surprised if students simply don't complete it. As a very basic survey, you can use these questions:

- On a scale of 1 to 10 (1 being the worst and 10 being the best), how would you rate this class?
- What did you like best about this class?
- If there was one thing that could be improved about this class, what would it be?
- Feel free to add any additional comments.

Another way to add some depth to the form is to use similar questions in three separate topics—the environment (the classroom), the course material, and the trainer—as shown below.

Classroom

- On a scale of 1 to 10 (1 being the worst and 10 being the best), how would you rate this classroom?
- What did you like best about this classroom?
- If there was one thing that could be improved about this classroom, what would it be?
- Feel free to add any additional comments.

Course Materials

- On a scale of 1 to 10 (1 being the worst and 10 being the best), how would you rate the course materials used in this class?
- What did you like best about course materials used in this class?
- If there was one thing that could be improved with these course materials, what would it be?
- Feel free to add any additional comments.

Trainer

- On a scale of 1 to 10 (1 being the worst and 10 being the best), how would you rate trainer that presented this class?
- What did you like best about this trainer?
- If there was one thing that this trainer could improve, what would it be?
- Feel free to add any additional comments.

Creating a Positive Learning Environment

A positive learning environment provides students with a safe place to learn that includes respect, understanding, and collaboration. Trainers are responsible for creating and maintaining this atmosphere, so it's important to understand the typical elements of a positive learning environment. They are:

- **Safe.** Students can freely participate and take risks by asking and answering questions. Trainers need to ensure that their responses to students encourage and reward the student's participation, and that other students do not belittle or attack any student. If a student does belittle or attack another student, the trainer needs to immediately let the attacking student, and the class, know that the behavior is unacceptable.

- **Respect.** The trainer should ensure that all students are respected and their input is treated as valuable, despite any diversity of knowledge, background, or experience. This ties into the element of safety, but stresses the importance of recognizing diversity and ensuring students respect each other.

- **Understanding.** The trainer and class are there for a common purpose: the trainer is attempting to provide training and the students are attempting to learn. Both the trainer and the students share an interest in, and a commitment to, student learning.

- **Collaboration.** The trainer and students are collaborators working together to transfer knowledge. While the trainer might have more knowledge about a specific topic than any single student in the classroom, all the students together typically have more combined knowledge than the trainer. Effective trainers are able to help the students collaborate with each other and share their knowledge, so it is typically a richer experience for everyone. Along these lines, trainers will often gain additional knowledge from the students by allowing and encouraging this collaboration.

One-on-One Training vs. Group Training

Most of the preceding topics in this chapter focused on classroom or group training. However, you can apply many of these same concepts to one-on-one training. One-on-one training refers to training computer users individually, or training other help desk personnel individually. This can be much easier than training an entire classroom because you are able to focus on the needs of just a single person. Also, you'll rarely need to create many additional training materials. For example, PowerPoint presentations are very effective when teaching groups but don't make much sense when teaching a single person.

Training Computer Users

Effective help desk specialists need to be able to provide basic training to computer users. They do so in one-on-one sessions where the technician helps the user perform a task or group of tasks. The technician might be working side-by-side with the user, or talking to the user over the phone. These sessions aren't usually planned, but instead, when users have a problem, they ask for help, and technicians can train them on how to resolve a problem.

Help desk specialists wouldn't train users how to do everything. For example, if a user is asking for help on configuring a newly installed application, and they'll never need to configure it again, a technician would just change the configuration and be done with it. However, if users need to perform a task regularly and are asking for help, it's best to show them how to perform the task on their own.

Understanding the Benefits of Training Users

A primary benefit of training users is that it can reduce help desk calls. This reduces the workload on the help desk and, in turn, reduces the help desk costs. Help desk employees will have more time to manage other incidents.

As an example, imagine an organization has implemented an automated password change system allowing users to reset their password without the assistance of a technician. When users understand how to use it, they are more likely to use it rather than call the help desk for assistance. Additionally, once a few users understand how to use it, they are more likely to assist fellow employees when needed.

A side effect of having users solve basic problems on their own is that help desk technicians are able to focus on mastering the skills for higher-level problems. In some cases, they might be able to resolve more issues that they might otherwise have escalated to a higher tier.

Using Steps When Training Users

One of the best ways to train users is to lead them through the steps one by one and allow them to do the task. As long as these steps are either well understood or written out, this becomes a very basic process.

ON THE SIDE:
When you realize that there isn't any need to train the user and you can simply make the change yourself, ask before you take control of their computer. For example, if you're working with a user side-by-side, ask if it's OK to use their mouse and keyboard. If you're talking over the phone and you realize you can perform the task by taking control of their system remotely, ask before you do so.

8

As an example, imagine that user accounts lock when users enter the wrong password too many times. Further, users can either unlock the account themselves, or call the help desk and ask the help desk to unlock their account. Admittedly, for any individual call, the technician could unlock the account much quicker than the time it takes to train the user. However, training the user saves time in the end, because a trained user is less likely to call back for the same issue. The technician might use the following steps to train the user:

1. Ask the user to open a web browser.

2. Ask the user to enter the following URL into the browser: "passreset"

> **ON THE SIDE:**   This example assumes a server named passreset is reachable within the network and provides password reset capabilities. In an actual network, the server might have a different name, and users might use a fully qualified domain name (such as passreset.com), depending on how administrators configured the server. The point is that the technician knows the URL, tells the user, and the user enters it into the browser.

3. A page appears asking the user, "Do you want to reset your password?." Tell the user to press the "Yes" button.

4. A textbox labeled "Username" appears. Tell the user to type his or her username.

5. Have the user press the "Go" button.

6. A message appears telling the user their account is locked. It then asks the user to enter their last name, username, and secret personal identification number (PIN). Tell the user to enter this information and then press the "Go" button.

> **ON THE SIDE:**   There are multiple methods used to ensure users can only reset their own password. A PIN issued to the user for other purposes is one way. Another might be for the user to enter one or more questions that only the user would know, such as the name of their first boss, or the name of their first pet.

7. Two text boxes appear labeled "Password" and "Confirm Password." Tell the user to enter the same new password in each text box.

   Note: Remind the user to make the password sufficiently complex with at least one uppercase letter, one lowercase letter, one special character, and one number, and be at least eight characters long, as described on the password reset page.

8. After the user enters the password two times, tell the user to press the "Reset Password" button. Note: If the user receives an error, have the user read the error and then help the user resolve it. The most common error is when the user doesn't enter the same password in both text boxes. If necessary, have the user reenter the password as described in the previous step.

9. When the password reset is complete, the user will be able to log on using this new password.

10. Ask the user if there is anything else you can help with. If not, wish them a good day and complete the call.

While the previous explanation assumed that the user called the help desk, technicians can use similar procedures when helping a user at the user's desk. The key is to ensure that the user performs the steps. If the technician takes control of the user's system and does the steps, it becomes a demonstration and the user is less likely to remember how to do it the next time.

Training Help Desk Personnel

Successful help desk technicians often train other help desk personnel one-on-one in **on-the-job training**. With on-the-job training, an experienced employee trains a new employee. For example, when a company hires a new technician, they will often assign a successful technician to train the new hire. One of the keys to success when using this method is to use a checklist. The checklist includes a list of knowledge and skills that a new technician should master within a given period.

In contrast, if managers don't take the time to identify what should be taught and communicate their expectations, the experienced technicians will make their own decisions about what they think is important. They'll provide some training to the new hire but probably won't cover all of the topics as adequately as they would if they had a checklist to follow.

Another challenge with on-the-job training is that the experienced technicians often aren't given enough time to properly train a new hire. As an example, a manager might introduce a new hire to a technician and tell the technician something like, "Sally's a new technician and she will work side-by-side with you for a couple of days. Show her everything she needs to know for the job." At the same time, the technician's normal job responsibilities don't change, so the technician needs to complete the normal work routine while also showing the new hire how to accomplish these tasks. While the new hire will likely gain some knowledge about the job requirements, this knowledge is typically limited to the very basics, and only the tasks performed by the experienced technician during the side-by-side training.

Developing a Checklist

The first step is to identify the needs and objectives of the one-on-one training, and a checklist is an ideal way to document these needs and objectives. The checklist might look similar to objectives for a course and include some of the verbs from Bloom's Taxonomy. As an example, here's the beginning of a checklist an organization might use for new hires that will handle help desk incidents with the telephone:

- Repeat the words used when greeting a caller.
- List the minimum amount of information that must be entered when opening an incident.

- Open a test incident for a test customer.
- Log appropriate information in the test incident.
- Close the test incident.
- Discuss the possible reasons why you should escalate an incident.
- Describe how to escalate an incident.
- Locate the online help file for the SalesApp application.
- Evaluate the symptoms given by a customer and help the customer resolve the issue.
- Demonstrate how to lead a customer through the process of a resetting a password.
- Repeat the words used when ending a customer call.

This list is not comprehensive, but it does show the start of a possible checklist. An experienced technician would know exactly what to teach the new hire and could easily determine if the new hire has the knowledge. Similarly, new hires would know exactly what they are expected to learn.

Some checklists are short and used for quick training sessions of new hires. For example, a supervisor might spend a few hours with a new hire and then have the new hire start work with an invitation to come back with any questions. Other checklists are more comprehensive and completed in stages. For example, the first stage might be a quick training session with a supervisor, followed by regular one-on-one sessions with experienced technicians for progressively more complex knowledge and tasks. Technicians might not complete the full checklist for a month or more.

A key point here is that the checklist documents the needs and objectives of the training. Without any specific objectives, there is no way to know what the training should, or will, accomplish. As Laurence J. Peter, developer of the Peter Principle management theory, wrote, "If you don't know where you are going, you will probably end up somewhere else." The checklist lets everyone know exactly where new hires should be going in terms of their knowledge and abilities.

Training by Using the Checklist

After creating the checklist, just about any experienced technician should be able to train others based on the checklist. This training would be one-on-one and the process might be similar to training computer users, though it wouldn't necessarily be as regimented. For example, when training users how to perform a task, technicians might follow a specific checklist. In contrast, when training other help desk personnel, technicians might just walk the other person through the task from memory. Trainees might take notes to ensure they remember the appropriate knowledge.

This type of training rarely requires any formal setting or pre-created materials. Instead, one technician shares knowledge with another to help the new technician learn the job tasks. Another benefit of this method is that day-to-day procedures often change over time. Technicians that do these procedures regularly know about the changes. In contrast, documentation for day-to-day procedures can easily become outdated due to changes.

Chapter Review Activities

Use the features in this section to study and review the topics in this chapter.

Answer These Questions

1. What is the combination of attributes needed by an effective trainer?

   a. Attitude, skills, and knowledge

   b. Knowledge and teaching ability

   c. Positive attitude and knowledge

   d. Positive attitude and teaching ability

2. Which of the following is NOT one of the skills needed by an effective trainer?

   a. The ability to project their voice and vary their tone and volume

   b. A wide body of knowledge and concepts related to the topic

   c. An understanding of how to ask questions

   d. The ability to tell analogies or stories

3. After a student asks a question, what should the instructor do first?

   a. Answer the question

   b. Postpone the question

   c. Redirect the question

   d. Repeat the question

4. After redirecting a question, and hearing from two or more students, what should the trainer do?

   a. Repeat the question

   b. Give the definitive answer

   c. Postpone the question

   d. Thank the student that asked the question

5. What is the primary purpose of telling stories during a training topic?

   a. To entertain

   b. To bridge the topic

   c. To enhance the learning

   d. As a segue

6. A classroom size is about 20 feet by 20 feet. When writing text on the white board, how large should the letters be?

   a. At least 1 inch

   b. At least 2 inches

   c. At least 3 inches

   d. At least 4 inches

7. Of the following choices, what is a primary benefit of bridging topics?

   a. It provides a segue from topic to another.

   b. It creates a positive, upbeat atmosphere.

   c. It helps students understand a course is a group of interrelated topics.

   d. It helps students engage in conversations.

8. Of the following choices, what is NOT one of the skills or techniques that effective trainers use?

   a. Make comfortable eye contact with students

   b. Use comfortable gestures when speaking

   c. Step away from the podium

   d. Use filler words as often as possible

9. The following statements refer to adult learning principles. Which one is NOT true?

   a. Adult learners have a need to know why they should learn something.

   b. Adult learners have a need to be self-directing.

   c. Adult learners have a need for self-paced learning.

   d. Adults want to be able to apply knowledge as soon as possible.

10. Which type of learner is most likely to attend a technical training course?

   a. Visual learners

   b. Auditory learners

   c. Kinesthetic learners

   d. A mixture

11. What can a trainer include in a course to help kinesthetic learners learn the material?

   a. PowerPoint presentations with graphics

   b. Stories and analogies

   c. Student handouts

   d. Exercises

12. Of the following choices, what should be created FIRST when creating course materials?

   a. Objectives

   b. PowerPoint slides

   c. Instructor guide

   d. Student handouts

13. Of the following choices, what is most commonly used when creating objectives?

   a. Bloom's Taxonomy

   b. Pedagogy

   c. Andragogy

   d. Learning styles

14. Bloom's Taxonomy refers to learning and understanding on six different levels. Of the following choices, which level has the most depth of learning?

   a. Knowledge

   b. Comprehension

   c. Application

   d. Analysis

15. Of the following choices, what BEST describes blended learning?

   a. A type of learning employing video and online applications

   b. A type of learning combining instructor-led and self-directed learning

   c. A type of learning using videos and tutorials

   d. A type of learning using visual, audio, and experiential methods

16. When is a help desk specialist MOST likely to provide one-on-one training to users?

   a. When the user calls the help desk

   b. When the specialist visits the user at the user's desk

   c. When the user is asking for help performing a repeatable task

   d. When the user is asking for help performing any task

17. Of the following choices, which represents the best organizational benefit for training users?

   a. Reduces costs

   b. Helps them understand

   c. Increases their independence

   d. Allows them to be help desk specialists

18. Of the following choices, what is NOT is a benefit of a checklist when training a new employee?

   a. It documents the objectives of the training.

   b. It informs new employees what they should learn.

   c. It informs existing employees what they should train new employees.

   d. It relieves supervisors of the responsibility of training new employees.

19. How should you determine how long a person should spend with on-the-job training?

   a. It is based on the objectives of the training.

   b. It is based on who is responsible for the training.

   c. It should last at least one full day.

   d. It should last at least one full month.

20. When training a user how to perform a task, when should a technician take over control of the user's computer?

   a. Only after asking the user for permission

   b. Only when the user can't see how to perform a task

   c. Only when it's clear the user will perform this task regularly

   d. The technician should avoid taking control of the user's computer

Answers and Explanations

1. **a.** Trainers need a combination of a positive upbeat attitude, effective teaching skills, and knowledge of the topic. Without a combination of all three, trainers are not able to effectively transfer the knowledge to the students.

2. **b.** Professors and instructors possess a wide body of knowledge, concepts, and theories, but trainers only need a narrow level of knowledge on the topic they are presenting. The other answers represent skills needed by trainers.

3. **d.** Instructors should repeat the question so that all the students can hear it and benefit from the answer. After repeating the question, the trainer can choose to answer it, postpone it, or redirect it.

4. **b.** The trainer should give the definitive answer to the question as the authority, using similar words and phrases provided by the students that answered the redirected question. This is especially important when more than one student responds and their answers appear to conflict with each other. The trainer should repeat the question before redirecting it and can thank the student then. The question shouldn't be redirected if you want to postpone it.

5. **c.** The primary purpose of telling stories during training is to enhance learning. The stories should be relevant to the topic, and the trainer should make the point of the story quickly. While stories might entertain, that is not the primary purpose. Similarly, a story might help bridge topics or be used as a segue into a new topic, but that isn't the primary purpose.

6. **b.** Lettering should be at least two inches to ensure it is readable from 20 feet away. A one-inch letter is readable from 10 feet away. Larger letters are useful for larger classrooms.

7. **c.** Bridging topics helps students understand that a course is comprised of interrelated topics. Bridging is unrelated to using segues between topics or the attitude of the trainer or the classroom. While students that understand how the topics are connected might engage in more conversations, that isn't a primary benefit of bridging topics.

8. **d.** Filler words (such as "uh" and "um") should be avoided, not used as much as possible. The other answers represent valid skills and techniques used by effective trainers.

9. **c.** Adult learners do not require self-paced learning and can learn in a classroom environment at the pace set by the trainer. The other statements are true.

10. **d.** Any course is likely to have a mixture of learners. Any class might include at least one student with each of the four learning styles. The reading/writing learning style is the only not mentioned in the possible answers.

11. **d.** Kinesthetic learners learn best by doing, so labs and exercises where they can perform a task are helpful for these learners. Visual learners learn best with graphics and charts. Auditory learners learn best by the spoken word, including stories and analogies. Reading/writing learners learn best by reading topics.

12. **a.** Objectives should be created before creating any other course materials. This helps ensure that all of the course materials (such as the PowerPoint slides, the instructor guide, and the student handouts) support the objectives of the course.

13. **a.** Bloom's Taxonomy is most commonly used by course developers when creating objectives for a course. Pedagogy is the science and art of education, and andragogy is the art and science of helping adults learn. Learning styles refer to preferred methods of learning, such as seeing, hearing, and doing.

14. d. Analysis is the fourth level in Bloom's Taxonomy and has the most depth of learning from the listed answers. The order is knowledge, comprehension, application, analysis, synthesis, and evaluation.

15. b. Blending learning combines instructor-led and self-directed learning. The self-directed learning might be from videos, online applications, or tutorials. Blending learning will often include elements appealing to visual, auditory, and kinesthetic learners, but so will other delivery methods.

16. c. The most likely time when a help desk specialist will provide one-on-one training to users is when the users need help performing a task that they are likely to repeat again in the future. If a task only needs to be performed once, the specialist can perform the task and doesn't need to train the user. Training can be in person or over the phone.

17. a. A primary benefit of training users is that it can reduce costs by reducing help desk calls. Training users does help them understand some technical issues better and can increase their ability to solve problems independently, but these are not the primary benefits for the organization. You would not train users to be help desk specialists unless they were hired to be help desk specialists.

18. d. A checklist makes training easier for all involved, but it does not relieve supervisors from the responsibility of training new employees or ensuring they are trained. The other answers are valid benefits.

19. a. The length of time for any training is based on the objectives and how long it takes to teach the objectives. It isn't based on who teaches the objectives, and any set amount of time will not match all situations.

20. d. When training a user how to perform the task, the technician should avoid taking control of the user's computer and instead let the user perform the steps. If training isn't needed, the technician can ask the user for permission to take over the computer to do the task. If the user can't see how, the technician needs to lead the user through the task in separate steps. Training is needed especially if the user will perform the task regularly.

Define the Key Terms

The following key terms include the ideas most important to the big ideas in this chapter. To review, without looking at the book or your notes, write a definition for each term, focusing on the meaning, not the wording. Then review your definition compared to your notes, this chapter, and the glossary.

Key Terms for Chapter 8

analogy	empowering words	PowerPoint presentations
andragogy	filler words	rapport
auditory learner	kinesthetic learner	reading/writing learner
Bloom's Taxonomy	learning style	story
bridging	on-the-job training	trainer
eLearning	pedagogy	visual learner

List the Words Inside Acronyms

The following are the most common acronyms discussed in this chapter. As a way to review those terms, simply write down the words that each letter represents in each acronym.

Acronyms for Chapter 8

AUP	STP	UTP
NLP	TCP	VARK
PIN	UDP	WIIFM

Create Mind Maps

For this chapter, create mind maps as follows:

1. Create a mind map to list the six levels of understanding within Bloom's Taxonomy and list some of the verbs associated with each of the levels.

Define Other Terms

Define the following additional terms from this chapter, and check your answers in the glossary:

blended learning	instructor	teacher
facilitator	professor	tutorials

Case Studies

Case Study 1

Create a list of at least ten training objectives you could use for someone to learn your current job, or a job you have previously held. Each of these training objectives should include at least one of the verbs from Bloom's Taxonomy.

Case Study 2

Perform an Internet search on "PowerPoint Tips" and create a list of at least ten tips for creating effective PowerPoint presentations.

Case Study 3

Prepare to give a five-minute presentation on a topic using any training aids you determine to be appropriate. Ensure you have a polished intro of at least one minute and a planned finish of 45 seconds. This way, when you realize you've talked for four minutes, you can easily segue into your finish, and complete your presentation finish in under five minutes.

Chapter 9

Business Skills

Business skills are useful in organizations of any size and are increasingly important in larger organizations. Hiring managers expect prospective employees to have basic business skills, and managers require employees to have these skills before promoting them to managerial positions. While the help desk is a great place to start and build experience, many people want to build a career beyond the help desk. Understanding the value of these business skills will help them advance in their careers.

This chapter covers business skills in four major sections:

- The first section, "Reviewing Core Business Skills," reviews many of the core business skills covered throughout this book such as communication, writing, and presenting. However, the focus in this section is primarily on how individuals can use these skills to excel within the business.

- Most businesses take the time to create and publish vision statements, mission statements, and identify their values. The "Shaping the Business" section discusses these, along with explanations of why they are relevant for help desk professionals.

- Ideally, IT goals within an organization are aligned with the business goals. Unfortunately, these goals are often misaligned with the IT department pursuing goals that don't provide value to the organization. The "Aligning the Business" section introduces IT governance to help organizations achieve business alignment. This section also compares cost centers and profit centers.

- Last, "Understanding ITIL" introduces the Information Technology Infrastructure Library (ITIL) and how it helps IT organizations track and improve IT services through their lifecycle. This section also includes information on ITIL certifications such as the ITIL Foundations certification, which many help desk professionals obtain.

Chapter Outline

Objectives

- List and describe at least three core business skills needed by help desk professionals
- Define scope and scope creep in the context of project management
- Define a critical task and the critical path in the context of project management
- List and explain at least three methods people use for conflict management
- Discuss the impact of personal appearance on communication within a business
- Describe the difference between vision and mission

- List and describe values that might be important to an organization
- Summarize the goal of business alignment
- Define IT governance
- Discuss the differences between a cost center and a profit center
- Define a service in the context of ITIL
- Describe the ITIL lifecycle
- Identify the most common ITIL certification
- Define a service level agreement
- List common ITIL good practices used in organizations

Key Terms

acceptable usage policy (AUP)

business alignment

cost center

critical path

critical task

good practices

Information Technology Infrastructure Library (ITIL)

IT governance

milestone

mission statement

profit center

scope

scope creep

service

service level agreement (SLA)

stakeholder

values

vision statement

Reviewing Core Business Skills

Previous chapters cover many of the skills needed by help desk specialists, but they normally focus on using these skills when working with customers. However, these skills are also important for individuals to master when working with others in the business. This section reviews many of the skills previous chapters cover, but focuses on the value of these skills when working with others in the business.

Communicating Effectively in the Business

Help desk specialists need to communicate effectively in the business if they expect to excel in the job. Chapter 2, "Communication Skills," provides key information related to communication with a focus on using these skills when communicating with customers. Successful employees use many of the same communication elements when communicating with others in the business.

Verbal and non-verbal communications are both extremely important when communicating with customers and fellow employees. By paying attention to what you say and how you say it, you are more likely to communicate effectively with everyone in your organization. Similarly, when you include active listening skills in your communication, you let others know that you value what they're saying.

Communication barriers such as filters are one of the most common causes of miscommunication in the business world. These barriers frequently result in the sent message being different than the received message, as shown in Figure 9-1. Common filters are distractions, a person's emotional state, beliefs, and a preferred style of communication. When you're aware of filters, you have a better chance of ensuring they don't cause communication problems.

FIGURE 9-1

Communication barriers can change the message.

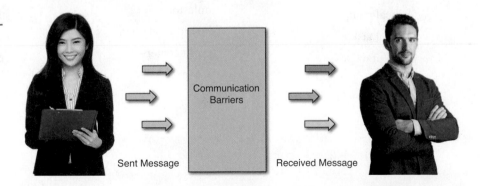

Sent Message   Communication Barriers   Received Message

Some communication is face-to-face, but people commonly communicate using other methods. Two additional methods of communication within the business are:

- **Telephone.** People often communicate with each other via the telephone in any business. It's relatively simple to pick up the phone and give someone a call. An important thing to remember is that non-verbal communication still comes across over the phone. Obvious elements of non-verbal communication are tone and volume, and these often communicate more than your words. Other non-verbal elements also come across over the phone. For example, even though you can't see someone's face, you've probably sensed when they were smiling.

- **Text-only.** Email has become one of the primary methods of communication for employees in many organizations. Employees typically use it for both official and unofficial correspondence within an organization. While not as popular as email, many employees also use chat and instant message (IM) systems for communication. In some cases, the chat and IM systems are internal, and in other cases, employees use external systems. However, the communication still flows through the network and is subject to the rules and policies of the organization. All text-only communication should be professional, especially when used to communicate with anyone other than very close friends. This means using proper grammar and punctuation, and avoiding text abbreviations. Even though some text abbreviations are perfectly clear to some people, many others have dual meanings and can prevent effective communication. For example, KKK means "over," as in my message is complete and I'm awaiting your reply. It also means Ku Klux Klan.

Many organizations require employees to read and acknowledge an **acceptable usage policy (AUP)**. An AUP describes the purpose of IT systems within the organization and user responsibilities related to these IT systems. An AUP typically includes acceptable use clauses related to text-only communications such as email, chat, and IM systems. Companies rarely tell employees they cannot use these systems for any personal purposes. However, an AUP usually informs employees that they should not use the systems for inappropriate use. Inappropriate use includes any illegal or unlawful activity such as harassment, libel, the use of obscenities, and any activity counter to the organization's policies.

Writing Skills in the Business

Chapter 7, "Writing Skills," includes detailed information on writing skills needed by help desk specialists. The most obvious task requiring effective writing skills is entering information into trouble tickets. Trouble ticket information is often used in a knowledge base used by others, so it's important for technicians to enter this information clearly and concisely.

Help desk technicians represent the organization when working with customers, and customers often view the entire organization based on their interaction with these technicians. This makes it that much more important for technicians to be clear and professional in their written communications with customers. This includes e-mail, chat, and IM communication.

While not all technicians will be writing tutorials, frequently asked question (FAQ) web pages, or white papers, some technicians will. These technicians require more extensive writing skills than a typical technician does. Chapter 7 discusses different writing styles and skills needed by technical writers, along with various methods used to create technical documents.

ON THE SIDE: It's important to remember that any correspondence sent through a company network is subject to monitoring. Many organizations use data loss prevention (DLP) systems to detect transmission of sensitive information and prevent data leakage. Additionally, organizations often retain email, chat, and IM transmissions, especially if they have had any problems with employees using these systems inappropriately. They don't necessarily review these transmissions regularly, but if necessary, they can easily retrieve and read all transmissions sent or received by any employee.

6

> **AUTHOR'S NOTE:**   I am frequently asked how a technician can get into technical writing. The short answer is that "writer's write"—so start writing! Also, be aware that everything you write is an audition. I remember a series of emails I received from a reader saying that no matter what he did, he couldn't get into writing. Each of his emails included multiple typos and grammar problems, and I wondered if all of his other attempts included these basic writing errors.

Understanding Presentation Skills in the Business

Employees frequently need to make presentations to others for a wide variety of topics. In some cases, technicians make presentations to other technicians to give them information on new technology. Other times, they make presentations to management or executives to request additional resources such as new systems to address a need, or to report on the status of a project. During disaster and crisis situations, technicians often brief managers and executives on the recovery progress. None of these are extensive presentations. They typically last about 10 to 20 minutes but become increasingly important for anyone trying to move up the promotion ladder.

Chapter 8, "Training Skills," provides key information related to training and includes many techniques you can use to make effective presentations. As a reminder, it's important to be aware of your voice and vary it appropriately. Make comfortable eye contact with the audience and ensure you make eye contact with the key players of the audience, such as the managers and executives wanting the information you're presenting. This helps you connect with them similar to how the presenter in Figure 9-2 is connected with his audience. Not only does he look comfortable, but the audience also looks like they're engaged with what he's saying. Use natural inviting gestures and ensure you eliminate any distracting mannerisms such as jiggling keys in your pocket or using placeholders such as "uh."

FIGURE 9-2

Making presentations.

If appropriate, use PowerPoint slides in your presentations. However, avoid the common mistakes many new presenters make during presentations using Power-Point, such as reading from the slides and turning their backs on the audience. It's also important to ensure the information is viewable to the audience and enhances the presentation without being distracting.

Many presentations are short 15-minute presentations. Similarly, TED talks are limited to 18 minutes, so it's worthwhile looking at what makes a TED talk successful. TED began in 1984 as a conference where Technology, Entertainment, and Design converged, and today TED talks cover almost any topic. TED is devoted to spreading ideas that have the power to change attitudes, lives, and ultimately, the world.

Videos hosted on TED.com are viewed at a rate of about 1.5 million times per day. Some presentations have been viewed more than 15 million times. The reason is simple: There are many great presentations delivered by skilled presenters. Author Carmine Gallo identified nine common elements shared in the most popular TED presentations and documented them in his book *Talk Like TED: The 9 Public-Speaking Secrets of the World's Top Minds*. It's an excellent book overall. As a short introduction, here are the nine common elements Gallo identified:

- **Unleash the master within.** When you speak with passion, it fires you up and you are more likely to inspire others to take action. In contrast, if you don't believe in the topic, your talk will lack passion and it'll reflect poorly in your talk. With this in mind, include topics that you care about in any talk you do.

- **Master the art of storytelling.** Stories engage people and have the power to ignite their imagination and move them to action. Look for relevant stories that you can add to your presentation to help you make meaningful points.

- **Have a conversation.** Take the time to know the details of the presentation inside and out so that you can deliver it as effortlessly as you can have a conversation with your best friend. Obviously, it doesn't take practice to talk with your best friend. However, it does take relentless practice to know your presentation that well.

- **Teach me something new.** Give your audience something new—or at least packaged differently. For example, your presentation might offer a fresh or novel way to solve an older problem. If your presentation only includes information they already know, their attention will drift and they'll begin to question why they are wasting their time.

- **Deliver jaw-dropping moments.** Include an emotionally charged event that your audience members will be talking about later. Include unexpected or shocking statistics. For example, many people still remember the speech when Steve Jobs introduced the iPod with the shocking statistic (at the time) that it could hold over 1,000 songs in your pocket. If possible, create powerful quotes that others can repeat, such as the ones documented on TED (http://www.ted.com/quotes). Many speakers end their talk with a signature story that is both memorable and inspiring. For example, Anthony Robbins has often ended presentations with his "There are no vans" story, which is both emotional and inspirational.

ON THE SIDE:
You can read a version of Anthony Robbins story in the book *Chicken Soup for the Soul: Stories to Open the Heart and Rekindle the Spirit* by Jack Canfield and Mark Victor Hansen.

- **Lighten up.** Don't take yourself or your topic too seriously. People love humor, and if you can give them something to smile about, it helps your presentation become more memorable. A simple reason is that laughter releases endorphins, making people feel better. Humor also lowers people's defenses and makes the speaker more likable. You can also use humor in serious topics. In the Academy Award winning documentary "An Inconvenient Truth," former Vice President Al Gore successfully weaved humor into an otherwise serious topic.

- **Stick to the 18-minute rule.** This has been very successful for TED speakers and it is useful for any presentation, when possible. The reason is that actively listening to a speaker takes effort, and its difficult for people to stay focused for too long. This makes it that much more difficult for them to remember your message. Also, successful TED speakers realize that they need to focus their message to keep within this timeframe. You won't hear them ramble. They focus all their words on the message. If you're forced to give longer presentations, build in soft breaks such as videos, exercises, or demonstrations.

- **Paint a mental picture with multisensory experiences.** Whenever possible, engage multiple senses such as sight, sound, touch, taste, and smell. The more senses you engage, the easier it is for the audience to remember the presentation. It's relatively easy to include words, images, and videos within a PowerPoint presentation. The key is to ensure that these enhance your message and do not distract from it.

- **Stay in your lane.** Be authentic, open, and transparent in your presentations. People can tell when you're not being real and you lose their trust.

You may never be on a TED stage, but that doesn't mean that you can't give powerful presentations. Find ways to include these elements in your presentations. If you want to learn more, get Carmine Gallo's book and dig deeper into these topics. Then watch some popular TED talks to see how they use these elements in their presentations.

Solving Problems in the Business

Chapter 6, "Troubleshooting Skills," includes a section on problem-solving skills. Critical thinking is one of the most important skills related to problem solving. As a reminder, critical thinking typically includes actively thinking about the issue, asking questions, analyzing and evaluating evidence and symptoms, and seeking different perspectives. These activities help you identify and evaluate different options when faced with a problem.

Technicians need these skills when troubleshooting, but they are also valuable when solving any problems in a business. Technicians that are able to use and improve their critical thinking skills will find that they become more and more useful as they advance in their career.

As an example, imagine your company's success is a direct result of selling a high-volume of products, composed of cogs and widgets. The company purchases the cogs from the only vendor they know that creates them—CogsRUs. Unfortunately, CogsRUs recently suffered a major disaster and can no longer provide the cogs. What do you do?

You can't go to a book to find a ready-made answer to this problem. Instead, it requires actively employing problem solving skills to find a solution. Some options are:

- **Stop selling the products.** The company's success is a direct result of selling them, so this might result in bankruptcy.

- **Find another vendor that creates the cogs.** Currently, the original source is the only known source, so this might be challenging.

- **Find another vendor that can start making the cogs.** Another vendor might have the capacity to create the cogs, even though they don't currently manufacture them. However, it might be difficult to convince them to start, and they might charge more per cog so that they can recoup their startup costs.

- **Make them yourself.** Your company isn't currently set up to make them. Senior management needs to evaluate if they have the capability and desire to do so. If they decide to do so, it will take time and resources to put everything in place to start making them.

The previous list identified some possible solutions and then listed reasons why each solution is a problem. They represent a negative mindset, but it is possible to look at each of these solutions from a different perspective.

Successful people commonly view problems as challenges and opportunities. They look for different perspectives and question the status quo. For example, the company might have always created these products in a specific way, but it might be possible to create them differently.

People often make great discoveries when faced with challenges and adversity, and it's entirely possible that this challenge can help the company identify a solution that results in significant gains. The following list shows the same possible solutions, along with how critical thinking can help someone identify different alternatives. A key point with each of these options is that they require actively thinking about the issue and evaluating the options, rather than assuming statements and conclusions provided by others are accurate.

- **Stop selling the products.** Because this might result in bankruptcy, fear might cause some people to refuse to consider it. However, by actively thinking about the option, it's possible to evaluate the likelihood that it will cause bankruptcy. It's possible the company's original success was due to selling these products, but since then, the company has expanded its product offerings and now sells other products with higher profit margins. If the company stops selling these products, they might be able to focus their efforts on creating and selling other products that are more profitable.

- **Find another vendor that creates the cogs.** People might say "CogsRUs is the only source" and that might have been true years ago. But is it still true today? By simply questioning the assumption that CogsRUs is the only source, you can prompt some research that locates an alternate source. It's entirely possible that there are multiple sources to buy the cogs.

- **Find another vendor that can start making the cogs.** It could be that the company always created the products with metal cogs and widgets, and it might be difficult to find another company to create the metal cogs. However, is it possible to use a plastic cog instead? Instead of looking for a company to create metal cogs, you can find a company that can create plastic cogs. An existing company manufacturing other plastic products would probably be able to make plastic cogs rather easily.

- **Make them yourself.** This option might have sounded too difficult when the company originally started selling the products. It might have required the company to build a new manufacturing facility with all the required dies and molds. However, new manufacturing methods are available today. For example, the company might be able to create the cogs with a 3D printer at a fraction of the cost that they previously paid.

The company might not have needed to look for alternatives before. However, when the problem forced them to look for alternatives, some excellent opportunities appeared. Some people in the company might have viewed the issue as an insurmountable problem. However, the critical thinker looked at the problem differently and came up with solutions that provide new opportunities for the company.

You might not face a problem related to cogs, but you are sure to face problems within the business. Look around and see how others react to them. Some people repeatedly complain and look for reasons why various solutions won't work. Others look at these same problems as challenges and opportunities. They employ critical thinking and other problem solving skills to find solutions.

Working with Customers

Many of the chapters in this book intertwine customer service skills into different topics. For example, Chapter 2 mentions the importance of communication for any customer interaction and Chapter 3, "Personal Skills," includes a section on service attitude. Effective communication is a core requirement for effective customer skills. Successful help desk specialists take the time to understand customers and identify their needs.

Even if the customer's request is outside the scope of the help desk's responsibilities, technicians can still use customer service skills to manage the customer's expectations. Technicians can take the time to explain what they can do and provide guidance to the customer for other avenues of support.

Managing Projects in the Business

Successful organizations launch a myriad of different projects during their lifetime, and it is valuable for help desk specialists to understand some basics related to project management. Some organizations have one or more dedicated project managers that manage projects from beginning to end, while other organizations assign personnel within the organization to manage projects as the projects come up.

Stakeholders will often sponsor or oversee a project. A **stakeholder** is typically a high-level manager or executive who has a stake or vested interest in the project. When project managers have problems within the project, they can go to the stakeholder for assistance.

As a help desk specialist, you probably won't be assigned to manage a project. However, it's very likely that management will ask you to contribute to a project in one way or another. Because of this, you should be familiar with some common methods used to manage projects.

> **ON THE SIDE:** If a project manager invites you to work on a project, consider it a compliment. Someone sees skills in you that can be valuable to the project, or sees potential in you that the project will help you develop. Further, working on a project management team will often give you an opportunity to expand your skills and increase your career opportunities. Even if your role is small, it still gives you an opportunity to see how a project progresses.

Most organizations use some type of project management software, such as Microsoft Project Professional, when managing projects. This software makes it easier for project managers to track the progress of the project and identify problems before they seriously affect the project's completion date. One of the great strengths of this type of software is the ability to create various charts such as a milestone chart, a Gantt chart, or a critical path chart.

Avoiding Scope Creep

When planning a project, one of the first things that management does is identify the scope. The **scope** identifies the boundaries of the project, and it's extremely important to stay within these boundaries. When project members expand the scope of the project without permission, it causes a common problem known as scope creep. **Scope creep** is any additional activities that are beyond the approved scope of the project, and it results in missed deadlines and increased costs.

As an example, imagine a company is managing the development of an application with in-house programmers. During the project, one programmer thinks of an awesome feature that he can add to the program. He's relatively sure he can do so rather easily, so he does. Unfortunately, his feature had a bug that he didn't detect. Later, software testers didn't know about the feature, so they didn't test it and didn't detect the bug. When the application went live, users ran into the bug and it resulted in outages and it corrupted data.

On the surface, this might have sounded like the developer was taking initiative and his efforts should be applauded. In reality, companies often reprimand developers for doing something like this. Experienced application developers know how often scope creep has caused significant problems, and most of them have the discipline to stay within the scope of the project. That's not to say that initiative is discouraged. However, only a project manager can authorize such changes, so any recommendations to expand the scope of a project need to go through the project manager. In many cases, the project manager won't expand the scope without getting approval from managers or stakeholders that are sponsoring the project.

The primary point here is that if you're working on a project team and asked to do some project tasks, stick to those tasks. You often won't see the entire picture and won't know how your tasks fit in. However, if you do something different or embellish the tasks, it can negatively affect the overall project and your reputation within the organization.

Planning a Project

One of the key steps when planning a project is to create a list of steps or tasks needed to complete it. Project managers often group these together in separate sections using a timeline. The timeline includes milestones for different parts of the project. A **milestone** indicates a significant accomplishment within the project and includes a summary of completed task along with the target date.

> **ON THE SIDE:** Project managers and executives use the milestones to gauge the progress of a project. A project is often referred to as "in the red" when milestone dates pass without completing the required tasks within the milestone. Executives give more attention to projects in the red to help them get back on track. When a project meets its milestones, it is "in the green" and doesn't require attention from executives.

As an example, imagine that a company plans to replace 1,000 existing desktop computers running an older operating system with new computers running Windows 8. This project might include the following milestones:

- **Project start date.** This identifies the date when the company starts the project. The target date is January 5.

- **Milestone 1: Upgrade ten computers in test run.** The goal in this milestone is to identify any potential problems that might adversely affect users and slow down the project. The target date is January 31.

- **Milestone 2: Upgrade computers in the IT department.** Next, the project replaces the computers in the IT department. One of the goals is to ensure that IT personnel are familiar with the new computers and can help resolve problems. The target date is March 5.

- **Milestone 3: Upgrade computers in the Sales department.** This milestone represents the first major upgrade for the end user. The target date is April 10.

- **Milestone 4: Upgrade computers in the Marketing department.** Because marketing personnel often work with graphics, they might need extras on their PCs, such as more memory and different applications. Upgrading these computers might take more time and effort. The target date is May 15.

- **Milestone 5: Upgrade computers in the HR and Accounting departments.** As with the computers in the marketing department, some of these computers might require additional resources to accommodate special applications. The target date is June 15.

- **Milestone 6: Upgrade computers in the remote office.** IT will investigate if they want to ship the computers directly to the remote office or ship the computers to the main location first. If the computers are shipped directly to the remote office, someone will need to configure them there. If they are shipped to the main location first, IT personnel can configure and test them before reshipping them to the remote office for installation. The target date is July 15.

- **Project end.** The project manager ties up any loose ends to ensure the project has met all of its goals. The target date is July 31.

Project management software makes it easy to chart these milestones. For example, Figure 9-3 shows a milestone chart with these milestones and dates.

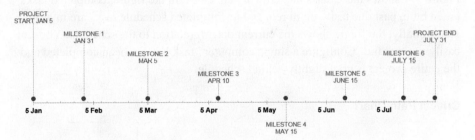

FIGURE 9-3

Milestone chart.

Obviously, each of these milestones includes several tasks within them that aren't listed. For example, Milestone 1 includes sub tasks such as identifying a standardized computer that supports the requirements, negotiating a price for 1,000 computers, and ordering ten of these computers. Administrators will likely use one computer as a standard to create an image. They'll install the operating system and all required applications on this computer, and configure it using appropriate security settings. Once they complete the configuration, they will capture an image of the computer, which they can apply to all the other computers.

Some organizations use a formal plan of actions and milestones (POA&M) document. It includes a listing of all the tasks needed for project completion along with the time needed to complete each task, and it groups these tasks within milestones. Additionally, the POA&M identifies who is responsible for completing these tasks. The project manager updates this document during the lifetime of the project.

AUTHOR'S NOTE:
I created the chart in Figure 9-3 using a free Microsoft Excel template named "Timeline with milestones." You simply enter the name of your milestones and their dates, and it automatically displays the chart. You can also manipulate the placement of the milestone labels.

Identifying Critical Tasks

Project managers often identify critical tasks in a project as early as possible. A **critical task** is any task that must be completed on time or it results in delaying the entire project. Consider Milestone 1. Each of the tasks within Milestone 1 is listed in the following bullets along with the time allotted to complete them.

- Identify a standardized computer—3 days
- Negotiate a price from a vendor—7 days
- Order and receive ten computers—7 days
- Configure a single computer for imaging—3 days
- Capture an image of the computer—3 days
- Deploy the image to the other nine computers—3 days

Each of these items is dependent on the completion of the previous task, so each of these items is a critical task. If any single item is delayed, it risks delaying the entire project. For example, you can't order the computers until you've negotiated a price. If you can't negotiate an acceptable price in the allotted timeframe, it delays all other tasks and you won't be able to meet the target milestone date.

Figure 9-4 shows these tasks in a critical path chart. In the figure, completed tasks are in blue, past due tasks are in red, and uncompleted schedule tasks are in gray. Additionally, the figure shows the current date in relation to the schedule. You can easily see that the "Configure a single computer" task has not been completed and the entire project is now slightly behind schedule.

FIGURE 9-4

Critical path chart.

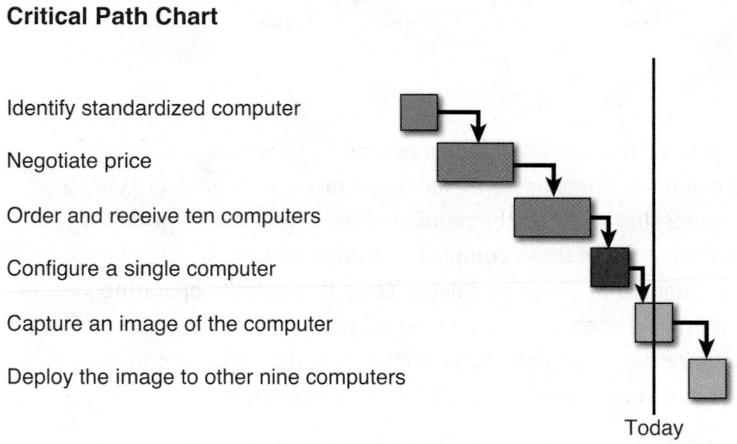

Critical Path Chart

Identify standardized computer

Negotiate price

Order and receive ten computers

Configure a single computer

Capture an image of the computer

Deploy the image to other nine computers

Today

While all the tasks in this milestone are dependent on each other, making each of them a critical task, this isn't always true. Many times, you can work on tasks simultaneously and the delay of one task doesn't delay other tasks.

Similarly, the delay of one milestone won't necessarily delay other milestones. As an example, Milestone 4 upgrades computers in the Marketing department. If the hardware requirements for their computers aren't identified on time, the project manager might shift resources to work on Milestone 5 for the HR and Accounting departments instead. Milestone 5 is not dependent on Milestone 4 and even with this adjustment, it's still possible to complete the overall project on time.

Again, as a single member on a project team, you probably won't see the entire picture and you won't know the reasoning behind some of the decisions. The best you can do is complete your assigned tasks on time whenever possible.

Working in Teams

Projects require people to work together in a team with the common goal of completing the project, or at the very least a common goal of completing certain tasks within a milestone. Ideally, everyone will contribute equally to the success of the project and do everything they can to help others. As you might guess, all teams don't work this well. However, just because others aren't effective team players, it doesn't mean you shouldn't be. As you advance in your career, you will likely begin to notice that effective team players advance quicker, and to higher positions within an organization, than individuals who are unable or unwilling to work with others.

Marty Brounstein wrote a helpful book titled *Managing Teams for Dummies*. In Chapter 18, "Ten Qualities of an Effective Team Player," he lists useful qualities for team members. You can look at this list from the perspective of a team member and from the perspective of a project manager. This list helps you identify qualities that make you a valuable member of a team. Project managers also look for these qualities when looking for team members to help on a project:

- Demonstrates reliability
- Communicates constructively
- Listens actively
- Functions as an active participant
- Shares openly and willingly
- Cooperates and pitches in to help
- Exhibits flexibility
- Shows commitment to the team
- Works as a problem-solver
- Treats others in a respectful and supportive manner

Even if you aren't working on a project, you often work within a team setting. For example, personnel working on a help desk are often part of the help desk team. Similarly, many class projects require classmates to work together on a team. Imagine how effortless these projects would be if everyone consistently demonstrated these qualities. Of course, you can't control everyone else. You can only control yourself, but if you choose to consistently demonstrate these qualities, you'll find that more people on your team will choose to do so, too.

Managing Conflict

Conflict is inevitable when working with others in a business and even when interacting with others in day-to-day relationships. Conflicts arise from differences and indicate a disagreement. People can disagree over just about anything, and simply disagreeing isn't a problem. However, when the disagreement continues, and people don't respect others opinions, it rises to the level of arguments and fights. Ideally, people address conflicts early to avoid allowing them to become destructive.

It's important to realize an important underlying issue related to conflict. It arises when one of the parties begins to feel threatened, even if the threat isn't real. The threat might make them feel as though they aren't respected or valued, and trigger stronger feelings from their personal history. The threat might make them fear a loss of safety and security, such as their physical safety and well-being, or the security of their job.

Every situation is different, but in general, people use one of the following strategies to manage conflict:

- **Collaborating.** An individual attempts to work with the other person to find a solution where both parties can win. Collaborators often view conflict resolution not as a problem, but as an opportunity to learn about the other person with the goal of identifying a mutually beneficial outcome. Collaboration requires time and a willingness for both parties to work with each other.

- **Compromising.** Not all problems have solutions where both parties come out as winners, or at least a win-win solution is not readily apparent. In some cases, both parties can identify a mutually acceptable compromise that ends the conflict. Compromise is often effective as a short-term resolution while both parties collaborate to identify a better resolution.

- **Forcing.** An individual uses authority or power over the other person to force a resolution to the conflict. For example, a supervisor can block any further conversation by saying something along the lines of, "A decision has already been made and it's time to move on so that we can complete something productive." While forcing a resolution can provide what appears to be a quick resolution to a conflict, it doesn't always resolve it. Instead, the other party might resent the forcing action, weakening the long-term relationship. Forcing isn't only from a position of authority. Some individuals simply use their will to force their position until the other party chooses to accommodate their position, or withdraw to avoid the conflict.

- **Withdrawing or avoiding.** It's possible to just ignore a conflict and not take any action to resolve it. This is useful if a person considers an issue trivial and simply not worth the effort to pursue. You can also use this if you're surprised by the conflict and want to postpone it until you get a better understanding of the issue. However, some people perceive withdrawing as tacit agreement.

- **Smoothing or accommodating.** You can address some situations by accommodating the concerns of the other party. This is certainly appropriate if you realize your position was wrong. From another perspective, some people use this strategy by verbally agreeing but not following it up with matching actions. The agreement sounds accommodating and avoids an immediate conflict. When the issue comes up again, the person offers a stream of excuses. Eventually, the other party sees through the tactic, which makes it that much more difficult to actually resolve it.

ON THE SIDE:
Many professionals specialize in conflict resolution. For example, arbitrators, mediators, and counselors act as a disinterested third party between two people in a dispute and help them find solutions to their problems. They help the two parties understand the root cause of the conflict and guide them to a resolution through reasoned negotiation. Managers use these same skills to resolve conflicts in the workplace.

ON THE SIDE: The movie *Game Change* had a perfect example of someone using accommodating to manipulate the conflict. Woody Harrelson played the role of campaign strategist Steve Schmidt and Julianne Moore played Governor Sarah Palin. Many times when Governor Palin made what Schmidt considered unreasonable demands in the movie, he simply agreed and used accommodating words. Eventually Governor Palin recognized the strategy and accused him of "managing" her.

Most people predominately use one or two of these strategies to resolve most of the conflicts in their lives. They have found these strategies effective and continue to use them. However, many successful people have learned all of the strategies. They consciously use the most appropriate strategy for any given situation.

Ideally, people would consistently use collaboration as their primary conflict resolution method. However, collaboration just takes more time than the other methods and some situations dictate an immediate resolution. Other significant considerations when choosing an alternate conflict resolution method include the importance of the issue and the relationship with the other party. If the issue isn't important, there's no need to continue the conflict. If the relationship is important, it's appropriate to compromise. Interestingly, when someone doesn't care about the relationship, they rarely compromise.

It's worth noting that not everyone has learned how to manage conflict. The perceived threat evokes a fight-or-flight response within them, and when they are unable to avoid the conflict with flight, they begin to fight. While this might sound like forcing, it is much more dramatic and typically elevates the conflict rather than managing it.

Maintaining Your Personal Appearance

Even though almost everyone has heard the phrase "You can't judge a book by its cover," people do so all the time. They also judge many other inner qualities about a person based on their outward personal appearance. Right or wrong, your personal appearance has a direct impact on your success. This doesn't mean you have to look like a model, but you do need to take the time to ensure your personal appearance conveys a positive overall image to others.

Some factors related to personal appearance are universal and apply to almost any job. For example, businesses expect people to be clean and groomed in a professional work environment. Managers do not enjoy having to tell a worker to take a shower before coming to work, but sadly, it is sometimes necessary. It shouldn't surprise anyone that these workers are not on the fast track for advancement.

Clothing norms are different from one organization to another. The most important consideration here is to understand and follow the organization's norms. Ideally, your clothes should help you fit in with other employees. If you underdress or overdress, it makes it harder for you to fit in. You don't need 30 different outfits to look professional. However, you do need to ensure the clothes you wear fit you, are clean, and don't look like you slept in them.

Many organizations have casual Fridays. Employees dress more formally from Monday through Thursday, and less formally on Friday. However, this means different things in different organizations. Flip-flops and a Hawaiian shirt might be acceptable in one organization but not another.

It's important to remember that your personal appearance has a direct effect on your communication with others in the business. If your appearance is distracting, people often focus on your appearance instead of focusing on you and your message.

Additionally, personal appearance includes your body language, and it affects how others perceive you. People often make both conscious and subconscious judgments about others based on how they sit or stand. For example, they might perceive someone that is slouching as lazy. Similarly, people pay attention to your facial expressions, especially when you're talking. They look for congruency between what you're saying verbally and your non-verbal expressions. When the two messages aren't congruent, they are more likely to believe your non-verbal expressions and have the impression that you are not being honest.

Shaping the Business

In addition to possessing core business skills as discussed in the previous section, it's also important to have a good understanding of the business, including its vision, mission, and values.

Figure 9-5 provides a generic overview. In general, a vision provides a big picture view of an end-result in the future, the mission focuses on activities in the present, and values identify traits, beliefs, and principles that the organization considers important. The following sections cover these in more detail.

FIGURE 9-5

Vision, mission, and values.

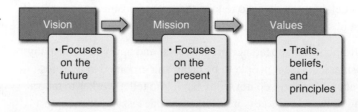

Many organizations spend a lot of time to define their vision statement, mission statement, and values and make them publically available. Ideally, everyone within the organization will understand and support them. Similarly, leaders within the organization strive to hire employees that can help them achieve their vision and share similar values. With this in mind, it's worth the time for prospective employees to understand an organization's vision, mission, and values before a job interview.

Creating Vision Statements

A **vision statement** defines or describes where an organization wants to be or what it wants to achieve at some point in the future. A vision statement is typically a single sentence, and it describes the long-term result of the organization's work. From a broader perspective, leaders within the organization can use the vision statement to help them decide if they should pursue an opportunity. If the opportunity won't help an organization get closer to its vision, they shouldn't pursue it.

Ideally, a vision inspires employees and they work together to achieve it. As an example, Bill Gates, founder of Microsoft, originally had a vision of "a computer on every desk and in every home." It was clear and inspired people to help him achieve it. They sought to create useful operating systems and applications helping people be more productive. They recognized that when computers were useful and affordable, everyone would want one. At the time, the term *personal computer* was foreign to most people. Instead, typical computers were the size of refrigerators, and only large organizations had them. While Bill Gates's original vision hasn't been achieved, most people would agree that Microsoft has made significant strides toward achieving it.

The guidelines for creating vision statements aren't consistent, and if you look around, you'll find that companies view them differently. Some companies start with an overriding vision statement and then formulate their goals and objectives to achieve this vision. Other companies identify their goals and objectives first and then summarize them in their vision statement.

As an example, Apple's current vision statement is, "Apple designs Macs, the best personal computers in the world, along with OS X, iLife, iWork and professional software. Apple leads the digital music revolution with its iPods and iTunes online store. Apple has reinvented the mobile phone with its revolutionary iPhone and App Store, and is defining the future of mobile media and computing devices with iPad." This is significantly different from the vision statement Steve Jobs had for Apple in 1980: "To make a contribution to the world by making tools for the mind that advance humankind."

The vision statements that provide the most inspiration to others are typically short, clear, and memorable. The following list shows some vision statements from several organizations that follow this formula:

- **National Multiple Sclerosis Society:** A World Free of MS.
- **Alzheimer's Association:** Our vision is a world without Alzheimer's.
- **Habitat for Humanity:** A world where everyone has a decent place to live.
- **Google:** Focus on the user and all else will follow.

ON THE SIDE: Interestingly, Microsoft's current vision statement is not so direct or succinct. It is: "Global diversity and inclusion is an integral and inherent part of our culture, fueling our business growth while allowing us to attract, develop, and retain this best talent, to be more innovative in the products and services we develop, in the way we solve problems, and in the way we serve the needs of an increasingly global and diverse customer and partner base."

6

You might notice that the Google vision statement doesn't focus on a future outcome as the others do. It's a good example of how an organization isn't constrained by guidelines written in books telling them what to do. Google reported net revenues of $59.7 billion in 2013 and had a market capitalization of almost $395 billion in early 2014. Their success might be due to their vision statement or despite it.

Creating Mission Statements

The **mission statement** focuses on the present and identifies what an organization hopes to achieve and/or how it hopes to achieve it. In some cases, it clarifies what the organization does, how it does it, and who they serve. Ideally, mission statements are clear and memorable, though they are typically longer than vision statements. As a comparison, the following list shows the mission statements from the same organizations mentioned in the vision section:

- **National Multiple Sclerosis Society:** We mobilize people and resources to drive research for a cure and to address the challenges of everyone affected by MS.

- **Alzheimer's Association:** To eliminate Alzheimer's disease through the advancement of research; to provide and enhance care and support for all affected; and to reduce the risk of dementia through the promotion of brain health.

- **Habitat for Humanity:** Seeking to put God's love into action, Habitat for Humanity brings people together to build homes, communities, and hope.

- **Google:** Google's mission is to organize the world's information and make it universally accessible and useful.

> **ON THE SIDE:**   Many people debate the required components in vision and mission statements and it's relatively easy to find conflicting information. As an example, Strategic Management Insight evaluated a variety of mission statements for many well-known companies based on guidelines published by Strategic Management Insight. Even though they mention that Google made a profit of $10.7 billion in 2012, they state that Google's 2013 mission statement (which is the same as it was in 2012) is a poorly created statement. You can read their full evaluation here: http://www.strategicmanagementinsight.com/mission-statements/google-mission-statement.html.

Note the differences between the vision and mission statements. The vision statement defines what the organization strives to achieve at some point in the future. The mission statement defines the organization's purpose and what it strives to do in the present.

Some companies use a vision or mission statement but not both. For example, TED has a simple mission—"Spread ideas"—but they do not have a published vision statement.

Just as the guidelines for vision statements aren't consistent, the guidelines and usage for mission statements aren't consistent. For example, Amazon doesn't have a published vision statement, but their published mission statement is "to be Earth's most customer-centric company, where customers can find and discover anything they might want to buy online, and endeavors to offer its customers the lowest possible prices." Some might argue that this is a combination of a vision statement and a mission statement because it includes both a future end-result and includes statements identifying how they want to operate in the present. However, most people agree that Amazon is on the right track as a customer-centric company. Executives within any organization can create their mission statement to meet their needs.

Identifying Values

Values identify the traits that a person or an organization considers important. On a personal level, they represent a person's core beliefs based on life experiences, and they typically guide a person's principles and standards of behavior. People make everyday decisions based on what they value.

Table 9-1 identifies many value pairs that might compete with each other in different situations. For example, many men know the answer to the question "Do this outfit make me look fat?" is almost always "No." Even when people value honesty, they might value compassion more and choose a compassionate answer rather than a truthful answer. In some situations, men might value friendship, family, or love higher than honesty and choose a diplomatic or well-intentioned answer.

TABLE 9-1
Potentially Conflicting Value Pairs

Value Pair	Comments
Honesty vs. Compassion	One person might be brutally honest, while another might be willing to tell a lie to show compassion.
Acceptance vs. Beauty	One person might easily accept another despite their appearance, while another might only accept those that meet their definition of beauty.
Religious faith vs. scientific knowledge	One person might value the faith they learned from their religious teachings more than knowledge they gain from science.
Career vs. family	One person might put career pursuits first, while another might put their family first.

ON THE SIDE:
Table 9-1 only lists a few values. Steve Pavlina (author of *Personal Development for Smart People*) created a comprehensive list of values you can view here: http://www.stevepavlina.com/articles/list-of-values.htm.

Governing Core Values

Many people take the time to identify the values that are important to them. They create and prioritize a list of these values and use them as their governing core values. When faced with difficult decisions, they consciously think about their values and make decisions based on the values they consider most important to them.

For example, if their job requires them to miss a big moment in one of their children's lives, it causes a dilemma. Someone that values career over family might choose the job requirement and promise to make it up to the child. In contrast, someone that values family over career might say "no" to the boss, realizing that it might affect a raise or promotion opportunity.

However, many other people don't take the time to identify and prioritize their values. Instead, they struggle with difficult decisions and don't consistently base their decisions on their values simply because their values aren't clear to them. One day, they might make decisions based on family values. Another day, they might make decisions based on career aspirations. Unfortunately, this inconsistency often confuses the people in their lives.

Similarly, executives within organizations often take the time to identify the values they consider important. They publish these values, letting others know what they are. When leaders, managers, and employees understand these values, they refer to them when making difficult decisions. For example, they might be faced with a decision between ensuring the organization's financial stability or ensuring customer safety. If the organization's values are clear to them, the decision is simple. However, if the organization's values aren't clear, the manager might make a decision based on their own values, or what they think the organization values.

Making Organizational Decisions Based on Values

Imagine that executives in Company A and Company B operate based on the values shown in Table 9-2. The companies might not have published these values, but they do reflect the values of the decision-making executives. These lists are prioritized, with number 1 considered the most important value and number 5 least important.

TABLE 9-2

Values of Two Different Companies

Company A	Company B
1. Financial stability	1. Customer safety
2. Dominant in marketplace	2. Employee satisfaction
3. Resourceful	3. Integrity and honesty
4. Employee respect	4. Provide quality service and products
5. Customer safety	5. Financial stability

Imagine that both companies compete with each other selling automobiles. Each company learns of a defect in one of its automobiles that causes an engine to catch fire when a rare set of circumstances occurs. To date, dozens of vehicles have caught fire, six people suffered severe injuries requiring hospitalization, and three people died. The injuries and deaths resulted from crashes after the fire and smoke overwhelmed or distracted the driver.

Each company also learned that they can fix the defect by replacing a part in the engine. They can announce a recall informing appropriate vehicle owners about the problem and pay dealerships to replace the part in all these cars. They also realize that once they announce the recall, they will be liable for the damages, injuries, and deaths related to past incidents caused by the defect.

Can you see how these companies will respond differently based on their values?

Company A values financial stability and marketplace domination and realizes that a recall will affect both negatively. Executives might do a cost-based analysis to determine the cost of acknowledging and repairing the defect. They might determine that the costs of the recall and all the related negative publicity might cause too much damage to their financial stability and market share. Instead, they choose to stay quiet about the issue. Even though customer safety isn't their top priority, they do care about customers, so they implement a fix in new cars to prevent future problems. However, cars bought by previous customers remain on the road at risk of the same fires that have injured and killed other customers.

In contrast, Company B values customer safety higher than its other values. As soon as executives learn about the problem, they set it as a top priority to investigate the issue, verify it is valid, and identify the specific conditions that cause the fire. They don't expect the investigation to take longer than a couple of days, but while they are investigating, they report their suspicions to the appropriate national agency. Once they verify the conditions that likely caused the fires, they notify customers of the problem with recommendations on how to avoid the conditions. They then verify they can resolve the problem by replacing the part and provide notifications to customers and dealerships on how to implement the fix. They are also concerned about financial stability and realize this will affect their bottom line, so they initiate a study to identify the costs of this recall. Later, they report these costs to their shareholders.

As an employee within an organization, you have the opportunity to observe their actions in relation to their values. There is bound to be some discrepancies in almost any organization as individuals act on their own values, instead of the organization's values. However, if you see these discrepancies very often, it might indicate two sets of values: a published set of values and a second set of values decision makers actually use to guide their decisions.

Making Personal Decisions Based on Values

Many individuals identify their guiding values similar to how a company does: they make conscious decisions to review different values, identify the values they consider important, and then prioritize them. Table 9-3 shows the values that two individuals have identified for themselves.

TABLE 9-3

Values of Two Different Individuals

Individual 1	Individual 2
1. Financial freedom	1. Family
2. Career success	2. Creative
3. Health and wellness	3. Honest but compassionate
4. Friends	4. Health and wellness
5. Family	5. Financial stability

Can you see how their lives would be different?

When faced with decisions between finances and family, they would make significantly different decisions. This isn't to say that either individual's values are more correct. What's most important is they both took the time to identify and prioritize their values, and when faced with conflicting choices, they make decisions based on these values.

Aligning the Business

Business alignment refers to how an organization is able to use IT resources to achieve its mission or business objectives. From the perspective of IT personnel, business alignment refers to how the IT side can produce value for the business.

Companies typically have a business side and an IT side. Both sides contribute to the success of the company, and both sides need each other. The primary purpose of IT is to support the business so that the business can make money. If the business doesn't make money, they can't afford IT, but they realize that IT helps them be more productive and make more money.

Ideally, everyone would recognize this symbiotic relationship is useful to both parties. Unfortunately, individual personalities often distort the relationship, causing people to view their contributions as more important than others. This often results in a misalignment of IT resources in relation to the goals of the organization.

> **AUTHOR'S NOTE:**   The conflict between business and IT isn't unique. Almost any partnership is subject to the same types of problems. Growing up in a restaurant, I saw endless conflicts between cooks and waitresses. Later, I saw similar conflicts between programmers and administrators. What I learned is that the people that can understand the perspective of "the other side" are often the most valuable to the organization. For example, an administrator that understands programming concepts can bridge the communication gap between the two. Similarly, an IT professional that understands business concepts can help ensure that IT systems support the vision and mission of the organization.

Governing IT

IT governance refers to the processes organizations use to ensure IT resources are efficient and contribute to the success of the organization. Organizations use these processes to ensure that funds spent on IT resources will contribute to the organization's goals. Similarly, they use these processes to ensure that IT has adequate funding to purchase necessary resources. Without active IT governance processes, IT funding is sometimes out of alignment with the organizations goals. Here are two examples:

- **IT sometimes buys expensive IT systems that don't provide value for the organization.** For example, IT might buy an expensive server to host files, even though existing servers are adequately meeting the company's needs.

- **The business sometimes refuses to pay for IT systems needed to meet key business goals.** For example, IT might request a new firewall to protect against new threats but the business side refuses. Without adequate security, attackers are able to cause outages.

Incidents such as these lead to mistrust that builds over time. The business suspects that the IT side has no concept of money and instead wants to spend without considering the return on investment. The IT side suspects the business side is miserly and is unwilling to pay for needed improvements.

Many organizations implement management frameworks to help them with IT governance. For example, **Control Objectives for Information and related Technology (COBIT)** is a set of good practices organizations can apply to IT management and IT governance. The current version (COBIT 5) is based on five principles:

- **Meeting stakeholder needs:** In this context, stakeholders are typically decision makers on the business side who benefit from IT resources. They can also be external stakeholders such as investors.

- **Covering the enterprise end-to-end:** The goal is to maintain a balance between all areas of the organization so that IT resources provide value to the organization and risk levels are optimized.

- **Applying a single integrated framework:** COBIT 5 has integrated previous versions of COBIT with some other frameworks. This helps avoid conflicts when using multiple disjointed frameworks.

- **Enabling a holistic approach:** COBIT 5 covers all functional areas of responsibility, including both internal and external stakeholders.

- **Separating governance from management:** COBIT stresses that governance and management are not the same thing but an organization can implement both holistically.

Comparing a Cost Center to a Profit Center

Chapter 1, "Introduction to Help Desk Support Roles," mentions profit centers and cost centers, and it's worth repeating that the IT department (including the help desk) is a cost center. A **cost center** generates costs for a company and does not bring in any direct revenue. In contrast, the business side is a **profit center**, which generates revenue for the company.

Successful companies make more money than they spend, so it's natural for executives to look for ways to increase profit and decrease costs. When IT professionals understand this, they learn to adjust their language and help ensure that IT resources are contributing to the business goals. Instead of just suggesting ways to spend money, they talk about ways that an investment can help reduce costs or increase profits.

Additionally, most executives understand the need to align the business and IT goals. When the goals are aligned, they view the IT side as more than just a cost center, but instead as a resource that produces value for the organization. Similarly, successful IT managers take the time to understand the vision, mission, and values of the organization, and strive to ensure that IT resources are aligned with the business goals.

Understanding ITIL

ON THE SIDE: The Official ITIL Website (http://www.itil-officialsite.com/) and other sources stress that the 2011 updates are minor. Editors reorganized the content to improve its flow and readability and standardized the information so that it is consistent in each of the publications and the ITIL glossary.

The **Information Technology Infrastructure Library (ITIL)** is a group of books written and released by the United Kingdom's Office of Government and Commerce (OGC). The original version came out in the 1980s, but it has gone through several updates since then. HM Government (short for Her Majesties Government) is now listed as the owner. HM Government published ITIL 2011 in July 2011. Most people know the previous version as ITIL v3, but ITIL 2011 renamed ITIL v3 to ITIL 2007.

ITIL began in response to the realization that many UK government agencies and private sector companies were creating their own set of best practices to manage IT services, and they were thriving. Other organizations didn't have a set of best practices and they were often faltering due to a lack of maturity with their IT services. ITIL documented many standard practices that any organization could adopt as their own best practice.

While early versions of ITIL used the term *best practices,* this later morphed into **good practices**. ITIL authors recognized that a best practice in one organization was not necessarily a best practice in another organization. A good practice is a proven, generally accepted practice. Good practices aren't required in every organization, but they are implemented whenever possible. ITIL is not a tool in itself, but instead is a collection of good practice concepts that any organization can implement. This is similar to how COBIT is a set of good practices that organizations can apply to IT management and IT governance.

These good practices often increase alignment of the goals between business and IT elements of an organization. In some organizations that don't adapt ITIL practices, IT departments forget that their primary goal is to support the business in achieving its objectives. Instead, IT focuses on its own internal goals, such as security, without considering the impact on the business.

Organizations often use ITIL to help them identify functions, roles, and processes that can benefit from formal IT Service Management (ITSM) concepts. The organization then uses ITSM concepts to help ensure that the IT department can provide IT services on a consistent basis.

Help desk specialists might not immediately recognize the purpose or importance of specific steps in some business processes. However, if they are able to dig into them deeper, they will often find that many of them have their roots in ITIL good practices.

Defining an ITIL Service

Service is a key term used throughout ITIL, so it's important to know what a service is in the context of ITIL. In short, a service is something that provides value to customers. These customers can be external customers paying for a service such as access to a website, or internal employees using services such as email. Business services are the services that customers can directly utilize or consume. ITSM is the implementation and management of these services.

As an example, payroll is a business service used within many organizations. Payroll requires different IT components such as access to employee databases and time tracking data. The payroll service consolidates this information, calculates compensation, and generates paychecks. Most of today's payroll services include a significant amount of automation, reducing the amount of labor required to ensure employees are paid accurately and on time.

Some organizations outsource this service. For example, Paychex provides a full suite of payroll services for small and large organizations. They can also manage various employee benefits such as 401K contributions, insurance offerings, and more, depending on the actual services the organization desires and purchases.

Tracking Services Through Their Lifecycle

ITIL is based on a five-phase lifecycle approach of IT services. Organizations identify the services they want to offer, design these services, implement the services, manage the services on a day-to-day basis, and then regularly review them for opportunities to improve them. These phases are documented in five separate ITIL publications:

- **ITIL Service Strategy.** In the first step of the lifecycle, organizations take steps to identify their customers and their service needs. The organization uses this knowledge to identify the services it plans to provide.

- **ITIL Service Design.** In this stage, the organization takes the time to design new and modified services. Goals include ensuring that the services meet the customer needs, are cost effective, and include processes to manage the services.

- **ITIL Service Transition.** Next, new and modified services are built, tested, and moved into production. A key goal in this phase is ensuring that implementing the service is smooth and changes do not result in unintended service outages.

- **ITIL Service Operation.** Once the services are in operation, an organization needs to take steps to ensure the service continues to operate as expected. In this phase, the organization oversees the health of the service, manages outages, and handles routine end-user requests. This phase is most closely associated with help desk services.
- **ITIL Continual Service Improvement.** The ITIL lifecycle is a continuous process, and in the service improvement stage, the organization takes steps to measure and improve services.

Figure 9-6 shows one way to think about these five phases, by starting at the top and moving clockwise. The organization identifies the service it wants to provide in the Service Strategy phase and then designs the service in the Service Design phase. Next, they put the service into operation during the Service Transition phase and then begin day-to-day operations in the Service Operation phase. Last, the Continual Service Improvement phase uses data from the other phases and provides input into adding or modifying a service in the Service Strategy phase.

FIGURE 9-6

Five phases of ITIL lifecycle.

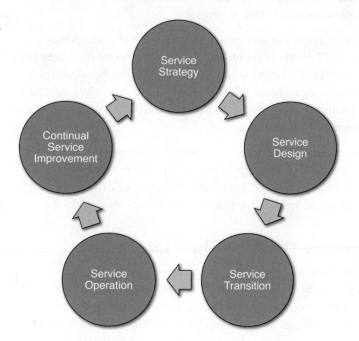

Understanding ITIL Certifications

There are several ITIL certifications individuals can earn to demonstrate their understanding and mastery of ITIL concepts. The most popular ITIL certification is ITIL Foundation, previously known as ITIL Foundations v3. It was renamed to ITIL Foundation in ITIL 2011.

Candidates earn the ITIL Foundation Certificate by passing a multiple choice exam. While it's strongly recommended that candidates attend an accredited ITIL foundation course, it is not a requirement. Many organizations bring in approved trainers to teach a three-day ITIL Foundation course and students take the exam at the end of day three.

Organizations that have adopted ITIL practices often require IT professionals to earn the ITIL Foundation certification to get a basic understanding of the ITIL framework. It also helps these IT professionals to understand how they participate in the various phases of the ITIL lifecycle, including continual service improvement.

Global Knowledge conducts annual surveys to identify the skills and salaries of IT professionals. In the 2013 IT Skills and Salary Survey (completed in a partnership with Windows IT Pro), they found that the ITIL Foundation certification was highly relevant. Individuals with this certification reported median salaries of $92,500 in the US. However, it's worth emphasizing that most of these respondents have multiple certifications and other technical skills. They didn't start with an ITIL certification but instead became proficient in at least one area of IT and then expanded their knowledge of business process improvement, which increased their earning potential.

While the ITIL Foundation certification provides a foundation for the full ITIL qualification scheme, there are several others ITIL certifications. Figure 9-7 shows the ITIL qualification scheme with each of the ITIL certifications included.

FIGURE 9-7

ITIL qualification scheme.

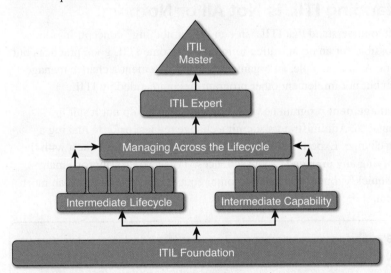

The following list describes these other certifications:

- **Intermediate Level (Service Lifecycle).** This certification focuses on the five phases of the ITIL service lifecycle and the use of processes and practice elements within it. It also includes the management capabilities needed to deliver quality Service Management practices in an organization. This is one path in the Intermediate Level, which gives individuals a deeper understanding of ITSM elements and how to implement them in an organization.

- **Intermediate Level (Service Capability).** This provides an alternate path in the Intermediate Level and focuses on four subject areas covering process activities, as well as the execution and use of processes throughout the Service Lifecycle. Both of the Intermediate Level certifications require individuals to take a group of courses in the desired path and then pass an exam.

- **Managing Across the Lifecycle.** After earning one of the Intermediate Level certifications, individuals can pursue this certification. It requires attending an approved course and passing an exam based on a case study and additional short scenarios. Individuals responsible for integrating and managing ITSM processes and services pursue this.

- **ITIL Expert.** After completing the Managing Across the Lifecycle certification, individuals can pursue the ITIL Expert certification. Candidates earn this certification by earning credits from ITIL qualifications and some complementary products.

- **ITIL Master.** The highest ITIL certification is ITIL Master and it validates the capability of an individual to apply ITIL principles, methods, and techniques in the workplace. Candidates must have first earned the ITIL Expert certification, and they can then submit a portfolio documenting a proposal for business improvement and a work package demonstrating the effectiveness of the proposal.

Understanding ITIL Is Not All or Nothing

It's important to understand that ITIL isn't an "all or nothing" concept. In other words, it's possible for an organization to implement some ITIL good practices but not all of them. As an example, an organization can implement a change management program but not implement other programs recommended by ITIL.

A **change management** program helps ensure that changes do not result in unintended outages. Administrators submit a change request prior to making a configuration change. Experts within the organization review the request with the goal of identifying any unintended consequences. These experts approve many requests very quickly, but they postpone some requests until the experts can meet to discuss them.

> **ON THE SIDE:**   Many organizations have suffered excessive outages after administrators completed well-meaning changes that resulted in disastrous consequences. These organizations have since implemented strict change management programs. They reprimand administrators that make unapproved changes, and if an administrator repeatedly makes unapproved changes, the organization terminates them.

Consider an administrator that manages an email server. Users are complaining that their emails are not reaching them and the administrator discovers that a new unified threat management (UTM) device is blocking many legitimate emails.

To resolve the problem, the administrator reconfigures the network to bypass the UTM, thinking that this step returns the network to its previous configuration. However, a UTM is a next generation firewall with multiple capabilities, including the ability to detect and block anti-spam, and in this situation, the UTM also replaced the existing firewall. While bypassing the UTM resolves the problem of blocking legitimate emails, it also causes significant other problems, such as leaving the network without firewall protection. If attackers discover the network no longer has a firewall, the damage can be extensive.

Now consider this same situation in an organization with a mature change management program that administrators understand and follow. The administrator sees the same problem but submits a change request instead of making the change. Experts managing the UTM will easily see the problem and deny the request, but they will also be able to help the original administrator resolve the problem of blocked emails. Most UTMs include sensitivity settings that administrators can adjust to allow more spam, but not block legitimate emails.

Change management is one example of many different ITIL processes, and most organizations implement more than just a change management process. The point is that you won't find any specific requirement mandating the implementation of different processes. Instead, ITIL documents many good practices, and organizations implement them based on their needs.

Understanding Service Level Agreements

Chapter 1 introduced service level agreements as Tier 4 within an IT support hierarchy. As a reminder, a **service level agreement (SLA)** defines a specific level of reliability for a service. ITIL formally describes an SLA as "an agreement between an IT service provider and a customer. The SLA describes the IT service, documents service level targets, and specifies the responsibilities of the IT service provider and the customer." Service contracts often include SLA clauses, which specify these requirements.

Many web site hosting providers use SLAs as promises or guarantees of service for some customers. As an example, LiquidWeb includes the following guarantees in its SLA for customers with dedicated servers:

- Guarantees that in the event of a dedicated server hardware failure, the faulty hardware will be replaced within 30 minutes of identifying the problem.
- Guarantees network uptime to be 100%. This guarantee assures that all major routing devices within our network are reachable from the global Internet 100% of the time.
- Guarantees an initial response by their help desk within 30 minutes.
- Guarantees they will answer phone calls within 59 seconds.
- Guarantees an initial response by their LiveChat system within 59 seconds.

Some of these guarantees, such as answering the phone or a live chat request within 59 seconds, might not sound like much. However, when compared to some other hosting providers, they really are significant.

AUTHOR'S NOTE:
I do not have any ownership in LiquidWeb, but I have experienced their customer service firsthand. Compared to many other hosting providers, their service truly lives up to their promise of heroic support.

6

Many SLAs also include a monetary penalty or remedy if the contractor is unable to meet the responsibilities or guarantees specified in the contract. As an example, LiquidWeb provides customers with a credit for ten times the actual amount of downtime beyond the guarantee.

Using Good Practices

This section introduced several good practices related to ITIL, such as implementing a change management program and using SLAs. The following list briefly describes some other good practices organizations often implement:

- **Configuration management.** Personnel document the configuration of systems and services. They then ensure that new systems include the same configuration settings as similar systems. Periodic checks detect unauthorized modifications of the configuration settings.

- **Event management.** An event is any detectable or discernible occurrence that might be of interest to IT management. Events do not necessarily affect the current operation of an IT service, but they might give insight into a potential problem later. Organizations often use monitoring tools to detect and report events. Administrators configure them to report events of interest based on the data collected by the tools. These tools can report significant events in real time so that administrators can address them immediately. Less important events are included in summary reports, making it easier for management to detect deviations in the IT environment.

- **Incident management.** An incident is any unplanned interruption to an IT service or reduction in the quality of an IT service. Users often report incidents to the help desk and help desk technicians enter the incident into an incident management application. Incident management applications help personnel manage incidents through their lifecycle. Note that an event can be an incident, but not all events are incidents.

- **Asset management.** Any organization has a wide variety of assets such as hardware, software, data, and personnel. Asset management includes ensuring that the organization has an adequate inventory of their assets, and they take steps to protect them. Many organizations use database programs to track their inventory. Critical business functions and processes are also assets because they contribute the overall mission of the organization. Organizations implement business continuity and disaster recovery plans to ensure these assets continue to operate, even after a disaster.

- **Knowledge management.** As philosopher George Santayana once said, "Those who cannot remember the past are condemned to repeat it." Knowledge management ensures that appropriate data is captured and available to personnel within the organization. As a simple example, organizations often manage a knowledge base, which provides help desk personnel with information to resolve many problems quicker than they could without the knowledge base.

- **Service level management.** This provides a clear definition of service level goals and expectations. It includes SLAs, but also much more, such as service targets defined with key performance indicators and operational level agreements for internal customers and external suppliers.

- **Information security management.** IT security focuses on protecting the confidentiality, integrity, and availability of the organization's assets. This has a broad scope including network security, personnel security, physical security, environmental security, data and application security, creating and enforcing security policies, risk management, and responding to security incidents.

Understanding the ITIL Service Desk

Some organizations expand their help desk into an ITIL service desk. The service desk includes all basic help desk functions but also integrates many of the ITIL processes, such as the good practices mentioned previously in this chapter.

As an example, the ITIL service desk can oversee the change management process. They accept the change requests and route them to the appropriate experts for review and approval. When approved, ITIL service desk personnel are aware of the changes or at least have access to the status of the changes. If a change causes an unexpected problem, the ITIL service desk personnel can often identify the cause by identifying a recent change.

In one incident where change requests were not routed to the help desk, it caused a significant amount of unnecessary work. First, IT technicians spent several hours on a Friday reconfiguring a system as part of a change. They were unaware it caused a problem. The help desk received a trouble call later on Friday night and spent much of the weekend troubleshooting it. Eventually, help desk technicians identified the changes in the system and spent the weekend returning the system to the original configuration. On Monday, the IT technicians that started the changes on Friday were upset that help desk technicians reversed their work. Additionally, the help desk technicians were upset that the IT technicians made the changes without notifying the help desk. An ITIL service desk could have prevented this incident and all of the needless rework.

Admittedly, adding these additional requirements does add to the help desk's workload. However, centrally managing these services can often provide significant benefits that save costs for the organization overall.

Comparing ITIL to ITL

ITIL originated with the UK government and is used around the world. The US government also publishes documents that provide both public and private organizations with insight into how to manage their IT systems effectively. Specifically, the Information Technology Laboratory (ITL) at the National Institute of Standards and Technology (NIST) regularly publishes documents based on ITL's research. It's important to realize that ITIL and ITL are *not* the same thing.

NIST is a division of the US Department of Commerce and it includes ITL. ITL develops standards and guidelines with a goal of improving IT security and the privacy of information on IT systems. ITL was created in response to the Federal Information Security Management ACT (FISMA) and publishes its findings in the Special Publication (SP) 800 series of publications.

6

As an example, SP 800-53, "Security and Privacy Controls for Federal Information Systems and Organizations," provides detailed information on security controls organizations use to reduce IT-related risks. It includes a catalog of security controls organized in 18 separate families of controls such as access control, configuration management, personnel security, and risk assessment. Appendixes in this document provide detailed information on more than 200 specific security controls.

> **ON THE SIDE:** All of the SP 800 reports, including SP 800-53, are freely available from here: http://csrc.nist.gov/publications/PubsSPs.html.

Some of the key differences between ITIL and ITL are:

- **ITL documents are free.** NIST provides free online access to all ITL SP 800 documents. In contrast, ITIL publications are rather expensive. You can purchase the five ITIL publications for approximately $550.

- **ITIL includes certifications but ITL does not.** While you can pursue several ITIL certifications, there aren't any ITL specific certifications. However, some security-related certifications such as the (ISC)2 Certified Information Systems Security Professional (CISSP) require test takers to understand many of the concepts discussed in SP 800 publications.

- **They each have a different focus.** ITIL is broader and focuses on good practices for identifying, designing, transitioning, managing, and improving services. ITL documents often provide very specific guidance related to an IT security concern. For example, SP 800-83, "Guide to Malware Incident Prevention and Handling for Desktops and Laptops," is very specific in the content, as you can tell from the title.

- **ITL includes dozens of publications.** ITIL concepts are published in five documents documenting the five phases of a service lifecycle, but ITL has many more documents covering a wide variety of focused topics.

- **ITIL documents are interdependent while ITL documents are independent.** While some SP 800 documents reference others, they are not dependent on each other. In contrast, the five ITIL books are part of a matched set designed around the ITIL lifecycle.

- **ITL updates documents individually.** Many ITL SP 800 documents have gone through revisions and when the revision is complete, NIST publishes them on their website. ITL is typically working on reviews and revisions to several documents at a time. In contrast, updates to ITIL books are completed and released at the same time. For example, ITIL version 3 (released in 2007 and later renamed to ITIL 2007) included updates to all the books in the ITIL set. Similarly, ITIL 2011 (released in 2011) included updates to all of these books.

Chapter Review Activities

Use the features in this section to study and review the topics in this chapter.

Answer These Questions

1. Many organizations have specific rules regarding the use of IT systems when communicating with others. They document this in a policy and require employees to read and acknowledge it. What is this?

    a. ITIL

    b. AUP

    c. IT governance

    d. Values

2. You plan to do a 15-minute presentation to others within your company on the importance of backing up data. Of the following choices, what is NOT one of the techniques you'd use to you ensure you engage the audience?

    a. Tell one or more relevant stories within the presentation

    b. Teach something new

    c. Stay serious

    d. Stick within a 15 minute timeframe

3. What, or who, defines the boundaries of a project?

    a. The scope

    b. The project manager

    c. Team members

    d. Time, because it will always vary

4. What is the result of scope creep? (Choose TWO.)

    a. Missed deadlines

    b. Increased productivity

    c. Increased costs

    d. Increased benefits from project

5. A project manager needs to identify tasks that must be completed on time to avoid a delay in the project completion. Of the following choices, what would be the BEST choice?

    a. Gantt chart

    b. Milestone chart

    c. Critical path chart

    d. Stakeholder list

344 CHAPTER 9 Business Skills

6. Which of the following is NOT one of the common conflict resolution strategies people use to resolve conflicts successfully?

   a. Collaborating

   b. Compromising

   c. Forcing

   d. Fighting

7. Which of the following statements is the MOST accurate related to personal appearance in a business?

   a. Personal appearance doesn't have an impact on promotions.

   b. Personal appearance isn't only clothes but also body language.

   c. Personal appearance doesn't have any impact on communication.

   d. Personal appearance is judged during hiring interviews but not on the job.

8. Of the following choices, what most accurately describes where an organization wants to be at some point in the future?

   a. Values

   b. Vision statement

   c. Mission statement

   d. Business alignment

9. A company wants to create a vision statement that provides inspiration to its employees. Which of the following guidelines should they use?

   a. Include as many company goals as possible in the statement

   b. Describe how the company plans to operate

   c. Include benefits to employees

   d. Keep it short, clear, and memorable

10. Of the following choices, what most accurately describes how an organization plans to operate in the present so that it can achieve its long-term objective?

    a. Values

    b. Vision statement

    c. Mission statement

    d. IT governance

11. Which of the following statements BEST describe business alignment?

    a. Ensuring IT goals match up with business goals.

    b. Ensuring business goals match up with the company's vision.

    c. Ensuring business goals match up with the company's mission.

    d. Ensuring business goals match up with the company's values.

12. Which of the following statements BEST describe IT governance?

    a. Processes used to learn of governing laws

    b. Processes used to ensure an organization follows governing laws

    c. Processes used to ensure IT resources abide by governing laws.

    d. Processes used to ensure IT resources add value to the organization

13. What benefit would a management framework such as COBIT provide?

    a. IT governance

    b. Decreasing profits

    c. Increasing costs

    d. Creating vision and mission statements

14. Which of the following statements is true related to cost centers and profit centers?

    a. The help desk is a profit center and the business side is a cost center.

    b. The help desk is a cost center and the business side is a cost center.

    c. The help desk is a cost center and the business side is a profit center.

    d. The help desk is a profit center and the business side is a profit center.

15. How many books are in the Information Technology Infrastructure Library?

    a. Three

    b. Four

    c. Five

    d. Six

16. Within the context of ITIL, what is a service?

    a. Something that provides value to an organization

    b. Something that provides value to customers

    c. The implementation and management of processes

    d. A process running on a computer

17. What is tracked through the different phases of the ITIL lifecycle?

    a. Processes

    b. Functions

    c. Good practices

    d. Services

6

18. Which of the following is the most likely ITIL certification that a help desk specialist would hold?

   a. Foundation

   b. Intermediate (Service Lifecycle)

   c. Intermediate (Service Capability)

   d. Managing Across the Lifecycle

19. An organization is contracting with an IT service provider for email services. The organization wants to ensure the IT service provider meets a minimum level of reliability for this service. What should they include in the IT contract?

   a. ITSM

   b. NIST

   c. ITL

   d. SLA

20. Which of the following best defines configuration management?

   a. Helps ensure changes do not cause unintended outages

   b. Ensures that new systems include the same settings as similar systems

   c. The ability to track an incident through its lifecycle

   d. Ensures that appropriate data is captured and available to personnel

Answers and Explanations

1. **b.** An acceptable use policy (AUP) describes the purpose of IT systems and user responsibilities when using these systems. This includes using the IT systems to communicate with others, such as with email. ITIL is a set of good practices published in books by the U.K. IT governance refers to the processes used to ensure IT resources are in alignment with the business. Values identify what an organization considers important, but they are not rules.

2. **c.** This presentation would benefit from techniques used by TED speakers, and one of the techniques successful TED speakers include in their talks is to lighten up and not take themselves or the topics too seriously. Storytelling is effective in presentations when the stories are relevant. Teaching something new makes it valuable to the audience. Respecting people's time is always important, and if you're asked to do 15 minutes, you should stick within that time limit.

3. **a.** Scope identifies the boundaries of a project. Management or stakeholders identify the scope and the project manager documents the scope in the project plan. However, the project manager doesn't define the boundaries. Team members do not define the boundaries either. If the boundaries vary, it results in scope creep and associated problems.

4. **a, c.** Scope creep occurs when project team members perform activities beyond the scope or boundaries of a project and it results in missed deadlines and increased costs. It doesn't result in increased productivity because people are working on unauthorized activities. Individuals might think they are providing increased project benefits, but unauthorized changes cause problems that far outweigh any potential benefits.

5. **c.** A critical path chart lists all the critical tasks within a project and a critical task is any task that must be completed on time to ensure the project is completed on time. A stakeholder list identifies the project stakeholders that have a stake or vested interest in the project.

6. **d.** Fighting is not a common conflict resolution strategy and it rarely resolves the conflict, escalating it instead. Collaborating, compromising, and forcing are three of the five strategies people often use.

7. **b.** Personal appearance includes clothes, grooming, cleanliness, and body language. People that don't follow the organization's norms related to personal appearance find it more difficult to fit in and are less likely to get promoted than individuals that follow the organizations norms. Distracting personal appearance can be a barrier in communication, and managers do judge people based on their personal appearance on the job.

8. **b.** A vision statement defines or describes where an organization wants to be at some point in the future. The mission is focused on the present, and values identify traits and beliefs an organization considers important. Business alignment refers to aligning the goals of IT resources with the goals of the business.

9. **d.** The most inspiring vision statements are short, clear, and memorable. Including multiple goals makes it longer. A mission statement and values describe how a company plans to operate. It's rare to include employee benefits in a vision statement.

10. **c.** A mission statement focuses on the present and identifies how an organization plans to operate. A vision statement focuses on the future. Values identify traits and beliefs an organization considers important. IT governance refers to the processes used to achieve business alignment.

11. **a.** Business alignment tries to ensure that the IT goals match up with business goals. It is not related to the vision, mission, or values of an organization.

12. **d.** IT governance refers to the processes organizations use to ensure IT resources are efficiently contributing to the success of the organization by adding value. It is not related to laws.

13. **a.** COBIT is a management framework that helps an organization with IT governance. It is not directly related to profits and costs, but when used effectively, it can help increase profits and decrease costs. It is not related to vision and mission statements.

14. **c.** The help desk does not generate revenue, so it is a cost center. The business side does generate revenue, so it is a profit center.

15. **c.** There are five books in the Information Technology Infrastructure Library, with one book for each of the five service phases.

16. **b.** ITIL defines a service as something that provides value to customers, and the customers can be external customers or internal employees. Some services provide value to an organization, but other services provide value to external customers. IT service management (ITSM) is the implementation and management of IT services but not processes. Operating systems do have software services that are processes running on a computer, but ITIL does not define a service that way.

17. **d.** Services are tracked through the five phases of the ITIL lifecycle. Services often include processes and functions and ITIL helps identify them, but they are not tracked in the different phases. ITIL recommends good practices but they are not tracked in the different phases.

18. **a.** The ITIL Foundation certification is the first certification in the ITIL qualification scheme and is the most likely ITIL certification a help desk specialist would hold. The other certifications are more advanced and pursued by some employees as they advance in their IT career.

19. **d.** A service level agreement (SLA) defines a specific level of reliability for a service and is included in many contracts. IT service management (ITSM) is the implementation and management of IT services. National Institute of Standards and Technology (NIST) is a US government agency that sponsors the Information Technology Laboratory (ITL). ITL publishes IT-related special publications.

20. **b.** Configuration management ensures that new systems include the same configuration settings as similar systems. It also helps ensure that unauthorized configuration changes are detected. Change management helps ensure changes do not cause unintended outages. Incident management is the process of tracking an incident through its lifecycle. Knowledge management ensures that appropriate data is captured and available to personnel.

Define the Key Terms

The following key terms include the ideas most important to the big ideas in this chapter. To review, without looking at the book or your notes, write a definition for each term, focusing on the meaning, not the wording. Then review your definition compared to your notes, this chapter, and the glossary.

Key Terms for Chapter 9

acceptable usage policy (AUP)	Information Technology Infrastructure Library (ITIL)	scope creep
business alignment		service
cost center	IT governance	service level agreement (SLA)
critical path	milestone	stakeholder
critical task	mission statement	values
good practices	profit center	vision statement
	scope	

List the Words Inside Acronyms

The following are the most common acronyms discussed in this chapter. As a way to review those terms, simply write down the words that each letter represents in each acronym.

Acronyms for Chapter 9

AUP	ITIL	OGC
COBIT	ITL	POA&M
DLP	IM	SLA
FAQ	ITSM	UTM
FISMA	NIST	

Create Mind Maps

For this chapter, create mind maps as follows:

1. Create a mind map to list the five methods people often use to manage conflict. Start with a circle labeled conflict and draw five lines out from the circle. Label these lines with the conflict resolution methods and then write short phrases of incidences where you've seen people use these methods.

2. Create a mind map to list the five phases of a service as described by ITIL. Start with a circle labeled lifecycle and create five labels around the circle (such as 1 through 5). Next, identify each of the labels.

Define Other Terms

Define the following additional terms from this chapter, and check your answers in the glossary:

change management

Control Objectives for Information and related Technology (COBIT)

Information Technology Laboratory (ITL)

National Institute of Standards and Technology (NIST)

Case Studies

Case Study 1

Use the Internet to find the "There are no vans" story told by Tony Robbins at many of his presentations. Think of a story in your life that you could tell to inspire others.

Case Study 2

Go to ted.com and watch at least one 18-minute video. Document how the speaker used the nine elements mentioned in the "Understanding Presentation Skills in the Business" section of this chapter.

Case Study 3

Think about where you want to be five years from now. Write down as many key words and short statements you can think of to describe your career position, your financial standing, your relationships, your standing or contributions in the community, your health and physical fitness, and things you're regularly doing for fun and recreation. Next, write a vision statement for each of these areas for yourself.

Case Study 4

Do an Internet search on "values" and make a list of at least ten values you consider important. Next, prioritize these values with your top five. If desired, you can read Steve Pavlina's articles on Living Your Values to help you with the process: http://www.stevepavlina.com/articles/living-your-values-1.htm.

Chapter 10

Calculating Help Desk Value

While the help desk is a cost center and doesn't generate any direct revenue, it still has value. This value isn't always apparent to personnel outside the help desk center, so it's important for help desk managers to understand how to communicate its value. The most common method is with the use of performance metrics. However, help desk managers also need to be aware of help desk costs and know how to create a cost benefit analysis when necessary.

This chapter includes three sections:

- The first section, "Calculating Value with Performance Metrics," describes many of the key metrics used to measure the performance of the help desk. Several of these metrics demonstrate what help desk personnel accomplish on a regular basis. Help desk managers also use many of them to identify trends within the help desk center and address issues before them become problems.

- Next, "Identifying Help Desk Costs" discusses the common costs associated with the help desk, along with a discussion on budgets. This section also includes methods used to calculate the cost per ticket metric.

- Last, the "Creating a Cost Benefit Analysis" section describes the purpose of a cost benefit analysis and the steps used to create one. It includes an example scenario comparing costs and benefits to show the value of an acquisition. This section also demonstrates how to calculate a return on investment.

Chapter Outline

Objectives

- Describe the purpose of metrics
- Define backlog and predicted backlog
- Compare and contrast reply time, wait time, and resolution time
- List and describe metrics used to measure technician performance
- Describe available metrics with computer telephony integration
- Discuss the differences between intrinsic and extrinsic motivation
- List and describe common help desk costs
- Discuss cloud-based and server-based help desk software
- Explain the cost per ticket and how to calculate it
- Discuss the purpose of a cost benefit analysis
- List and describe the three primary steps used in a cost benefit analysis
- Summarize the primary differences between tangibles and intangibles
- Discuss the purpose of a return on investment value

Key Terms

abandoned call	cost benefit analysis (CBA)	return on investment
abandon rate	intangibles	tangibles
answer time	new tickets	ticket
backlog	payback period	tickets solved
budget	performance metric	trend analysis
computer telephony integration (CTI)	reply time	wait time
	resolution time	

Calculating Value with Performance Metrics

Performance metrics measure various activities and management personnel commonly use them to determine the effectiveness of different areas of an organization, including the help desk. A **performance metric** provides quantifiable data on the performance of a process, and many help desk metrics help to calculate the overall value of the help desk.

Metrics also help an organization justify costs. The primary purpose of the help desk is to assist customers, and technicians commonly log each request into an application as a **ticket** or incident. The number of tickets the help desk handles can be used to justify costs, especially if this number drastically increases.

Imagine that a help desk normally handles about 1,000 tickets a month and maintains a high customer satisfaction rating. However, recent customer growth resulted in an increase in the number of tickets to about 1,500 tickets a month. Further, this increase correlates with a decrease in customer satisfaction. A help desk manager can use this data to justify a change such as implementing a telephone integration system or hiring more help desk technicians.

Without any metrics, senior management might only hear about an increase in customer complaints without a clear idea of the problem. They can easily get a perception of poor performance from the help desk personnel, along with inadequate management skills by help desk managers.

Metrics are also useful at identifying the effectiveness of new procedures and techniques. As an example, if you have a growing backlog of tickets, you might look for some creative solutions to reduce them, such as adding or updating a frequently asked question (FAQ) page, training one or more technicians, or implementing an online knowledge base. With metrics, you can compare before and after performance to measure the effectiveness of the solutions. If they're effective, keep doing them. If they're not effective, stop.

> **ON THE SIDE:**
> Successful people often repeat three simple behaviors: 1) Identify what works and keep doing it; 2) Identify what doesn't work and stop; and 3) Try new things. Help desk managers can implement new processes and procedures and use metrics to determine what they should continue and what they should stop.

Measuring the Performance of Your Help Desk

Chapter 1, "Introduction to Help Desk Support Roles," introduces a few key metrics used to measure the effectiveness of a help desk. This section goes into more depth for these metrics and adds some additional metrics commonly available in many help desk applications.

It's worth noting that if you try to collect these metrics manually, it becomes extremely time consuming. Instead, most organizations use an application to manage tickets, and these applications automatically record data and include reporting capabilities to view specific metrics. For example, Zendesk and Freshdesk are two companies that host cloud-based help desk software, and each product includes a wide variety of built-in metrics. Similarly, server-based help desk applications such as BMC Remedy installed on servers within an organization also include built-in metrics.

In general, any help desk application includes the ability to track and report metrics. However, they don't necessarily use the same names for similar metrics. For example, one application might use a Customer Satisfaction Report derived from a Customer Satisfaction metric, while another might use a Satisfaction Ratings Report derived from a Satisfaction Rating metric. Both reports provide the same type of data related to customer satisfaction, but the metric names and reports are slightly different. The following sections identify some common metrics that help desk managers can use to measure the help desk performance, but don't be surprised if you see any of these metrics with a different name somewhere else.

New Tickets or New Incidents

In the context of the help desk, an incident is the same thing as a ticket. Users request assistance and logging the request into the application creates a ticket. The **new tickets** metric shows the volume of these requests. It provides insight into the workload requirements of the help desk personnel, and when you compare the volume over time, it helps identify trends.

As an example, Figure 10-1 shows the number of new tickets logged each month for a year. Looking at the figure, two trends might jump out at you. First, there's a sharp drop in the number of tickets in April and the tickets progressively declined until August. Next, the tickets started to increase in September and reached a high in December. The volume stayed lower for most of the year and then began rising in October with a peak in December.

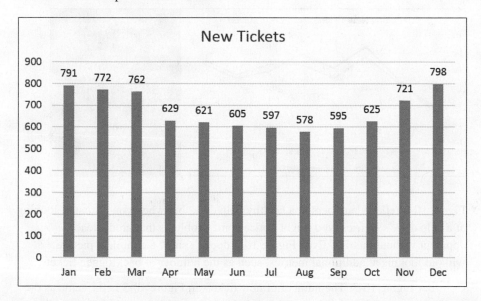

While the chart doesn't indicate the cause of these trends, it does give management insight into trends that are worth investigating. For example, April shows a sharp drop in new tickets that persisted for several months. An investigation into what changed between March and April might show that the company posted a new frequently asked question (FAQ) page and this page is helping many users solve the problems for themselves.

354   CHAPTER 10   Calculating Help Desk Value

The spike in October, November, and December sales is worth investigating too. Imagine that the company enjoys increased holiday sales between October and December and they hire seasonal employees to assist during this time. This spike in tickets is very likely due to the increased sales and seasonal employees. Proactive managers can use this data to ensure the help desk has appropriate staffing levels to meet the increased demand during this time.

Tickets Solved or Resolved Incidents

Another important metric is **tickets solved**, or resolved incidents. It identifies the number of customer requests that technicians addressed and solved during a period. Help desk managers often look at this on a weekly basis and compare it to the number of new tickets. Ideally, the help desk should solve about the same number of tickets as they receive. In some weeks, they might resolve more as they work on backlogged tickets. In other weeks, they might resolve less, resulting in an increase in the number of backlogged tickets.

Figure 10-2 shows the progress of a relatively healthy help desk over the past eight weeks. The two trend lines in the graph identify new tickets and tickets solved. Ideally, these trend lines should be similar, with only minor deviations as they are in the graph. The Weekly Progress table next to the chart also shows the actual percentage of tickets solved compared to the number of new tickets. The percentage of solved tickets is consistently above 98 percent, which is excellent.

FIGURE 10-2

Comparing new tickets
and tickets solved on a
healthy help desk.

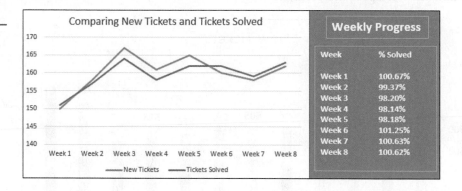

Figure 10-2 reflects numbers in a healthy help desk, but when you first start looking at a help desk's metrics, you might notice some problems that aren't readily apparent without metrics. Even Figure 10-2 doesn't show a complete picture without looking at additional metrics, such as the number of backlogged tickets.

Consider Figure 10-3. The number of new tickets in Figure 10-3 is the same as the number of new tickets in Figure 10-2, but the tickets solved metric is drastically different. For some reason, this help desk has a dip in the number of tickets solved every other week, and the number of tickets solved is not trending with the number of new tickets. Further, the percentage of tickets solved clearly shows significant inconsistencies from one week to another.

> **ON THE SIDE:** Figures 10-2 and 10-3 are using different scales, causing the New Tickets trend line to look different in each, even though the New Tickets values are the same in each figure. Figure 10-2 has a scale of 140 to 170 and shows how closely the two trend lines are to each other. Figure 10-3 has a scale of 80 to 180 to accommodate the drastic deviations in the Tickets Solved trend line.

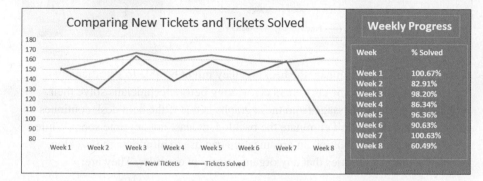

FIGURE 10-3

Comparing new tickets and tickets solved on a help desk with problems.

Of course, these graphs don't identify the cause of a problem. However, they do make it easy to identify potential problems worth investigating. A help desk manager seeing the graph in Figure 10-3 knows that something is causing these dips in productivity every other week, and this is worth the manager's time to investigate. In contrast, a help desk manager seeing the graph in Figure 10-2 can quickly see that the help desk is consistently solving the tickets they're receiving, and sometimes more.

Backlog and Predicted Backlog

The **backlog** identifies the number of open or unsolved tickets in a help desk's system. In simplest terms, it is the total number of new tickets minus the total number of tickets solved. Most help desk applications allow you to track the backlog for different periods, such as monthly or weekly. This allows you to see if the backlog is growing, shrinking, or staying the same. Additionally, some systems can automatically predict the expected backlog at some point in the future based on past trends.

As an example, Figure 10-4 shows the backlog in comparison with New Tickets and Tickets Solved. Even though the New Tickets and Tickets solved graphs indicate the help desk is solving about the same number of tickets they're receiving, the backlog graph indicates the backlog is staying relatively the same. You can see the average number of new tickets is hovering around 160 a week, and the average backlog is about 130 tickets. Assuming the help desk is assisting users on a first-come first-served basis, this indicates most customers are waiting over a week before receiving assistance. If the current trends continue, you can expect the average backlog will stay at about 130 six months from now.

10

FIGURE 10-4

Backlog.

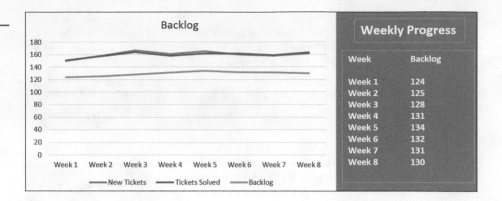

If this help desk can eliminate the backlog, they might be able to significantly reduce the amount of time customers are waiting before technicians solve their problems. One clear message from these graphs is that if the help desk continues on the same path, they won't eliminate the backlog, at least not anytime soon. While there isn't any single solution an organization can use to eliminate the backlog, there are some possibilities that any organization can consider. They are:

- **Increase the number of tickets solved.** A help desk manager might be able to create a vision of reducing this number to less than 10 and enlist the help desk technicians in the vision. The technicians might have ideas on exactly how they can do so and might truly appreciate being asked for their input. The manager might set some interim goals, such as less than 100 by a certain date, less than 75 by a certain date, and so on. It's possible that some technicians might need some training or coaching so that they can solve more tickets, or possibly solve tickets quicker. If the backlog is significant, you might choose to supplement the help desk for a short time. You can hire a contractor, a part-time employee, or possibly transfer an employee from another IT department to the help desk for a short time.

> **ON THE SIDE:** It's important not to put too much external pressure on technicians involved in a job requiring creative thinking. However, by enlisting the technicians in a vision that the entire team can pursue, you are able to inspire intrinsic or internal motivators for the technicians. The "Comparing Intrinsic and Extrinsic Motivation" section later in this chapter expands on some of the unexpected drawbacks of extrinsic, or external, motivators.

- **Solve problems before they become tickets.** You might be able to add or update FAQs on your website. You could start by simply asking technicians what problems they're solving most often and then add questions to the FAQ page to address these problems. You might also be able to make your knowledge base publicly accessible, so that users can search it and find their own answers.

- **Reduce customer requests for status.** When customers have to wait a long time to get a problem solved, they often want to know the status of their request. If they don't hear from the help desk, many of them will follow-up. Each time a customer follows-up asking for status, it takes time for a technician to respond. Depending on how long customers are waiting, some of them might be irate. In addition, to causing intangible losses to the organization's reputation, it also adds stress and more time when technicians and management personnel need to spend more time with irate customers. You can avoid much of this with simple status messages to customers to set their expectations. This can be as simple as an email giving the customer an estimated date when they can expect to hear back from the help desk. Of course, it's important for help desk personnel to ensure they do follow-up with the customer by that time.

- **Consider categorizing tickets.** Some help desks assign tickets to technicians using a round-robin method. The first ticket goes to technician 1, the second one goes to technician 2, and so on. However, you can categorize tickets and assign them to technicians based on their experience and expertise. This allows each technician to work on familiar problems and solve each problem quicker. Once you clear the backlog, you can switch back to the original method if desired, giving technicians some variety and an opportunity to learn and grow in the job.

Submission Methods

Some help desks only accept tickets in-person or via a phone call. However, many other help desks accept tickets from a wide variety of methods. These include in-person, phone, e-mail, web page forms, instant messages, chat windows, automated reports from monitoring systems, and some social media outlets such as Twitter.

Ideally, customers want to report tickets using the method that's easiest to them. If that method is available, that's the method they'll most likely use. When you look at this metric, it gives you insight into your customer's preferred method of communication, at least for tickets. Also, when you look at this metric over time, it will help you identify any changes in trends. When you see a trend, you can ensure the help desk staff is adequately equipped to handle these changes.

Reply Time

The **reply time** refers to how long it takes before a customer receives a reply from a live person. Long reply times often result in dissatisfied customers, so organizations seek to have low or quick reply times. Reply times vary significantly based on the help desk system and the primary method customers use to report incidents. Many Internet service providers (ISPs) use automated telephone systems and have reputations for longer reply times. Other systems include text-based systems such as email, instant message, and web page submissions.

As an example, consider an organization that uses an automated telephone system to queue calls before a technician responds. The initial reply time might be long.

ON THE SIDE: Some organizations use computer telephony integration (discussed later in this chapter) and can record when a customer calls and match this up to when a technician answers. However, without such a system, it's difficult to accurately know the reply times for phone calls.

10

Many organizations use automated messages saying something like, "Your call is important to us." They also combine it with a message about the wait time such as, "You are fifth in the queue" or, "Your wait time is expected to be about ten minutes." This isn't an actual reply, but it does help set the customer's expectations about how much they time they need to wait.

It's also worth pointing out that the longer it takes for a technician to reply, the more likely it is for a customer to expect an immediate resolution to the problem. For example, if a customer waits 10 minutes to talk to a technician, the customer typically expects the technician to resolve the problem. However, if a technician answers the phone within 30 seconds, customers are often willing to accept a delay in the resolution. In the latter example, the technician collects information on the problem to create a ticket and then asks the customer for some time to investigate it and get back to the customer.

> **ON THE SIDE:**   When providing estimates of reply times, it's best to over-estimate these times. Customers are more likely to be irritated if they hear a message indicating their wait time will be about five minutes but they actually end up waiting ten minutes. In contrast, customers will be pleasantly surprised if you tell them their wait time will be ten minutes but someone starts helping them after only five minutes. If asked, technicians can explain that some incidents are easy to resolve, allowing them to get to other customers quicker.

Organizations that use text-based systems for initiating tickets often allow the help desk to reply quicker. Technicians can quickly acknowledge the ticket. If the customer reports the problem via instant message or chat, a technician can collect information to initiate the ticket and then ask for time to investigate it and get back to the user. Similarly, if the customer reports the problem via email or a web page, a technician can quickly reply to indicate the ticket is logged and a technician will be looking into the problem. Remember, though, that this reply needs to come from a live person, not an automated response.

Of course, lower reply times are better. However, it's worth comparing the average of this metric over a given time such as a week, with the reply times during any specific time period. For example, you might notice that the average response time is about five minutes for any given week. Looking closer, you might see that the response times between 8 AM and 10 AM Monday through Friday is about 15 minutes or longer, and the response times between 6 PM and 8 PM is typically only a minute. With this information, you can focus on improving the response times between 8 AM and 10 AM, but you probably won't want to spend any time trying to improve the response times between 6 PM and 8 PM.

Wait Time

The **wait time** refers to how long it takes before a problem is resolved. Most help desk systems calculate this as the time between the ticket creation and its resolution.

When looking at this time, it's important to understand how a ticket is created in the help desk system and how it compares to the reply time.

If customers create the ticket themselves, such as via a web page, the wait time includes the reply time. For example, a customer could create a ticket via a web page, and then receive a reply in 10 minutes. The technician then resolves the problem in 20 minutes. In this scenario, the wait time includes the reply time and is a total of 30 minutes.

As another example, imagine a customer calls the help desk and waits on the phone for 20 minutes before talking to a technician. The technician then creates the ticket and is able to solve the customer's problem in 10 minutes. In this scenario, the help desk system reports the wait time as 10 minutes.

Resolution Time

The **resolution time** metric looks at two times within a ticket: first resolution time and full resolution time. Ideally, the times are always the same. The first resolution time is the time between ticket creation and its resolution. Technicians close the ticket when they resolve it and in most situations, they never open it again. If the ticket is never opened again, the full resolution time will be the same as the first resolution time. However, there are many situations when a technician closes a ticket but someone later reopens the same ticket.

As an example, imagine a user named Bob calls and asks for help configuring email settings. A technician helps Bob configure Simple Mail Transfer Protocol (SMTP) and then closes the ticket. An hour later, Bob realizes that while his system is sending email, it isn't receiving any email, so he calls the help desk again. Another technician receives the call and reopens the previous ticket. The second technician helps Bob configure Post Office Protocol (POP). After verifying that Bob can send and receive email, the technician ends the call and closes the ticket.

When the first resolution and full resolution times are different, it indicates a potential problem. In the example, the customer asked for help configuring his system to send email. Even though Bob didn't specifically ask for help configuring his system to receive email, it's reasonable for a technician to predict this need. The second technician verified Bob could send and receive email, and if the first technician took this step, it would have avoided the second help desk call. An obvious question is, "Why didn't the first technician take the additional steps needed to avoid the second call?" Two common reasons are:

- **Technicians pressured to close tickets quickly:** When management pressures technicians to close tickets quickly, technicians can perceive this as more important than customer service. Instead of taking the time to ensure customers are fully satisfied, technicians rush the customer so that they can close the ticket quicker. While this does reduce the wait times for many tickets, some customers will contact the help desk again later to try to get the problem resolved completely, or ask another question.

ON THE SIDE:
Many help desk systems identify users with customer numbers and automatically reopen recently closed tickets when customers call back within a certain period. For example, if a user calls back within 24 hours, the system automatically reopens the previous ticket. This gives the second technician easy access to all the information from the original call.

10

- **Technicians don't fully understand the problem or problem resolution:** In many situations, technicians might be doing the best they can, but they lack the expertise to fully resolve many problems. The solution is often to provide additional training or coaching to these technicians to improve their skills. Many times, this can be used as a teaching opportunity, letting the first technician see both what happened and how to avoid a repeat of a similar situation in the future.

Obviously, customers would rather have a problem completely resolved in a single ticket. They don't want to call back asking for help again. When they're forced to do so, they're bound to make less than favorable judgments on the competency of the help desk and attribute these same judgments to the organization as a whole. Organizations often train technicians to ask something like, "Is there anything else I can help you with?" before ending the call.

Satisfaction Ratings

The primary purpose of the help desk is to assist customers, and the best way to determine how effective they are doing so is with customer evaluations. This provides direct insight into customer satisfaction and can often give the organization valuable feedback on what the help desk is doing well and what they might want to improve.

You typically only hear how satisfied customers are when you ask. Additionally, you are much more likely to get an answer when your question is simple. With this in mind, you get the best feedback on customer satisfaction when you ask your customers to provide feedback and you give them a simple method to do so.

> **ON THE SIDE:**
> Remember, help desk customers can be internal employees and external paying customers. It's possible to ask for feedback from both types of customers.

For example, if you want to get feedback on the help desk after a ticket is closed, you could ask, "Overall, how would you rate this support request?" You could then give them two choices, "Bad" or "Good," and then include a section for them to provide a comment. If desired, you can expand this with a scale, such as 1 to 5 with 1 being the worst, and 5 being the best. You ask the same question, but then let them click on the screen to indicate the rating.

While this one question survey is better than nothing, it often raises questions. For example, if the average rating hovers around 3, you might want to know what's stopping it from being a 4 or a 5. However, unless customers provided detailed comments, you might not know why.

Many organizations expand the survey by asking a few questions. For example, they might ask "Please rate your experience on a scale of 1 to 5 (with 5 being the best) for the following three questions":

- Was the technician helpful?
- Was the technician courteous?
- Overall, how satisfied were you with the service?

The benefit of this is that you might find that the technician was helpful but rude, or very courteous but not very helpful. This gives you some insight into what the help desk, or individual technicians, can work on improving. Technicians might need training or coaching on communications so that customers perceive them as being more helpful or courteous.

Technician Performance

You can often get details on individual technician performance by drilling down into some of the previous metrics. For example, you can identify the following metrics for any individual technician:

- **Resolved tickets.** Assuming all technicians work 40-hour weeks and have similar skills, they would each resolve about the same number of tickets. However, there is bound to be some variance, primarily because not all technicians have the same level of expertise and some are bound to be better than others. As an example, Figure 10-5 shows the distribution of resolved tickets by five help desk technicians. While Lisa is a superstar, the graph also shows that Homer and Bart might need some assistance to increase their performance.

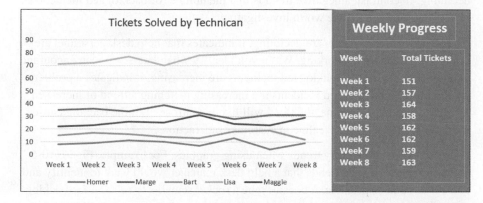

FIGURE 10-5

Tickets solved by technician.

- **Wait times.** Some technicians might be solving problems very quickly, while others might be taking a significant amount of time with each ticket. For example, if you look at Homer's performance on week 7, it looks like he only resolved five tickets. If you drilled into the wait times for these five tickets, you might find that he's taking as long as eight hours for each ticket. While this might be justified for some problems, it isn't justified for all the problems. If you checked and discovered that these tickets were for simple password resets, it might indicate that Homer needs more than just training.

- **Satisfaction ratings.** Satisfaction ratings for individual technicians can give you insight into their customer service skills. For example, if most of the technicians had an average satisfaction rating between 4.5 and 4.8, but Bart's satisfaction rating consistently hovers at around 2.3, it indicates a problem worth investigating.

10

ON THE SIDE: When looking at technician performance, it's just as important to recognize the top performers as it is to identify the technicians at the bottom of the scale. For example, Maggie might have the ability to double her performance, but if she sees that Lisa is not benefiting from all her work, Maggie might conclude she's better off staying in the middle of the pack. Recognition can come in many forms, including public acknowledgment, private conversations offering words of appreciation and encouragement, salary raises, bonuses, increased responsibility, and promotions.

Analyzing Trends

A significant benefit of using metrics is the ability to spot trends. **Trend analysis** uses existing tools and statistics to identify consistent movement in one direction or another. A trend is not just a blip, such as an increase one week and a decline the next week. Instead, a trend reflects a consistent increase over time or a consistent decrease over time.

As an example, a positive trend can be that the number of backlogged incidents is declining. In contrast, a negative trend is that the number of backlogged incidents is increasing. Both trends are worth investigating.

If the backlogged incidents are declining, it indicates that help desk personnel are doing something that's working. When you identify what that is, you can encourage them to continue. If the backlogged incidents are increasing, it indicates a problem. It might be that backlogged incidents are increasing matching a trend of increased incidents. If nothing is done, the trend will likely continue until the backlog causes more problems, such as a decline in customer satisfaction.

It's often easiest to identify trends when using graphics. For example, Figure 10-6 shows three interrelated trends that a help desk manager would want to identify and address as soon as possible. It doesn't take a rocket scientist to see that the backlog is becoming a serious problem, but when combined with the other two lines, it provides insight into the possible cause.

FIGURE 10-6

Identifying trends.

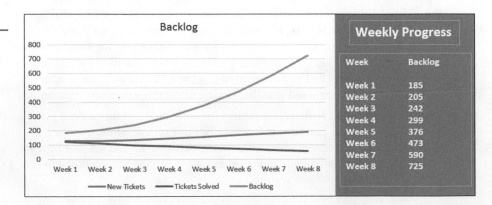

At week 1, the three metrics are relatively close, though the backlog is high. The middle line shows the number of new tickets is steadily increasing, while the bottom line shows the number of tickets solved is steadily declining. Customers with open tickets are probably following up with the help desk, asking for more help or at least some type of status, and many of them are frustrated with the situation. Technicians are spending time with these customers and have less time to solve new tickets. This isn't a fun working environment for them, so they are probably struggling with the situation too. They can see that they are solving progressively fewer tickets, and they frequently have to deal with irate customers.

Imagine that the manager didn't have this graph but instead looked at reports separately. The manager might notice that technicians are solving fewer and fewer tickets and increase pressure on them to do more. Of course, this won't help, because the problem isn't due to the technicians not doing their job. Instead, management needs to take proactive steps to decrease the backlog.

Capturing Statistics with Computer Telephony Integration

Computer telephony integration (CTI) is a technology that connects the telephone system with a computer system. Many help desk systems that interact with customers via telephone use a CTI system. As a simple example, when a user calls into the help desk, the telephone system captures the user's phone number and passes it to the help desk application. The help desk application can use this to identify the caller and retrieve the caller's customer information. When a technician answers the call, the help desk application can pop up a window providing the customer's information.

CTI systems help automate many of the initial help desk processes. As a reminder, the first three steps in a typical incident process are Receiving, Validating, and Logging. When the customer calls, the CTI system can receive the call. Next, it can verify the caller is a valid customer for the help desk. Some systems require users to enter additional information such as a personal identification number (PIN) or customer access number when they call. The CTI can capture this and use it to verify the customer is a valid help desk customer. After validating the caller, the CTI system can log the customer's information into a ticketing system. A technician still needs to log additional details on the incident, but the CTI system logs the customer information.

In addition to automating the first three steps of a typical incident, the CTI system can also capture some metrics. Some of the common metrics you can capture with a CTI are:

- **Abandoned calls.** An **abandoned call** is a call where the caller hangs up before a live person answered the phone, and the abandoned calls metric identifies the total number of abandoned calls for a given period. If this number is high, it's worth investigating to determine the cause.

ON THE SIDE:
Many times when you call into any type of service center, technicians start by asking a few qualifying questions, such as your name and address. They aren't recording this information. Instead, they are verifying the information they see on the screen to ensure they have the correct customer record open.

10

- **Abandon rate.** The **abandon rate** identifies the percentage of abandoned calls compared to the total number of calls. If the rate is high, you can look at the abandoned calls closer to determine when they are happening most often. For example, you might find a large volume of abandoned calls between 8 AM and 10 AM correlating with a long reply time during these hours. You can then take steps to improve the reply time during these hours.

- **Answer time or queue time.** The **answer time** identifies the amount of time customers wait before a live person answers the call. Some help desk systems express this as queue time. It is the same as the reply time in a help desk system, but the reply time can refer to replies from other methods instead of just a telephone. You can typically look at the average, shortest, and longest times with this metric, and chart the times over hourly periods to identify when customers are waiting the longest. By adding technicians during these times, you might be able to improve the overall answer times.

Comparing Intrinsic Motivation to Extrinsic Motivation

Managers often try to motivate employees to accomplish work in the best interest of the company. However, some methods of motivation work better than others in certain situations. More specifically, some situations require intrinsic motivators and others require extrinsic motivators, and successful managers know when to use each.

Intrinsic motivation comes from within a person. People often take action for their own personal reasons, such as finding it enjoyable, feeling like they are contributing to something bigger than themselves, or gaining a sense of accomplishment. **Extrinsic motivation** comes from outside a person. Incentives and rewards for achieving certain milestones are examples. These can be monetary incentives such as bonuses or pay raises, or non-monetary incentives such as a grade in a course. Similarly, threats of discipline or punishment also provide extrinsic motivation for people.

It's important to be careful when using metrics to incentivize help desk technicians as extrinsic motivation because there are many situations where they are counter-productive. As an example, some managers might offer monetary incentives for technicians to get them to improve their metrics, or penalize technicians if their metrics are too low. However, the added stress from these extrinsic motivators decreases performance in many typical help desk scenarios. The following sections describe a famous cognitive performance test, which applies directly to the creative problem-solving skills needed by help desk technicians in many of their day-to-day tasks.

Understanding the Candle Problem

Psychologist Karl Duncker published the candle problem in his 1926 thesis, and social scientists have repeated it many times. It provides insight into how people perform when they have incentives under different situations.

In the candle problem, participants are given the following three items (also shown in Figure 10-7):

- A candle
- A box of thumbtacks
- A book of matches

> **ON THE SIDE:**   Best-selling author Dan Pink presented an outstanding TED talk in 2009, titled The Puzzle of Motivation. He explains the candle problem and its implications in an informative and entertaining 18-minute talk. You can view the talk here: http://www.ted.com/talks/dan_pink_on_motivation.

FIGURE 10-7

The three items for the candle problem.

They are then asked to affix a lit candle onto a corkboard wall in such a way that candle wax doesn't drip onto a table below. People commonly try to tack the candle to the wall. It's a good idea, but it doesn't work. Other people light the candle and attempt to use some of the candle's wax to stick it to the wall. Another good idea, but it doesn't work either.

Instead, the solution is to empty the box of tacks, attach the box to the corkboard wall, and place the lit candle into the box. This isn't obvious at first because people don't recognize the box as an available tool.

Testers time two different groups of participants to see how long it takes them to solve the problem. They tell one group that they'll be timed to obtain norms or average solution times. They are not offered any type of incentives. The second group gets an incentive. Testers tell them they can win a prize based on how quickly they solve the problem. For example, in one experiment with the candle

10

test, participants were told that individuals that finish in the top 25% win $40.00 and the person with the best time wins $156.

Business people often think that incentives such as these will result in better performance. They assume the incentivized group does better, but they are wrong. This test repeatedly shows that people in the incentivized group consistently take longer to find the solution. That's correct. Offer them money to do it quicker and they do it slower. The reason is related to functional fixedness.

Understanding Functional Fixedness

Functional fixedness is a mental block against using an object differently than its obvious use. In the candle problem, people commonly view the box only as the container for the tacks rather than as a tool they can use to solve the problem. In reality, they have four items they can use to solve the problem: the candle, tacks, a box, and a book of matches. However, functional fixedness reduces this to only three items: the candle, tacks, and a book of matches.

Participants need to think creatively to overcome this functional fixedness related to the box. However, the incentive limits their creative thought process. The possibility of getting money for completing the task is a stressor that motivates them to complete it quicker. However, the added stress from the incentive hinders use of brain areas in the prefrontal cortex used for creative thinking and problem solving. This slows people down.

Removing Functional Fixedness

Here's a twist. When testers eliminate functional fixedness related to the box, it negates the need for creative thinking and the incentives are effective motivators. Instead of giving the participants three items, testers give them four items:

- A candle
- An empty box
- Thumbtacks
- A book of matches

Author Dan Pink humorously calls this *The Candle Problem for Dummies*. While that's an exaggeration, it does emphasize the point that this problem is simpler. Participants no longer view the box as a container for the thumbtacks, and they don't have to overcome functional fixedness to solve the problem. The testers present the box as one of the available tools and participants quickly see the solution. They don't need to count on creative thought to view the box from a different perspective.

When testers offer the participants incentives, they consistently complete the task quicker. They are motivated to complete the task quicker, and this motivation doesn't hinder them. When the challenge is simple and doesn't require creative thought, extrinsic motivators are effective.

Learning from the Candle Problem

This knowledge can be valuable for managers if they understand the concepts. There are two key points:

- **Incentives hinder performance for creative problems.** If employees need to work on tasks or projects requiring creative thought, incentives hinder them and slow them down. Yes, employees will still accomplish the tasks. However, the incentives don't help them complete them quicker—they instead slow them down.

- **Incentives can be useful in non-creative problems.** If employees need to work on simple tasks that don't require creative thought, incentives are effective motivators. For example, if employees need to complete a simple task repeatedly, incentives might motivate them to complete the tasks quicker.

Help desk personnel often need creative thought when troubleshooting and solving technical problems. Even if a customer complains of a problem that a technician has seen before, customers rarely present the problem in the same manner. Instead, the technician needs to use customer service and communication skills to identify the problem completely, and these skills often require some creativity when working with different customers.

With this in mind, extrinsic motivators used to get technicians to improve their metrics are rarely effective. At best, technicians get better with time and managers might believe the incentives are working. At worst, technicians begin to resent the system and look for ways to game it. For example, they might start looking for ways to improve their metrics artificially.

Even though extrinsic motivators are rarely effective for help desk employees, it doesn't mean that managers cannot appeal to a person's intrinsic motivation. Managers can recognize and applaud a technician's accomplishments; this often takes no more than offering authentic compliments. Technicians feel good about themselves and their contribution to the organization's mission, and are motivated to continue doing so. However, this internal motivation is not stressful for most people and does not hinder creative thought.

Identifying Help Desk Costs

If you want to calculate the help desk value accurately, you also need to understand the costs. One good thing about costs is that they are easy to quantify. The organization is spending a specific amount of money for various resources, and you can normally look at past expenditures to identify them. This makes it relatively easy to identify costs associated with the help desk. When necessary, managers can use this information to predict future expenditures for budget estimates.

The following sections identify many of the common costs associated with any help desk. When you have these costs available and know how many tickets help desk personnel are solving, you are able to calculate and track the cost per ticket and similar metrics.

Personnel Costs

Personnel costs include the costs associated with the technicians, supervisors, and/or managers working on the help desk. Payroll is the most obvious cost here, but it's important to understand that an organization also pays additional costs associated with payroll. For example, employers must match some taxes paid by employees.

Many organizations offer matching contributions for 401K or similar retirement plans. For example, an organization might offer as much as five percent of matching contributions. If employees invest five percent or more of their salary to a qualified plan, the organization matches that five percent, effectively doubling the employee's investment. Based on the percentage, and how many employees actually take them up on this offer of free money, this amount can vary from one organization to another.

Organizations commonly offer insurance benefits and supplement the cost of these plans. This includes health, dental, vision, life, and disability insurance. Employers are also required to pay worker compensation insurance. If the employer offers paid holidays, vacations, and sick days, this also goes into the mix.

Some organizations build incentives for employees to work overtime rather than hire additional employees. This can save money in some situations by reducing the overall costs of benefits, even when employees earn additional money per hour for overtime work.

Hardware Costs

The hardware costs include the computers and peripherals used by help desk personnel. If the help desk is a 24-hour operation, help desk technicians will share computers. However, if they all work a specific shift, such as nine to five Monday through Friday, each technician might have a dedicated computer. Peripherals include printers and scanners.

Organizations often have a planned schedule for replacing computers on a regular basis, such as every five years. They then spread the cost of the hardware over this five-year period.

Software Costs

Software costs include all of the software required on the help desk computers. In some cases, this might require a Microsoft Office suite including Microsoft Word, Microsoft Excel, and more. However, if help desk personnel don't need this software, the company might choose to forgo these costs.

A bigger software cost is associated with the help desk software. Technicians will use this to enter and track tickets, and management will use it to measure the effectiveness of the help desk. There are many options for this, including cloud-based software such as Zendesk and Freshdesk, and server-based software such as BMC Remedy.

One advantage to using cloud-based software is that your organization doesn't need to host and maintain the software. You simply rent access to it, the external company handles all the details, such as maintaining the servers and implementing fault tolerance methods to ensure the servers are highly available. Technicians and managers access the service over the Internet and rarely need to worry about outages. A disadvantage is that the company pays for it on a monthly basis, typically with a fee for each help desk technician and manager, and this fee sometimes appears to be high.

> **ON THE SIDE:** While the per-technician costs of cloud-based software often looks high initially, many organizations have found that it is worthwhile in the end. Zendesk was founded in 2007 and now boasts more than 40,000 companies are using its services, including Sears, Groupon, 20th Century Fox, Elance, and more. Similarly, Freshdesk launched in 2011 and boasts that more than 17,000 companies are using its services, including Enterprise Rent-a-Car, Goodreads, Unicef, and more.

In contrast, server-based software is typically a one-time fee that includes free updates. However, internal administrators must install it on an available server and maintain it. Additionally, administrators typically need to install and maintain associated applications on the help-desk computers. Technicians use the local application to access the server application.

Facility Costs

Facility costs refer to the space used by the help desk personnel when they are assisting customers. It also includes the supporting facility services, such as the network infrastructure, power, heating, and air conditioning. In some cases, additional facility costs might be required, such as security services.

It's rare for help desk personnel to operate independently away from the rest of the organization. Instead, they operate in the same building, and financial personnel typically know exactly how much a square foot of space costs in any building they own or rent. In other words, you can often get this figure from someone in the finance department if necessary.

The help desk benefits from economies of scale with most facility costs. **Economies of scale** refers to the cost savings gained by an increase in production. In this example, the facility costs are already in place, and if you are adding a help desk employee, you won't have additional costs associated with the network infrastructure, power, heating, and air conditioning. Depending on standards used within an organization, facility costs might not need to be included in help desk costs.

> **ON THE SIDE:**
> Many organizations allow personnel to work from home, and this includes some help desk personnel. It results in direct savings for the organization related to facility costs and reduces an employee's travel time to and from work. The challenge from the organization's point of view is ensuring that personnel are actually working, but metrics can help an organization verify employee productivity no matter where they are working.

10

Overhead Costs

Some organizations simplify cost calculations by just using an overhead percentage. For example, they can identify payroll costs and then add in an extra 30 percent. The extra 30 percent addresses all the extra overhead items such as facility, hardware, and software costs.

It also addresses some of the overhead that isn't readily apparent, such as payroll. Ensuring employees are consistently paid on time is extremely important. However, payroll doesn't happen magically. Instead, an organization employs personnel to manage the payroll, or they outsource the payroll to another organization such as Paychex. The cost of this is typically minimal for the relatively few employees working on the help desk, but it's not the only overhead cost within an organization.

Budgeting

Organizations put a lot of time and effort into creating budgets and normally create them on an annual basis. A **budget** identifies the money needed for a specific purpose, such as to run a department or fund a project. Department heads project their needs for the following year and submit their requests in a budget. They often query managers within a department for input to ensure they accurately reflect the department's needs.

Some budget items, such as consumable items, are easy to predict. You can normally look at the expenditures from the previous year and predict the costs for the next year. However, some costs are not readily apparent without some forethought. For example, if you want to add additional software, hardware, or personnel, you'll need to evaluate these extra costs to get an accurate estimate.

Ideally, managers identify their needs and include a request for them in a budget. This makes it easier to fund the request. In contrast, unbudgeted items are often difficult to get approved, and are sometimes postponed to the following budget year.

Calculating Cost per Ticket

Another cost-related key to the help desk is the cost per ticket, or the cost per resolved ticket. You won't find a standard formula used to measure this cost in every organization. However, as long as an organization calculates it the same way over time, they will be able to identify trends using this metric. Some items to consider when calculating this cost are:

- **Personnel costs.** This includes the payroll of all personnel working on the help desk. One organization might use a simple calculation of hourly pay or salaries. Another organization might add in the additional overhead such as taxes and benefits.

- **Facility costs.** Smaller organizations with one or two help desk technicians might skip this cost because it is minimal, or add in an overhead percentage. However, larger organizations employing dozens of technicians would typically include this cost because the technicians require so much space.

ON THE SIDE: A similar metric is cost per contact, which generically refers to any contact with a help desk technician. It includes inbound calls, outbound calls, email responses, chat responses, and so on. Organizations that provide assistance primarily over the phone typically use the term cost per call instead. Also, organizations that respond to customers in multiple ways sometimes choose to measure each method separately, such as cost per inbound call or cost per email response.

- **Hardware and software costs.** This includes all the hardware and software technicians require on-the-job. Instead of a lump-sum cost, organizations typically identify the replacement cost and the replacement time period to identify a monthly cost. For example, if they plan to replace the hardware every five years and estimate the replacement cost as $15,000, the annual cost is $3,000. If cloud-based software is used, that fee needs to be included in this cost. Similarly, if upgrades to the server-based software are required, that cost needs to be included.

The next step is to add all the costs together to identify a total. One method is identify the annual costs and use this figure to identify the monthly costs by dividing by 12, or the weekly costs by dividing by 52. As an example, imagine the annual cost is $120,000. This equates to a monthly cost of $10,000 and a weekly cost of $2,308.

A common method is to use the resolved tickets metric when identifying the cost per ticket. However, if you want to use another metric, such as the cost per contact, you need to have a good understanding of how your organization handles tickets. For example, if a caller's problem is typically resolved on the first call, you can use the resolved tickets metric. If technicians record the ticket on the first contact but resolve them during the second contact, you'd add the number of new tickets with the number of resolved tickets. Notice that these methods don't account for the occasional deviations. For example, even if technicians resolve most tickets on the first contact, some require two or more calls. If you want to be more exact, you can use a different measurement, such as inbound calls.

Figure 10-8 shows a Cost per Ticket chart for a year. You can see some increases between April and October and a decrease in November and December. While this might look like a problem, it is entirely possible that there isn't a problem at all. Still, it is important to understand the reasons for these changes. For this example, the total costs haven't changed, but instead, the number of tickets resolved has decreased between April and October, as shown in Figure 10-9.

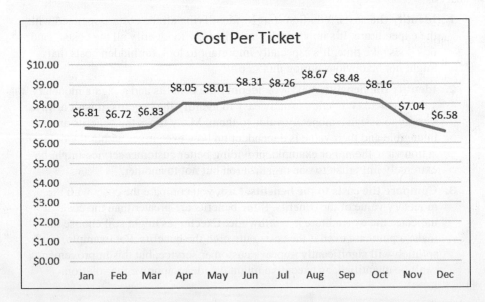

FIGURE 10-8

Identifying cost per ticket.

10

FIGURE 10-9

Tickets resolved.

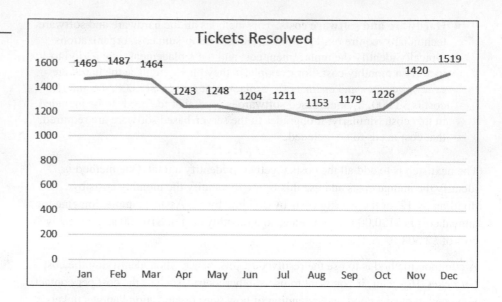

The two most important things to remember when calculating the cost per ticket are 1) account for any changes in costs, and 2) use a consistent calculation. The most common reason for a change in costs is either pay changes or new hires. When people get raises, or new people are added to the help desk, these changes need to be added into the mix. If you originally calculate the cost based on resolved tickets, but later change this to inbound calls, you won't be able to use the two calculations for reliable comparisons between each other.

Creating a Cost Benefit Analysis (CBA)

Managers use a **cost benefit analysis (CBA)** to compare costs and benefits when making business decisions. When done accurately, a CBA makes it relatively easy to make many decisions. In general, there are three steps to create a cost benefit analysis:

1. **Identify the costs.** You first start by identifying all the costs associated with the expenditure. It's important to take the time to identify all the costs—and this does take time. It's especially important to look for hidden costs that might not be obvious during this step.

2. **Identify the benefits.** Next, you identify the benefits and assign a monetary value to them. While it's usually easy to identify the benefits, it isn't always so easy to assign a monetary value to them. Many times the benefits are intangible and their value is dependent on how executives within the organization view them. For example, providing better customer service might be extremely important to one organization but not to another.

3. **Compare the costs to the benefits.** Last, you compare the costs with the monetary value of the benefits. If the benefits are greater than the costs, it indicates the expenditure is worthwhile. Executives might still choose to make a purchase even if the costs outweigh the benefits. For example, if a solution will significantly improve customer service, but this improvement can't be quantified, an executive might decide to approve the solution.

It's common to look at a year-long period when creating a CBA. In other words, you would identify the annual costs and the annual benefits rather than the lifelong costs and lifelong benefits. This makes it easier to create the CBA and complete the analysis. As long as the benefits are greater than the costs, or the costs are greater than the benefits, the decision is clear. However, if the two are relatively equal, the decision isn't clear and might require a deeper analysis.

Comparing Tangibles and Intangibles

When calculating costs and value, you often need to consider both tangibles and intangibles. **Tangibles** are costs, benefits, and asset values that are easy to quantify in monetary terms. For example, the cost of help desk software and the cost of a server to host it are both specific costs represented by a monetary value.

Intangibles are costs, benefits, and asset values that are not easy to quantify because they do not directly equate to monetary values. For example, if a company loses access to help desk software and can no longer assist any customers, it results in the loss of customer confidence. This loss of goodwill is an intangible loss because there isn't a clear monetary value associated with the loss.

When a company loses the goodwill of a customer, it risks losing the customer. Companies often spend a lot of time and money to attract new customers, and they typically view this as an investment because they recognize that it is easier to sell to a repeat customer than it is to acquire a new customer. With this in mind, losing a customer doesn't just represent the lost revenue from this customer. It also represents losing the investment of attracting the customer.

Help desk managers typically don't need to calculate the intangible costs and values. However, they do need to be aware of them as hidden costs that often drive executive decisions. More, they need to be aware of the intangible values that a help desk provides to an organization.

An Example CBA

As an example, consider a company that has recently expanded its help desk operations but doesn't have any help desk software. Instead, help desk technicians enter data into Microsoft Excel spreadsheets and Microsoft Word documents.

Sam, the help desk manager, finds it difficult to track incidents and doesn't have any simple way of retrieving metrics on help desk performance. He doesn't have accurate data indicating how much time technicians spend on incidents or even how many tickets each technician resolves. Sam knows that the number of backlogged tickets is high and is causing problems, but he doesn't have accurate information on the number of backlogged tickets. Additionally, technicians often lose track of incidents until an irate customer calls back asking for status.

ON THE SIDE: Organizations commonly follow the financial guidelines outlined in the generally acceptable accounting principles (GAAP) framework. GAAP includes references to customer goodwill and accountants often attempt to quantify customer goodwill, or loss of goodwill, by assigning values and costs to them. However, even though they do estimate a monetary value for goodwill, it is still recognized as an intangible value.

10

Sam researched possible solutions and wants funding to purchase Zendesk help desk software. He recognizes that simply asking to spend money without showing value for the expenditure is an easy way to hear the answer "no." Sam knows that an educated manager takes the time to complete a cost benefit analysis, and that's what he decides to do.

Identifying Costs

Sam reviewed the Zendesk plans and determined that the Plus version is the best option to meet his needs. The cost is $69 a month for each technician and manager that accesses the service, but Zendesk offers a discount reducing this to $59 when paying for it annually. The help desk currently has three technicians and one help desk manager, so this results in a cost of $2,832 annually (59 × 4 × 12) with the annual discount.

When identifying costs, it's also important to look for hidden costs. For example, when adding in new software, it's possible that personnel might need training. However, in this example, the manager spent time familiarizing himself with Zendesk using their free trial. He found it easy to use and knows the help desk technicians will be able to use it without any formal training.

Zendesk does require Internet access. However, the company already has Internet access for all computers, so this requirement does not add any additional costs.

In some cases, you can address intangible costs within the CBA. In this example, many customers are not happy with the service they're currently receiving, and it's possible some customers left. If you can identify how many customers left the company, you can list this as an intangible cost.

Identifying Benefits

The next step is to identify benefits and, when possible, assign a monetary value to them. After giving it some thought, the manager identified the following tangible benefits:

- **Less time updating and tracking tickets.** Currently, technicians spend an excessive amount of time finding files when they need to update the tickets. The help desk manager also spends a lot of time going through the files to track them. An automated system will save an average of two hours of labor time for each employee each week, or eight hours total. On a monthly basis, this equates to approximately 32 hours of saved labor.

- **Cost benefit of $640 monthly.** The average salary of technicians and the help desk manager is $20 per hour (including benefits and additional costs). This solution reduces the workload by 32 hours a month, providing a monthly cost benefit of approximately $640.

When identifying benefits, it's important to also look for intangible benefits. Even if you aren't able to quantify them, you should still list them. Intangible benefits that directly support the organization's vision, mission, and values are especially important to include. As an example, if the organization is focused on customer service and their vision, mission, and value statements stress this, then intangible benefits related to customer service are highly relevant.

For this example, some of the intangible values are:

- **Better customer service.** The built-in metrics make it easier to track backlogged tickets and prevent tickets from being lost. Management can ensure technicians are working on older and/or high priority tickets when necessary. Additionally, this method makes it easier to contact customers and set their expectations for tickets that will take longer to resolve.

- **Improved customer satisfaction metrics.** The tool includes the ability to measure customer satisfaction with simple surveys and automatically records the responses. Available reports allow management to review customer satisfaction for any given period and for any specific technician.

- **Enhanced work environment.** Technicians will be able to focus on the primary job of meeting customer needs rather than spending excessive time looking for the correct documents. This will decrease their frustration with the current system, decrease the number of irate customers, and overall improve the technician's morale.

- **Built-in tools to measure performance.** Several metrics are automatically tracked and easily viewable in the interactive reporting dashboard. Management will be able to identify the performance of the help desk overall, and of individual technicians. While the manager is currently tracking the help desk performance with rudimentary tools, the current method doesn't provide the same capabilities as the Zendesk software.

- **Easily accessible knowledge base.** Zendesk allows technicians to search the online database of past incidents through a simple interface. The current system requires the technicians to manually search through files, which often doesn't give them the information they need. Admittedly, this knowledge base isn't readily available, but as technicians use Zendesk, the knowledge base will grow and become more useful.

Comparing Costs to Benefits

The next step is to compare the costs and the benefits. In simple terms, the purchase makes sense if the benefits are greater than the cost, and the purchase doesn't make sense if the benefits are less than the cost. While a cost benefit analysis often does make a decision simple, there are many times when the answer isn't as clear. For example, if you're unable to quantify the intangible benefits, but they appear to be significant, management might decide to go ahead with the purchase, even when the costs outweigh the tangible benefits.

For the example in this section, you can summarize the costs and benefits as:

- **Zendesk cost:** $2,832 annually ($236 per month)
- **Tangible benefit:** $7,680 annually ($640 monthly)
- **Savings:** $4,848 annually ($404 monthly)

10

In other words, the CBA shows that this $2,832 investment will provide a cost savings of $4,848 annually. This expenditure makes sense as long as the data is accurate. However, you can expect executive decision makers to analyze the data, and they might ask probing questions on how it was obtained. Ideally, the CBA addresses data collection methods and eliminates any need for executives to question its validity.

With that in mind, do you notice a hole in this CBA?

The tangible benefit isn't providing any direct savings to the organization. Assuming technicians and the manager all work 40-hour work weeks now, they will also be working 40-hour work weeks after the purchase. Yes, the technicians will be more productive and will be able to use their time more efficiently, but the organization isn't paying them any less. In this scenario, it's important to point out how the technicians extra time equates to real savings.

One possibility is to point out the current problem and include alternatives in the CBA. In this situation, the manager can cite the number of times irate customers called in asking for status on lost tickets and mention that the current help desk staff cannot adequately handle the workload unless something changes. He can include some alternatives such as:

- **Add another help desk technician:** One option is to add another help desk technician to address these problems. This option does not bring in any of the intangible benefits of the Zendesk software, such as better customer service and tools to measure the performance of the help desk. The estimated costs and benefits are:
  - **Technician cost:** $32,000 annually (for entry-level technician)
  - **Tangible benefit:** None
  - **Savings:** None

> **AUTHOR'S NOTE:** Salaries vary in different organizations and in different locations. However, you can often find the average salary for jobs using online searches. In the CBA example, I searched on Glassdoor.com (http://www.glassdoor.com/Salaries/index.htm) and identified an average annual salary of $40,000 for help desk employees. Dividing this by 2,080 (40 hours × 52 weeks) gives an hourly wage of $19.23 and I rounded it up to $20. I then used a lower salary of $32,000 for the entry level technician. Of course, these estimates are not necessary if you're the manager in a company—you can use the actual salaries of help desk technicians to identify the average.

However, when comparing this option against the Zen desk software, here are the costs and benefits:

- **Zendesk cost:** $2,832 annually
- **Tangible benefit:** $32,000 annually (by not hiring another technician)
- **Savings:** $29,168

- **Hire a part-time technician:** Another option is to hire a part-time technician. A part-time technician wouldn't have the same level of expertise as full-time help desk employees but would still reduce the workload. To provide the same value, this technician would need to work at least 10 hours weekly. With an estimated pay of $15 per hour, this equates to approximately $150 weekly and $7,800 annually. This option does not bring in any of the intangible benefits of the Zendesk software. The estimated costs and benefits are:

  - **Part-time technician cost:** $7,800 annually

  - **Tangible benefit:** None

  - **Savings:** None

  When comparing this option against the Zendesk software, here are the costs and benefits:

  - **Zendesk cost:** $2,832 annually

  - **Tangible benefit:** $7,800 annually (by not hiring a part-time technician)

  - **Savings:** $4,968

With all this information included in the CBA, the decision to purchase Zendesk becomes even clearer. It provides both tangible and intangible benefits to the organization and is better than the alternatives.

Calculating Return on Investment (ROI)

An alternative to a CBA is a **return on investment (ROI)** value. An ROI assesses the worth of an investment and expresses it as a ratio or a percentage. The simplest method uses this formula to calculate a ratio: Benefits ÷ Costs = ROI ratio.

This formula calculates a percentage: Benefits ÷ Costs × 100 = ROI percentage.

The following bullets show the ROI using the values from the CBA example:

- **Purchasing Zendesk**
  $7,680 ÷ $2,832 = 2.7 (or 270%)

- **Comparing Zendesk with hiring full-time technician**
  $32,000 ÷ $2,832 = 11.3 (or 1,130%)

- **Comparing Zendesk with hiring part-time technician**
  $7,800 ÷ $2,832 = 2.75 (or 275%)

Each has a ratio greater than 1 indicating they have a positive return on investment.

From another perspective, imagine that you are unable to use a cloud-based solution. Instead of evaluating Zendesk, you are evaluating a server-based product that has a higher startup cost but provides the same benefits. Imagine that the initial cost includes the following items, but the ongoing costs are negligible:

- **Server:** $10,000

- **Server-based application:** $6,000

10

ON THE SIDE:
These figures are purposely elevated to show a contrast with the previous examples.

- **Administrator training:** $4,000
- **Total initial costs:** $20,000

You can then calculate the ROI for each of the same options. The following calculations show that this server-based application is preferable to hiring a full-time technician with a ratio of 1.6, but it is not necessarily preferable to the other two options. Remember, though, these examples are only evaluating the tangible benefits.

- **Purchasing server-based application**
  $7,680 ÷ $20,000 = .384 (or 38.4%)
- **Comparing server-based application and hiring full-time technician**
  $32,000 ÷ $20,000 = 1.6 (or 160%)
- **Comparing server-based application and hiring part-time technician**
  $7,800 ÷ $20,000 = .39 (or 39%)

These calculations show that the server-based application is preferable over hiring a full-time technician. However, the other two options give lower ratios. Even though the ROI ratios are low, an organization might still want to consider them. In this scenario, they are considering a $20,000 one-time investment, but they reap the benefits every year, and it might result in a positive return on their investment over time.

The **payback period** identifies how long it takes until the investment starts providing a positive return. If the initial cost is higher than the benefits, you can calculate the payback period as:

Payback period = Cost ÷ Benefits

- **Purchasing server-based application**
  $20,000 ÷ $7,680 = 2.6 years payback period
- **Comparing server-based application and hiring part-time technician**
  $20,000 ÷ $7,800 = 2.5 years payback period

If desired, you can express the payback period in months with this calculation:

Payback period = Cost ÷ Benefits × 12

Chapter Review Activities

Use the features in this section to study and review the topics in this chapter.

Answer These Questions

1. Of the following choices, what is NOT a purpose of help desk metrics?

    a. Help justify costs

    b. Help calculate the value of the help desk

    c. Provide sales information

    d. Identify effectiveness of the help desk

2. How do you calculate a help desk's backlog?

    a. New tickets - tickets solved

    b. Tickets solved - new tickets

    c. Cumulative number of tickets received

    d. Cumulative number of tickets solved

3. You've determined that the number of new tickets and the number of tickets resolved is about the same. What does this tell you about the backlog?

    a. The backlog is close to zero.

    b. The backlog is too high.

    c. The backlog will be about the same six months from now if current trends continue.

    d. Unable to determine.

4. A customer calls the help desk and waits on the phone for 10 minutes before talking to a technician. The technician then creates the ticket and solves the customer's problem in 20 minutes. What is the wait time?

    a. 10 minutes

    b. 20 minutes

    c. 30 minutes

    d. 40 minutes

5. A customer creates a ticket via a web page and a technician responds after 10 minutes. The technician solves the problem and closes the ticket after working on it for 20 minutes. What is the wait time?

    a. 10 minutes

    b. 20 minutes

    c. 30 minutes

    d. 40 minutes

6. When does the resolution time indicate a possible problem?

   a. When the resolution time is greater than the reply time

   b. When the resolution time is greater than the wait time

   c. When the first resolution time is greater than the final resolution time

   d. When the final resolution time is greater than the first resolution time

7. Which of the following metrics could you use to identify a top-performing technician?

   a. New tickets

   b. Tickets solved

   c. Backlog

   d. Wait time

8. Which of the following metrics could you use to identify a top-performing technician?

   a. New tickets

   b. Tickets solved

   c. Backlog

   d. Reply time

9. Which of the following CTI metrics identifies the amount of time customers wait before a live person answers the call?

   a. Abandoned calls

   b. Wait time

   c. Abandon rate

   d. Queue time

10. What is the impact of extrinsic motivators on tasks requiring creative thought?

    a. They decrease performance.

    b. They increase performance.

    c. They don't have any effect.

    d. They stimulate creative thought.

11. When calculating personnel costs for hourly employees, what should you include?

    a. The hourly pay

    b. The hourly pay and taxes

    c. The hourly pay, taxes, and insurance costs

    d. The hourly pay, taxes, insurance costs, and benefits

12. Who is responsible for ensuring cloud-based help desk software is highly available?

    a. The organization using it

    b. Help desk technicians

    c. Help desk managers

    d. The vendor selling access to it

13. How do technicians typically access server-based help desk software?

   a. Via the cloud

   b. From the server

   c. From applications on their help desk computers

   d. Via the Internet

14. Which of the following calculations provides the BEST formula for calculating the cost per ticket?

   a. Facility costs × 1.3 ÷ backlogged tickets

   b. Personnel costs × 1.3 ÷ backlogged tickets

   c. Facility costs × 1.3 ÷ resolved tickets

   d. Personnel costs × 1.3 ÷ resolved tickets

15. Which of the following BEST identifies the purpose of a CBA?

   a. To compare costs and benefits when making business decisions

   b. To identify the cost of backlogged tickets

   c. To compare costs during a budget analysis

   d. To assess the worth of an investment

16. What are the three steps you must take when creating a CBA?

   a. Identify costs, identify backlog, and analyze the two

   b. Identify costs, identify benefits, and compare the two

   c. Collect data on tickets, balance this data over time, and analyze the results

   d. Collect value information, budget for costs, and analyze previous budgets

17. Which of the following is an example of an intangible value?

   a. Server hardware

   b. Cloud-based software

   c. Desktop PCs

   d. Customer confidence

18. What should be included when identifying costs for a CBA?

   a. Tangible costs only

   b. Intangible costs only

   c. Tangible, intangible, and potential hidden costs

   d. Tangible and intangible costs only

19. What should be included when identifying benefits for a CBA?

   a. Tangible benefits only

   b. Intangible benefits only

   c. Tangible and intangible benefits

   d. Only benefits that can be quantified

10

20. Which of the following BEST defines an ROI?

    a. It compares costs and benefits when making business decisions.

    b. It calculates the cost of a ticket.

    c. It calculates the cost of backlogged tickets.

    d. It assesses the worth of an investment and expresses it as a ratio or a percentage.

Answers and Explanations

1. **c.** Help desk metrics do not provide any sales information. However, they can be used to justify costs, calculate the value of the help desk, and identify the effectiveness of the help desk.

2. **a.** The backlog is the number of new tickets - the number of tickets solved.

3. **c.** This indicates the backlog will stay relatively the same in the future unless something changes. If it's 100 now, it will probably be 100 six months from now. The scenario doesn't indicate the actual value of the backlog, so you don't know if it's close to zero or too high, but you do know that it will stay relatively constant.

4. **b.** The wait time refers to how long it takes before a problem is resolved and is calculated as the time between ticket creation and ticket resolution. In this scenario, the technician created the ticket and solved the problem in 20 minutes. While the customer waited on the phone for 10 minutes, this isn't included because the ticket wasn't created. The resolution time is 30 minutes.

5. **c.** The wait time refers to how long it takes before a problem is resolved and is calculated as the time between ticket creation and ticket resolution. Since the customer created it on the web site, the resolution time includes the reply time of 10 minutes.

6. **d.** If the final resolution time is greater than the first resolution time, it indicates the ticket had to be reopened and indicates a possible problem. It isn't possible for the first resolution time to be greater than the final resolution time. The resolution time isn't compared with the reply time or the wait time.

7. **b.** The tickets solved metric shows the number of closed tickets, and it can be broken down to show how many tickets each technician has solved. Technicians do not have a direct impact on new tickets or the backlog. Wait time indicates how quickly a technician resolves tickets, but it doesn't necessarily reflect top performance.

8. **b.** The tickets solved metric shows the number of closed tickets, and it can be broken down to show how many tickets each technician has solved. Technicians do not have a direct impact on new tickets, the backlog, or the replay time.

9. **d.** The queue time in a computer telephony integration (CTI) system identifies the amount of time customers wait before a live person answers the call. An abandoned call is a call where the caller hangs up before a live person answered the phone, and the abandon rate identifies the percentage of abandoned calls compared to the total number of calls. The wait time refers to how long it takes before a problem is resolved.

10. **a.** Extrinsic motivators decrease performance with tasks requiring creative thought. They do not stimulate creative thought.

11. **d.** Personnel costs include hourly pay, the company's share of matching taxes, insurance costs such as unemployment insurance and donations to supplement other employee insurance, and any additional benefits offered to employees.

12. **d.** The vendor of the cloud-based software is responsible for ensuring its availability. This is a primary benefit of cloud-based software. Personnel within the organization are not responsible for any of its maintenance.

13. **c.** Technicians typically access server-based help desk software from applications on their help desk computers. These applications interact with the server-based software. Cloud-based software is accessed via the Internet. The technicians would not access the software directly from the server.

14. **d.** You can calculate the cost per ticket using personnel costs × 1.3 ÷ resolved tickets. The 1.3 multiplier adds in a 30 percent overhead cost to account for items such as facility costs. Personnel costs are most important and cannot be omitted. Backlogged tickets do not provide an accurate view of how many tickets the organization is receiving or resolving.

15. **a.** Managers use a cost benefit analysis (CBA) to compare costs and benefits when making business decisions. A CBA is not related to backlogged tickets and it doesn't compare costs during a budget analysis. A return on investment (ROI) assesses the worth of an investment.

16. **b.** When creating a cost benefit analysis (CBA), you identify costs, identify benefits, and compare the two. A CBA is not related to tickets or backlogged tickets.

17. **d.** Customer confidence is an example of an intangible value because it isn't easy to quantify it in monetary terms. The other items have specific values based on their cost.

18. **c.** When creating a cost benefit analysis (CBA), you should attempt to identify tangible, intangible, and potential hidden costs.

19. **c.** When creating a cost benefit analysis (CBA), you should attempt to identify tangible and intangible benefits. You should include intangible benefits even if you can't quantify them.

20. **d.** A return on investment (ROI) assesses the worth of an investment and expresses it as a ratio or a percentage. Managers use a cost benefit analysis (CBA) to compare costs and benefits when making business decisions. An ROI is unrelated to tickets.

Define the Key Terms

The following key terms include the ideas most important to the big ideas in this chapter. To review, without looking at the book or your notes, write a definition for each term, focusing on the meaning, not the wording. Then review your definition compared to your notes, this chapter, and the glossary.

Key Terms for Chapter 10

abandoned call	cost benefit analysis (CBA)	resolution time
abandon rate		return on investment
answer time	intangibles	tangibles
backlog	new tickets	ticket
budget	payback period	tickets solved
computer telephony integration (CTI)	performance metric	trend analysis
	reply time	wait time

10

List the Words Inside Acronyms

The following are the most common acronyms discussed in this chapter. As a way to review those terms, simply write down the words that each letter represents in each acronym.

Acronyms for Chapter 10

CBA	GAAP	POP
CTI	ISP	ROI
FAQ	PIN	SMTP

Create Mind Maps

For this chapter, create mind a map as follows:

1. Create a mind map to list the available ticket-related metrics. Start with a circle labeled Help Desk and draw at least five lines out from the circle. Label each of the lines with a metric related to tickets.

Define Other Terms

Define the following additional terms from this chapter, and check your answers in the glossary:

economies of scale   functional fixedness   intrinsic motivation

extrinsic motivation

Case Studies

Case Study 1

Perform an Internet search on "the candle problem" and research its validity. Also, go to ted.com and watch Dan Pink's talk on The Puzzle of Motivation.

Appendix

Figure	Photo Credit
Figure 1-6	DURIS Guillaume
Figure 2-1	Gajus
Figure 2-2	berc
Figure 2-3	berc
Figure 2-4	Faber Visum
Figure 2-5	Cello Armstrong Minerva Studio
Figure 3-5	ianrward
Figure 4-1	naraz
Figure 4-2	Oleksiy Mark
Figure 4-3	Amy Walters
Figure 4-4	Horticulture
Figure 4-5	Ruslan Kudrin
Figure 4-8	Christos Georghiou
Figure 4-9	Christos Georghiou
Figure 4-10	Christos Georghiou
Figure 4-12	Christos Georghiou
Figure 4-8	singkham
Figure 4-9	singkham
Figure 4-10	singkham
Figure 4-12	singkham
Figure 4-12	ray8
Figure 4-13	Soul wind
Figure 5-3	Rafal Olechowski
Figure 5-4	Gunnar Assmy
Figure 5-5	freshidea Bobboz tiero
Figure 5-6	davidevison

Figure	Photo Credit
Figure 7-2	Lisa F. Young
Figure 8-1	photo5963
Figure 8-1	slaved
Figure 8-2	Rtimages
Figure 8-3	Rtimages
Figure 8-6	Rtimages
Figure 9-1	ruigsantos
Figure 9-1	leungchopan
Figure 9-2	Andres Rodriguez
Figure 10-7	Alexandar Iotzov

Glossary

A

abandon rate   The percentage of abandoned calls compared to the total number of calls received by a help desk.

abandoned call   A help desk phone call where the caller hangs up before a live person answers. Some help desk systems include the abandoned calls metric to identify the total number of abandoned calls for a given period.

acceptable usage policy (AUP)   A written company policy that describes the purpose of IT systems and user responsibilities when using them. Organizations typically require employees to read and acknowledge the policy annually.

active listening   Focusing on the entire message during communication. Active listening involves listening to the words, paying attention to the non-verbal messages, making eye contact, and responding to show understanding.

active writing   A form of writing that follows the order of subject, verb, and object. It focuses on what a subject does rather than vaguely saying something was done. Most technical documents use an active writing style as much as possible. Compare to passive writing.

advanced persistent threat (APT)   A group or entity that has the capability and intent to persistently target a specific organization. They typically have the backing of an organization with almost unlimited resources, such as a government. Some organized cyber-criminals fund APTs.

adware   Malware that displays unwanted advertisements to users. Adware might install itself as additional toolbars, change a user's home page, and display pop-up windows with advertisements.

analogy   A comparison between two things. Analogies provide a comparison between two things and can help people connect known concepts with unknown concepts. Analogies often make it easier for someone to understand new concepts.

andragogy   The art and science of helping adults learn. It is similar to pedagogy but refers to adult learning

answer time   The amount of time customers wait before a live person answers the call into a help desk. Some help desk systems express this as queue time or wait time.

aptitude   A person's innate ability or talent related to a particular field of study. It identifies the ease with which a person can learn a topic. Compare to attitude.

attitude   The way a person looks at things such as events in their lives. It is their manner or disposition. Compare to service attitude and aptitude.

auditory learner   A learner who learns best by hearing information. Other learning styles are visual learner, reading/writing learner, and kinesthetic learner.

availability   Part of the security triad. Security programs attempt to ensure IT systems and data are available when needed. *See also* confidentiality and integrity.

B

backlog   The number of open or unsolved incidents. It is a running count of the difference between new tickets and tickets resolved.

black-hat   A knowledgeable individual that attempts to break into computer systems for malicious reasons or personal gain. Black-hat hackers break existing laws. When media refer to hackers involved in cyber-crime, they are normally referring to black-hat hackers. Compare to white-hat and gray-hat.

blended learning   A combination of instructor-led class sessions and self-directed eLearning. Students are able to learn some topics at their own pace and an instructor teaches other topics in classroom sessions.

Bloom's Taxonomy   A classification of learning objectives with six levels of learning. The six levels are knowledge, comprehension, application, analysis, synthesis, and evaluation.

body language   Facial expressions, body movement, and placement of arms and legs, which combine to indicate subtle messages. Body language is part of non-verbal communication and can make up as much as 55 percent of a communicated message. Other non-verbal communication is vocal tone.

botnet   A robotic network of computers. Criminals use malware to join computers to a botnet and then direct these computers to launch attacks or send spam. Computers joined in a botnet are zombies.

bridging   A technique used to help students connect different topics between multiple sessions in a course. Trainers bridge topics by mentioning how a current topic is related to a past topic students have covered or a future topic.

budget   The amount of money needed for a specific purpose such as running a department or funding a project.

burnout   A state of mental, emotional, or physical exhaustion. It is often the result of long-term distress that hasn't been effectively managed.

business alignment   Ensuring that IT goals line up with the business goals of an organization. Organizations often use IT governance frameworks to help them with business alignment.

business continuity planning (BCP)   Overall planning lifecycle dedicated to analysis, design, implementation, testing, and maintenance of various elements designed to keep the organization operating even after a significant outage. Business continuity planning is a continuous process.

business impact analysis (BIA)   A process used to analyze the business and identify critical functions and services. The BIA also helps the organization determine the cost impact of losing these functions and services. Organizations use the results as part of an overall business continuity plan.

business skills   One of the key hard skills needed by successful help desk technicians. It refers to the technician's understanding of the organization's vision, mission, and values, in addition to the ability to use tools available within the organization.

C

central processing units (CPUs)   Sophisticated chips that plug into motherboards and perform the majority of processing for a computer. Intel and AMD are the primary manufacturers of CPUs.

change management   A program designed to prevent unintended outages from changes. Personnel submit change requests, and appropriate experts review them to identify unintended consequences. Personnel do not make changes until the change goes through the change management process.

closed-ended question   A question that can be answered with a one- or two-word response. *See also* open-ended questions.

communication   Communication is the process of sharing information between two or more people. People commonly share information through speech, writing, and images. *See also* verbal and non-verbal communication.

CompTIA A+   An entry-level CompTIA certification. It focuses on the basic operation of a computer including hardware and operating system concepts.

CompTIA Network+   A CompTIA certification. It builds on knowledge from A+ and focuses on networking concepts such as hardware, cabling, and protocols.

CompTIA Security+   A CompTIA certification. It builds on the Network+ certification and focuses on IT security concepts such as risk and risk mitigation using various controls.

computer telephony integration (CTI)   Technology that connects a telephone system with a computer system. Many CTI systems can capture customer information such as the calling phone number and/or a customer access number. The CTI system can then pass this information to a computer and pop up the customer data when a technician takes the call. CTI systems can also capture metrics related to phone calls.

confidentiality   Part of the security triad. Security programs attempt to ensure confidentiality by preventing unauthorized disclosure of data. *See also* availability and integrity.

content management system (CMS)   An application used to manage content on a website. Content managers enter the data and the CMS handles the delivery of the content to the users. Most CMSs support a search engine so that users can search for content. Many blogs use a CMS-based application.

continuing education (CE)   A process where individuals continue to learn after becoming certified. Individuals are often required to earn a specific number of CE credits to retain a certification.

Control Objectives for Information and related Technology (COBIT)   A management framework used for IT governance. COBIT 5 is based on five principles and provides organizations with a set of good practices they can apply to IT management and IT governance.

cost-based analysis (CBA)   An analysis of costs and benefits related to an expenditure. A CBA identifies and analyzes the costs and benefits to simplify the decision-making process.

cost center   A cost center generates additional costs for an organization. Cost centers provide indirect support for an organization's mission, but they do generate direct revenue. Compare to a profit center.

critical path   A graphic showing all of the critical tasks within a project. Project managers use it to easily identify the critical tasks within a project.

critical task   Any task within a project that must be completed on time to avoid delaying a project. Project managers focus more attention on critical tasks to ensure they are completed on time.

critical thinking   The ability to use your personal experience, logical thought processes, and creativity to analyze and evaluate situations. Further, critical thinking allows you to use the information gathered to reach a conclusion or answer.

cyber theft   The theft of financial or other personal information through cyberspace. Many criminals operate in organized cyber gangs and steal millions of dollars annually.

cyber vandalism   Cyber-attacks by vandals with the intent to destroy, deface, or spoil IT resources without permission. Modifying or defacing a website is cyber vandalism.

cyber-attacks   Attacks on an organization's IT resources through cyberspace. The purpose of the attacks might be for monetary gain, intelligence gathering, or vandalism.

cybercrime   Any type of crime that targets computers, or uses computer networks or devices, and violates existing laws. Cybercrime includes cyber vandalism, cyber theft, and cyber-attacks.

cyber-criminal   Criminals that break into computer systems for malicious reasons and/or personal gain. They typically launch attacks through cyberspace.

cyberspace   The online world of computer networks where people can interact with others without physically being with them. People commonly interact with cyberspace via the Internet.

D

denial of service (DoS)   An attack from a single attacker designed to disrupt or disable the services provided by an IT system. Compare to distributed denial of service (DDoS).

Denial of Service (DoS) attack   Attacks designed to disable a resource such as a server, network, or any other service provided by the company. If the attack is successful, the resource is no longer available to legitimate users.

distress   A negative form of stress that indicates anxiety, pain, or sorrow. Distress can cause physical ailments and should be managed to resolve the issue causing it. *See also* stress and eustress.

distributed denial of service (DDoS)   A denial of service (DoS) attack that comes from multiple sources at the same time. Attackers often enlist computers into botnets after infecting them with malware. Once infected, the attacker can then direct the infected computers to attack other computers.

drive-by download   Malware that attempts to infect a user's system when the user visits a malicious website.

E

economies of scale   Cost savings gained by an increase in production. As an example, adding one help desk technician increases the productivity of the help desk, but it does not add to facility costs such as network infrastructure, power, heating, and air conditioning costs.

eLearning   Electronic learning. Refers to any method where students learn through an electronic source, such as with a computer-based application or via a web page.

electrostatic discharge (ESD)   A discharge of static electricity that can harm electronic components. RAM and CPUs are highly susceptible to ESD damage, but all electronic components are also susceptible to ESD damage. Technicians commonly use tools such as ESD wrist straps to prevent ESD damage.

empowering words   Words or phrases of encouragement spoken by a trainer in response to student interaction. These positive words encourage more interaction and positive responses from students.

escalate   Referring an incident to a technician at a higher-level tier. Technicians at lower-level tiers might refer the incident if the problem is beyond their experience or knowledge level. They can also escalate problems that require higher levels of privileges that they do not possess.

eustress   A positive form of stress resulting from a positive event in someone's life or an enjoyable challenge. For example, sports players experience eustress as they prepare for and compete in a sports event. *See also* stress and distress.

expository writing   A style of writing that focuses on a subject and omits the opinions of the author. Expository writing provides facts and is often used in business settings.

extrinsic motivation   Motivation that comes from outside a person. Incentives and rewards for achieving certain milestones are examples. These can be monetary, such as bonuses or pay raises, or non-monetary, such as a grade in a course. Similarly, threats of discipline or punishment also provide extrinsic motivation for people.

F

facilitator   Someone who moderates sessions to help participants share their knowledge with each other. Facilitators provide guidance and supervision to help the group reach a specific outcome, such as learning about a topic or communicate more effectively.

fault tolerance   The ability of a system to tolerate a fault and continue to operate. Fault tolerance systems often use redundant hardware, such as additional hard drives or additional servers, to eliminate a single point of failure.

filler words   Short meaningless words such as "uh" and "um." Speakers and trainers often use these unconsciously and it can distract from the message.

filters   Communication filters block or change the meaning of messages. They can be external (such as outside noise or other distractions) or internal (such as the emotional state or internal beliefs of a person).

firewall   Software or hardware designed to control traffic. A network-based firewall is typically hardware, and it controls traffic in and out of a network. A host-based firewall is software installed on individual systems and it controls traffic in and out of individual systems.

firmware   Software embedded in hardware. Desktop PCs include Basic Input/Output System (BIOS), which is the firmware used to start PCs.

flow chart   A diagram that represents an algorithm or process. Some organizations use flow charts in troubleshooting guides to help technicians diagnose problems. They are also useful when developing expert systems.

frequently asked questions (FAQs)   A list of questions frequently asked by users or customers, along with the answer. Many websites include a FAQ page.

functional fixedness   A mental block against using an object differently than its obvious use. Individuals need to exercise creative thinking to overcome this mental block.

G

general adaptation syndrome   A model used to describe how bodies react and adapt to stressors. It includes three stages: alarm, resistance, and exhaustion. Symptoms of distress begin to appear while in the exhaustion phase.

good practices   Defined in ITIL as a proven, generally accepted practice. ITIL originally called these best practices but realized that many of the practices are not required in every organization and so renamed them to good practices. Ideally, organizations implement good practices whenever possible.

gray-hat   A knowledgeable individual that attempts to break into computer systems, but not for malicious reasons. Gray-hat hackers break into systems for the fun of exploration and often report their findings to the organization after breaking in. Their actions often break laws, and law enforcement authorities can prosecute them for their actions. Compare to white-hat and black-hat.

H

hard skills   Specific, measurable skills such as configuring and troubleshooting systems. Technicians need a mix of both hard skills and soft skills. Compare to soft skills.

help desk   A division of an IT department that provides direct support to end users. Support can be provided directly to users in person, over the phone, via chat or instant messages, via email, or via web page posts. End users might be workers within the organization or external customers such as ISP subscribers.

hub   A basic networking device. Hubs connect computers together in a network. Hubs have no intelligence and cannot analyze traffic. All traffic received on one port goes to all other ports. Many organizations replace hubs with switches for better performance.

I-J

incident   A problem affecting a user. It can be any unplanned interruption or reduction in the quality of an IT service.

incident management   Process of managing incidents or problems affecting users. It includes the processes and procedures used to deal with incidents. Incidents might be reported by users, technical staff, or from automated systems that monitor and report incidents.

inflection   Refers to the modulation of different words in a sentence. Statements with a rising inflection at the end of a sentence indicate a question. Statements with a falling inflection at the end indicate a statement.

Information Technology Infrastructure Library (ITIL) A group of books written and released by the United Kingdom's Office of Government and Commerce (OGC). ITIL documents best practices organizations can implement to provide consistent IT services. The library includes five books.

Information Technology Laboratory (ITL) Part of NIST. ITL develops standards and guidelines with a goal of improving IT security and the privacy of information on IT systems. ITL publishes its findings in the Special Publication (SP) 800 series of publications.

instructor Someone with a wide body of knowledge, concepts, and theories who instructs, or teaches, others. Instructors might use only lecturing or presentations when teaching. Synonymous with teacher. Compare to trainer, who has a narrower level of knowledge and experience.

intangibles Costs, benefits, and asset values that are not easy to quantify because they do not directly equate to monetary values. A CBA will normally include intangibles along with tangibles. Compare to tangibles.

integrity Part of the security triad. Security programs attempt to ensure integrity by providing assurances that data and IT systems are not modified. *See also* availability and confidentiality.

Internet service provider (ISP) A telecommunication company that provides Internet access to its subscribers. ISPs employ help desk personnel to assist ISP subscribers having problems with their Internet access.

intrinsic motivation Motivation that comes from within a person. People often take action for their own personal reasons. Individuals might do so simply because they enjoy it or to gain a sense of accomplishment.

IT governance Processes used to ensure that IT resources are aligned with the goals of the organization. Organizations often use frameworks to help them with IT governance.

K

keylogger Malware or hardware that captures keystrokes. Some keyloggers send the logged data to criminals. Criminals attempt to install software keyloggers onto systems to capture credentials such as usernames and passwords for banking sites.

kinesics The study of body movements such as gestures and facial expressions. These movements are also known as body language and make up part of non-verbal communications.

kinesthetic learner A learner who learns best by performing a task. Also known as an experiential learner. Other learning styles are visual learner, auditory learner, and reading/writing learner.

knowledge base A collection of data in searchable form. IT-based knowledge bases include information technicians use to troubleshoot problems. For example, it could include symptoms and solutions for known problems, along with tutorials or procedures. Knowledge bases can be internal and only available within the organization or external and available to anyone.

L

learning style Refers to the primary learning styles related to hearing, seeing, reading, and doing. People learn using all the learning styles, but many people have a preferred learning style and learn best with this preferred learning style. *See* visual learner, auditory learner, reading/writing learner, and kinesthetic learner.

local area network (LAN) A group of computers and other IT resources connected together in the same location, such as within an office or within a building. Compare to WAN and MAN.

GL

M

malware   Malicious software (malware) includes viruses, worms, Trojans, logic bombs, rogueware, and more. Antivirus software helps protect against malware, but it is only useful when all appropriate systems have antivirus software installed with up-to-date signatures.

memorandum of agreement (MOA)   An agreement between one entity within an organization and another entity within the same organization. It stipulates performance expectations such as minimum uptime and maximum downtime levels, and is used instead of an SLA.

memorandum of understanding (MOU)
Same as MOA.

metric   A method of measuring something. It provides quantifiable data used to gauge the effectiveness of a process; metrics are commonly used to measure the effectiveness of a help desk.

metropolitan area network (MAN)   A group of LANs connected together in two or more buildings but in the same geographical location such as on the same campus or in the same city. Compare to LAN and WAN.

milestone   Target date for significant accomplishments within a project. A project will typically have several milestones. Project managers and executives use these milestones to determine if a project is on track or if it is behind schedule.

mission-critical functions or services   Activities integral to the organization performing its core business. Help desk personnel measure the effect of an incident against mission-critical functions or services to determine the priority of the incident.

mission statement   A statement that focuses on the present and identifies what an organization hopes to achieve and/or how it hopes to achieve it. In contrast, a vision statement focuses on the future.

N

National Institute of Standards and Technology (NIST)   A division of the U.S. Department of Commerce. NIST includes the Information Technology Laboratory (ITL), which publishes IT standards and guidelines in the Special Publication (SP) 800 series of publications.

new tickets   The number of new tickets received by a help desk. It shows the overall workload volume, and help desk managers compare it to the tickets solved metric. Some systems refer to this as new incidents.

non-verbal communication   The body language and tone of voice that combine with the spoken words to communicate a message. In many situations, non-verbal communication can be as much as 93 percent of an overall message.

O

on-the-job training   Training from an experienced employee to a new employee while working on the job. This is a form of one-on-one training.

open-ended question   A question that cannot be answered with a one- or two-word response. Open-ended questions help technicians get more information on a problem. *See also* closed-ended questions.

P-Q

passive writing   A form of writing using a passive voice rather than an active voice. It indicates action but is vague on what caused the action. Most writers discourage the use of passive writing in technical documents. Compare to active writing.

Patch Tuesday   The day when Microsoft sends out updates in North America. This is the second Tuesday of every month.

payback period   The length of time it takes until you start seeing a positive return on an investment. It is calculated as Payback period = Cost ÷ Benefits.

pedagogy   The science and art of education. Pedagogical principles are used to develop and deliver most courseware.

performance metric   A method of measuring performance. It provides quantifiable data used to gauge the effectiveness of a process. Several performance metrics measure the effectiveness and overall performance of a help desk.

persuasive writing   A form of writing that attempts to convince the reader of a specific point of view. It is often used in white papers and marketing materials.

phishing   Specialized type of spam designed to trick users into giving up sensitive information such as usernames and passwords. Spear-phishing targets a group of users in an organization. Whaling targets high-level executives.

PowerPoint presentations   Presentations created in Microsoft PowerPoint to create training slides. PowerPoint presentations include multiple pages or slides, sometimes called slide decks.

principle of least privilege   Ensuring that users have access to only the resources they need for their job. Privileges include both rights and permissions.

professor   A faculty member at a college or university who instructs or teaches. Professors are a step above instructors and have a wide body of knowledge, concepts, and theories. Professors might use only lecturing or presentations when teaching.

profit center   A profit center generates direct revenue for an organization. Compare to a cost center, which does not provide any direct revenue but instead provides indirect support at additional costs.

protocol analyzer   Also called a sniffer. A protocol analyzer is software used to capture and analyze traffic sent over a network. When data is sent in clear text, the text can be read using a protocol analyzer.

R

random access memory (RAM)   Memory used within computers. Desktop PCs commonly use dual inline memory modules (DIMMs) and laptops use small outline dual inline memory modules (SO DIMMs). Both have memory chips soldered on circuit cards that can easily be installed in computers.

rapport   A close or harmonious relationship where people or groups understand each other's feelings or ideas and communicate effectively based on this mutual understanding. Successful technicians build rapport with customers while assisting them resolve problems. Similarly, trainers typically try to build rapport with students so that students are in a more receptive frame of mind.

reading/writing learner   A learner that learns best by reading and/or writing information. Other learning styles are visual learner, auditory learner, and kinesthetic learner.

reply time   How long it takes a customer to receive a reply from a live person when requesting assistance. Depending on the method a customer uses to contact the help desk, this might be the amount of time before a technician answers the phone, replies via email, or via any other method.

residual risk   The risk that remains after implementing security controls to mitigate risk. Senior management is responsible for deciding what security controls to implement, and for any losses related to residual risk.

resolution time   How long it takes to resolve a problem completely. Normally, this will be the same as the wait time. However, if a technician closes a ticket indicating it's resolved but the customer contacts the help desk again for the same problem, the original ticket is opened again. Compare to wait time.

return on investment   A calculation to assess the worth of an investment. ROI is expressed as a ratio or a percentage. The formula is Benefits ÷ Costs = ROI ratio, or Benefits ÷ Costs × 100 = ROI percentage.

risk   The likelihood that a threat will exploit a vulnerability resulting in a loss. Organizations use risk mitigation techniques to reduce risk.

GL

risk management   The process of reducing risk to an acceptable level by implementing security controls. Organizations implement risk management programs to identify risks and methods to reduce it. The risk that remains after risk has been mitigated to an acceptable level is residual risk.

rogueware   A type of Trojan horse that presents itself as free antivirus software. It attempts to trick users into thinking their computers are infected, and encourages users to pay to remove the malware. Sometimes called ransomware or scareware.

router   A networking device used to connect networks together. Hubs or switches connect devices in networks and routers connect these networks together.

S

scope   The boundaries of a project. Projects include a scope definition so that personnel understand the project boundaries. Identifying the scope helps prevent scope creep.

scope creep   Additional activities beyond the defined or expected scope of a project. Scope creep often results in missed deadlines and increased costs.

security skills   One of the key hard skills needed by successful technicians to recognize threats and vulnerabilities. Attackers and criminals launch malicious attacks on systems, and security professionals implement controls to protect these systems.

self-talk   The internal dialog that runs through a person's mind. Self-talk forms and reinforces a person's self-image, which affects their performance and stimulates more self-talk. Negative self-talk can be replaced with positive self-talk.

service   Defined in ITIL as something that provides value to customers. These customers can be external customers paying for a service, such as access to a website, or internal employees using a service, such as email. IT Service Management (ITSM) is the implementation and management of these services.

service attitude   A caring attitude related to customers. It goes beyond just a positive attitude and includes a sense of caring for the customer along with a desire to solve the customer's problem.

service level agreement (SLA)   An agreement between an IT service provider and a customer to provide a specific level of reliability for a service. It stipulates performance expectations such as minimum uptime and maximum downtime levels. Many SLAs include monetary penalties if the IT service provider does not provide the service as promised.

single point of failure (SPOF)   Any component that can cause an entire system or service to fail if it fails. An SPOF can be a single hard drive in a system, a single server for a critical service such as a website, or even a single location. Redundant techniques help eliminate SPOFs.

soft skills   Refers to the ability to communicate effectively with others. Technicians need a mix of both hard skills and soft skills. Compare to hard skills.

spam   Unwanted email. Spam often includes malicious components, such as links to drive-by downloads. Infected systems joined to a botnet often send out spam at the bidding of the criminal controlling the botnet.

spyware   Malware that collects information about users without their knowledge or consent. Extreme versions of spyware use keyloggers to capture user keystrokes, including usernames and passwords.

stakeholder   Someone that has a vested interest in a project. Stakeholders are often high-level managers or executives with authority to resolve problems within a project.

story   An account of a real-life event. When used by trainers and leaders, stories have the power to ignite people's imagination and move their hearts, minds, and feet into action.

stress A state of mental tension and worry causing problems or potential problems. Stress can cause strong feelings of worry or anxiety. Stress is often described as either positive stress (eustress) or negative stress (distress). *See also* distress and eustress.

stress management A combination of techniques and practices used to reduce the negative effects of stress. Some techniques people use for stress management are exercise, tai chi, yoga, meditation, breathing exercises, taking a walk, taking a bath, engaging in a hobby, adopting a different routine, and looking at events with a different perspective.

switch A networking device used to connect computers together in a network. Switches analyze traffic and only send traffic to destination ports. In contrast, hubs send traffic to all other ports.

T-U

tangibles Costs, benefits, and asset values that are obvious and easy to quantify in monetary terms. A CBA attempts to identify all the tangible costs and benefits in its calculations. Compare to intangibles.

teacher *See* instructor.

technical skills One of the key hard skills needed by successful help desk technicians to configure, maintain, and troubleshoot IT systems. Technical skill requirements vary between organizations and even between specific jobs within an organization.

technical support Support provided to personnel to resolve technical problems. Help desk personnel provide technical support to end users.

technical writing A form of expository writing which informs the reader with facts. Technical documents often include explanations to teach how to perform a task or procedure.

threat Anything or anyone that represents a danger to an organization's IT resources. Threats can exploit vulnerabilities, resulting in losses to an organization.

ticket An incident that has been logged into an incident management system. It might also be called a service ticket.

tickets solved The number of tickets closed by help desk personnel. Help desk managers often compare this to the new tickets metric. Some systems refer to this as resolved incidents.

trainer Someone with a narrow level of knowledge and experience on a topic, who transfers this knowledge by training others. Individuals providing technical training on specific technical topics are trainers.

training aids Anything used by a trainer to enhance training. Typical training aids are white boards, interactive white boards, PowerPoint presentations, videos, and any relevant hardware or equipment that a trainer shows to the students.

Transmission Control Protocol/Internet Protocol (TCP/IP) A suite of protocols used on the Internet and in many local area networks. Individual protocols within TCP/IP are defined in formal documents called RFCs.

trend analysis Using tools and statistics to identify consistent movement in one direction or another. The analysis might show a consistent upward trend or a consistent downward trend, but either way it indicates a change worth investigating.

Trojan (or Trojan horse) Malware that looks like something beneficial but has a malicious component. Users are tricked into downloading and installing the malware, thinking it's worthwhile. After the user installs the Trojan, the malicious component runs. Trojans are named after the Trojan horse from Greek mythology.

troubleshooting skills One of the key hard skills needed by successful help desk technicians to assess problems and identify solutions.

tutorials Self-guided materials that trainees use to learn new topics. Tutorials are typically written documents, such as manuals or study guides, but can also be presented through an application or online. Trainees learn at their own pace.

GL

V

values   Traits, beliefs, and principles that a person or an organization considers important. Many organizations publish their values along with their vision and mission statements.

verbal communication   The spoken words used when communicating. Communication in conversations between people includes both verbal and non-verbal communication. In many situations, verbal communication is as little as 7 percent of the total communicated message.

virtual private network (VPN)   A connection used by remote users to connect to an organization's internal resources. VPNs provide access to a private network over a public network such as the Internet.

virus   Malware that executes in response to user interaction. An infected application has malicious code that runs when the user runs the application. In some cases, a user action, such as inserting an infected USB flash drive into a system, causes the malicious code to run.

vision statement   A statement that describes where an organization wants to be or what it wants to achieve at some point in the future. It is normally a single sentence and provides inspiration to employees to help the organization achieve it. In contrast, a mission statement focuses on the present.

visual learner   A learner that learns best by seeing information. Other learning styles are auditory learner, reading/writing learner, and kinesthetic learner.

vocal tone   Refers to how a person's voice is modified by changing the volume, pitch, and inflection of words. The tone can imply a different message than the words, and individuals often pay more attention to the tone than the words. Vocal tone can make up as much as 38 percent of a message in communication.

vulnerability   A weakness. It can be a weakness in any organizational IT systems, networks, configurations, users, or data. If a threat exploits a vulnerability, it can result in a loss to an organization.

W-Z

wait time   How long it takes to resolve a ticket. It is typically calculated as the amount of time between ticket creation and ticket resolution. Compare to resolution time.

white paper   An informational document or report. White papers typically describe an issue and help the reader understand it and a solution. Many companies use white papers as sales tools.

white-hat   An IT professional working in IT security to protect systems from attacks. Sometimes referred to as a white-hat hacker. White-hat hackers do not break laws or attempt to break into systems without permission. Compare to black-hat and gray-hat.

wide area network (WAN)   A group of LANs connected together in two or more locations separated by a large geographical distance such as in different cities. Compare to LAN and MAN.

wireless access point (WAP)   A device used to provide network access to wireless devices. WAPs use a transceiver to send and receive data wirelessly.

wireless router   A router with wireless capabilities. Most wireless routers include a switch component, a router component, a firewall, services, and a wireless transceiver. The router component typically provides access to the Internet for internal devices.

worm   Self-replicating malware. Unlike a virus, a worm travels over a network without any user intervention. Many viruses include a worm component that starts after the initial virus starts.

Index

Symbols

C

D

X-Z